X GENDER

2

**Story and Art by
Asuka Miyazaki**

CONTENTS

Ep. 14: The "Coronavirus" Story

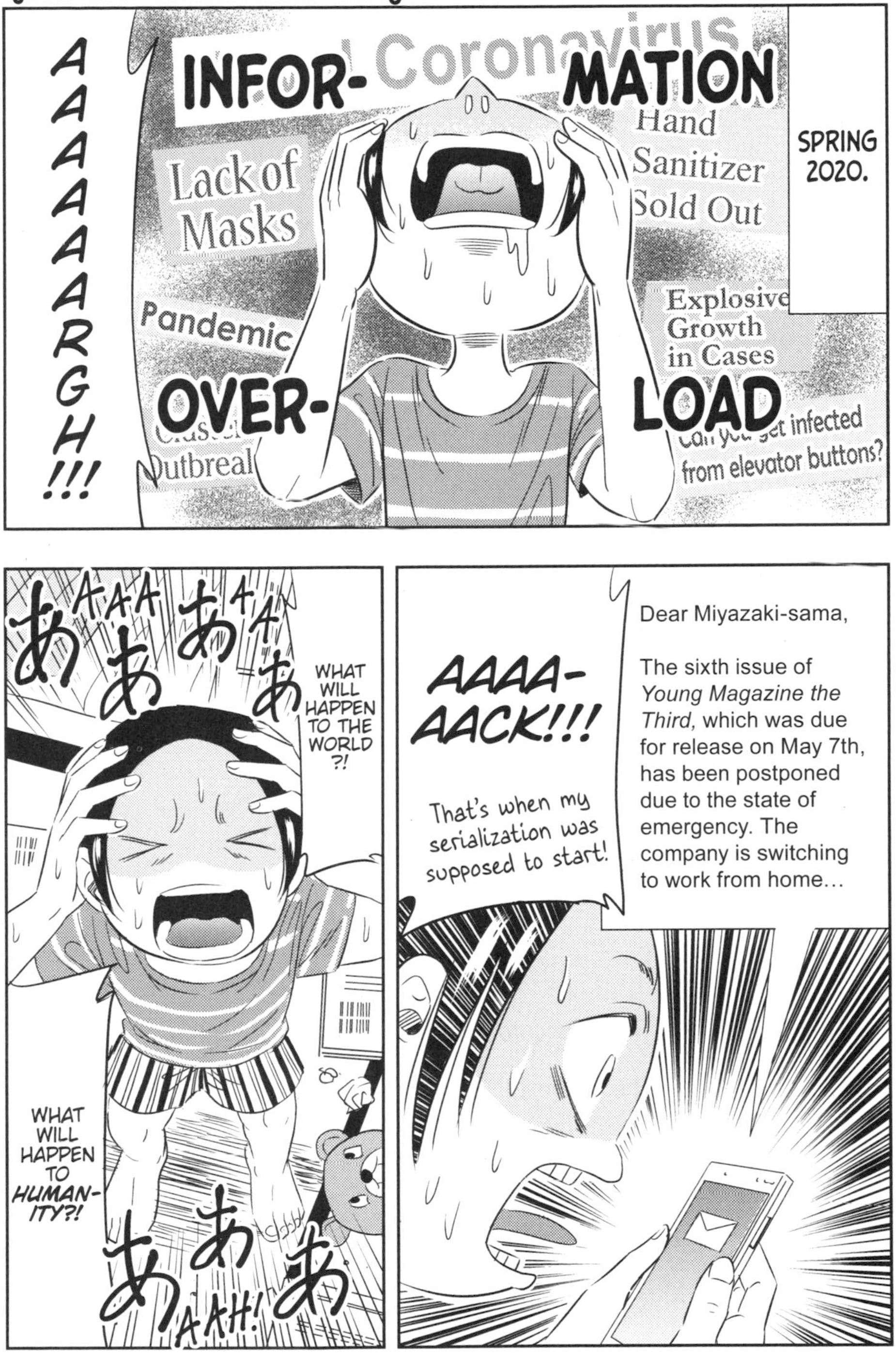

SPRING 2020.
Coronavirus
INFOR-MATION OVER-LOAD
Hand Sanitizer Sold Out
Lack of Masks
Explosive Growth in Cases
Pandemic
Can you get infected from elevator buttons?
AAAAAAARGH!!!
Dear Miyazaki-sama,
The sixth issue of *Young Magazine the Third,* which was due for release on May 7th, has been postponed due to the state of emergency. The company is switching to work from home…
AAAA-AACK!!!
That's when my serialization was supposed to start!
あAAAあAAあAあ
WHAT WILL HAPPEN TO THE WORLD?!
WHAT WILL HAPPEN TO *HUMANITY?!*
あAAH!あああ

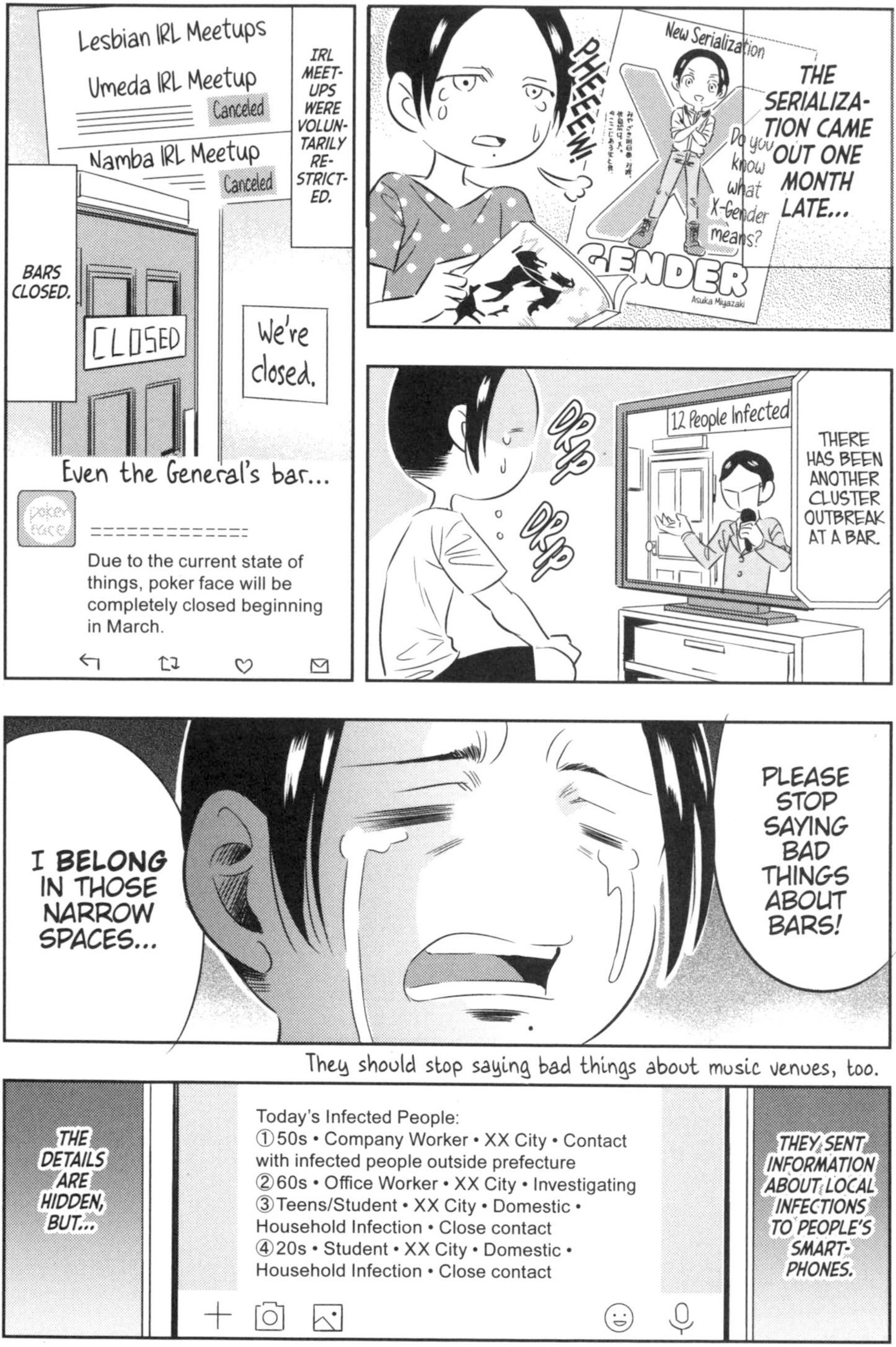
THE SERIALIZATION CAME OUT ONE MONTH LATE...
PHEEEW!
New Serialization
Do you know what X-Gender means?
X GENDER
Asuka Miyazaki
THERE HAS BEEN ANOTHER CLUSTER OUTBREAK AT A BAR.
12 People Infected
DRIP
DRIP
IRL MEET-UPS WERE VOLUNTARILY RESTRICTED.
Lesbian IRL Meetups
Umeda IRL Meetup
Canceled
Namba IRL Meetup
Canceled
BARS CLOSED.
CLOSED
We're closed.
Even the General's bar...
poker face
Due to the current state of things, poker face will be completely closed beginning in March.
PLEASE STOP SAYING BAD THINGS ABOUT BARS!
I BELONG IN THOSE NARROW SPACES...
They should stop saying bad things about music venues, too.
THEY SENT INFORMATION ABOUT LOCAL INFECTIONS TO PEOPLE'S SMARTPHONES.
Today's Infected People:
①50s • Company Worker • XX City • Contact with infected people outside prefecture
②60s • Office Worker • XX City • Investigating
③Teens/Student • XX City • Domestic • Household Infection • Close contact
④20s • Student • XX City • Domestic • Household Infection • Close contact
THE DETAILS ARE HIDDEN, BUT...

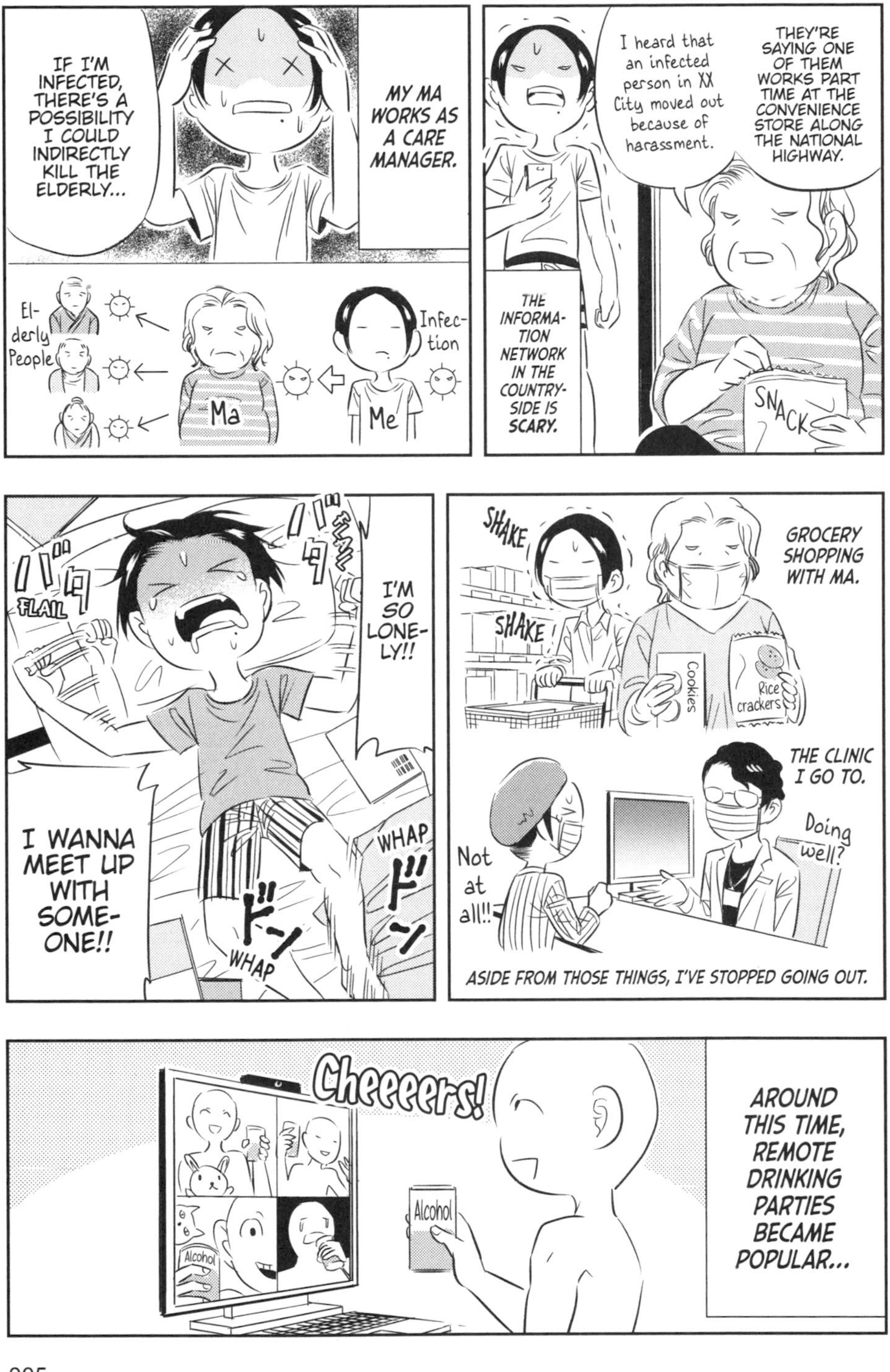
THEY'RE SAYING ONE OF THEM WORKS PART TIME AT THE CONVENIENCE STORE ALONG THE NATIONAL HIGHWAY.
I heard that an infected person in XX City moved out because of harassment.
THE INFORMATION NETWORK IN THE COUNTRYSIDE IS SCARY.
SNACK
MY MA WORKS AS A CARE MANAGER.
IF I'M INFECTED, THERE'S A POSSIBILITY I COULD INDIRECTLY KILL THE ELDERLY...
Infection
Me
Ma
Elderly People
GROCERY SHOPPING WITH MA.
SHAKE
SHAKE
Cookies
Rice crackers
THE CLINIC I GO TO.
Doing well?
Not at all!!
ASIDE FROM THOSE THINGS, I'VE STOPPED GOING OUT.
FLAIL
FLAIL
I'M SO LONELY!!
I WANNA MEET UP WITH SOMEONE!!
WHAP
WHAP
AROUND THIS TIME, REMOTE DRINKING PARTIES BECAME POPULAR...
Cheeeers!
Alcohol
Alcohol

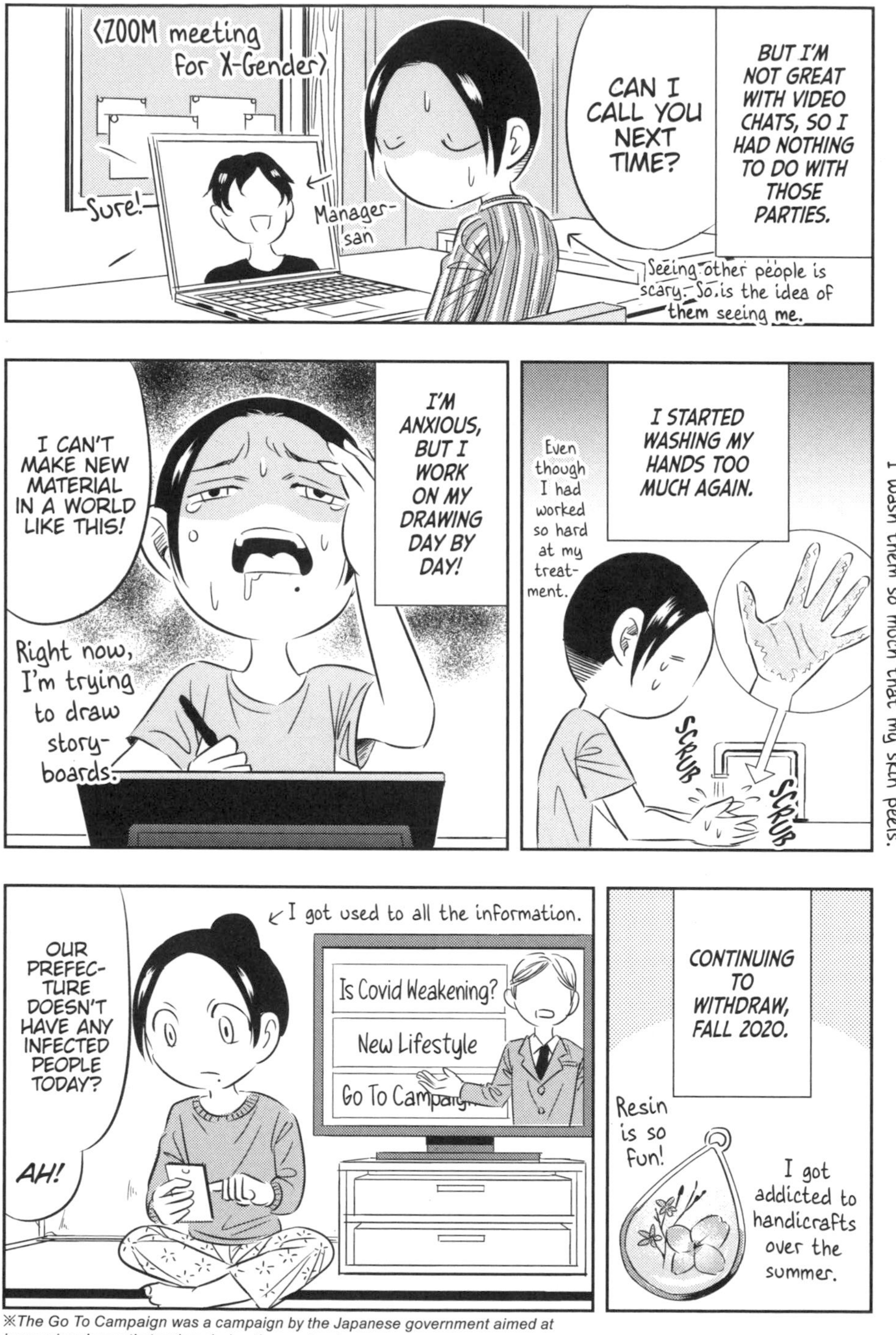
BUT I'M NOT GREAT WITH VIDEO CHATS, SO I HAD NOTHING TO DO WITH THOSE PARTIES.
CAN I CALL YOU NEXT TIME?
Seeing other people is scary. So is the idea of them seeing me.
‹ZOOM meeting for X-Gender›
Manager-san
Sure!
I wash them so much that my skin peels.
I STARTED WASHING MY HANDS TOO MUCH AGAIN.
Even though I had worked so hard at my treatment.
SCRUB
SCRUB
I'M ANXIOUS, BUT I WORK ON MY DRAWING DAY BY DAY!
I CAN'T MAKE NEW MATERIAL IN A WORLD LIKE THIS!
Right now, I'm trying to draw storyboards.
CONTINUING TO WITHDRAW, FALL 2020.
I got addicted to handicrafts over the summer.
Resin is so fun!
I got used to all the information.
Is Covid Weakening?
New Lifestyle
Go To Campai
OUR PREFECTURE DOESN'T HAVE ANY INFECTED PEOPLE TODAY?
AH!

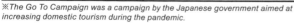

※*The Go To Campaign was a campaign by the Japanese government aimed at increasing domestic tourism during the pandemic.*

I DIDN'T HAVE THE WILL TO GO.

The Three Cs

Cluster

Splash

Eating and drinking with multiple people

Aerosol

Social Distancing Police

IT HAD BEEN OPENING BIT BY BIT SINCE THE END OF JULY, BUT...

bar Poker face Business Day Calendar	THE GENERAL'S BAR IS OPEN!
September 24th	
September 25th	open
September 26th	open

THIS TIME, I'LL GO!

Today's Infected People:
① 30s • Female • XX City • Infected at a bar

About me

Public Shunning

HISS

HISS

Stone throwing

GAGA

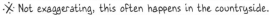

※ Not exaggerating, this often happens in the countryside.

I WILL GO LOSE MONEY AT THE BAR!!

FOR THE SURVIVAL OF THE BAR I LOVE...

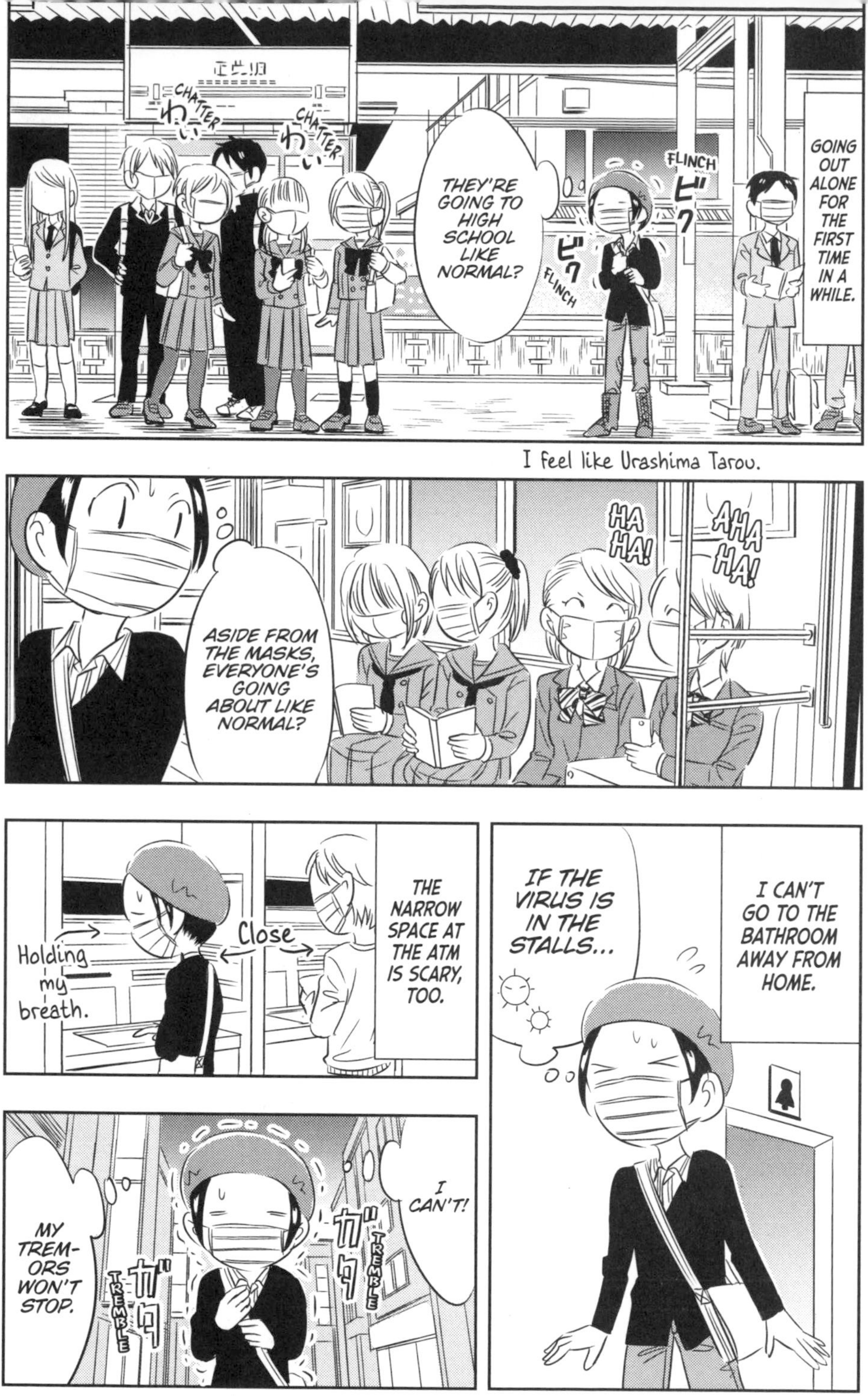
GOING OUT ALONE FOR THE FIRST TIME IN A WHILE.
FLINCH ビク
ビク FLINCH
THEY'RE GOING TO HIGH SCHOOL LIKE NORMAL?
CHATTER わい
CHATTER わい
I feel like Urashima Tarou.
AHA HA HA!
HA HA!
ASIDE FROM THE MASKS, EVERYONE'S GOING ABOUT LIKE NORMAL?
I CAN'T GO TO THE BATHROOM AWAY FROM HOME.
IF THE VIRUS IS IN THE STALLS...
THE NARROW SPACE AT THE ATM IS SCARY, TOO.
Close
Holding my breath.
I CAN'T!
ガタ TREMBLE
ガタ TREMBLE
MY TREMORS WON'T STOP.

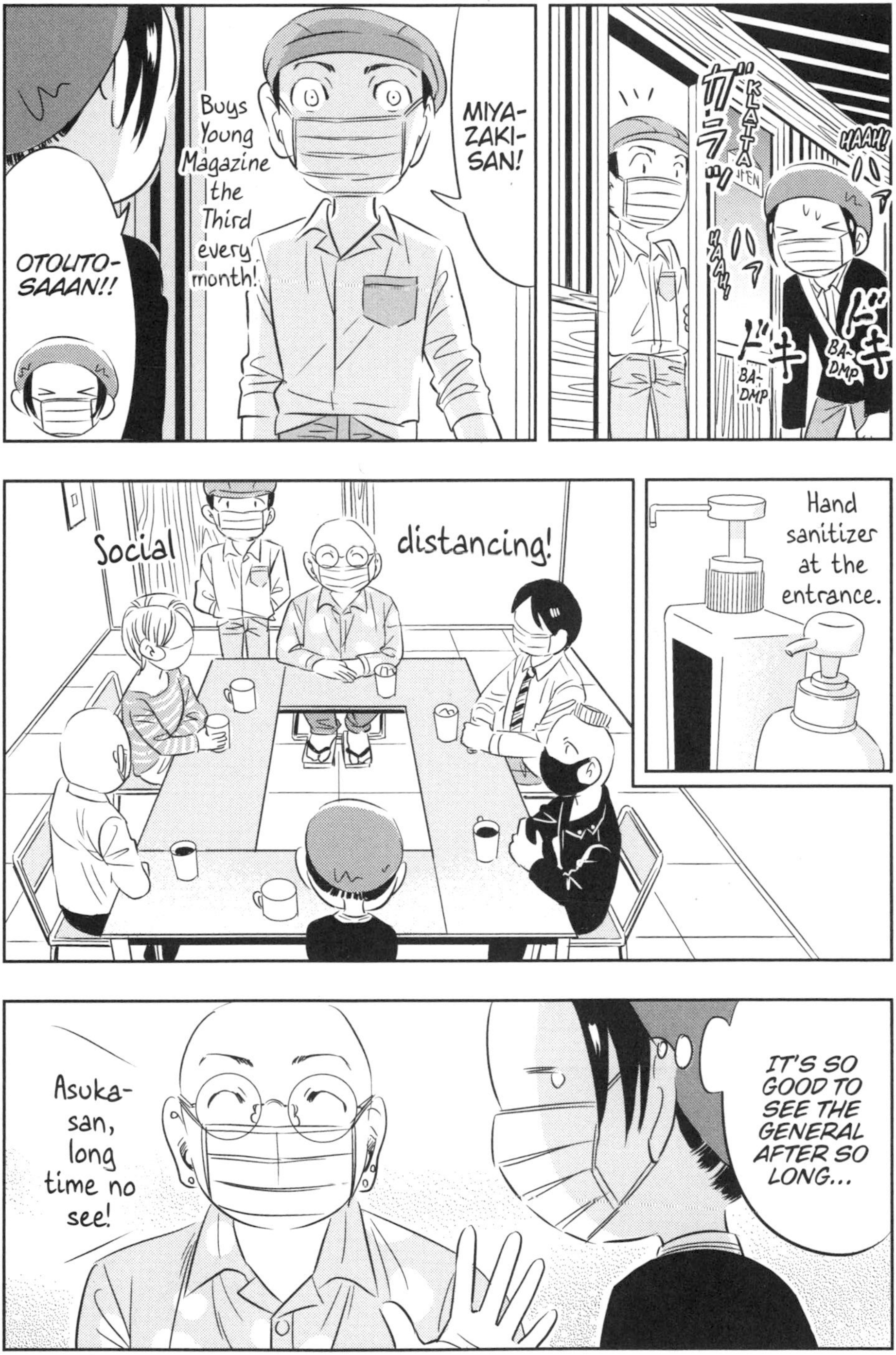
ガラッ
KLATTA
ハァ
HAAH!
ハァ
HAAH!
ドキ
BA-DMP
ドキ
BA-DMP
MIYA-ZAKI-SAN!
Buys Young Magazine the Third every month!
OTOUTO-SAAAN!!
Hand sanitizer at the entrance.
Social distancing!
IT'S SO GOOD TO SEE THE GENERAL AFTER SO LONG...
Asuka-san, long time no see!

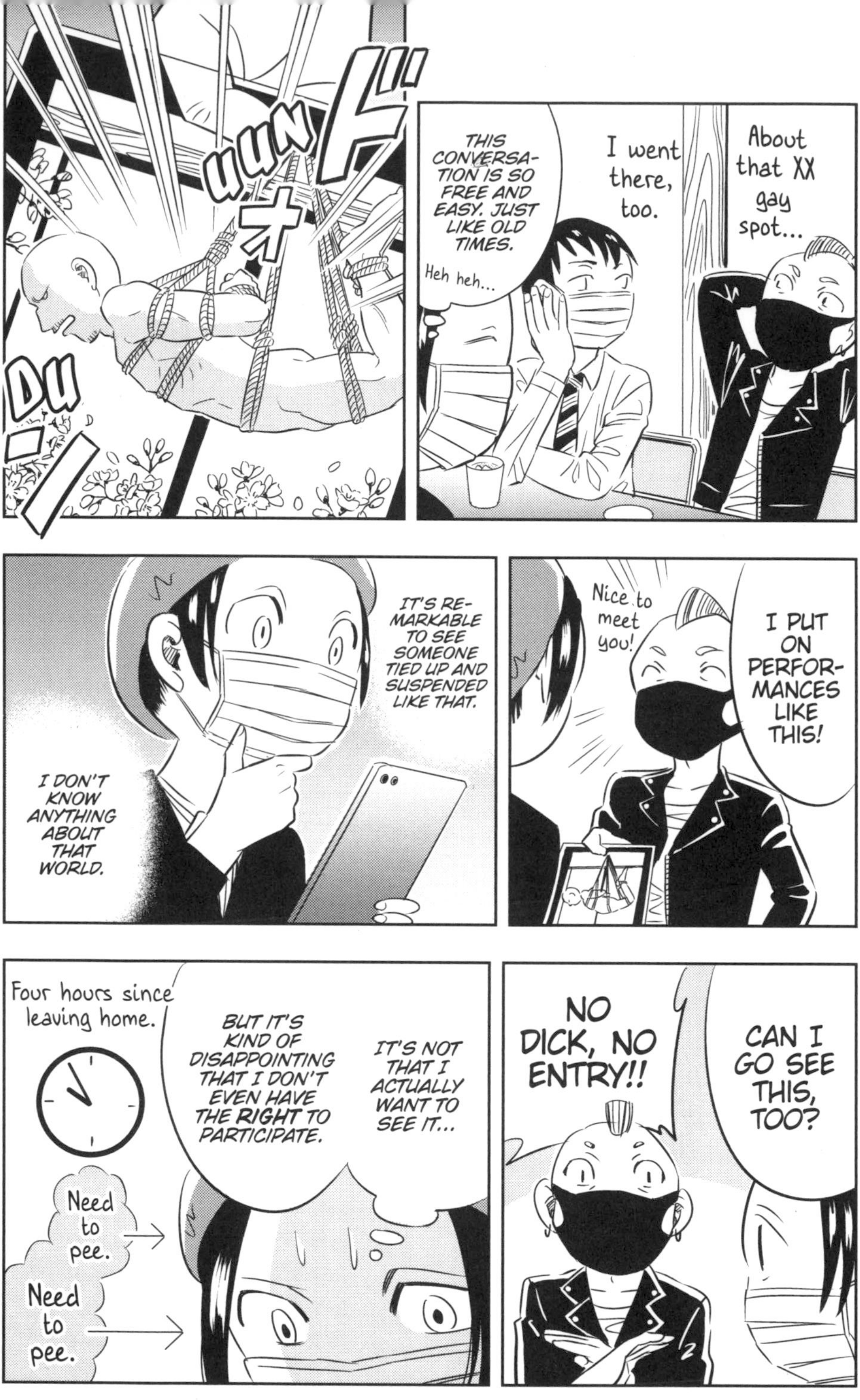
About that XX gay spot...
I went there, too.
THIS CONVERSATION IS SO FREE AND EASY. JUST LIKE OLD TIMES.
Heh heh...
UUN
DU
I PUT ON PERFORMANCES LIKE THIS!
Nice to meet you!
IT'S REMARKABLE TO SEE SOMEONE TIED UP AND SUSPENDED LIKE THAT.
I DON'T KNOW ANYTHING ABOUT THAT WORLD.
CAN I GO SEE THIS, TOO?
NO DICK, NO ENTRY!!
IT'S NOT THAT I ACTUALLY WANT TO SEE IT...
BUT IT'S KIND OF DISAPPOINTING THAT I DON'T EVEN HAVE THE **RIGHT** TO PARTICIPATE.
Four hours since leaving home.
Need to pee.
Need to pee.

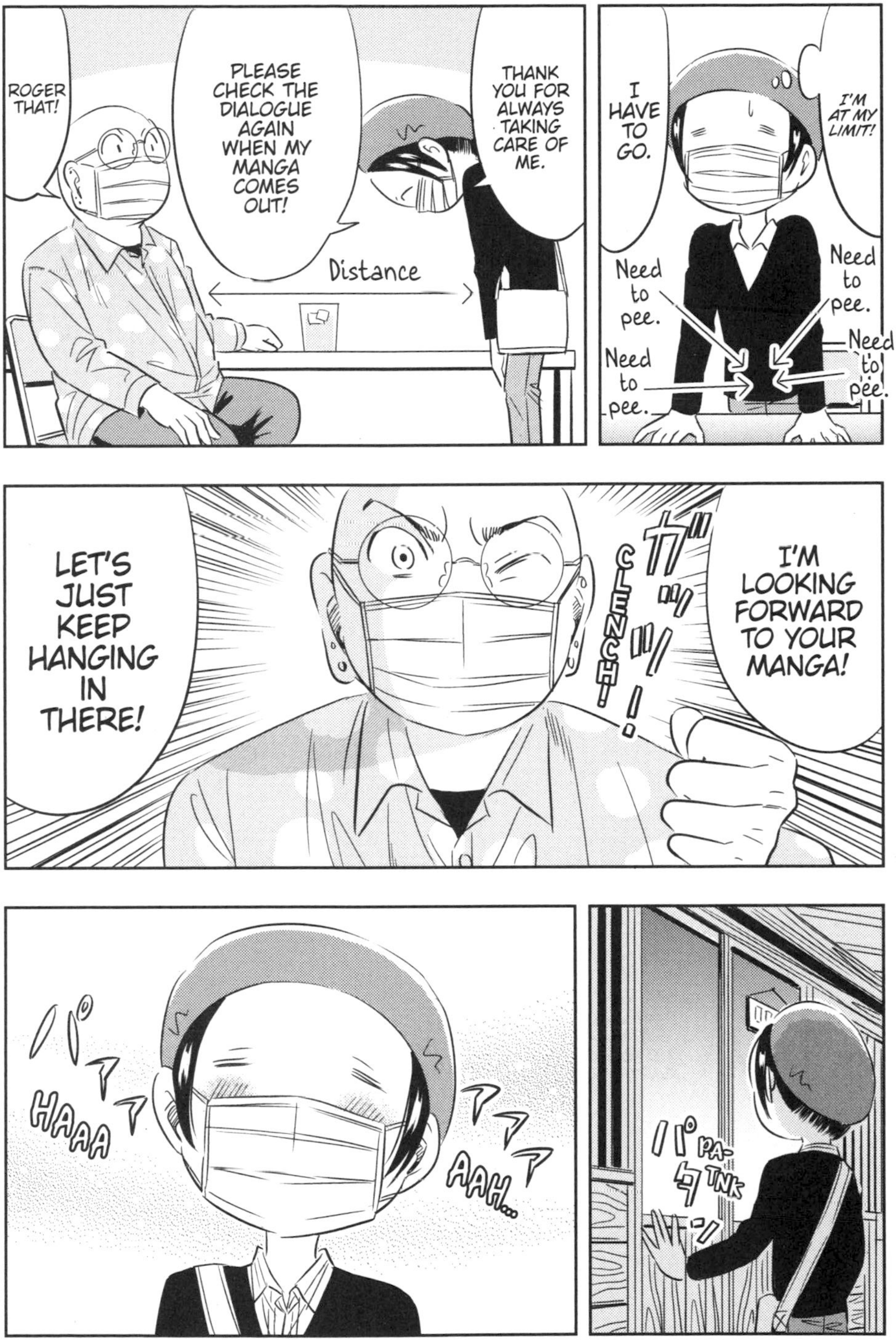
I'M AT MY LIMIT!
I HAVE TO GO.
Need to pee.
Need to pee.
Need to pee.
Need to pee.
THANK YOU FOR ALWAYS TAKING CARE OF ME.
PLEASE CHECK THE DIALOGUE AGAIN WHEN MY MANGA COMES OUT!
ROGER THAT!
Distance
I'M LOOKING FORWARD TO YOUR MANGA!
CLENCH!
LET'S JUST KEEP HANGING IN THERE!
PA-TNK
HAAAA
AAH...

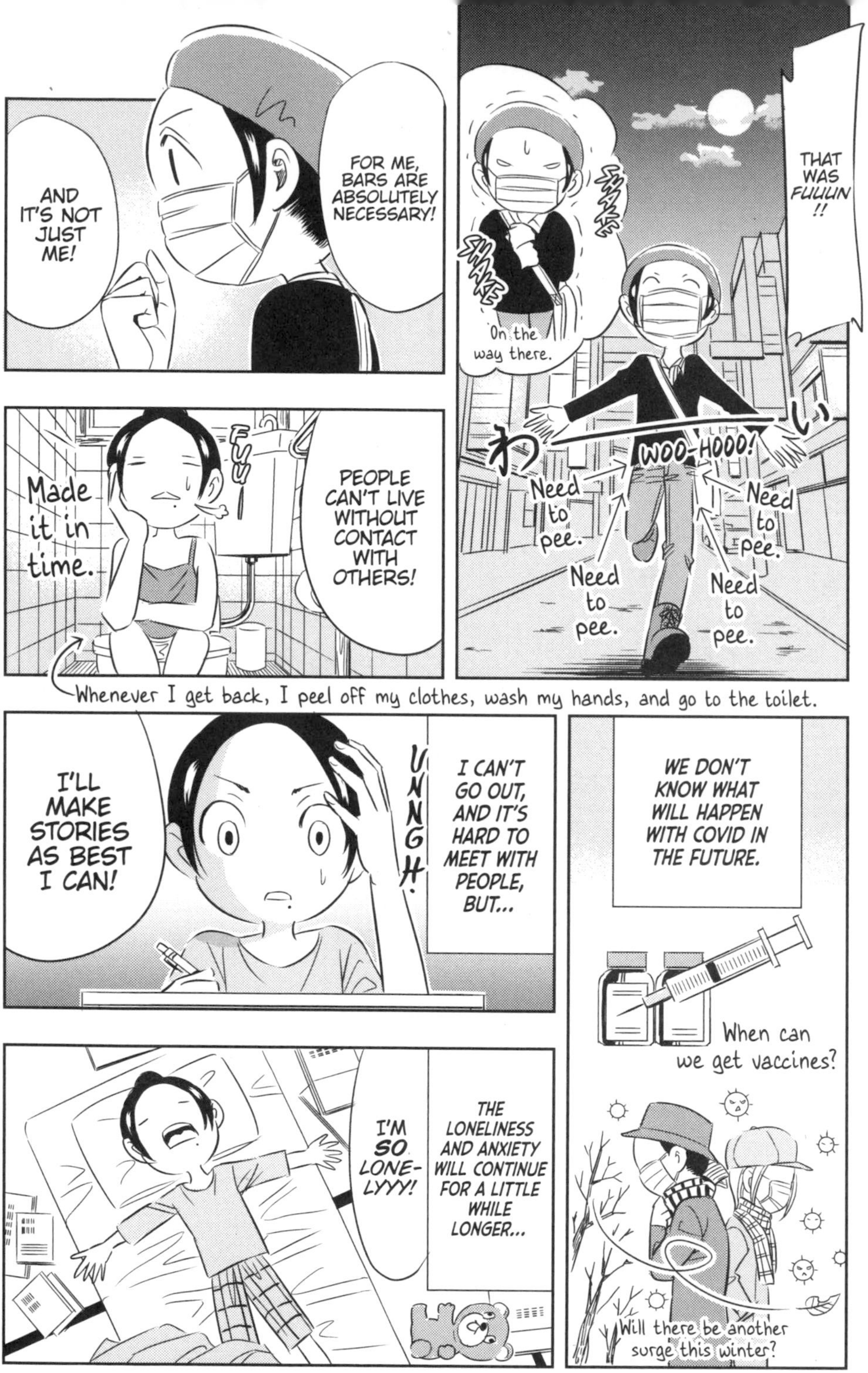
THAT WAS FUUUN!!
SHAKE
SHAKE
On the way there.
わ
WOO-HOOO!
い
Need to pee.
Need to pee.
Need to pee.
Need to pee.
FOR ME, BARS ARE ABSOLUTELY NECESSARY!
AND IT'S NOT JUST ME!
PEOPLE CAN'T LIVE WITHOUT CONTACT WITH OTHERS!
FUU
Made it in time.
Whenever I get back, I peel off my clothes, wash my hands, and go to the toilet.
WE DON'T KNOW WHAT WILL HAPPEN WITH COVID IN THE FUTURE.
When can we get vaccines?
Will there be another surge this winter?
I CAN'T GO OUT, AND IT'S HARD TO MEET WITH PEOPLE, BUT...
UNNGH!
I'LL MAKE STORIES AS BEST I CAN!
THE LONELINESS AND ANXIETY WILL CONTINUE FOR A LITTLE WHILE LONGER...
I'M SO LONE-LYYY!

Ep. 15: The "From a Female Perspective" Story

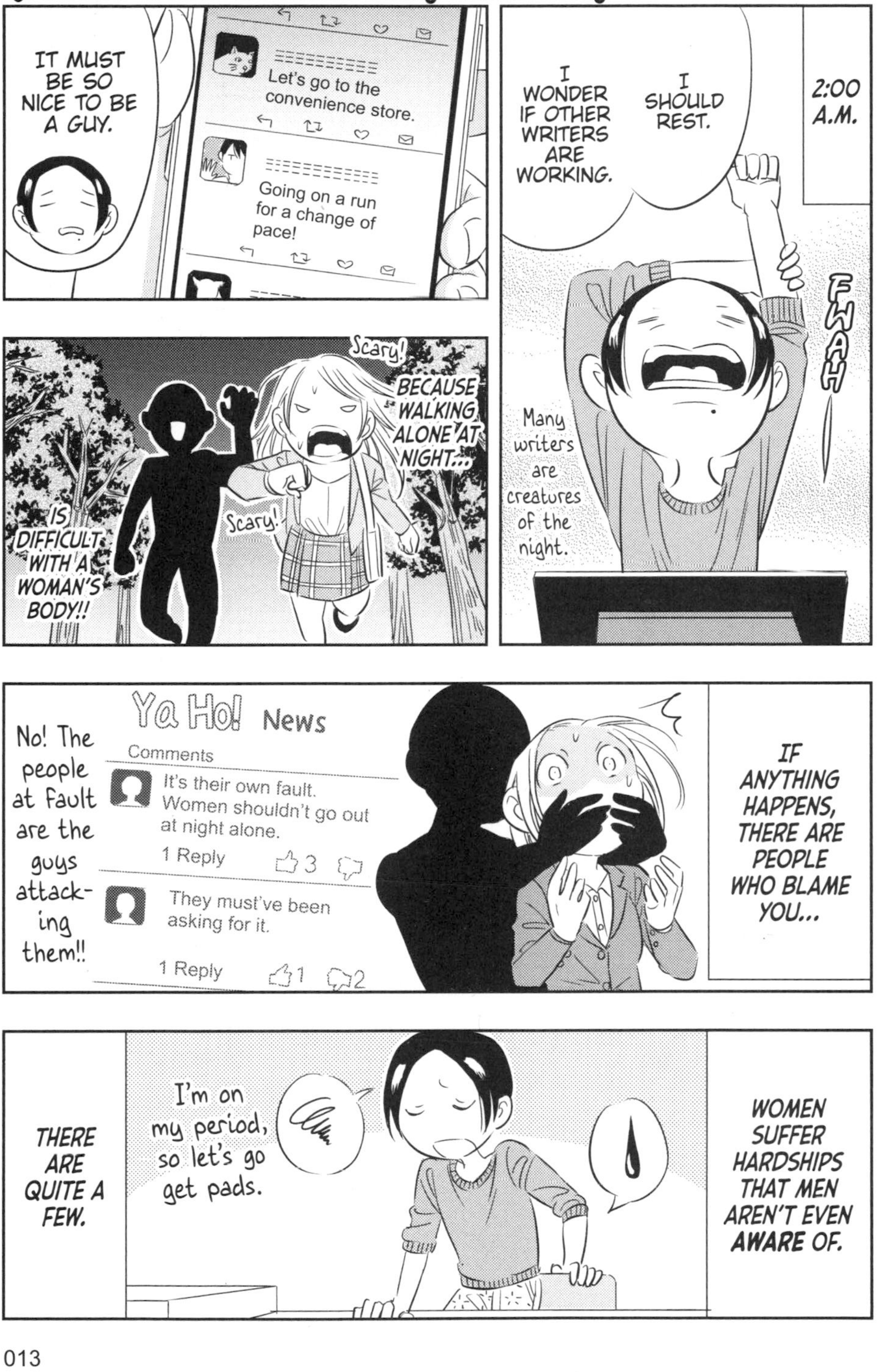
2:00 A.M.
I SHOULD REST.
I WONDER IF OTHER WRITERS ARE WORKING.
FWAH
Many writers are creatures of the night.
Let's go to the convenience store.
Going on a run for a change of pace!
IT MUST BE SO NICE TO BE A GUY.
Scary!
BECAUSE WALKING ALONE AT NIGHT...
Scary!
IS DIFFICULT WITH A WOMAN'S BODY!!
IF ANYTHING HAPPENS, THERE ARE PEOPLE WHO BLAME YOU...
Ya Ho! News
Comments
It's their own fault. Women shouldn't go out at night alone.
1 Reply
3
They must've been asking for it.
1 Reply
1
2
No! The people at fault are the guys attacking them!!
WOMEN SUFFER HARDSHIPS THAT MEN AREN'T EVEN AWARE OF.
I'm on my period, so let's go get pads.
THERE ARE QUITE A FEW.

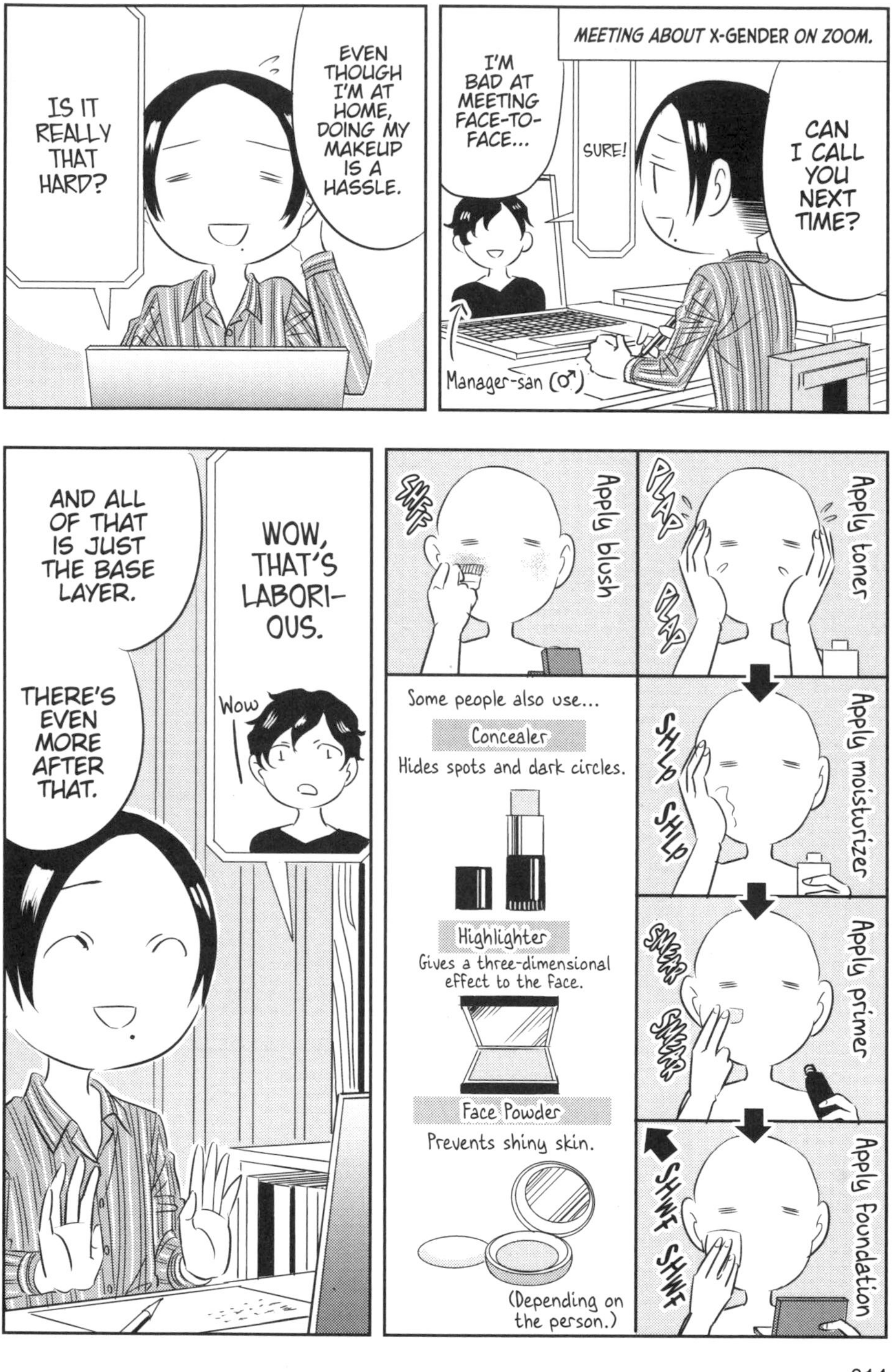
MEETING ABOUT X-GENDER ON ZOOM.
CAN I CALL YOU NEXT TIME?
SURE!
I'M BAD AT MEETING FACE-TO-FACE...
Manager-san (♂)
EVEN THOUGH I'M AT HOME, DOING MY MAKEUP IS A HASSLE.
IS IT REALLY THAT HARD?
Apply toner
PLAP PLAP
Apply moisturizer
SHLP SHLP
Apply primer
SMEAR SMEAR
Apply Foundation
SHWF SHWF
Apply blush
SHFF
Some people also use...
Concealer
Hides spots and dark circles.
Highlighter
Gives a three-dimensional effect to the face.
Face Powder
Prevents shiny skin.
(Depending on the person.)
WOW, THAT'S LABORI-OUS.
Wow
AND ALL OF THAT IS JUST THE BASE LAYER.
THERE'S EVEN MORE AFTER THAT.

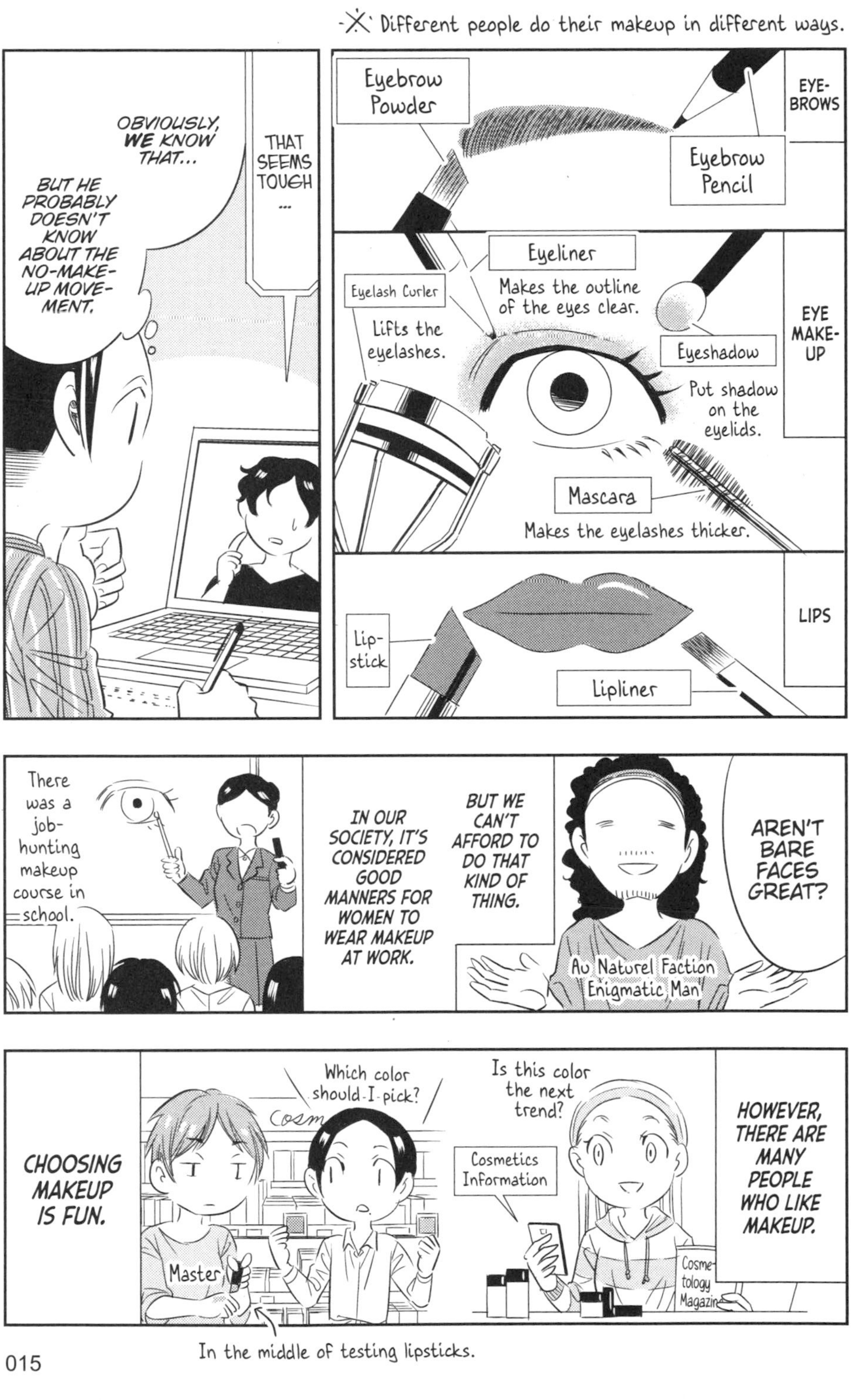
-※- Different people do their makeup in different ways.
EYE-BROWS
Eyebrow Pencil
Eyebrow Powder
EYE MAKE-UP
Eyeshadow
Put shadow on the eyelids.
Eyeliner
Makes the outline of the eyes clear.
Eyelash Curler
Lifts the eyelashes.
Mascara
Makes the eyelashes thicker.
LIPS
Lipliner
Lip-stick
THAT SEEMS TOUGH...
OBVIOUSLY, WE KNOW THAT...
BUT HE PROBABLY DOESN'T KNOW ABOUT THE NO-MAKE-UP MOVE-MENT.
AREN'T BARE FACES GREAT?
Au Naturel Faction Enigmatic Man
BUT WE CAN'T AFFORD TO DO THAT KIND OF THING.
IN OUR SOCIETY, IT'S CONSIDERED GOOD MANNERS FOR WOMEN TO WEAR MAKEUP AT WORK.
There was a job-hunting makeup course in school.
HOWEVER, THERE ARE MANY PEOPLE WHO LIKE MAKEUP.
Is this color the next trend?
Cosmetics Information
Cosme-tology Magazin
Which color should-I-pick?
Master
In the middle of testing lipsticks.
CHOOSING MAKEUP IS FUN.

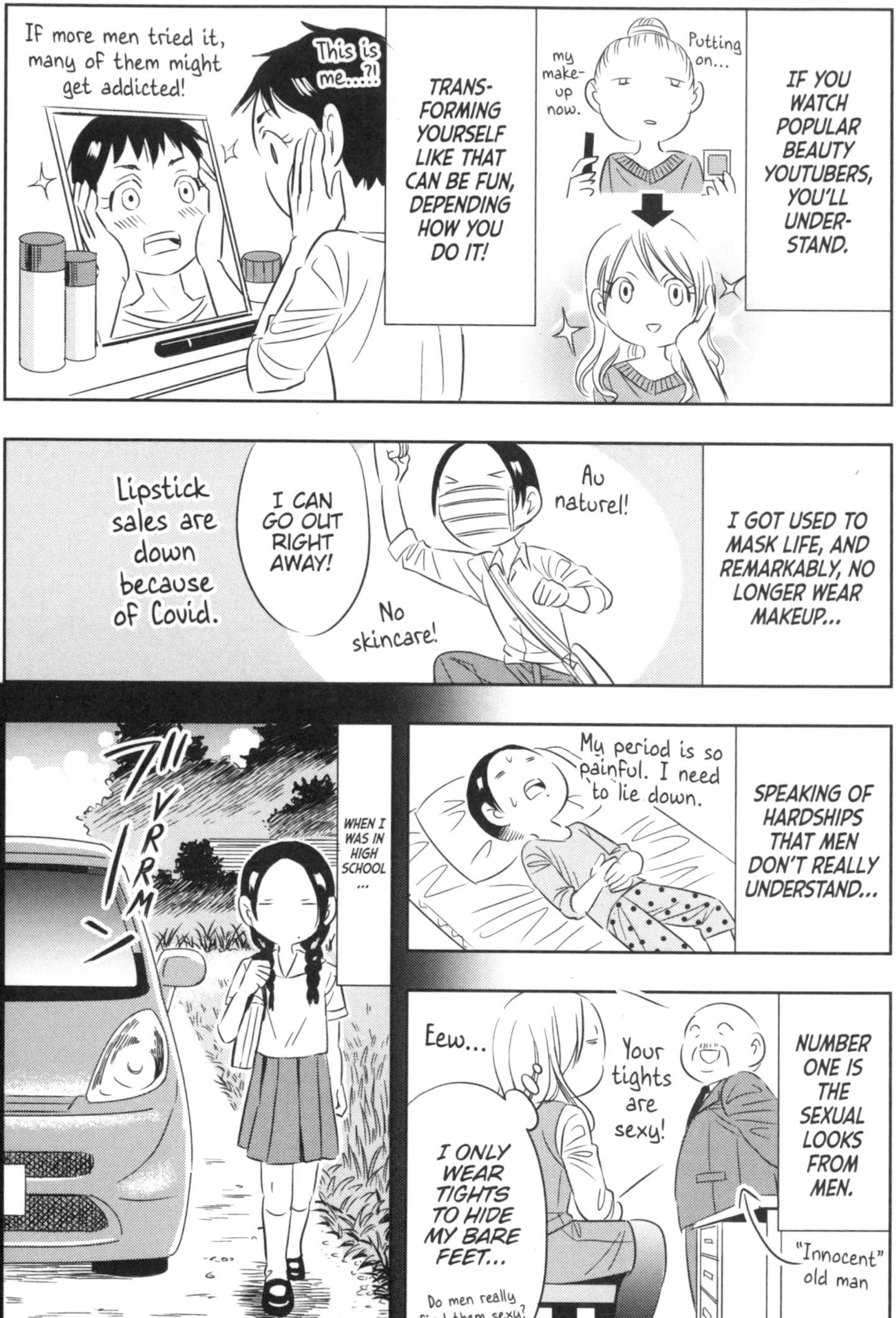
IF YOU WATCH POPULAR BEAUTY YOUTUBERS, YOU'LL UNDERSTAND.
Putting on...
my make-up now.
TRANS-FORMING YOURSELF LIKE THAT CAN BE FUN, DEPENDING HOW YOU DO IT!
This is me...?!
If more men tried it, many of them might get addicted!
I GOT USED TO MASK LIFE, AND REMARKABLY, NO LONGER WEAR MAKEUP...
Au naturel!
I CAN GO OUT RIGHT AWAY!
No skincare!
Lipstick sales are down because of Covid.
SPEAKING OF HARDSHIPS THAT MEN DON'T REALLY UNDERSTAND...
My period is so painful. I need to lie down.
NUMBER ONE IS THE SEXUAL LOOKS FROM MEN.
Your tights are sexy!
Eew...
I ONLY WEAR TIGHTS TO HIDE MY BARE FEET...
Do men really find them sexy?
"Innocent" old man
WHEN I WAS IN HIGH SCHOOL ...
VRRRM

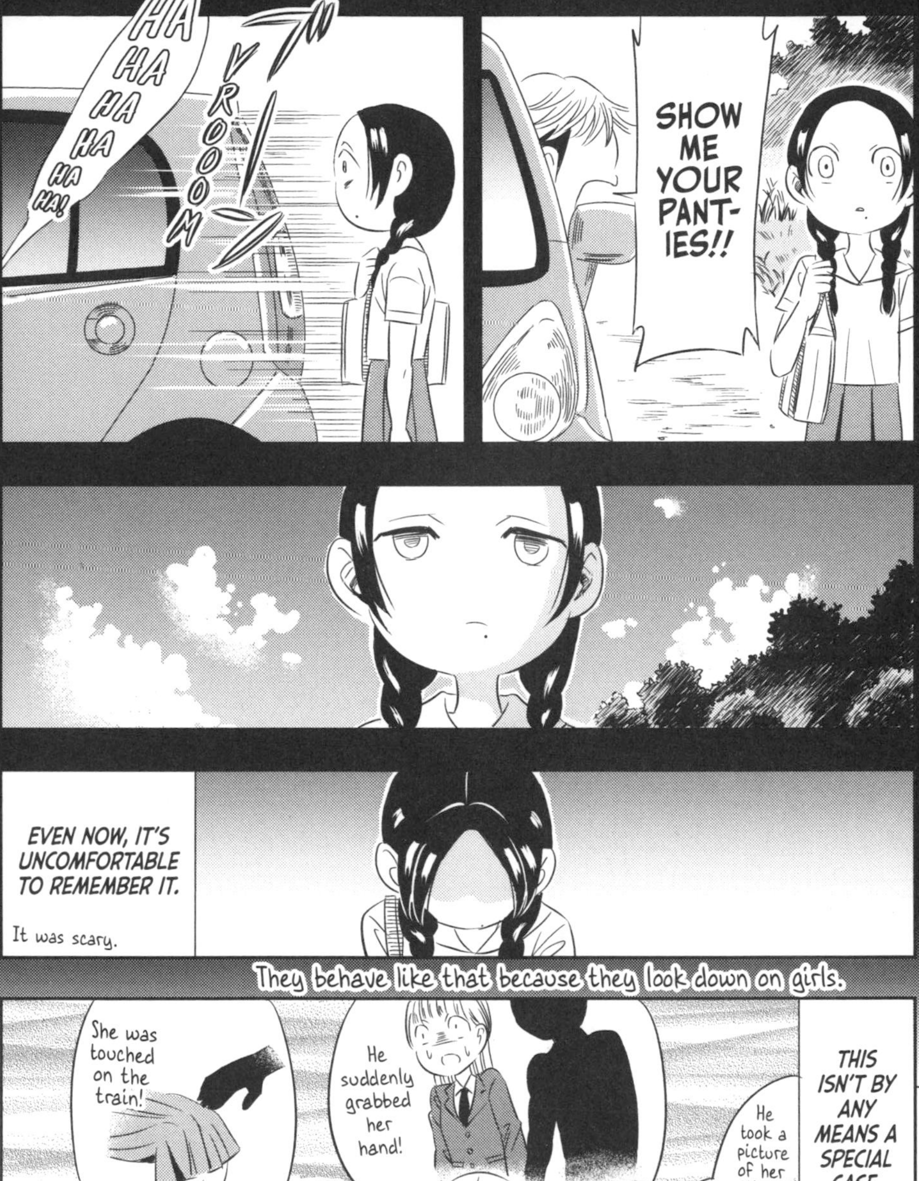
SHOW ME YOUR PANT-IES!!
VROOOOM
HA HA HA HA HA HA!
EVEN NOW, IT'S UNCOMFORTABLE TO REMEMBER IT.
It was scary.
They behave like that because they look down on girls.
THIS ISN'T BY ANY MEANS A SPECIAL CASE.
He took a picture of her with his phone!
He suddenly grabbed her hand!
She was touched on the train!
GIRLS HAVE PLENTY OF EXPERIENCES LIKE THESE.

Even though adults should be protecting them.

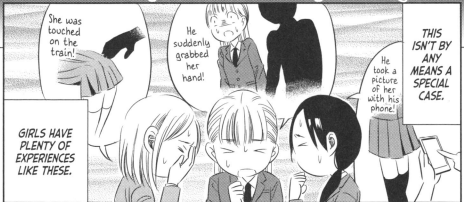

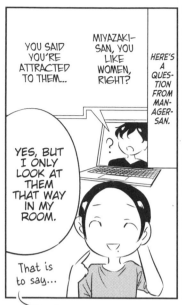

HIGH SCHOOL GIRLS ARE SEXUALIZED JUST FOR EXISTING.
. . .
Don't tempt me, girl!
Middle-Aged Man
She's not a virgin, right?
. . .
Middle-Aged Man
Do you wear school swimsuits in gym class?
Middle-Aged Man
How much will you give to me?
School uniforms are sexy, aren't they?
Middle-Aged Man
Middle-Aged Man
HERE'S A QUESTION FROM MANAGER-SAN.
MIYAZAKI-SAN, YOU LIKE WOMEN, RIGHT?
YOU SAID YOU'RE ATTRACTED TO THEM...
?
YES, BUT I ONLY LOOK AT THEM THAT WAY IN MY ROOM.
That is to say...
DAY TO DAY, I LIVE AS A WOMAN.
Man Switch OFF
Man Switch ON
HGWEEEE!
18+
GENERALLY, WHEN I WATCH PORN, I IMAGINE MYSELF WITH MALE GENITALIA.
BUT IN DAILY LIFE, I'M NOT EXCITED ABOUT WOMEN.
From a female perspective.
I WANT TO COVER HER UP...
There's this kind of thing.
Cleavage Cover
I ONLY GET EXCITED BY ACTRESSES IN PORN...
I MEAN.

If you have questions like this, please DM me on Twitter! Thinking about it helps me realize things about myself, and I'm grateful for it!

It's like this, so I'm "not quite a lesbian," I think.

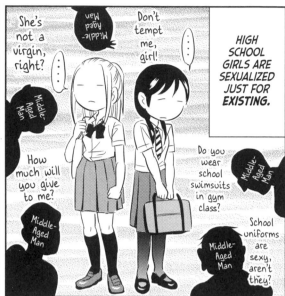

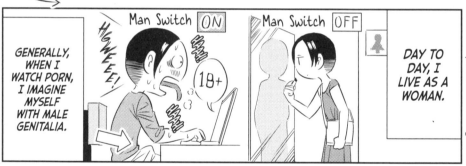

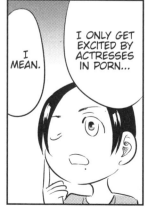

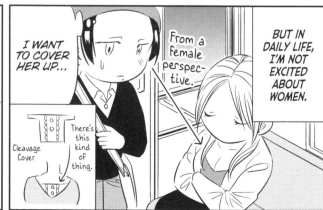

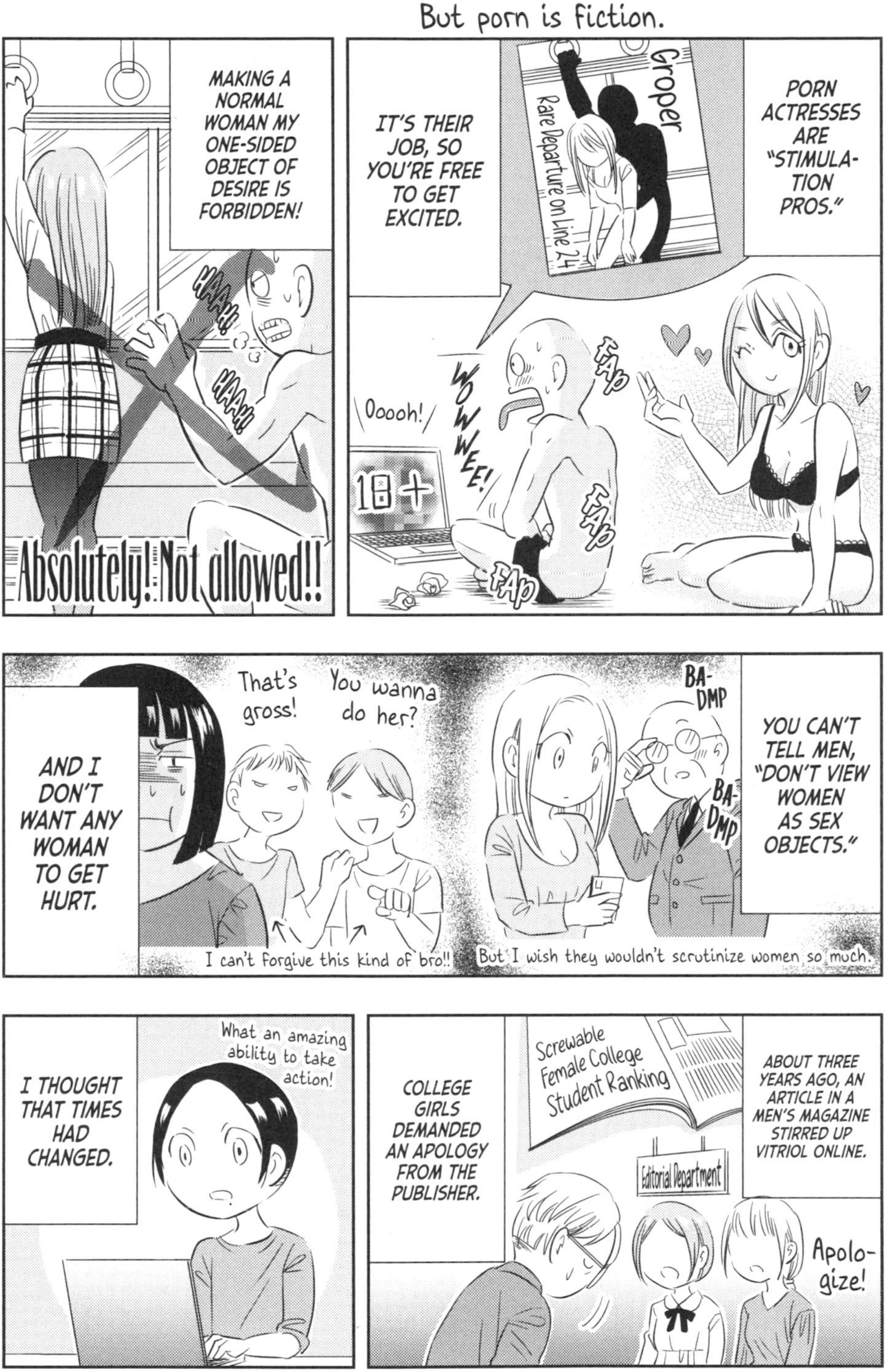
But porn is fiction.
PORN ACTRESSES ARE "STIMULATION PROS."
Groper
Rare Departure on Line 24
IT'S THEIR JOB, SO YOU'RE FREE TO GET EXCITED.
FAP
WOWWEE!
Ooooh!
18+
FAP
FAP
MAKING A NORMAL WOMAN MY ONE-SIDED OBJECT OF DESIRE IS FORBIDDEN!
HAAH!
HAAH!
Absolutely! Not allowed!!
YOU CAN'T TELL MEN, "DON'T VIEW WOMEN AS SEX OBJECTS."
BA-DMP
BA-DMP
But I wish they wouldn't scrutinize women so much.
You wanna do her?
That's gross!
AND I DON'T WANT ANY WOMAN TO GET HURT.
I can't forgive this kind of bro!!
ABOUT THREE YEARS AGO, AN ARTICLE IN A MEN'S MAGAZINE STIRRED UP VITRIOL ONLINE.
Screwable Female College Student Ranking
Editorial Department
COLLEGE GIRLS DEMANDED AN APOLOGY FROM THE PUBLISHER.
Apologize!
What an amazing ability to take action!
I THOUGHT THAT TIMES HAD CHANGED.

My high school era: the scenery I was often exposed to on the train.

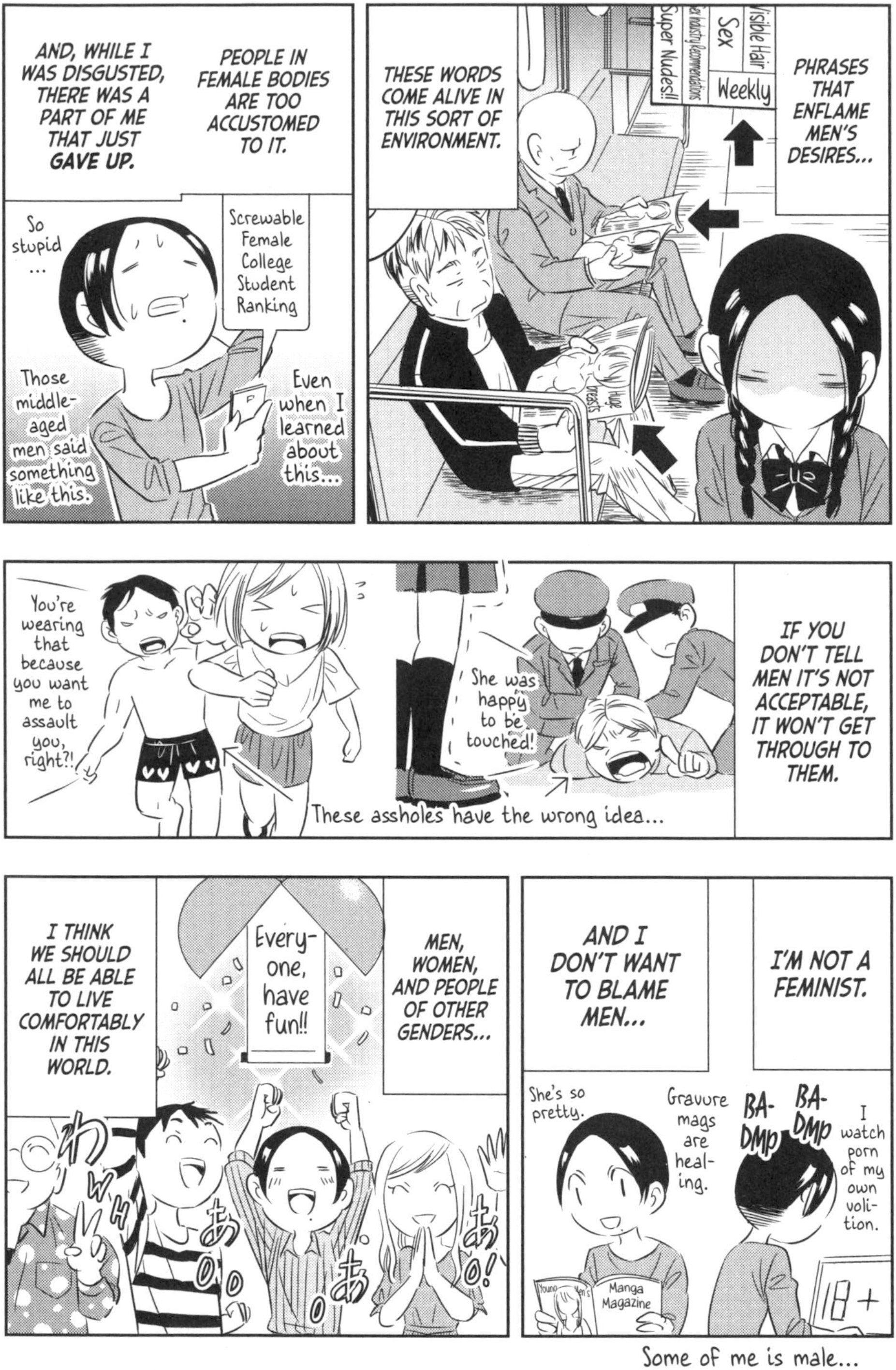
PHRASES THAT ENFLAME MEN'S DESIRES...
Weekly
Sex
Visible Hair
Sex industry Recommendations
Super Nudes!!
THESE WORDS COME ALIVE IN THIS SORT OF ENVIRONMENT.
Huge breasts
PEOPLE IN FEMALE BODIES ARE TOO ACCUSTOMED TO IT.
AND, WHILE I WAS DISGUSTED, THERE WAS A PART OF ME THAT JUST GAVE UP.
Screwable Female College Student Ranking
So stupid ...
Even when I learned about this...
Those middle-aged men said something like this.
IF YOU DON'T TELL MEN IT'S NOT ACCEPTABLE, IT WON'T GET THROUGH TO THEM.
She was happy to be touched!
You're wearing that because you want me to assault you, right?!
These assholes have the wrong idea...
I'M NOT A FEMINIST.
AND I DON'T WANT TO BLAME MEN...
BA-DMP
BA-DMP
I watch porn of my own volition.
Gravure mags are healing.
She's so pretty.
Young Men's Manga Magazine
18+
MEN, WOMEN, AND PEOPLE OF OTHER GENDERS...
Every-one, have fun!!
I THINK WE SHOULD ALL BE ABLE TO LIVE COMFORTABLY IN THIS WORLD.

Some of me is male...

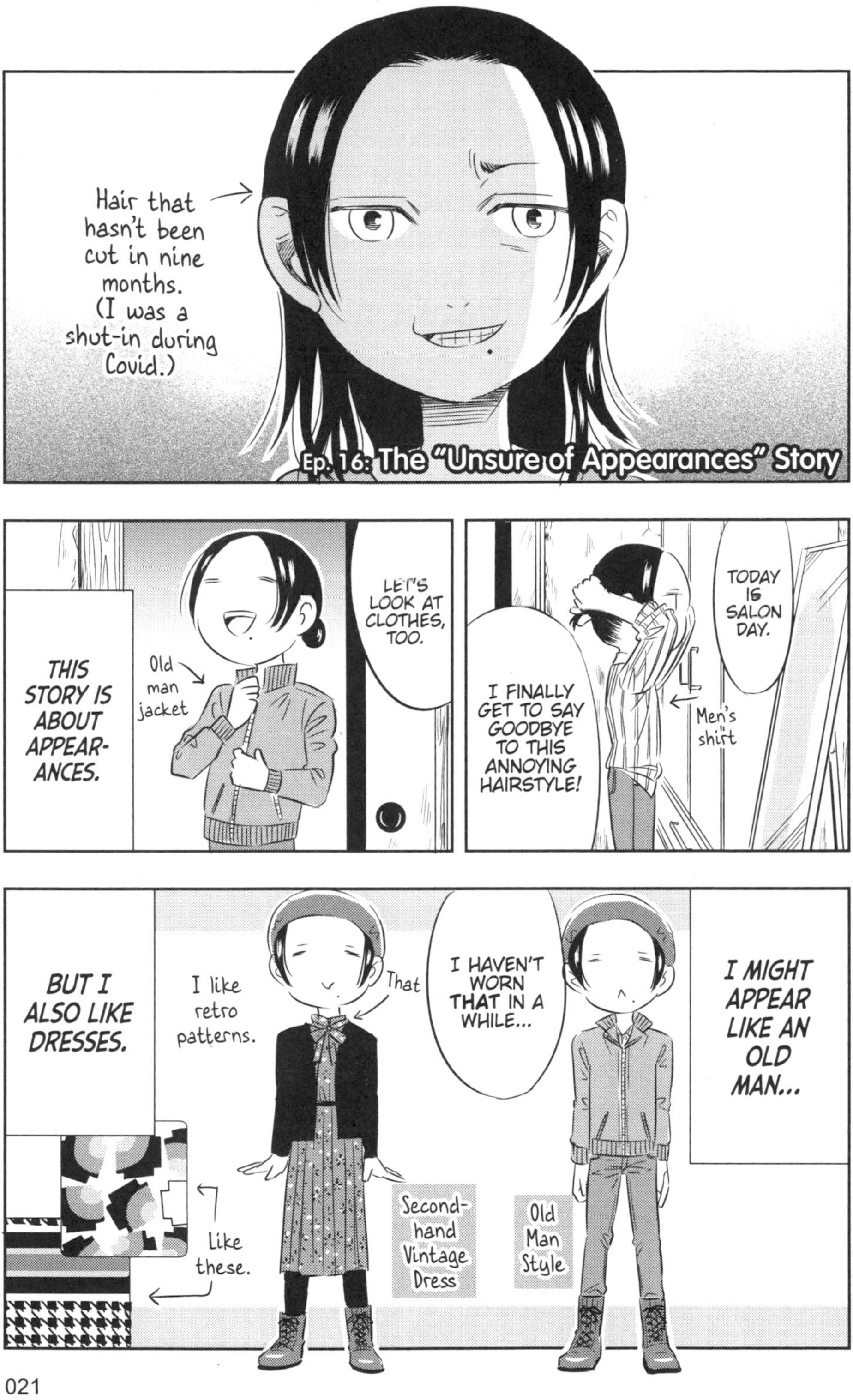
Hair that hasn't been cut in nine months. (I was a shut-in during Covid.)
Ep. 16: The "Unsure of Appearances" Story
TODAY IS SALON DAY.
I FINALLY GET TO SAY GOODBYE TO THIS ANNOYING HAIRSTYLE!
Men's shirt
LET'S LOOK AT CLOTHES, TOO.
THIS STORY IS ABOUT APPEARANCES.
Old man jacket
I MIGHT APPEAR LIKE AN OLD MAN...
Old Man Style
I HAVEN'T WORN THAT IN A WHILE...
That
Second-hand Vintage Dress
I like retro patterns.
BUT I ALSO LIKE DRESSES.
Like these.

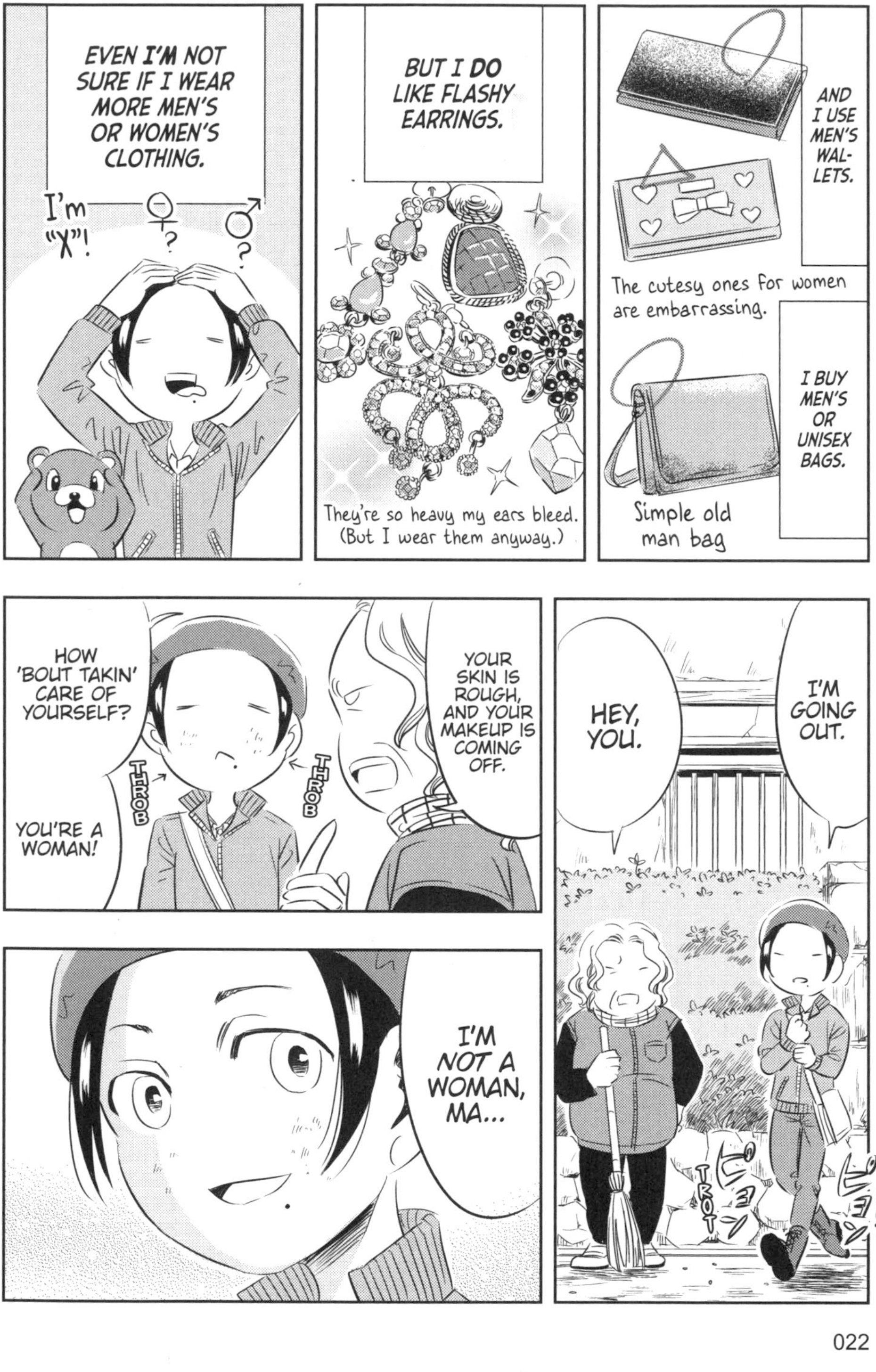
AND I USE MEN'S WAL-LETS.
The cutesy ones for women are embarrassing.
I BUY MEN'S OR UNISEX BAGS.
Simple old man bag
BUT I DO LIKE FLASHY EARRINGS.
They're so heavy my ears bleed. (But I wear them anyway.)
EVEN I'M NOT SURE IF I WEAR MORE MEN'S OR WOMEN'S CLOTHING.
I'm "X"!
♀?
♂?
I'M GOING OUT.
HEY, YOU.
TROT
TROT
YOUR SKIN IS ROUGH, AND YOUR MAKEUP IS COMING OFF.
THROB
THROB
HOW 'BOUT TAKIN' CARE OF YOURSELF?
YOU'RE A WOMAN!
I'M NOT A WOMAN, MA...

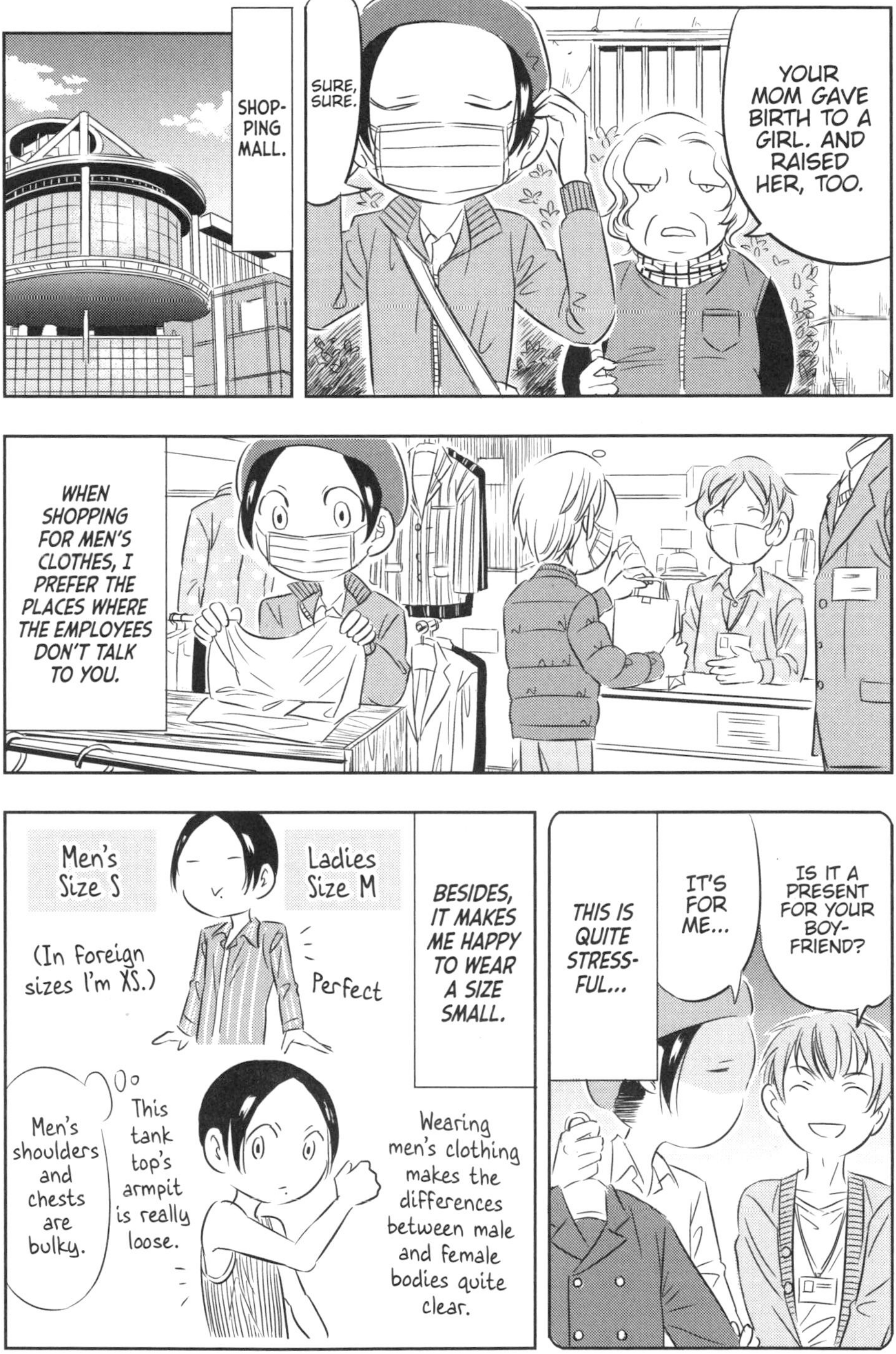
YOUR MOM GAVE BIRTH TO A GIRL. AND RAISED HER, TOO.
SURE, SURE.
SHOP-PING MALL.
WHEN SHOPPING FOR MEN'S CLOTHES, I PREFER THE PLACES WHERE THE EMPLOYEES DON'T TALK TO YOU.
IS IT A PRESENT FOR YOUR BOY-FRIEND?
IT'S FOR ME...
THIS IS QUITE STRESS-FUL...
BESIDES, IT MAKES ME HAPPY TO WEAR A SIZE SMALL.
Ladies Size M
Men's Size S
(In foreign sizes I'm XS.)
Perfect
Wearing men's clothing makes the differences between male and female bodies quite clear.
This tank top's armpit is really loose.
Men's shoulders and chests are bulky.

Now, would I be asked, "Is it for your husband?"

Groooss!!

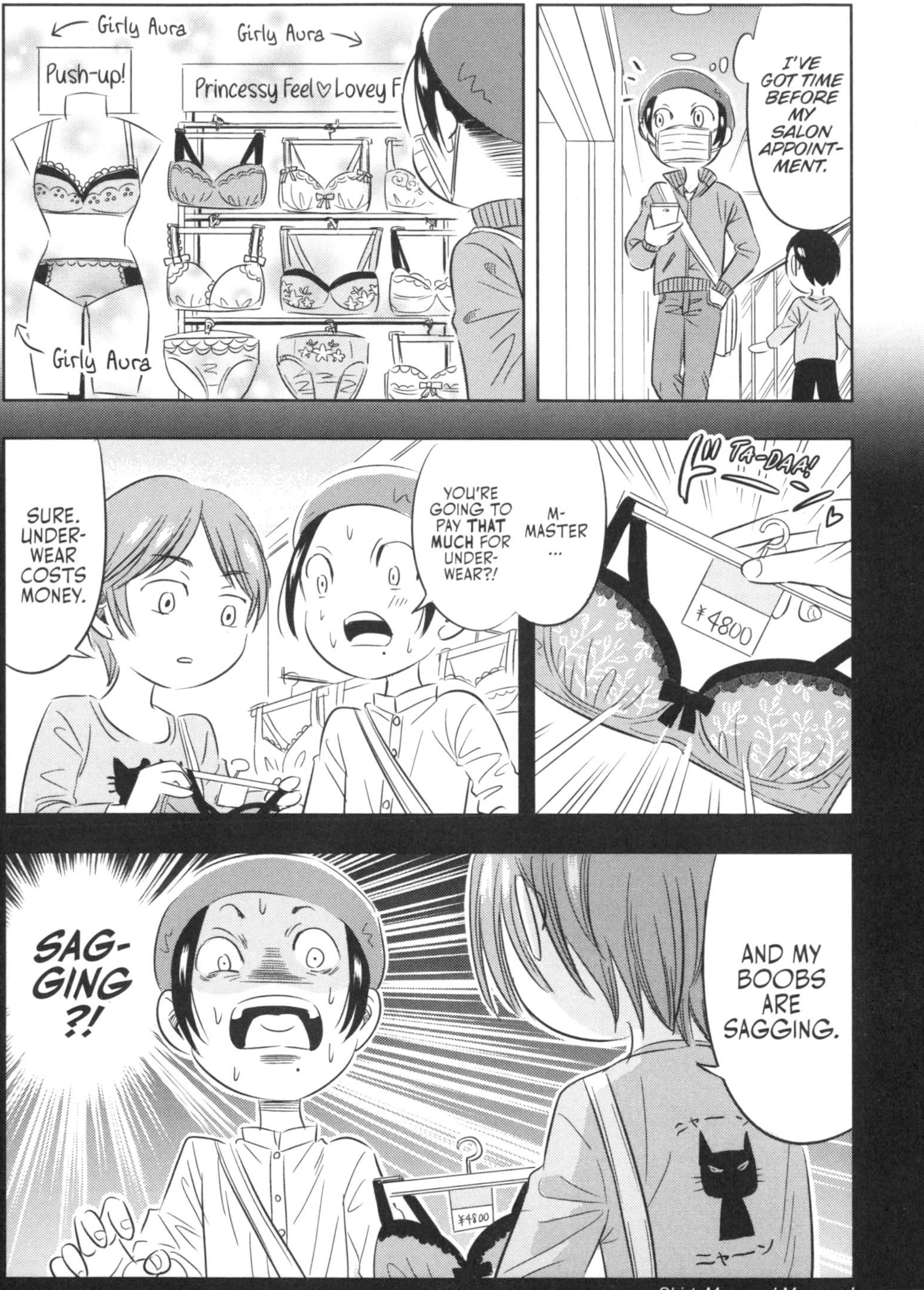
I'VE GOT TIME BEFORE MY SALON APPOINTMENT.
Girly Aura
Girly Aura
Push-up!
Princessy Feel♡Lovey F
Girly Aura
TA-DAA!
¥4800
M-MASTER...
YOU'RE GOING TO PAY **THAT MUCH** FOR UNDERWEAR?!
SURE. UNDERWEAR COSTS MONEY.
AND MY BOOBS ARE SAGGING.
SAGGING?!
¥4800
ニャーン
ニャーン

Shirt: Meooow! Meooow!

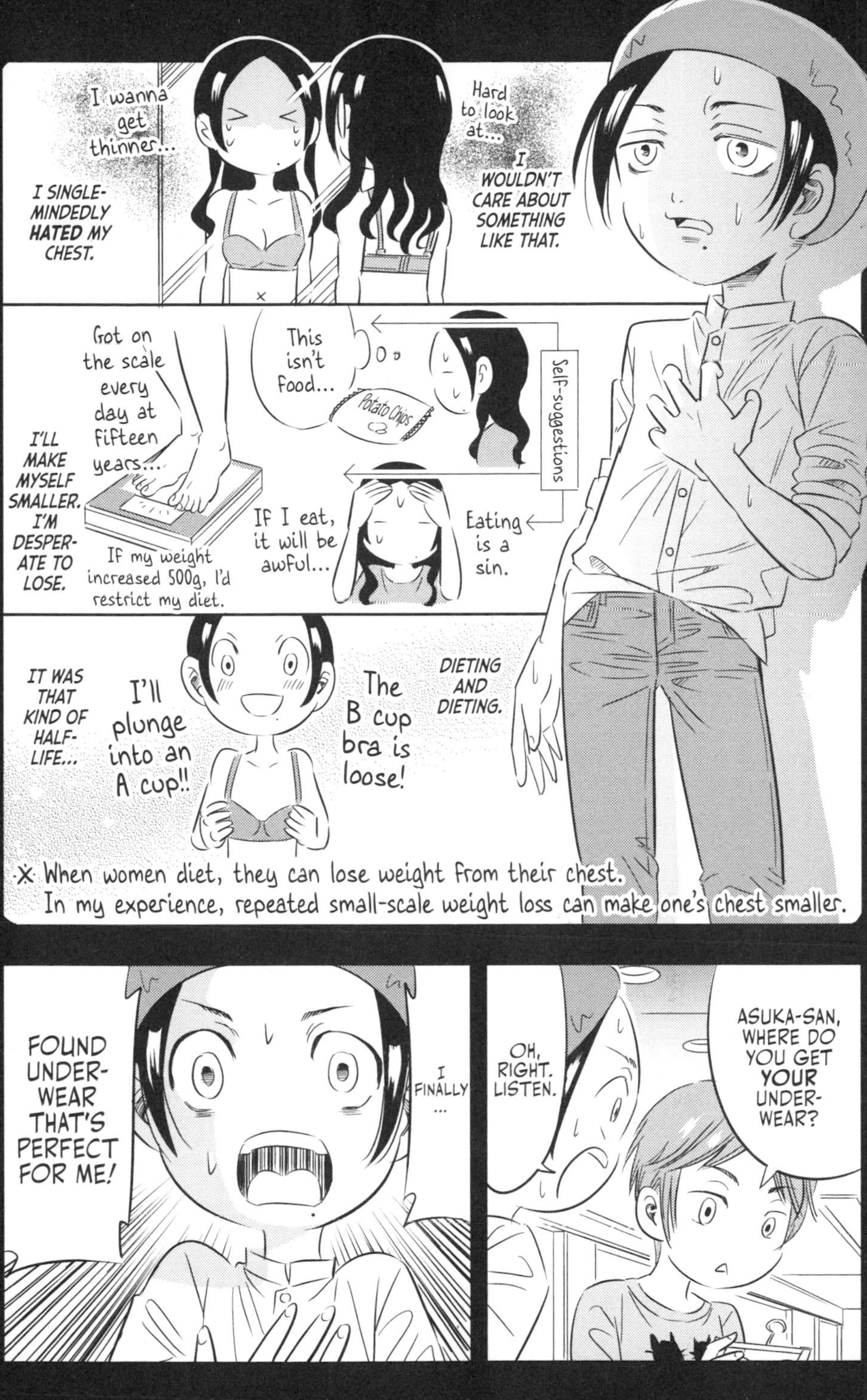

Hard to look at...
I WOULDN'T CARE ABOUT SOMETHING LIKE THAT.
I wanna get thinner...
I SINGLE-MINDEDLY HATED MY CHEST.
Self-suggestions
This isn't food...
Potato Chips
Eating is a sin.
If I eat, it will be awful...
Got on the scale every day at fifteen years...
If my weight increased 500g, I'd restrict my diet.
I'LL MAKE MYSELF SMALLER. I'M DESPERATE TO LOSE.
DIETING AND DIETING.
The B cup bra is loose!
I'll plunge into an A cup!!
IT WAS THAT KIND OF HALF-LIFE...
※ When women diet, they can lose weight from their chest. In my experience, repeated small-scale weight loss can make one's chest smaller.
ASUKA-SAN, WHERE DO YOU GET YOUR UNDERWEAR?
OH, RIGHT. LISTEN.
I FINALLY...
FOUND UNDERWEAR THAT'S PERFECT FOR ME!

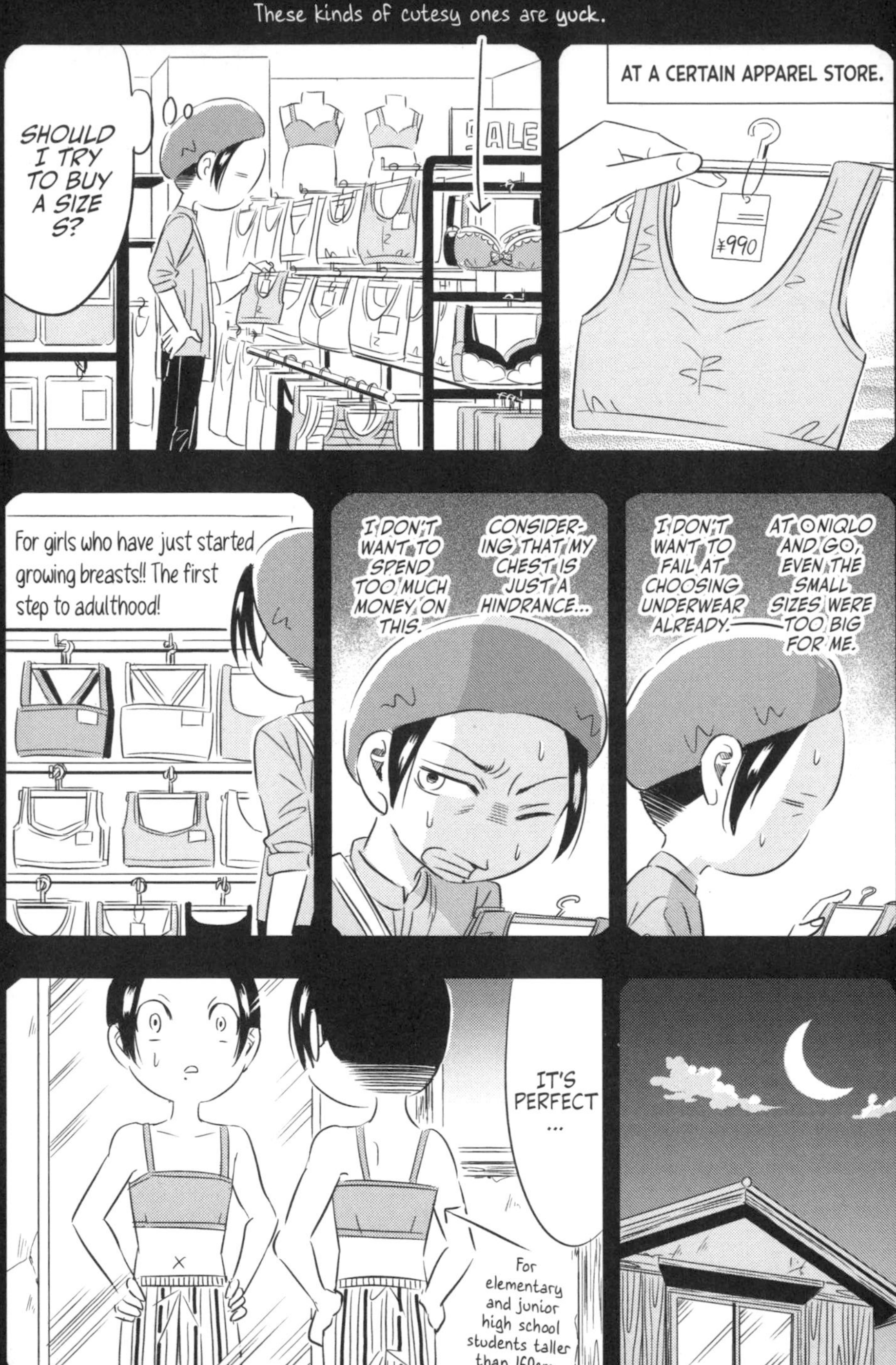
AT A CERTAIN APPAREL STORE.
¥990
These kinds of cutesy ones are yuck.
SALE
SHOULD I TRY TO BUY A SIZE S?
AT ONIQLO AND GO, EVEN THE SMALL SIZES WERE TOO BIG FOR ME.
I DON'T WANT TO FAIL AT CHOOSING UNDERWEAR ALREADY.
CONSIDERING THAT MY CHEST IS JUST A HINDRANCE...
I DON'T WANT TO SPEND TOO MUCH MONEY ON THIS.
For girls who have just started growing breasts!! The first step to adulthood!
IT'S PERFECT ...
For elementary and junior high school students taller than 160cm.

It's not that I'm petite, there just isn't anything for small breasts.

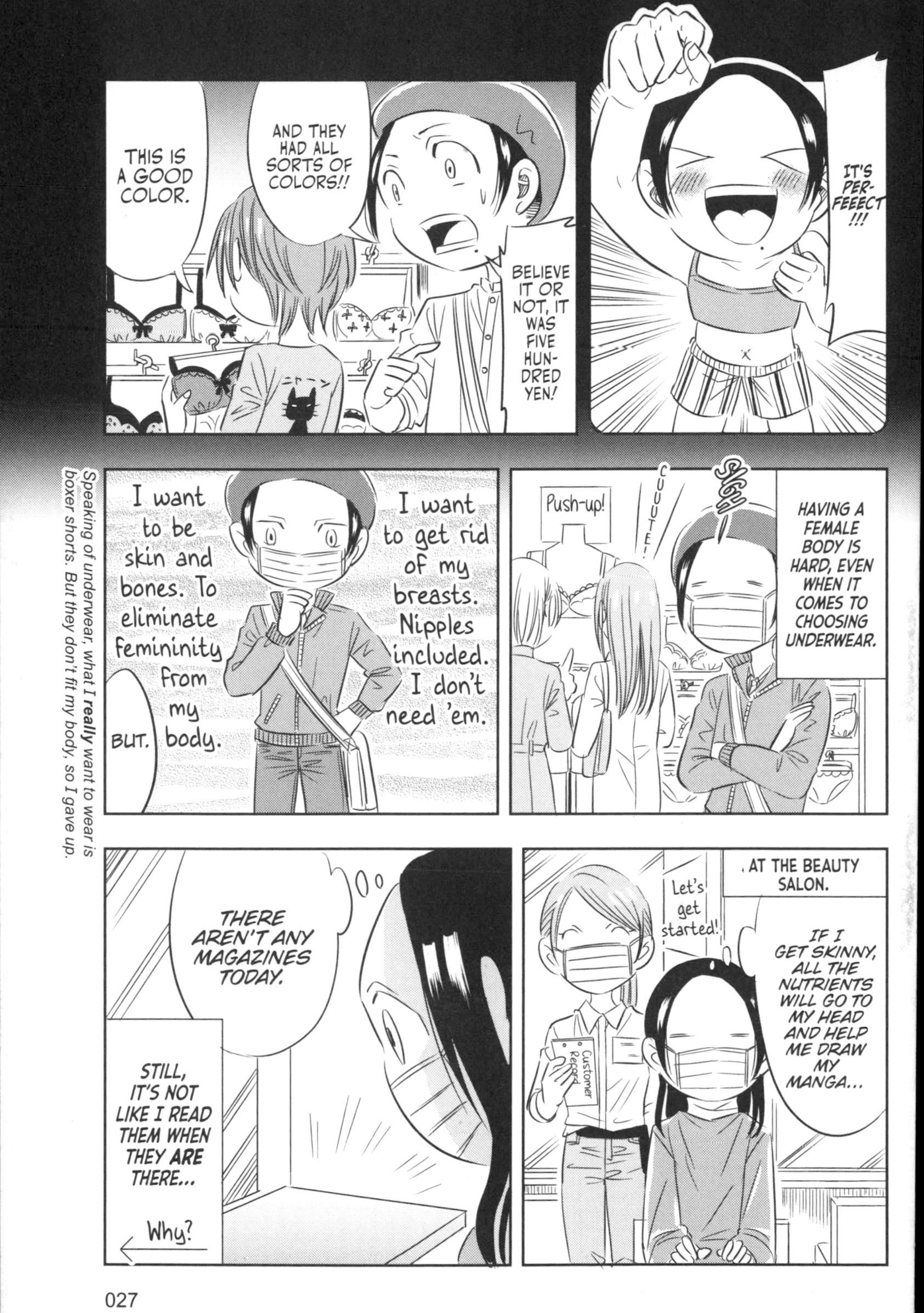
IT'S PER-FEEECT!!!
THIS IS A GOOD COLOR.
AND THEY HAD ALL SORTS OF COLORS!!
BELIEVE IT OR NOT, IT WAS FIVE HUNDRED YEN!
HAVING A FEMALE BODY IS HARD, EVEN WHEN IT COMES TO CHOOSING UNDERWEAR.
SIGH
CUUUTE!
Push-up!
I want to get rid of my breasts. Nipples included. I don't need 'em.
I want to be skin and bones. To eliminate femininity from my body.
BUT.
AT THE BEAUTY SALON.
IF I GET SKINNY, ALL THE NUTRIENTS WILL GO TO MY HEAD AND HELP ME DRAW MY MANGA...
Let's get started!
Customer Record
THERE AREN'T ANY MAGAZINES TODAY.
STILL, IT'S NOT LIKE I READ THEM WHEN THEY **ARE** THERE...
Why?

*Speaking of underwear, what I **really** want to wear is boxer shorts. But they don't fit my body, so I gave up.*

When I was a student, there were lots of sharp fashion magazines that didn't care about how men perceived them. Like KERA! and Zipper...

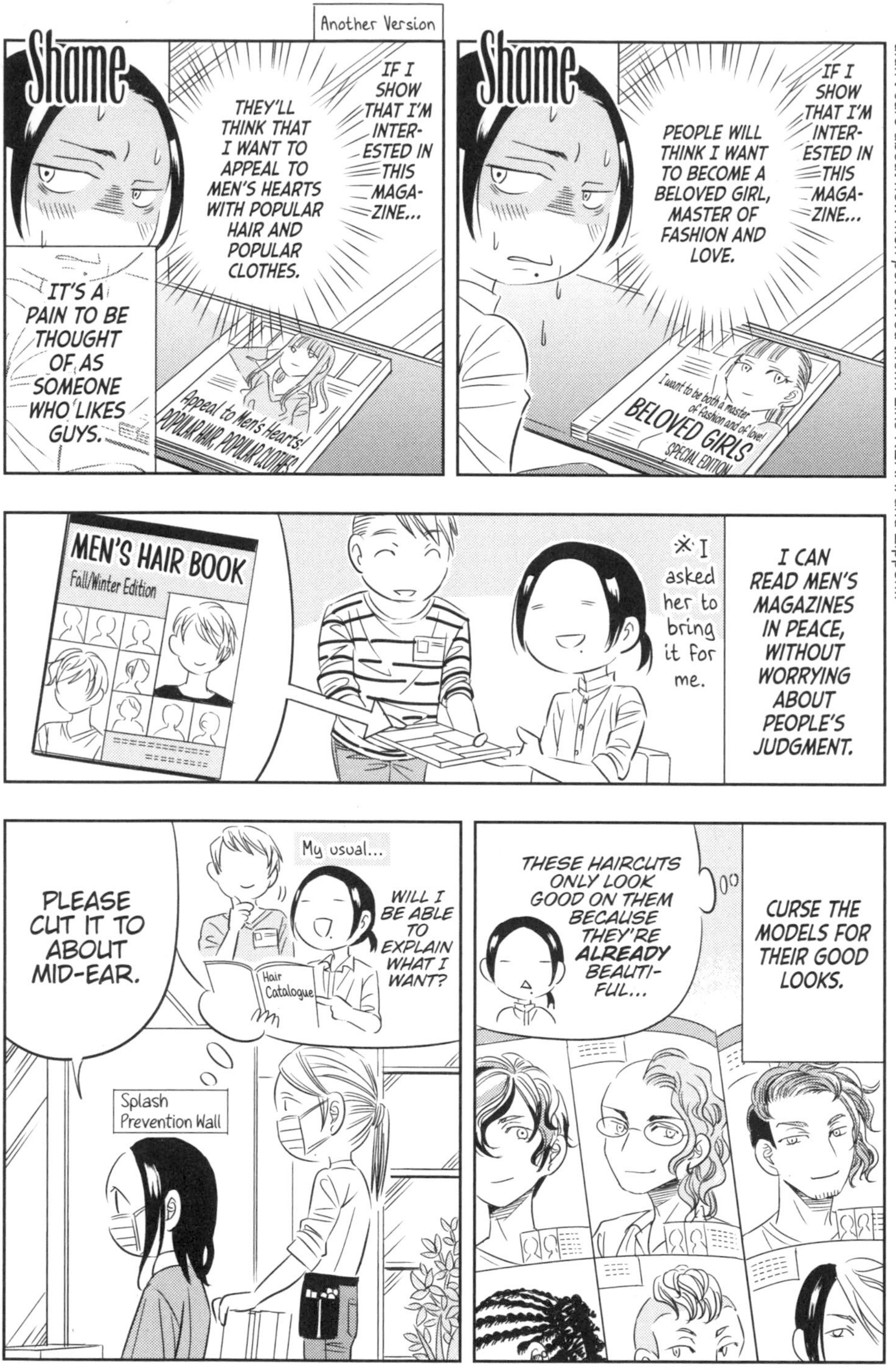

Shame
IF I SHOW THAT I'M INTERESTED IN THIS MAGAZINE...
PEOPLE WILL THINK I WANT TO BECOME A BELOVED GIRL, MASTER OF FASHION AND LOVE.
I want to be both a master of fashion and of love!
BELOVED GIRLS
SPECIAL EDITION
Another Version
Shame
IF I SHOW THAT I'M INTERESTED IN THIS MAGAZINE...
THEY'LL THINK THAT I WANT TO APPEAL TO MEN'S HEARTS WITH POPULAR HAIR AND POPULAR CLOTHES.
IT'S A PAIN TO BE THOUGHT OF AS SOMEONE WHO LIKES GUYS.
Appeal to Men's Hearts!
POPULAR HAIR, POPULAR CLOTHES
I CAN READ MEN'S MAGAZINES IN PEACE, WITHOUT WORRYING ABOUT PEOPLE'S JUDGMENT.
※I asked her to bring it for me.
MEN'S HAIR BOOK
Fall/Winter Edition
CURSE THE MODELS FOR THEIR GOOD LOOKS.
THESE HAIRCUTS ONLY LOOK GOOD ON THEM BECAUSE THEY'RE ALREADY BEAUTIFUL...
My usual...
WILL I BE ABLE TO EXPLAIN WHAT I WANT?
Hair Catalogue
PLEASE CUT IT TO ABOUT MID-EAR.
Splash Prevention Wall

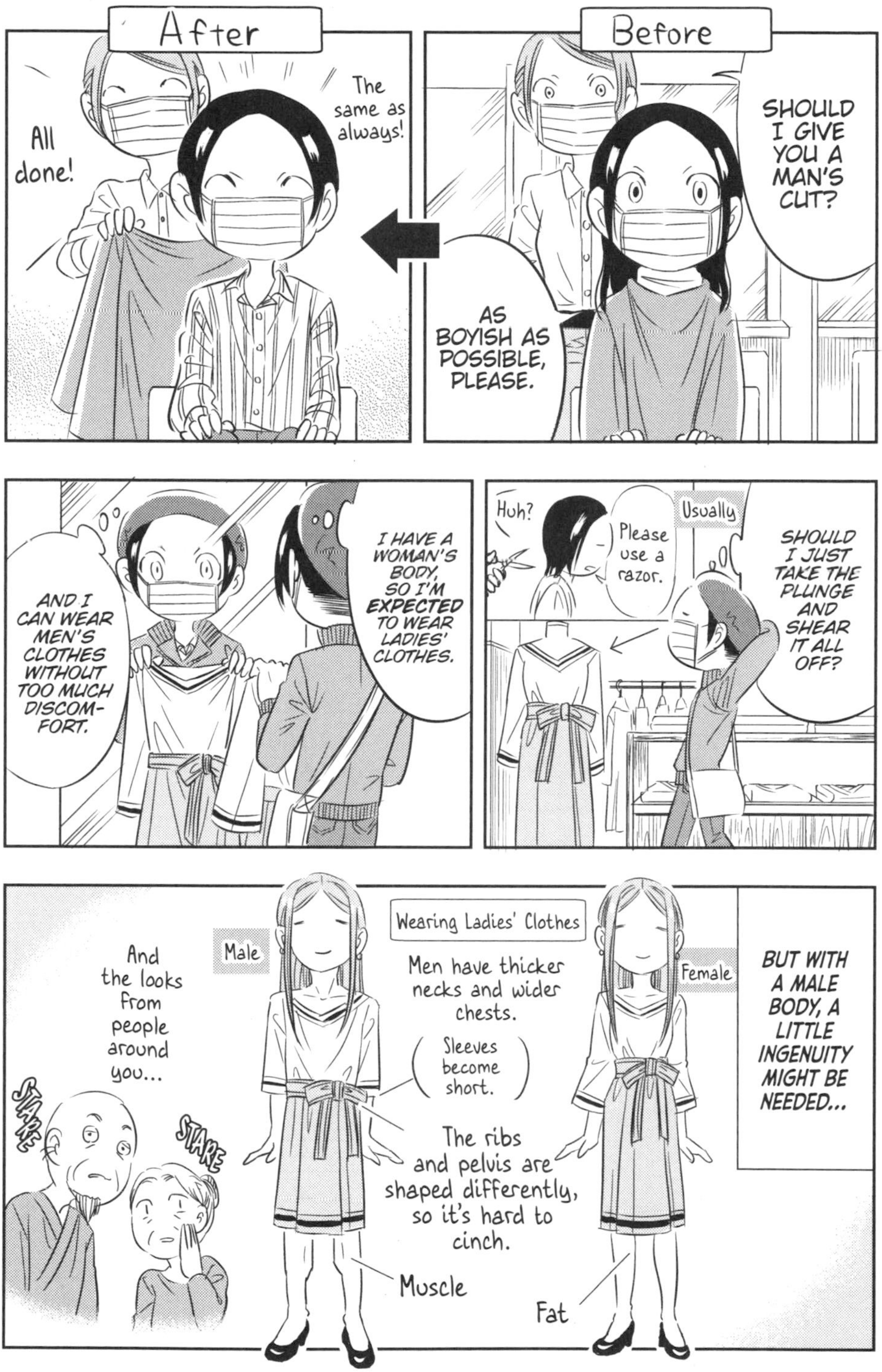
Before
SHOULD I GIVE YOU A MAN'S CUT?
AS BOYISH AS POSSIBLE, PLEASE.
After
The same as always!
All done!
Usually
SHOULD I JUST TAKE THE PLUNGE AND SHEAR IT ALL OFF?
Please use a razor.
Huh?
I HAVE A WOMAN'S BODY, SO I'M EXPECTED TO WEAR LADIES' CLOTHES.
AND I CAN WEAR MEN'S CLOTHES WITHOUT TOO MUCH DISCOMFORT.
BUT WITH A MALE BODY, A LITTLE INGENUITY MIGHT BE NEEDED...
Wearing Ladies' Clothes
Female
Male
Men have thicker necks and wider chests.
(Sleeves become short.)
The ribs and pelvis are shaped differently, so it's hard to cinch.
Fat
Muscle
And the looks from people around you...
STARE
STARE

Because the American Village was a playground, nothing that anyone wore surprised me.

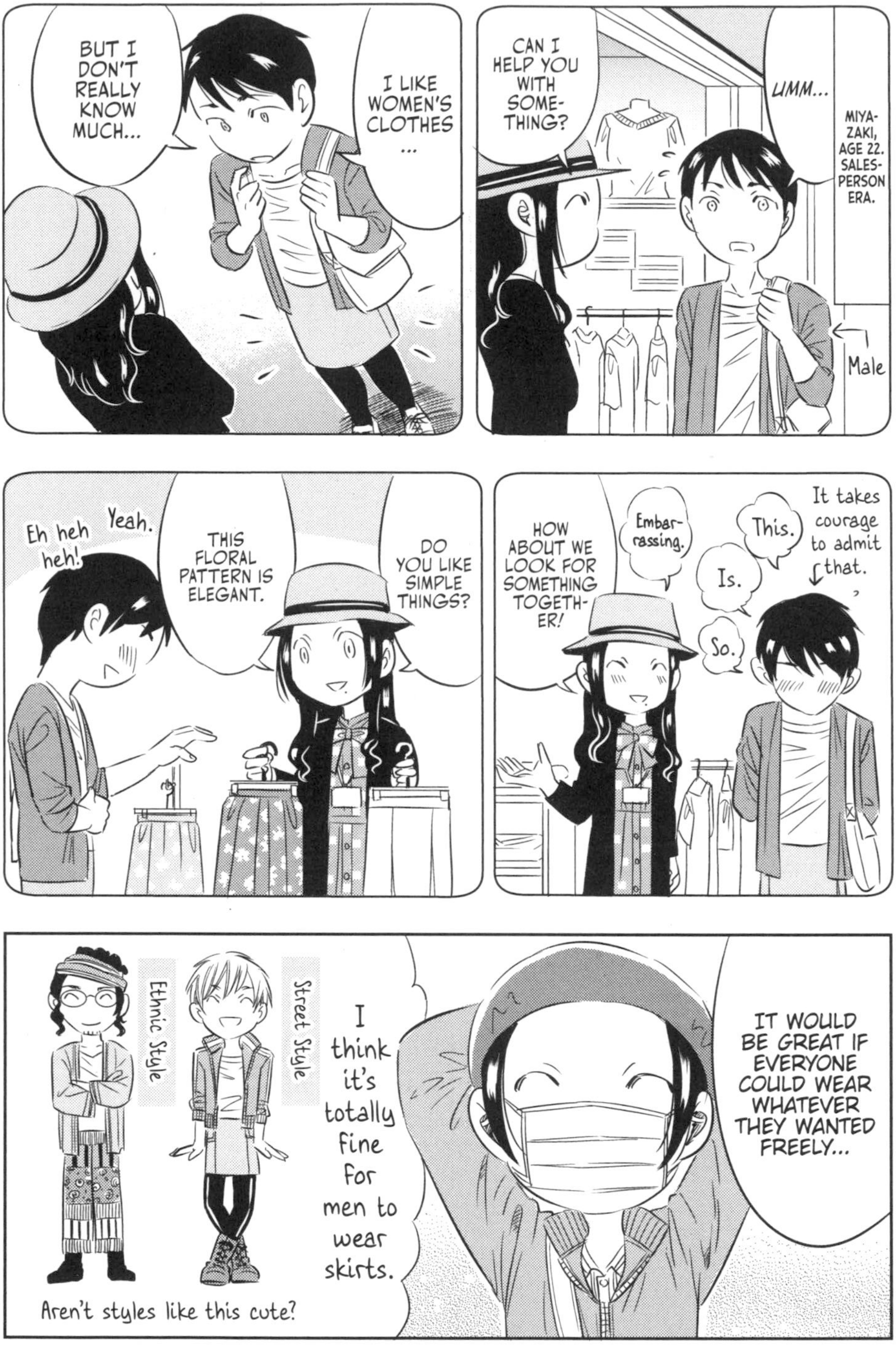
CAN I HELP YOU WITH SOMETHING?
UMM...
MIYAZAKI, AGE 22. SALESPERSON ERA.
Male
I LIKE WOMEN'S CLOTHES ...
BUT I DON'T REALLY KNOW MUCH...
It takes courage to admit that.
HOW ABOUT WE LOOK FOR SOMETHING TOGETHER!
This.
Is.
So.
Embarrassing.
DO YOU LIKE SIMPLE THINGS?
THIS FLORAL PATTERN IS ELEGANT.
Yeah.
Eh heh heh!
IT WOULD BE GREAT IF EVERYONE COULD WEAR WHATEVER THEY WANTED FREELY...
I think it's totally fine for men to wear skirts.
Street Style
Ethnic Style
Aren't styles like this cute?

Since the third semester of our third year in junior high doesn't affect our reports, we have some freedom.

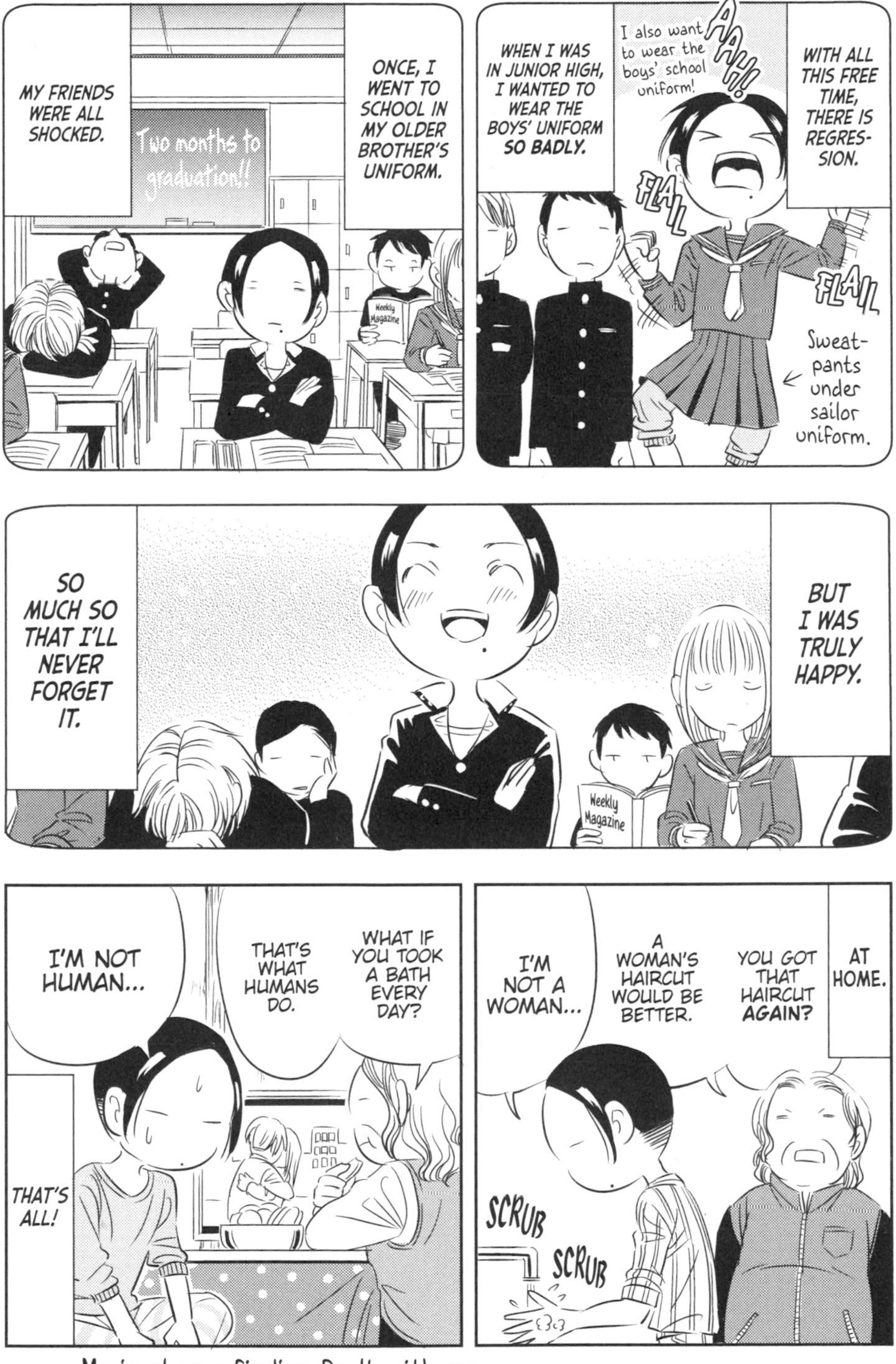
WITH ALL THIS FREE TIME, THERE IS REGRES-SION.
AAAH!!
I also want to wear the boys' school uniform!
WHEN I WAS IN JUNIOR HIGH, I WANTED TO WEAR THE BOYS' UNIFORM **SO BADLY.**
FLAIL
FLAIL
Sweat-pants under sailor uniform.
ONCE, I WENT TO SCHOOL IN MY OLDER BROTHER'S UNIFORM.
Two months to graduation!!
Weekly Magazine
MY FRIENDS WERE ALL SHOCKED.
BUT I WAS TRULY HAPPY.
SO MUCH SO THAT I'LL NEVER FORGET IT.
Weekly Magazine
AT HOME.
YOU GOT THAT HAIRCUT **AGAIN?**
A WOMAN'S HAIRCUT WOULD BE BETTER.
I'M NOT A WOMAN...
SCRUB
SCRUB
WHAT IF YOU TOOK A BATH EVERY DAY?
THAT'S WHAT HUMANS DO.
I'M NOT HUMAN...
THAT'S ALL!

Ma is always finding fault with me.

Ep. 17: The "Junior High School Girls" Story

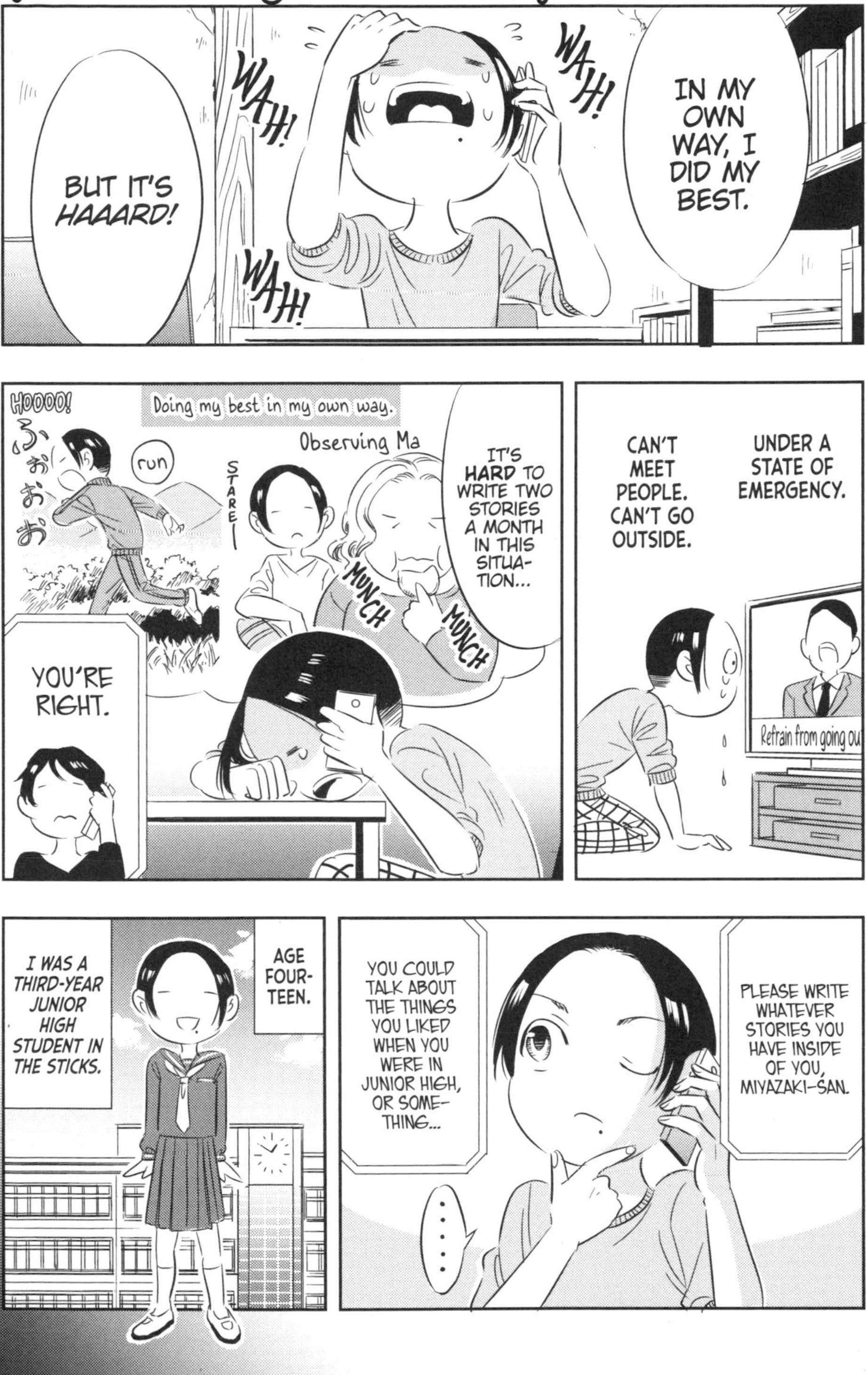

IN MY OWN WAY, I DID MY BEST.
WAH!
WAH!
WAH!
BUT IT'S *HAAARD!*
UNDER A STATE OF EMERGENCY.
CAN'T MEET PEOPLE. CAN'T GO OUTSIDE.
Refrain from going ou
Doing my best in my own way.
HOOOO!
ふおおお
run
Observing Ma
STARE
IT'S **HARD** TO WRITE TWO STORIES A MONTH IN THIS SITUATION...
MUNCH
MUNCH
YOU'RE RIGHT.
PLEASE WRITE WHATEVER STORIES YOU HAVE INSIDE OF YOU, MIYAZAKI-SAN.
YOU COULD TALK ABOUT THE THINGS YOU LIKED WHEN YOU WERE IN JUNIOR HIGH, OR SOMETHING...
......
AGE FOURTEEN.
I WAS A THIRD-YEAR JUNIOR HIGH STUDENT IN THE STICKS.

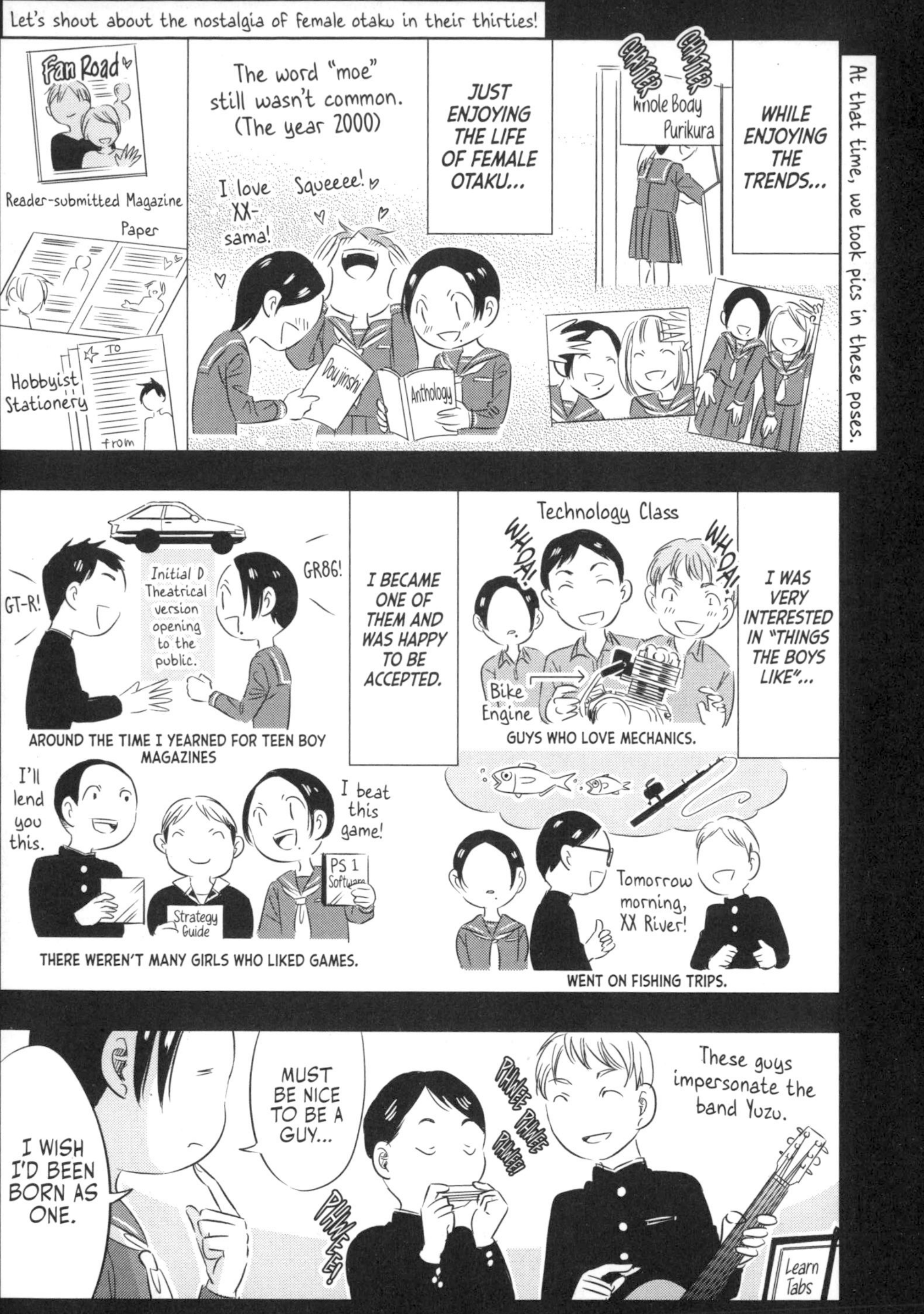
Let's shout about the nostalgia of female otaku in their thirties!
At that time, we took pics in these poses.
WHILE ENJOYING THE TRENDS...
CHATTER
CHATTER
Whole Body Purikura
JUST ENJOYING THE LIFE OF FEMALE OTAKU...
The word "moe" still wasn't common. (The year 2000)
Squeeee!
I love XX-sama!
Doujinshi
Anthology
Fan Road
Reader-submitted Magazine
Paper
Hobbyist Stationery
TO
from
I WAS VERY INTERESTED IN "THINGS THE BOYS LIKE"...
Technology Class
WHOA!
WHOA!
Bike Engine
GUYS WHO LOVE MECHANICS.
Tomorrow morning, XX River!
WENT ON FISHING TRIPS.
I BECAME ONE OF THEM AND WAS HAPPY TO BE ACCEPTED.
GR86!
Initial D Theatrical version opening to the public.
GT-R!
AROUND THE TIME I YEARNED FOR TEEN BOY MAGAZINES
I beat this game!
PS 1 Software
Strategy Guide
I'll lend you this.
THERE WEREN'T MANY GIRLS WHO LIKED GAMES.
These guys impersonate the band Yuzu.
Learn Tabs
PHWEE PHWEE PHWEE!
PHWEEE!
MUST BE NICE TO BE A GUY...
I WISH I'D BEEN BORN AS ONE.

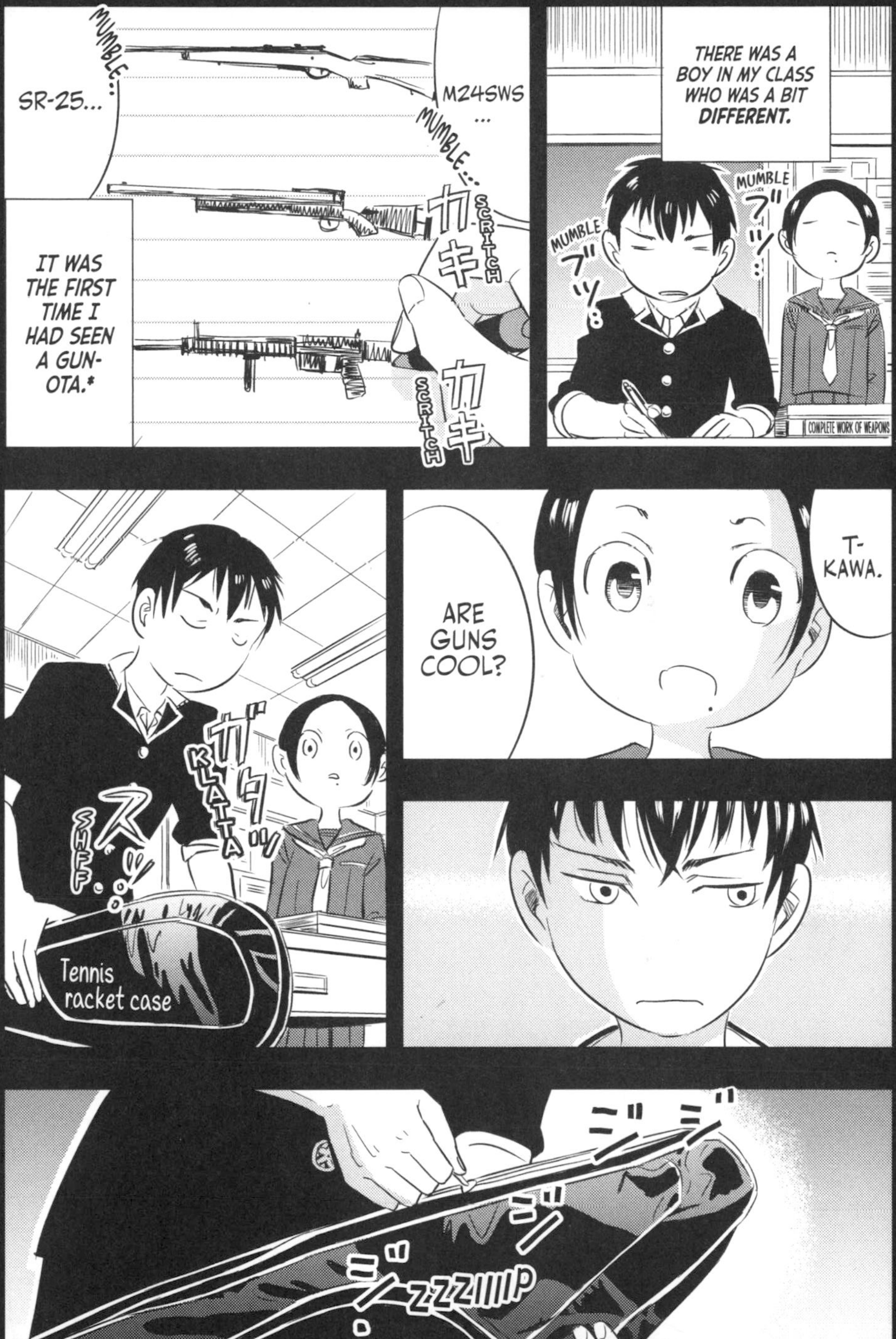
THERE WAS A BOY IN MY CLASS WHO WAS A BIT DIFFERENT.
MUMBLE
MUMBLE
COMPLETE WORK OF WEAPONS
MUMBLE...
SR-25...
M24SWS ...
MUMBLE...
SCRITCH
SCRITCH
IT WAS THE FIRST TIME I HAD SEEN A GUN-OTA.*
T-KAWA.
ARE GUNS COOL?
KLATTA
SHFF
Tennis racket case
ZZZIIIIP

*Military otaku. Although the term lumps them all together, they seem to have various preferences and types of knowledge.

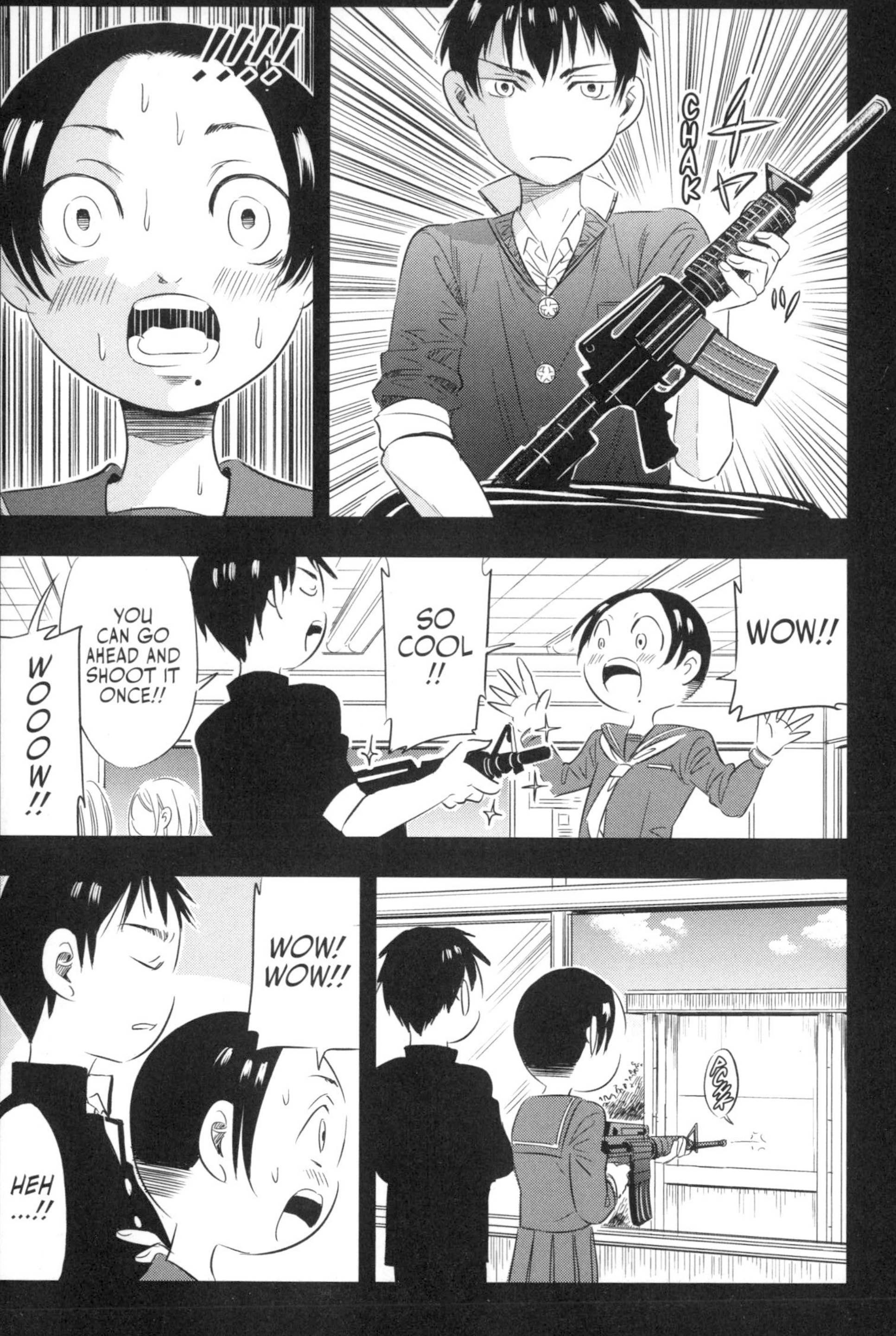
CHAK
...!!!!
WOW!!
SO COOL !!
YOU CAN GO AHEAD AND SHOOT IT ONCE!!
WOOOOW!!
PCHK
WOW! WOW!!
HEH ...!!

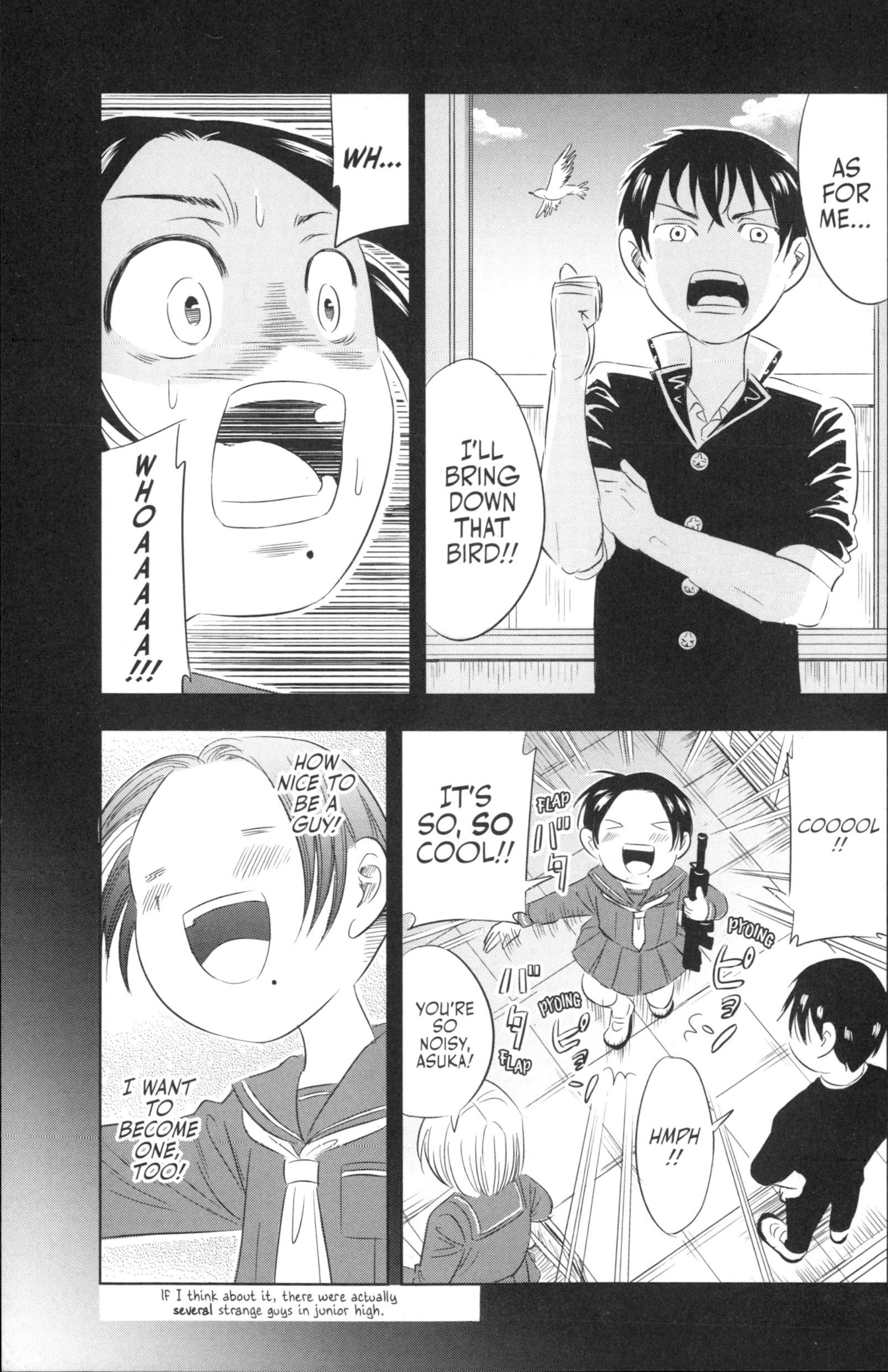
AS FOR ME...
I'LL BRING DOWN THAT BIRD!!
WH...
WHOAAAAAAA!!!
COOOOL!!
PYOING
IT'S SO, SO COOL!!
FLAP
PYOING
FLAP
HMPH!!
YOU'RE SO NOISY, ASUKA!
HOW NICE TO BE A GUY!
I WANT TO BECOME ONE, TOO!

If I think about it, there were actually **several** strange guys in junior high.

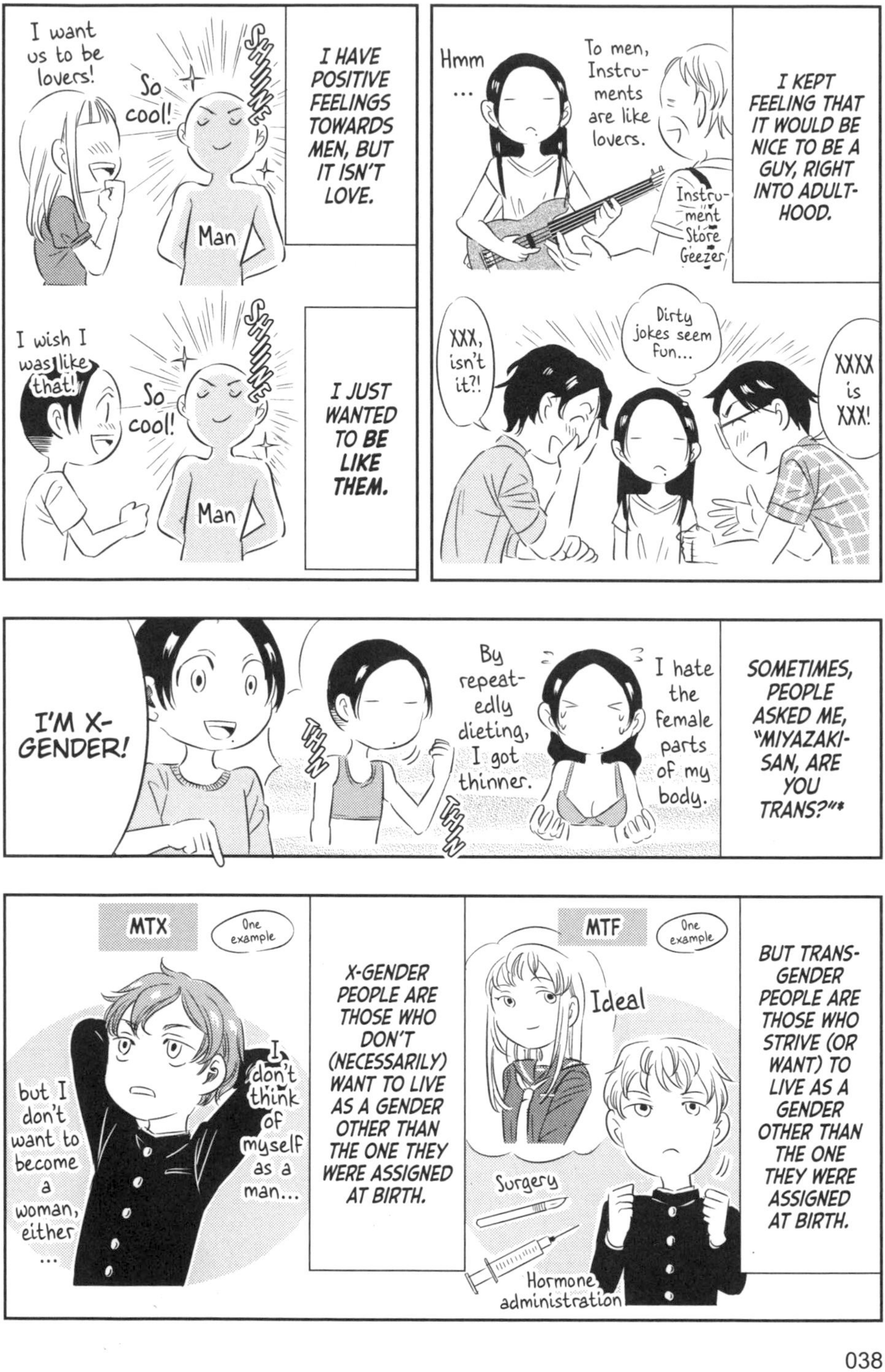
I KEPT FEELING THAT IT WOULD BE NICE TO BE A GUY, RIGHT INTO ADULTHOOD.
To men, Instruments are like lovers.
Instrument Store Geezer
Hmm ...
XXXX is XXX!
Dirty jokes seem fun...
XXX, isn't it?!
I HAVE POSITIVE FEELINGS TOWARDS MEN, BUT IT ISN'T LOVE.
SHIIINE
So cool!
Man
I want us to be lovers!
I JUST WANTED TO BE LIKE THEM.
SHIIINE
So cool!
Man
I wish I was like that!
SOMETIMES, PEOPLE ASKED ME, "MIYAZAKI-SAN, ARE YOU TRANS?"*
I hate the female parts of my body.
By repeatedly dieting, I got thinner.
THIN
THIN
I'M X-GENDER!
BUT TRANSGENDER PEOPLE ARE THOSE WHO STRIVE (OR WANT) TO LIVE AS A GENDER OTHER THAN THE ONE THEY WERE ASSIGNED AT BIRTH.
MTF
One example
Ideal
Surgery
Hormone administration
X-GENDER PEOPLE ARE THOSE WHO DON'T (NECESSARILY) WANT TO LIVE AS A GENDER OTHER THAN THE ONE THEY WERE ASSIGNED AT BIRTH.
MTX
One example
I don't think of myself as a man...
but I don't want to become a woman, either ...

*Trans = transgender.

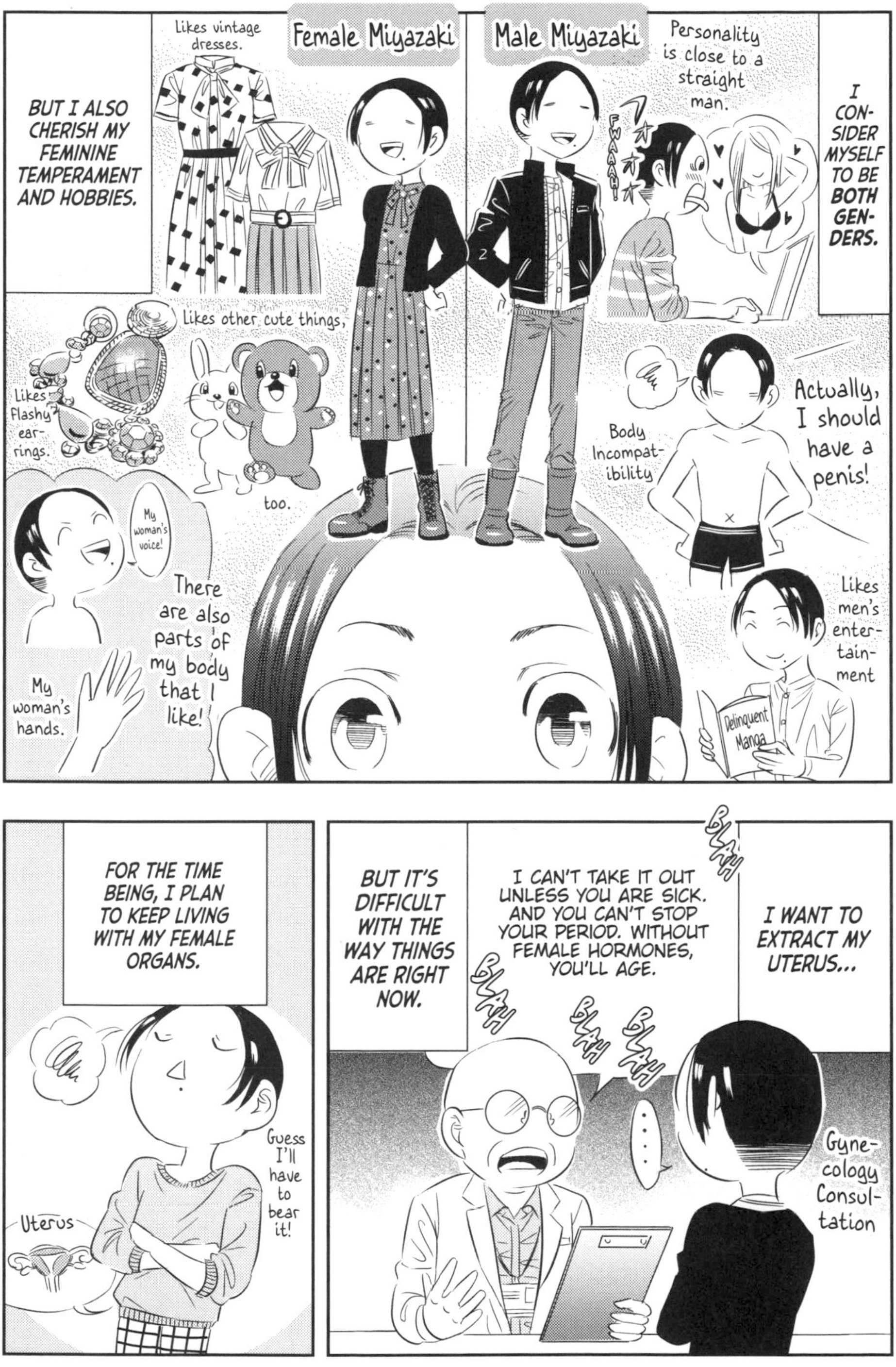
I CONSIDER MYSELF TO BE BOTH GENDERS.
Personality is close to a straight man.
FWAAAH!
Male Miyazaki
Female Miyazaki
Likes vintage dresses.
BUT I ALSO CHERISH MY FEMININE TEMPERAMENT AND HOBBIES.
Actually, I should have a penis!
Body Incompatibility
Likes other cute things,
too.
Likes flashy earrings.
Likes men's entertainment
Delinquent Manga
There are also parts of my body that I like!
My woman's voice!
My woman's hands.
I WANT TO EXTRACT MY UTERUS...
BLAH
I CAN'T TAKE IT OUT UNLESS YOU ARE SICK. AND YOU CAN'T STOP YOUR PERIOD. WITHOUT FEMALE HORMONES, YOU'LL AGE.
BUT IT'S DIFFICULT WITH THE WAY THINGS ARE RIGHT NOW.
BLAH
BLAH
BLAH
...
Gynecology Consultation
FOR THE TIME BEING, I PLAN TO KEEP LIVING WITH MY FEMALE ORGANS.
Guess I'll have to bear it!
Uterus

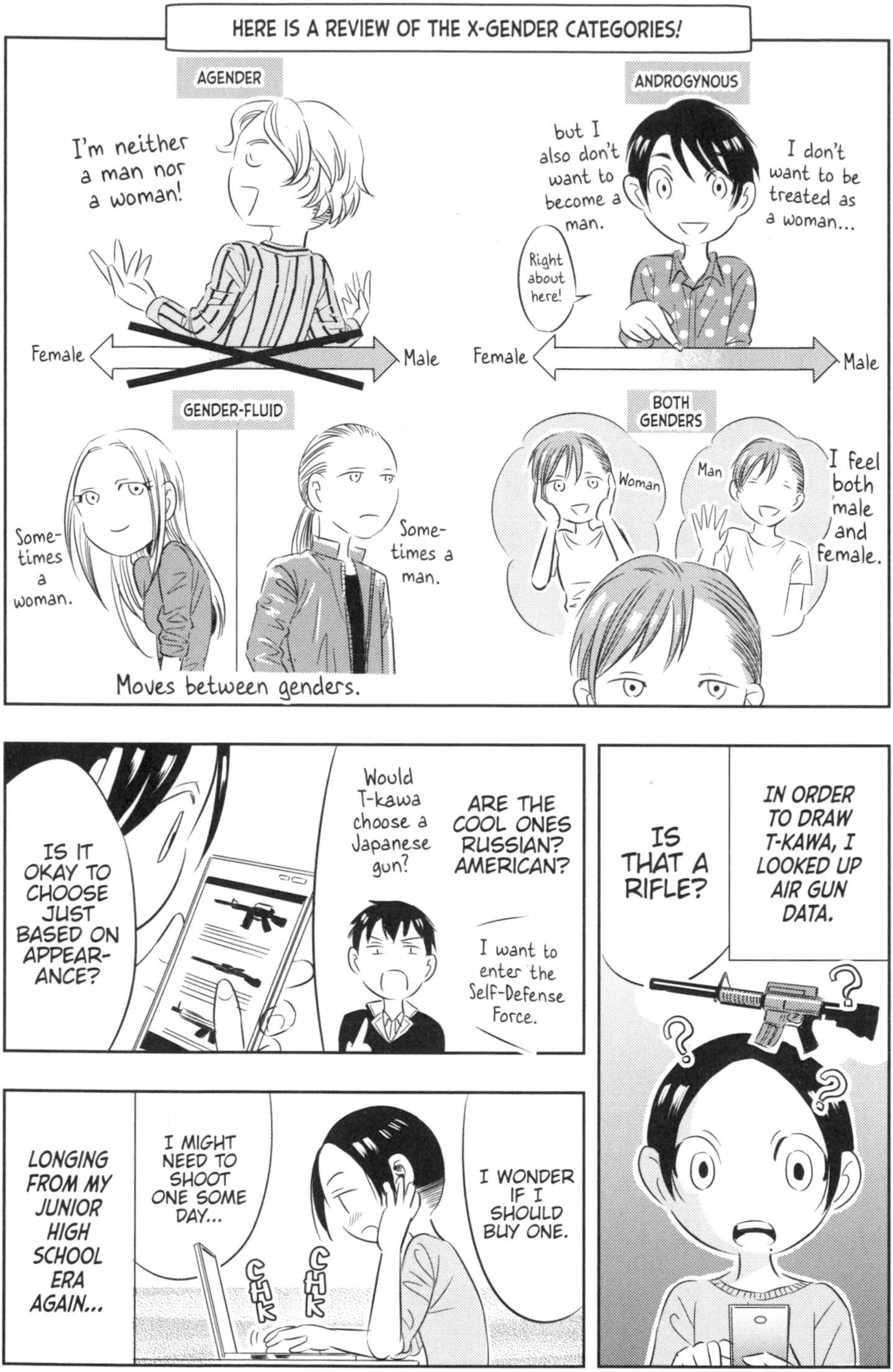
HERE IS A REVIEW OF THE X-GENDER CATEGORIES!
ANDROGYNOUS
I don't want to be treated as a woman...
but I also don't want to become a man.
Right about here!
Female
Male
AGENDER
I'm neither a man nor a woman!
Female
Male
BOTH GENDERS
I feel both male and female.
Man
Woman
GENDER-FLUID
Some-times a man.
Some-times a woman.
Moves between genders.
IN ORDER TO DRAW T-KAWA, I LOOKED UP AIR GUN DATA.
IS THAT A RIFLE?
ARE THE COOL ONES RUSSIAN? AMERICAN?
Would T-kawa choose a Japanese gun?
I want to enter the Self-Defense Force.
IS IT OKAY TO CHOOSE JUST BASED ON APPEAR-ANCE?
I WONDER IF I SHOULD BUY ONE.
CHK
CHK
I MIGHT NEED TO SHOOT ONE SOME DAY...
LONGING FROM MY JUNIOR HIGH SCHOOL ERA AGAIN...

Ep. 18: The "Sex" Story

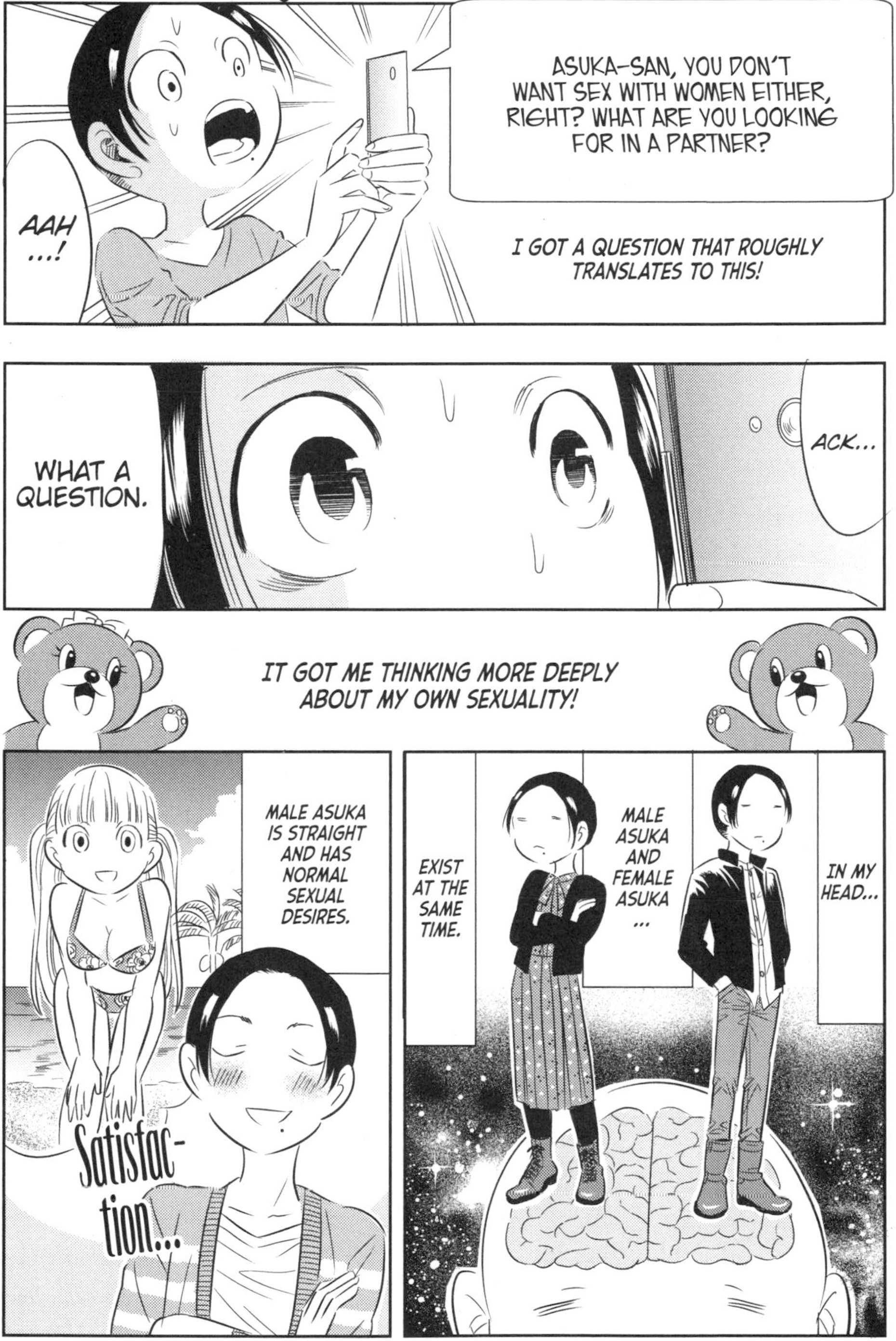
ASUKA-SAN, YOU DON'T WANT SEX WITH WOMEN EITHER, RIGHT? WHAT ARE YOU LOOKING FOR IN A PARTNER?
I GOT A QUESTION THAT ROUGHLY TRANSLATES TO THIS!
AAH ...!
ACK...
WHAT A QUESTION.
IT GOT ME THINKING MORE DEEPLY ABOUT MY OWN SEXUALITY!
IN MY HEAD...
MALE ASUKA AND FEMALE ASUKA ...
EXIST AT THE SAME TIME.
MALE ASUKA IS STRAIGHT AND HAS NORMAL SEXUAL DESIRES.
Satisfac-tion...

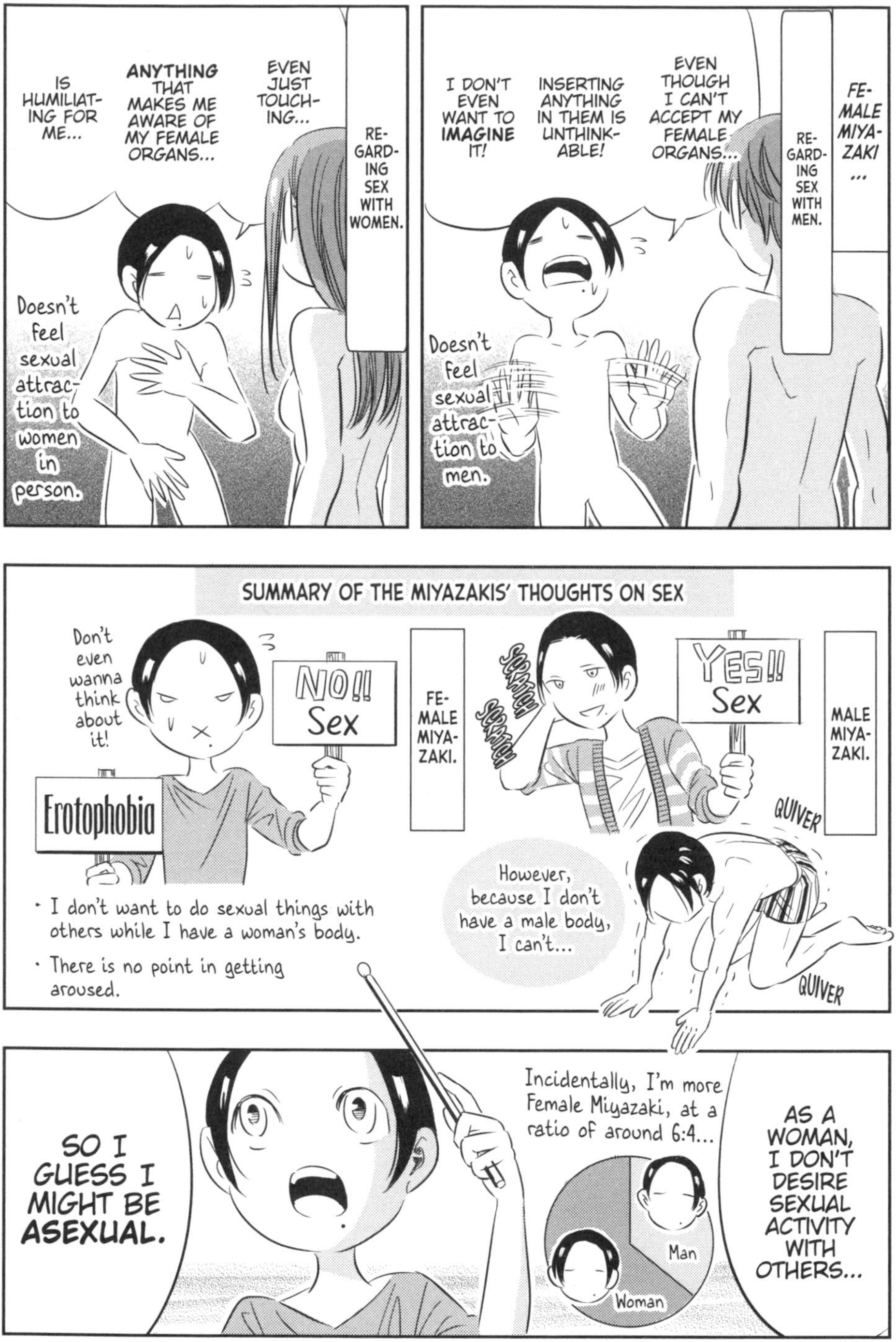
FEMALE MIYAZAKI...
REGARDING SEX WITH MEN.
EVEN THOUGH I CAN'T ACCEPT MY FEMALE ORGANS...
INSERTING ANYTHING IN THEM IS UNTHINKABLE!
I DON'T EVEN WANT TO IMAGINE IT!
Doesn't feel sexual attraction to men.
REGARDING SEX WITH WOMEN.
EVEN JUST TOUCHING...
ANYTHING THAT MAKES ME AWARE OF MY FEMALE ORGANS...
IS HUMILIATING FOR ME...
Doesn't feel sexual attraction to women in person.
SUMMARY OF THE MIYAZAKIS' THOUGHTS ON SEX
MALE MIYAZAKI.
YES!! Sex
SCRATCH SCRATCH
QUIVER
QUIVER
However, because I don't have a male body, I can't...
FEMALE MIYAZAKI.
NO!! Sex
Don't even wanna think about it!
Erotophobia
· I don't want to do sexual things with others while I have a woman's body.
· There is no point in getting aroused.
AS A WOMAN, I DON'T DESIRE SEXUAL ACTIVITY WITH OTHERS...
Incidentally, I'm more Female Miyazaki, at a ratio of around 6:4...
Man
Woman
SO I GUESS I MIGHT BE ASEXUAL.

For Female Miyazaki, even though other people are appealing, and even sexy, that doesn't mean Female Miyazaki wants to have sex with them. (Female Miyazaki considers both men and women with sex appeal to be "cool.") Incidentally, Female Miyazaki doesn't want to kiss, either.

Reference site: JobRainbow

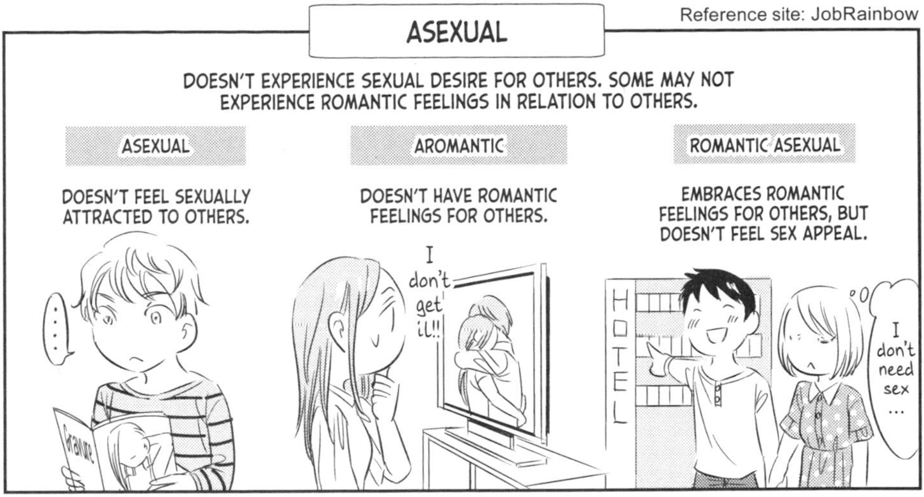
ASEXUAL
DOESN'T EXPERIENCE SEXUAL DESIRE FOR OTHERS. SOME MAY NOT EXPERIENCE ROMANTIC FEELINGS IN RELATION TO OTHERS.
ASEXUAL
DOESN'T FEEL SEXUALLY ATTRACTED TO OTHERS.
....
Gravure
AROMANTIC
DOESN'T HAVE ROMANTIC FEELINGS FOR OTHERS.
I don't get it!!
ROMANTIC ASEXUAL
EMBRACES ROMANTIC FEELINGS FOR OTHERS, BUT DOESN'T FEEL SEX APPEAL.
HOTEL
I don't need sex ...

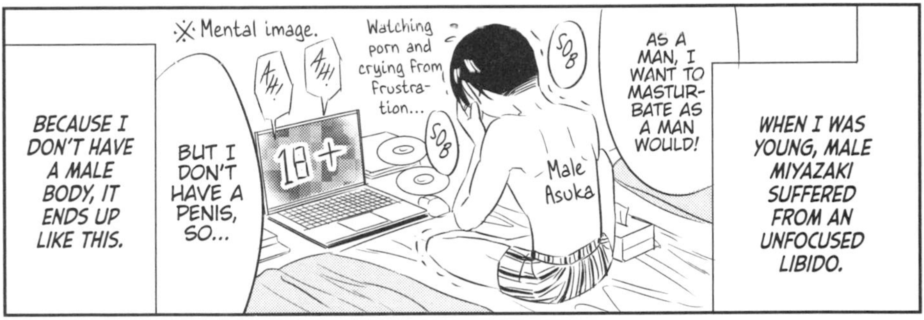
WHEN I WAS YOUNG, MALE MIYAZAKI SUFFERED FROM AN UNFOCUSED LIBIDO.
AS A MAN, I WANT TO MASTURBATE AS A MAN WOULD!
SOB
Male Asuka
Watching porn and crying from frustration...
※Mental image.
AH!
AH!
18+
SOB
BUT I DON'T HAVE A PENIS, SO...
BECAUSE I DON'T HAVE A MALE BODY, IT ENDS UP LIKE THIS.

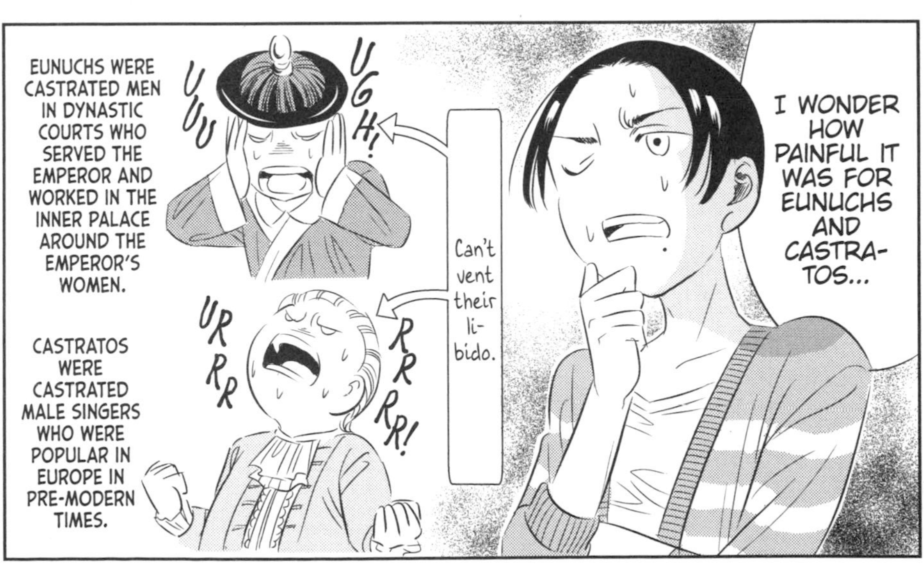
I WONDER HOW PAINFUL IT WAS FOR EUNUCHS AND CASTRATOS...
Can't vent their libido.
UGH!
UUU
EUNUCHS WERE CASTRATED MEN IN DYNASTIC COURTS WHO SERVED THE EMPEROR AND WORKED IN THE INNER PALACE AROUND THE EMPEROR'S WOMEN.
RRRRR!
URRR
CASTRATOS WERE CASTRATED MALE SINGERS WHO WERE POPULAR IN EUROPE IN PRE-MODERN TIMES.

I used to think that I had romantic feelings, but since I'm not interested in romantic entertainment, I've been wondering lately if I'm actually aromantic. Does romance feel similar to fraternity or longing...?

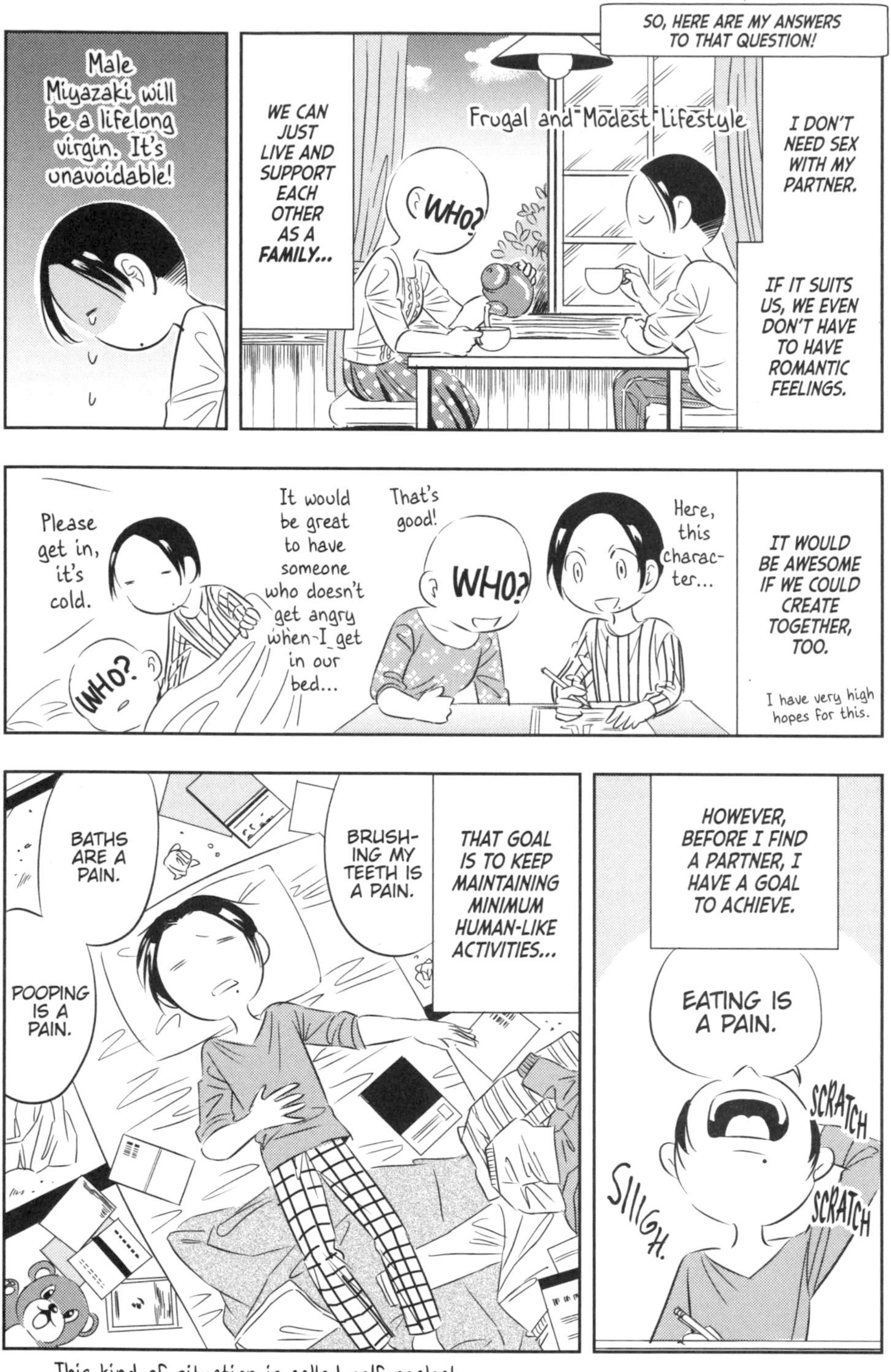
SO, HERE ARE MY ANSWERS TO THAT QUESTION!
I DON'T NEED SEX WITH MY PARTNER.
Frugal and Modest Lifestyle
IF IT SUITS US, WE EVEN DON'T HAVE TO HAVE ROMANTIC FEELINGS.
WE CAN JUST LIVE AND SUPPORT EACH OTHER AS A FAMILY...
WHO?
Male Miyazaki will be a lifelong virgin. It's unavoidable!
IT WOULD BE AWESOME IF WE COULD CREATE TOGETHER, TOO.
I have very high hopes for this.
Here, this character...
WHO?
That's good!
It would be great to have someone who doesn't get angry when I get in our bed...
Please get in, it's cold.
WHO?
HOWEVER, BEFORE I FIND A PARTNER, I HAVE A GOAL TO ACHIEVE.
EATING IS A PAIN.
SCRATCH
SCRATCH
SIIIGH.
THAT GOAL IS TO KEEP MAINTAINING MINIMUM HUMAN-LIKE ACTIVITIES...
BRUSHING MY TEETH IS A PAIN.
BATHS ARE A PAIN.
POOPING IS A PAIN.

This kind of situation is called self-neglect.

Ep. 19: The "Old Friend" Story

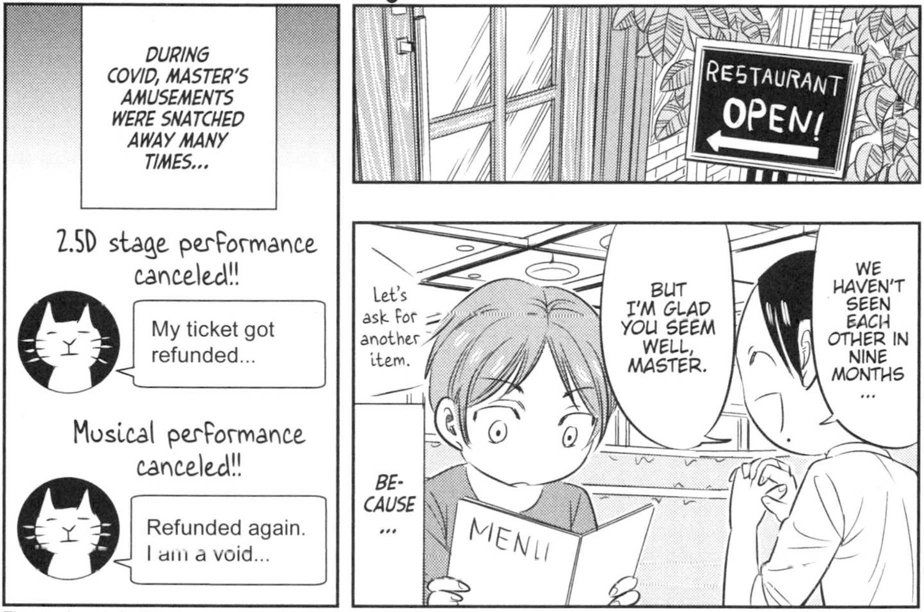
RESTAURANT OPEN!
WE HAVEN'T SEEN EACH OTHER IN NINE MONTHS...
BUT I'M GLAD YOU SEEM WELL, MASTER.
Let's ask for another item.
MENU
BE-CAUSE...
DURING COVID, MASTER'S AMUSEMENTS WERE SNATCHED AWAY MANY TIMES...
2.5D stage performance canceled!!
My ticket got refunded...
Musical performance canceled!!
Refunded again. I am a void...

The storyboards for this story were completed in December 2020.
This story took place when Covid patient numbers were low, before the mask recommendation for dining.

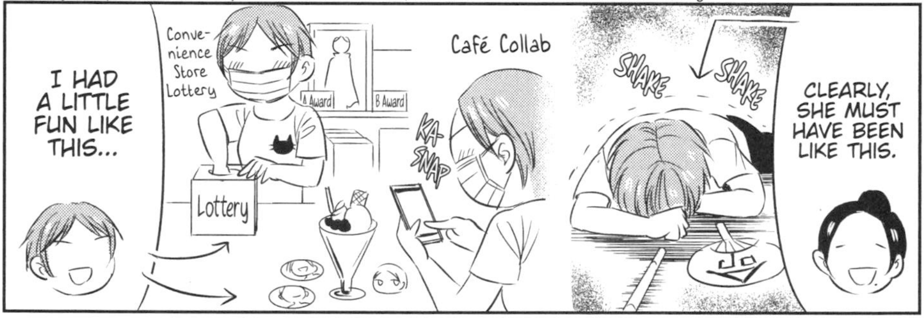
CLEARLY, SHE MUST HAVE BEEN LIKE THIS.
SHAKE
SHAKE
I HAD A LITTLE FUN LIKE THIS...
Café Collab
KA-SNAP
Convenience Store Lottery
A Award
B Award
Lottery

Fan: Life

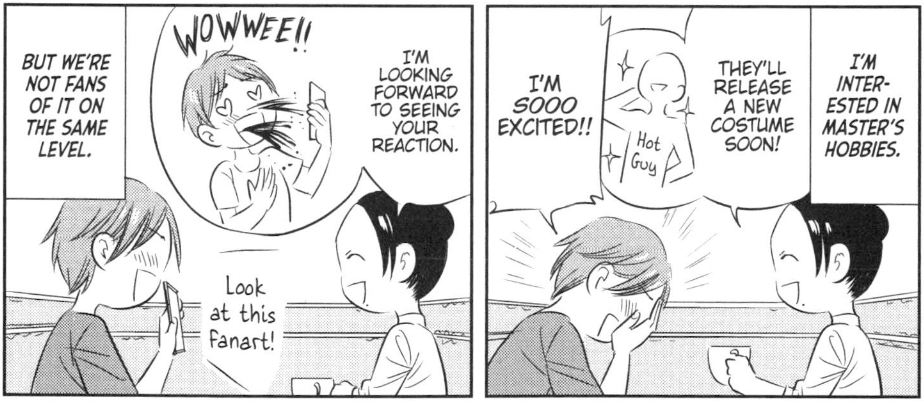
I'M INTERESTED IN MASTER'S HOBBIES.
THEY'LL RELEASE A NEW COSTUME SOON!
Hot Guy
I'M SOOO EXCITED!!
I'M LOOKING FORWARD TO SEEING YOUR REACTION.
WOWWEE!!
BUT WE'RE NOT FANS OF IT ON THE SAME LEVEL.
Look at this fanart!

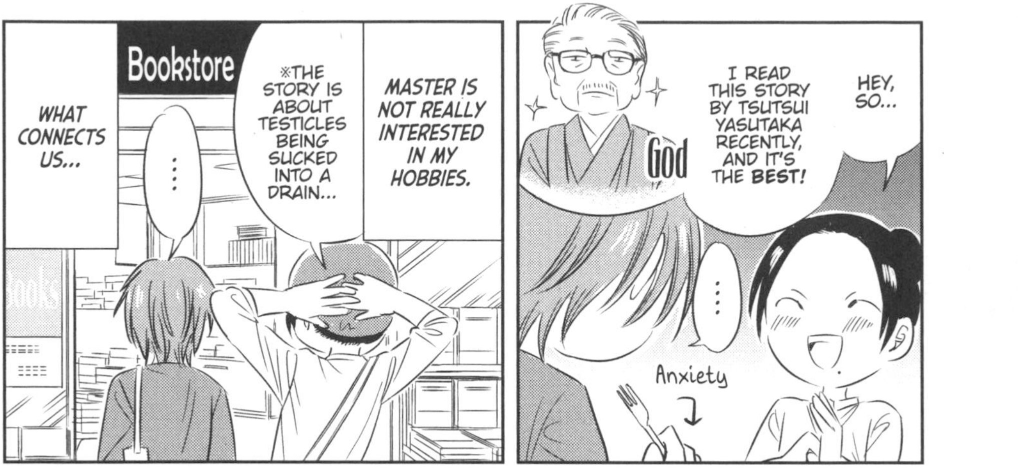
HEY, SO...
I READ THIS STORY BY TSUTSUI YASUTAKA RECENTLY, AND IT'S THE **BEST!**
God
...
Anxiety
MASTER IS NOT REALLY INTERESTED IN MY HOBBIES.
※THE STORY IS ABOUT TESTICLES BEING SUCKED INTO A DRAIN...
...
WHAT CONNECTS US...
Bookstore
Books

※*From the short story of the same name in the collection* Record of Dark Troubles *by Tsutsui Yasutaka (Kadokawa Bunko).*

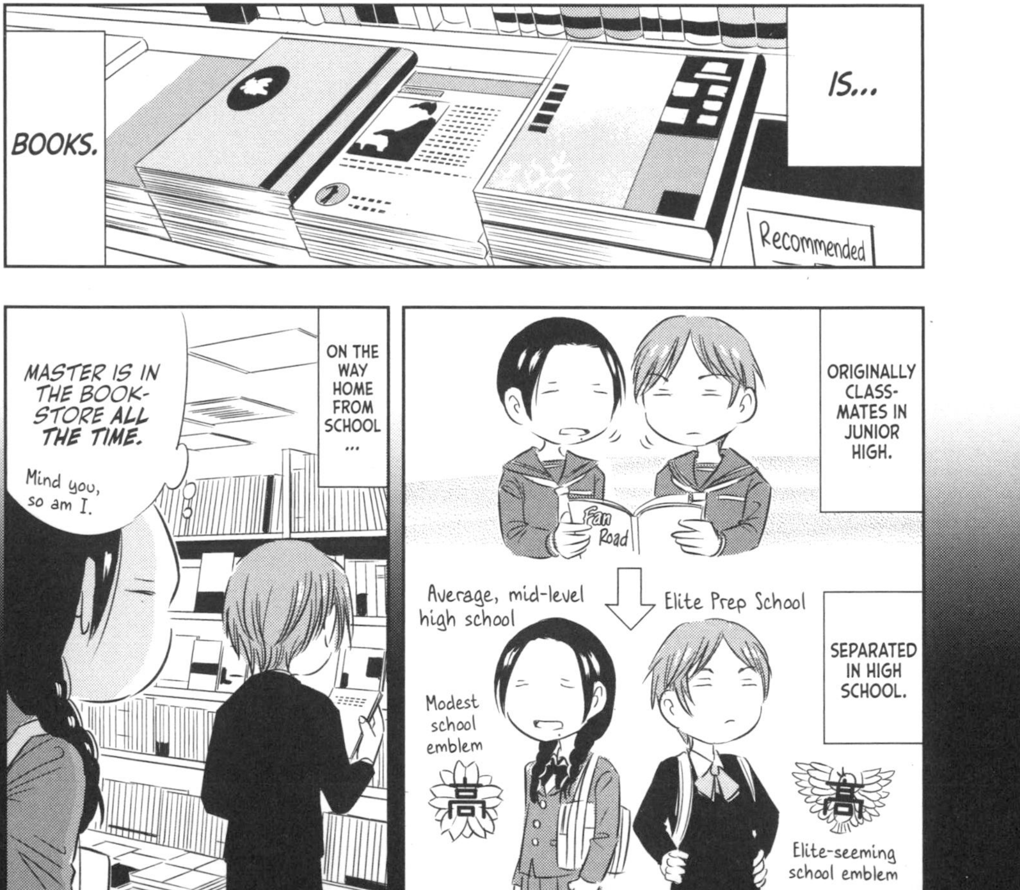
IS...
BOOKS.
Recommended
ORIGINALLY CLASSMATES IN JUNIOR HIGH.
Fan Road
Average, mid-level high school
Elite Prep School
SEPARATED IN HIGH SCHOOL.
Modest school emblem
Elite-seeming school emblem
ON THE WAY HOME FROM SCHOOL ...
MASTER IS IN THE BOOKSTORE **ALL THE TIME.**
Mind you, so am I.

Insignia: High School

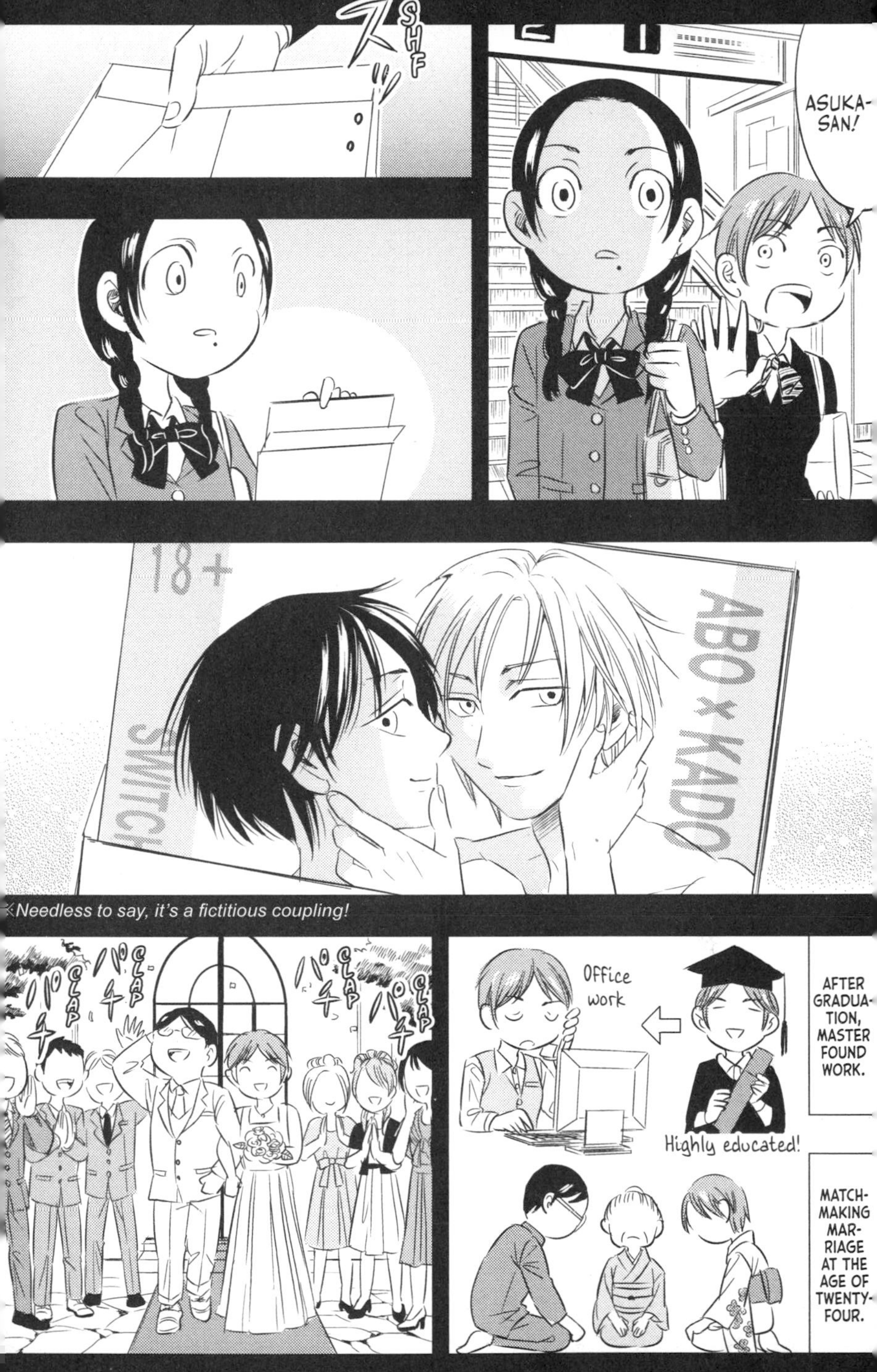
ASUKA-SAN!
ス SHF
18+
ABO x KADO
SWITCH
※Needless to say, it's a fictitious coupling!
AFTER GRADUATION, MASTER FOUND WORK.
Highly educated!
Office work
MATCH-MAKING MARRIAGE AT THE AGE OF TWENTY-FOUR.
パチ CLAP
パチ CLAP
パチ CLAP
パチ CLAP

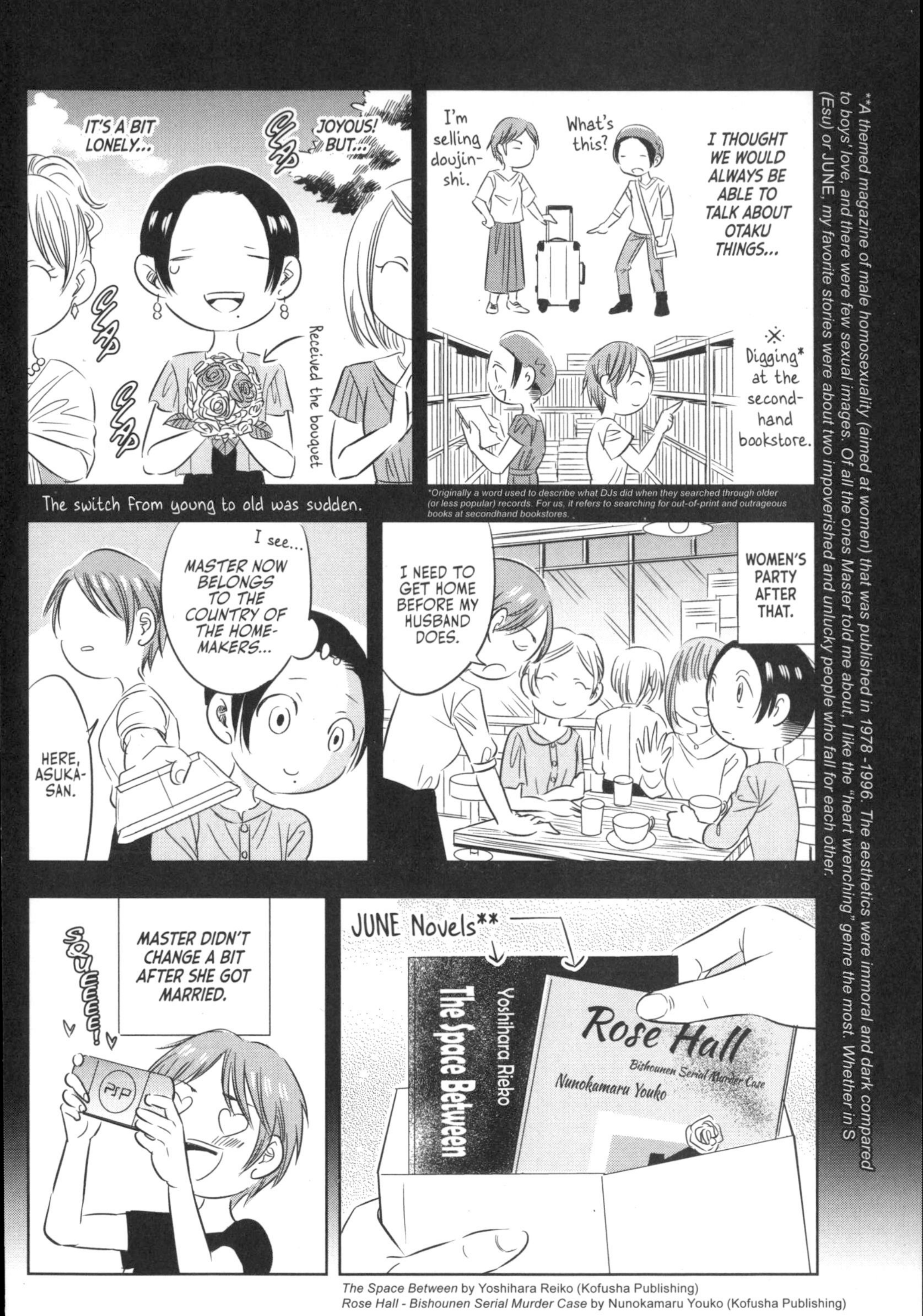

I THOUGHT WE WOULD ALWAYS BE ABLE TO TALK ABOUT OTAKU THINGS...
What's this?
I'm selling doujin-shi.
※ Digging* at the second-hand bookstore.
JOYOUS! BUT...
CLAP
IT'S A BIT LONELY...
Received the bouquet
CLAP
CLAP
The switch from young to old was sudden.
WOMEN'S PARTY AFTER THAT.
I NEED TO GET HOME BEFORE MY HUSBAND DOES.
I see... MASTER NOW BELONGS TO THE COUNTRY OF THE HOME-MAKERS...
HERE, ASUKA-SAN.
JUNE Novels**
Yoshihara Rieko
The Space Between
Rose Hall
Bishounen Serial Murder Case
Nunokamaru Youko
MASTER DIDN'T CHANGE A BIT AFTER SHE GOT MARRIED.
SQUEEEEE!
PSP

*Originally a word used to describe what DJs did when they searched through older (or less popular) records. For us, it refers to searching for out-of-print and outrageous books at secondhand bookstores.

The Space Between by Yoshihara Reiko (Kofusha Publishing)
Rose Hall - Bishounen Serial Murder Case by Nunokamaru Youko (Kofusha Publishing)

***A themed magazine of male homosexuality (aimed at women) that was published in 1978-1996. The aesthetics were immoral and dark compared to boys' love, and there were few sexual images. Of all the ones Master told me about, I like the "heart wrenching" genre the most. Whether in S (Esu) or JUNE, my favorite stories were about two impoverished and unlucky people who fall for each other.*

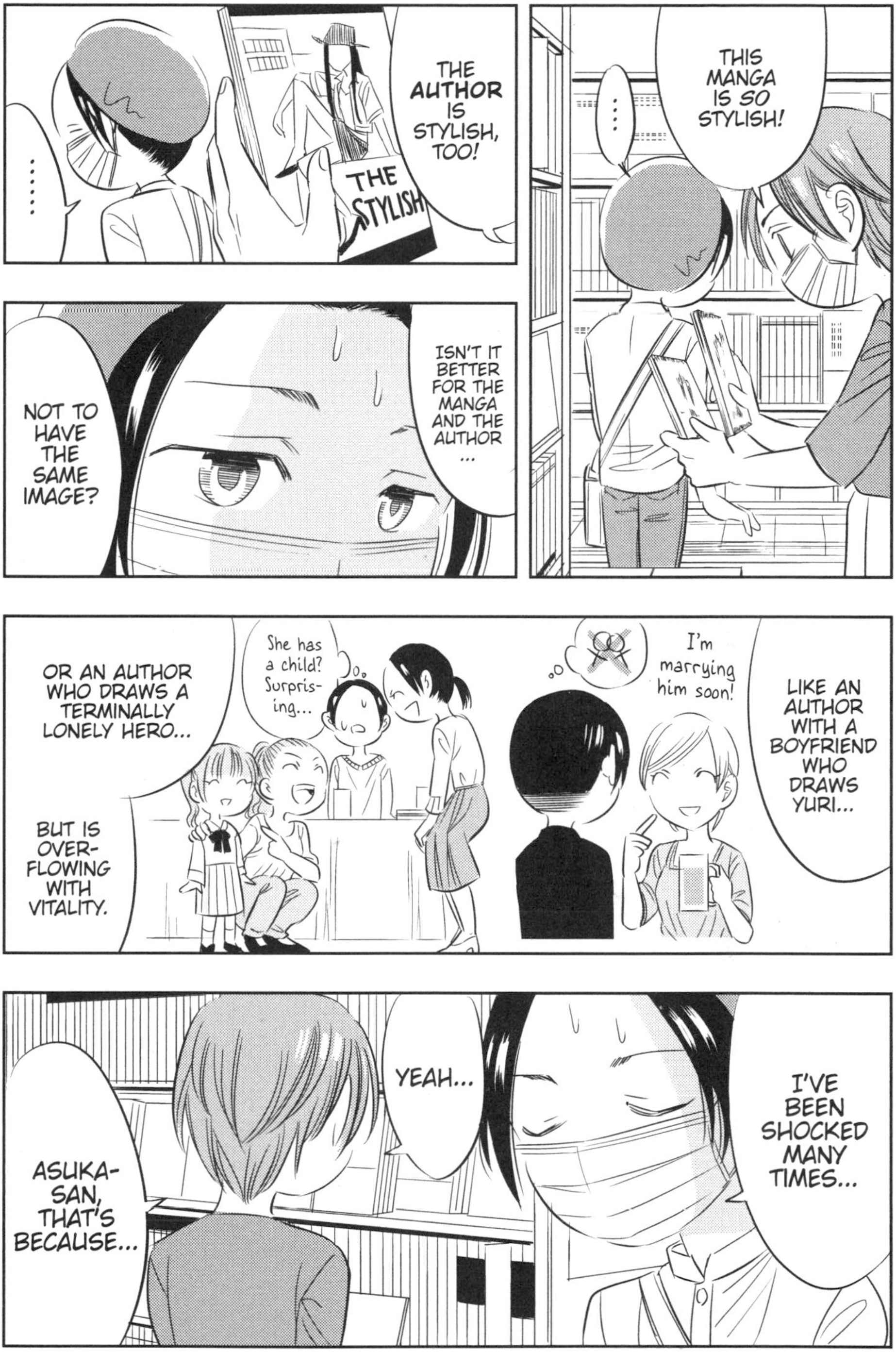

THIS MANGA IS SO STYLISH!
....
THE AUTHOR IS STYLISH, TOO!
......
THE STYLISH
ISN'T IT BETTER FOR THE MANGA AND THE AUTHOR ...
NOT TO HAVE THE SAME IMAGE?
LIKE AN AUTHOR WITH A BOYFRIEND WHO DRAWS YURI...
I'm marrying him soon!
She has a child? Surpris-ing...
OR AN AUTHOR WHO DRAWS A TERMINALLY LONELY HERO...
BUT IS OVER-FLOWING WITH VITALITY.
I'VE BEEN SHOCKED MANY TIMES...
YEAH...
ASUKA-SAN, THAT'S BECAUSE...

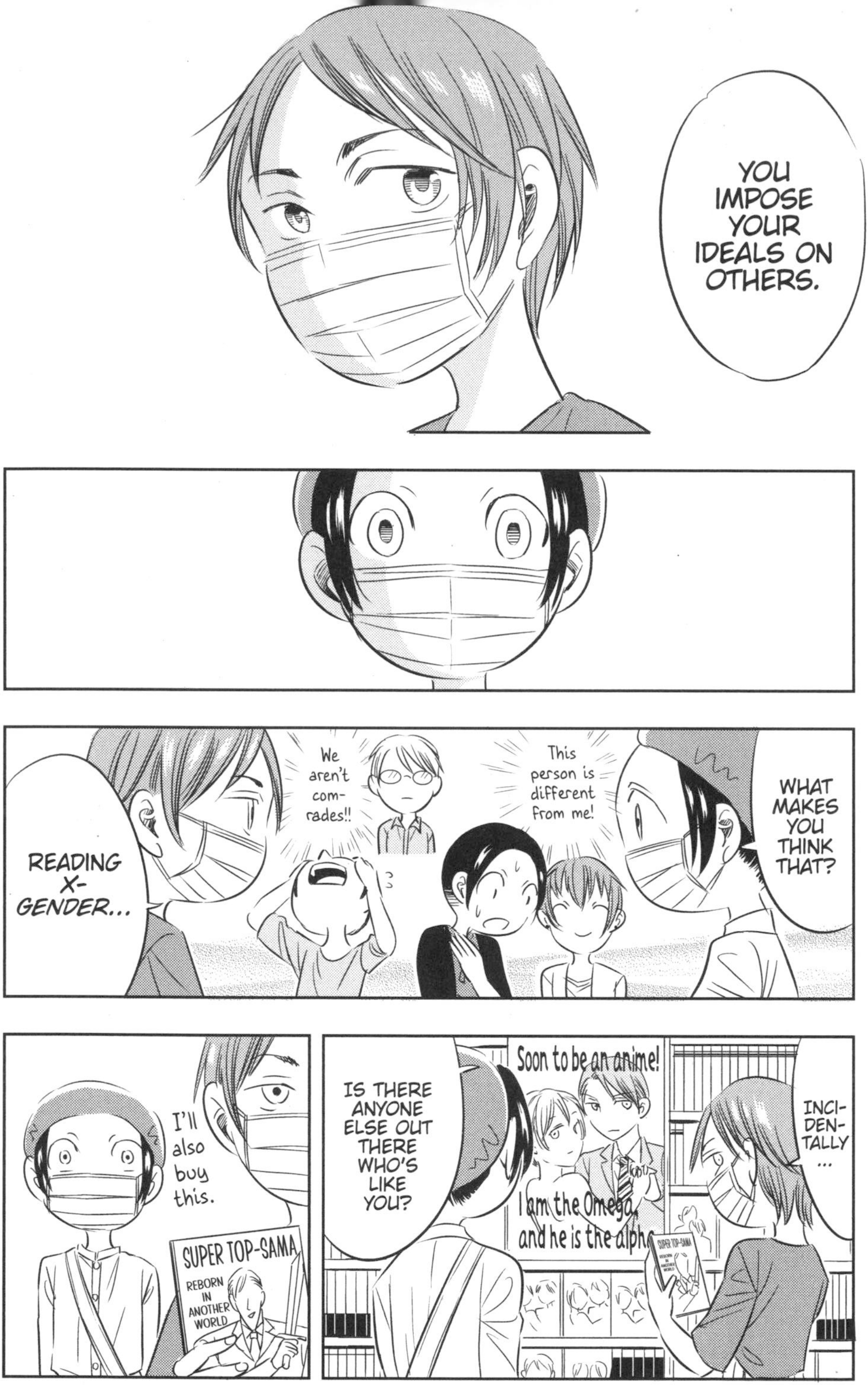
YOU IMPOSE YOUR IDEALS ON OTHERS.
WHAT MAKES YOU THINK THAT?
This person is different from me!
We aren't com-rades!!
READING X-GENDER...
INCI-DENTALLY...
Soon to be an anime!
IS THERE ANYONE ELSE OUT THERE WHO'S LIKE YOU?
I am the Omega, and he is the alpha
SUPER TOP-SAMA
I'll also buy this.
SUPER TOP-SAMA
REBORN IN ANOTHER WORLD

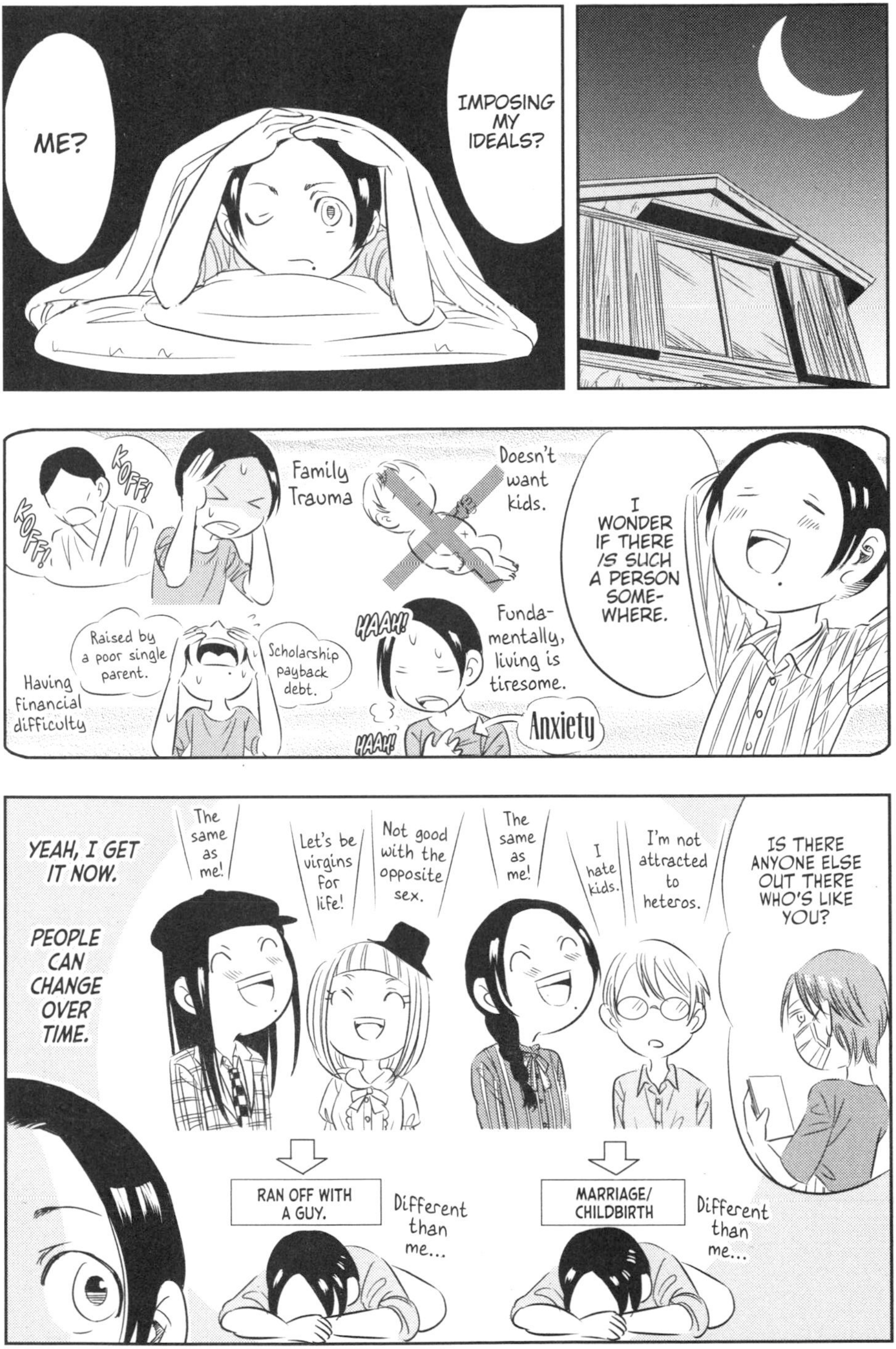
IMPOSING MY IDEALS?
ME?
I WONDER IF THERE IS SUCH A PERSON SOMEWHERE.
Doesn't want kids.
Family Trauma
KOFF!
KOFF!
Fundamentally, living is tiresome.
HAAH!
HAAH!
Anxiety
Scholarship payback debt.
Raised by a poor single parent.
Having financial difficulty
IS THERE ANYONE ELSE OUT THERE WHO'S LIKE YOU?
I'm not attracted to heteros.
I hate kids.
The same as me!
Not good with the opposite sex.
Let's be virgins for life!
The same as me!
YEAH, I GET IT NOW.
PEOPLE CAN CHANGE OVER TIME.
MARRIAGE/ CHILDBIRTH
Different than me...
RAN OFF WITH A GUY.
Different than me...

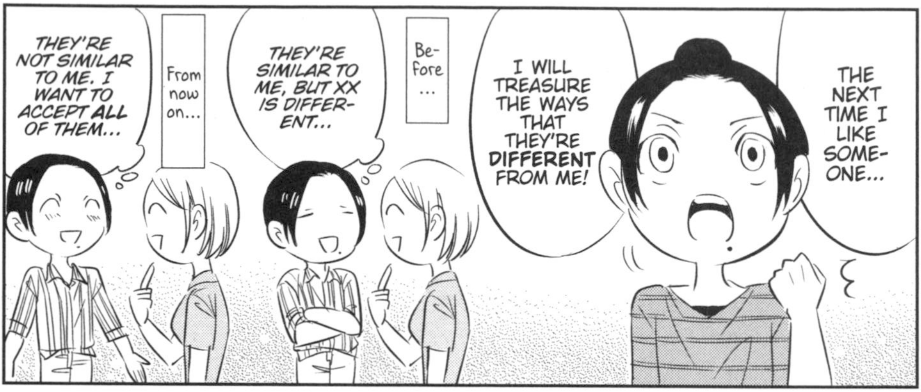
THE NEXT TIME I LIKE SOMEONE...
I WILL TREASURE THE WAYS THAT THEY'RE DIFFERENT FROM ME!
Before...
THEY'RE SIMILAR TO ME, BUT XX IS DIFFERENT...
From now on...
THEY'RE NOT SIMILAR TO ME. I WANT TO ACCEPT ALL OF THEM...

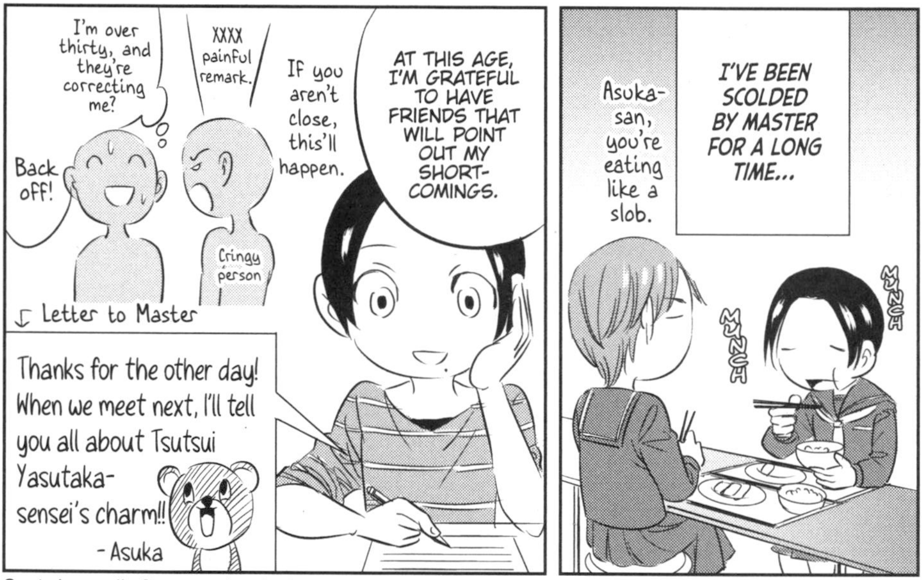
I'VE BEEN SCOLDED BY MASTER FOR A LONG TIME...
Asuka-san, you're eating like a slob.
MUNCH
MUNCH
AT THIS AGE, I'M GRATEFUL TO HAVE FRIENDS THAT WILL POINT OUT MY SHORTCOMINGS.
If you aren't close, this'll happen.
XXXX painful remark.
I'm over thirty, and they're correcting me?
Back off!
Cringy person
Letter to Master
Thanks for the other day! When we meet next, I'll tell you all about Tsutsui Yasutaka-sensei's charm!!
- Asuka

Sent via email after scanning the letter.

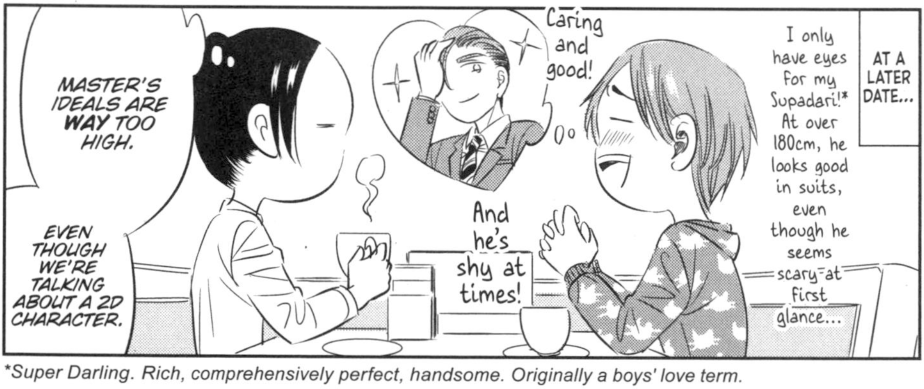
AT A LATER DATE...
I only have eyes for my Supadari!* At over 180cm, he looks good in suits, even though he seems scary at first glance...
Caring and good!
And he's shy at times!
MASTER'S IDEALS ARE WAY TOO HIGH.
EVEN THOUGH WE'RE TALKING ABOUT A 2D CHARACTER.

*Super Darling. Rich, comprehensively perfect, handsome. Originally a boys' love term.

Ep. 20: The "Aspiring Manga Artist" Story

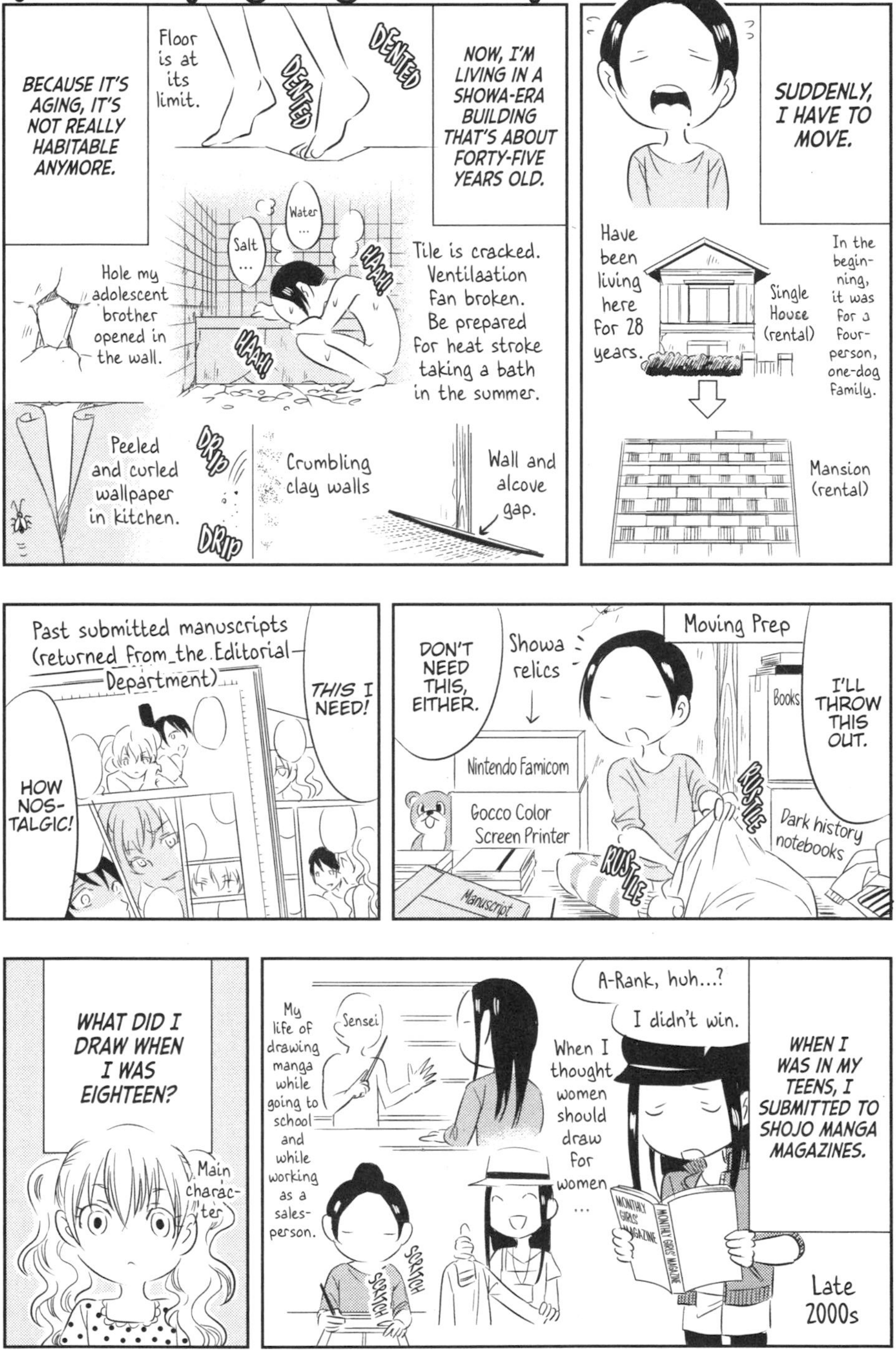

SUDDENLY, I HAVE TO MOVE.
In the beginning, it was for a four-person, one-dog family.
Have been living here for 28 years.
Single House (rental)
Mansion (rental)
NOW, I'M LIVING IN A SHOWA-ERA BUILDING THAT'S ABOUT FORTY-FIVE YEARS OLD.
DENTED
DENTED
Floor is at its limit.
BECAUSE IT'S AGING, IT'S NOT REALLY HABITABLE ANYMORE.
Tile is cracked. Ventilaation fan broken. Be prepared for heat stroke taking a bath in the summer.
HAAH
HAAH
Water...
Salt...
Hole my adolescent brother opened in the wall.
Wall and alcove gap.
Crumbling clay walls
DRIP
DRIP
Peeled and curled wallpaper in kitchen.
Moving Prep
I'LL THROW THIS OUT.
Books
Dark history notebooks
RUSTLE
RUSTLE
Showa relics
DON'T NEED THIS, EITHER.
Nintendo Famicom
Gocco Color Screen Printer
Manuscript
THIS I NEED!
Past submitted manuscripts (returned from the Editorial Department)
HOW NOS-TALGIC!
WHEN I WAS IN MY TEENS, I SUBMITTED TO SHOJO MANGA MAGAZINES.
Late 2000s
A-Rank, huh...?
I didn't win.
MONTHLY GIRLS' MAGAZINE
When I thought women should draw for women...
My life of drawing manga while going to school and while working as a sales-person.
Sensei
SCRATCH
SCRATCH
WHAT DID I DRAW WHEN I WAS EIGHTEEN?
Main character

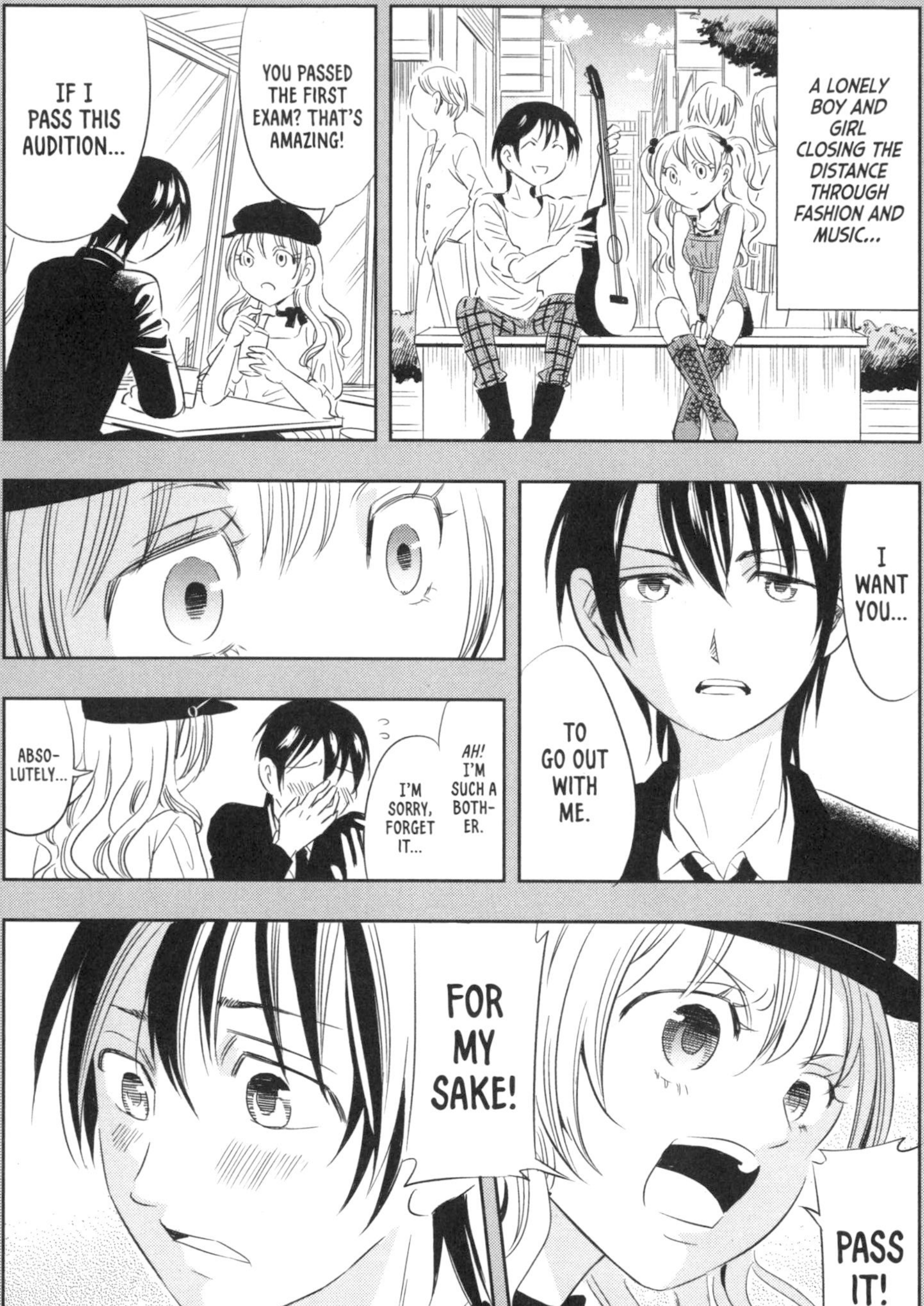
A LONELY BOY AND GIRL CLOSING THE DISTANCE THROUGH FASHION AND MUSIC...
YOU PASSED THE FIRST EXAM? THAT'S AMAZING!
IF I PASS THIS AUDITION...
I WANT YOU...
TO GO OUT WITH ME.
AH! I'M SUCH A BOTHER.
I'M SORRY, FORGET IT...
ABSO-LUTELY...
PASS IT!
FOR MY SAKE!

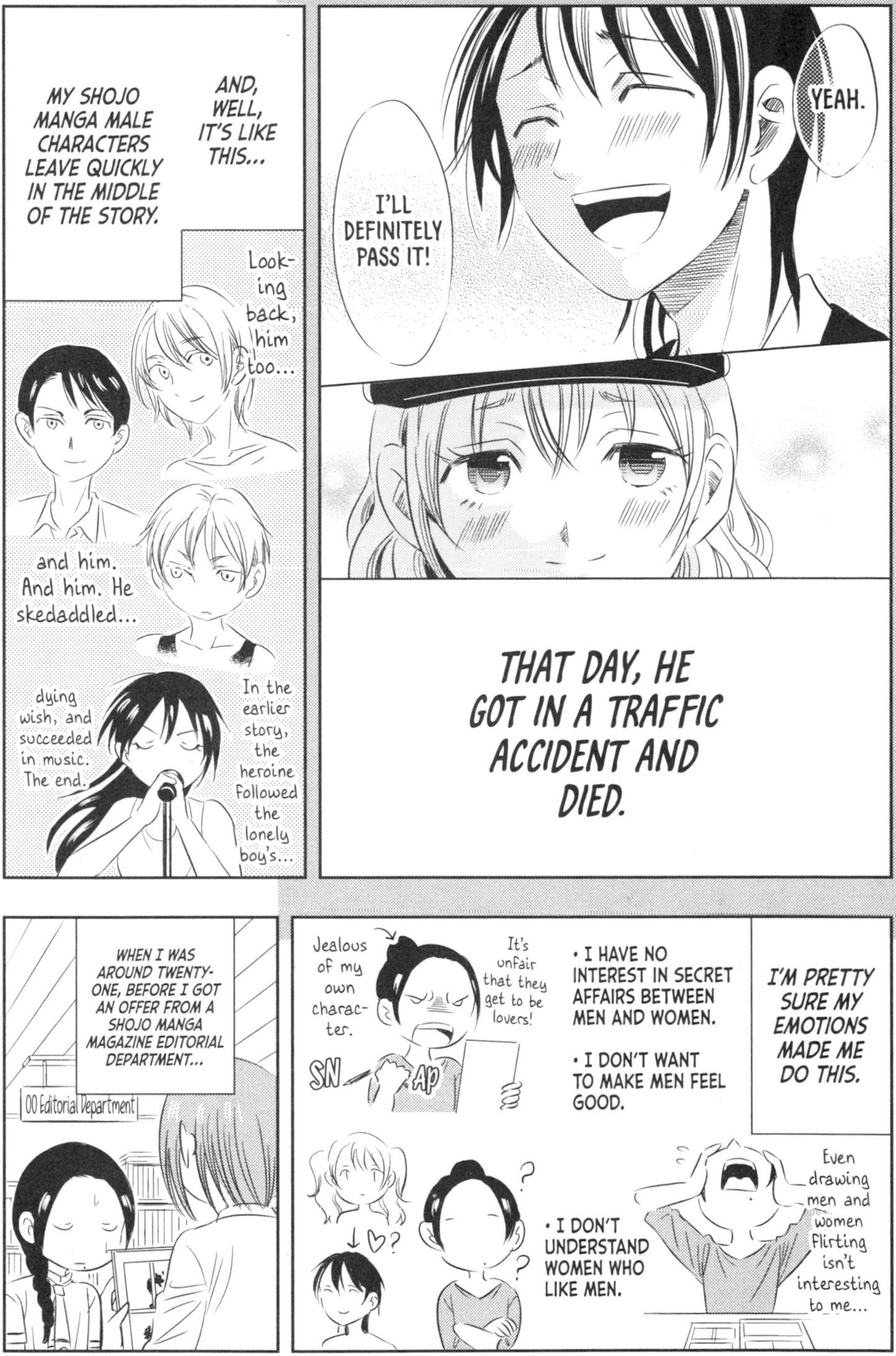
YEAH.
I'LL DEFINITELY PASS IT!
THAT DAY, HE GOT IN A TRAFFIC ACCIDENT AND DIED.
AND, WELL, IT'S LIKE THIS...
MY SHOJO MANGA MALE CHARACTERS LEAVE QUICKLY IN THE MIDDLE OF THE STORY.
Looking back, him too...
and him. And him. He skedaddled...
In the earlier story, the heroine followed the lonely boy's...
dying wish, and succeeded in music. The end.
I'M PRETTY SURE MY EMOTIONS MADE ME DO THIS.
• I HAVE NO INTEREST IN SECRET AFFAIRS BETWEEN MEN AND WOMEN.
• I DON'T WANT TO MAKE MEN FEEL GOOD.
It's unfair that they get to be lovers!
Jealous of my own character.
SNAP
Even drawing men and women flirting isn't interesting to me...
• I DON'T UNDERSTAND WOMEN WHO LIKE MEN.
WHEN I WAS AROUND TWENTY-ONE, BEFORE I GOT AN OFFER FROM A SHOJO MANGA MAGAZINE EDITORIAL DEPARTMENT...
OO Editorial Department

Even though they were all nice, kind guys...

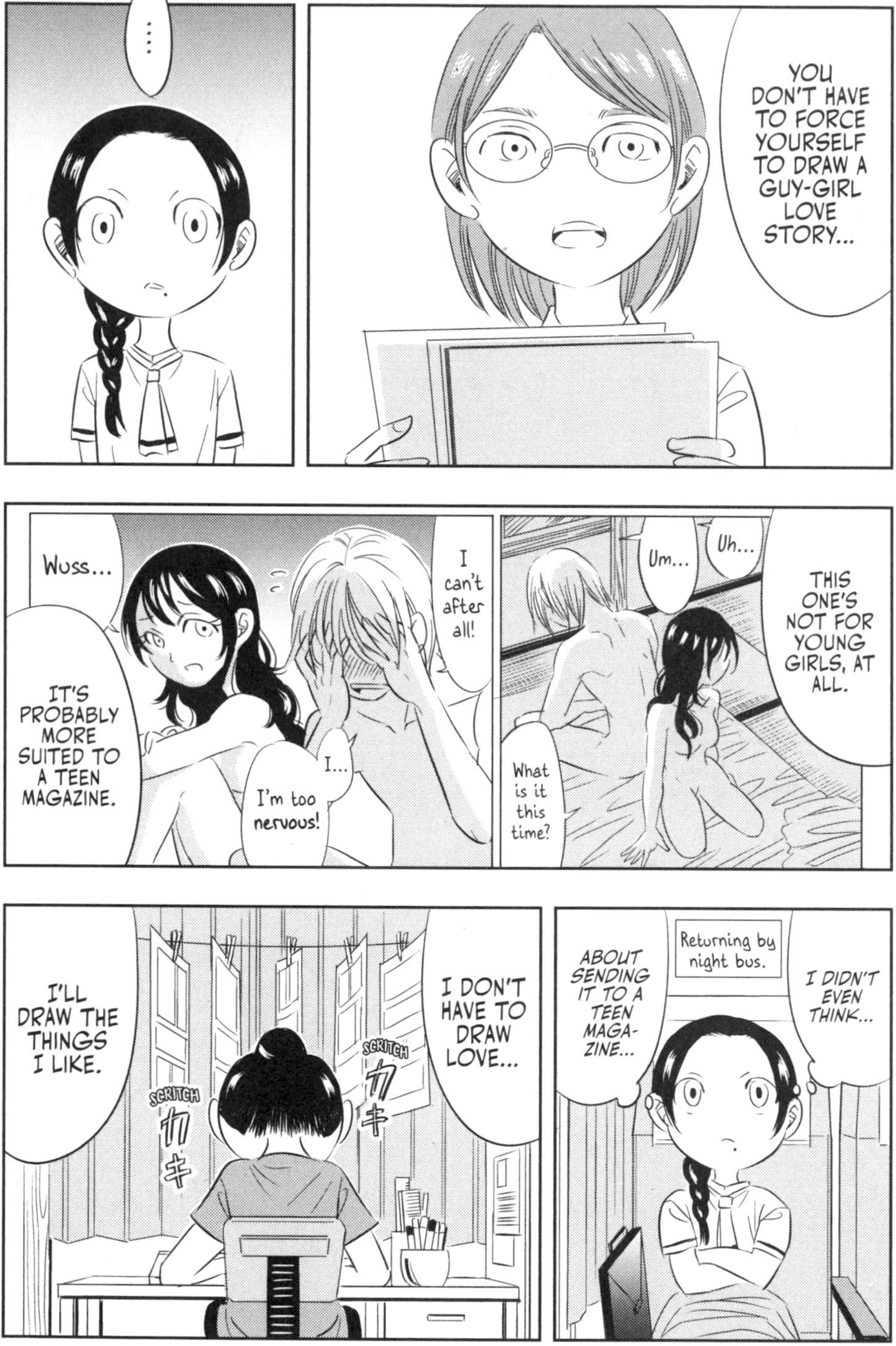
YOU DON'T HAVE TO FORCE YOURSELF TO DRAW A GUY-GIRL LOVE STORY...
……
Uh...
Um...
THIS ONE'S NOT FOR YOUNG GIRLS, AT ALL.
What is it this time?
I can't after all!
Wuss...
IT'S PROBABLY MORE SUITED TO A TEEN MAGAZINE.
I... I'm too nervous!
Returning by night bus.
I DIDN'T EVEN THINK...
ABOUT SENDING IT TO A TEEN MAGA-ZINE...
I DON'T HAVE TO DRAW LOVE...
SCRITCH カキ
SCRITCH カキ
I'LL DRAW THE THINGS I LIKE.

An editor's viewpoint is amazing!

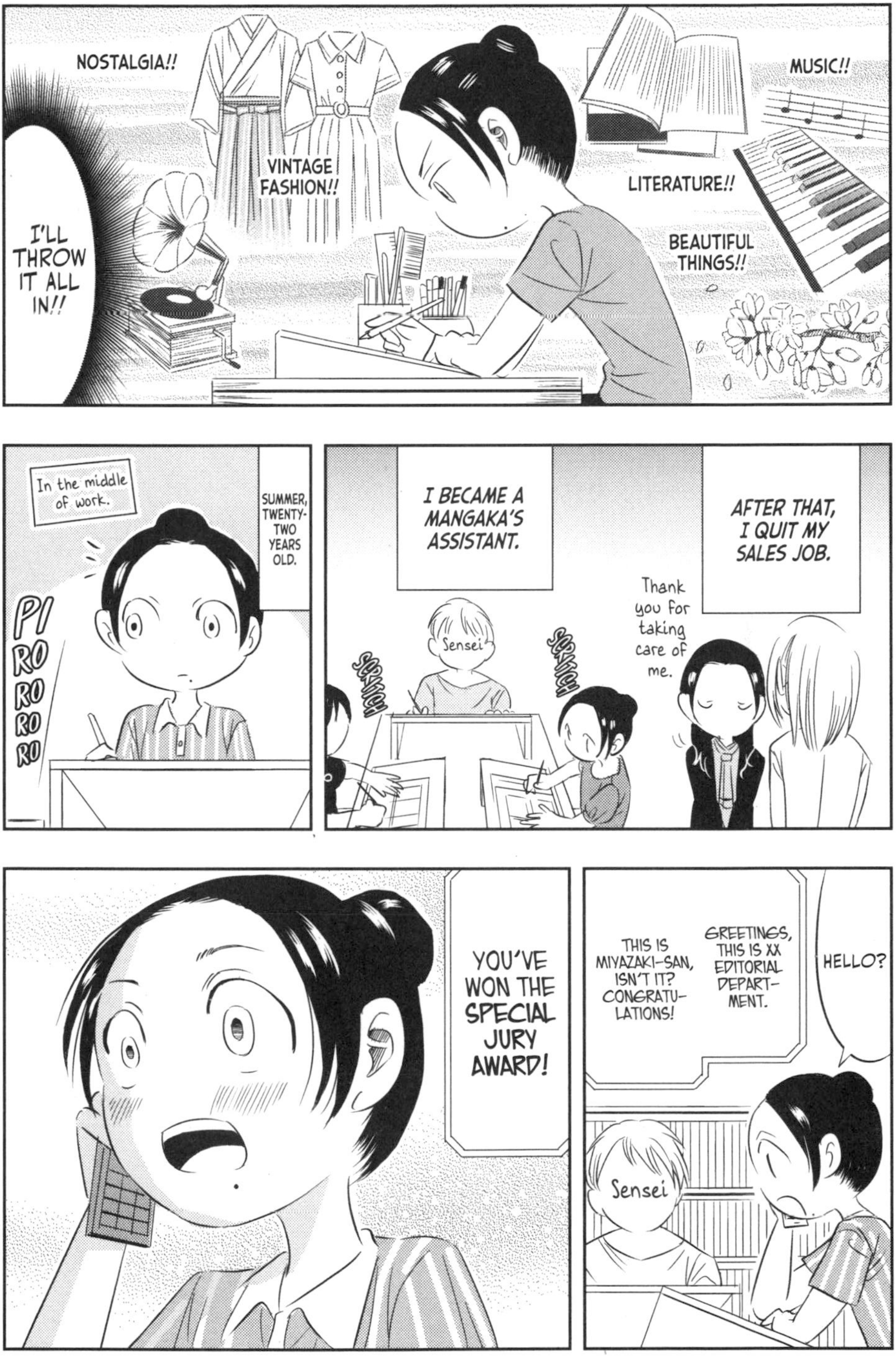
MUSIC!!
LITERATURE!!
BEAUTIFUL THINGS!!
NOSTALGIA!!
VINTAGE FASHION!!
I'LL THROW IT ALL IN!!
AFTER THAT, I QUIT MY SALES JOB.
I BECAME A MANGAKA'S ASSISTANT.
Thank you for taking care of me.
SCRITCH
Sensei
SCRITCH
SUMMER, TWENTY-TWO YEARS OLD.
In the middle of work.
PIROROROROR
HELLO?
GREETINGS, THIS IS XX EDITORIAL DEPARTMENT.
THIS IS MIYAZAKI-SAN, ISN'T IT? CONGRATULATIONS!
Sensei
YOU'VE WON THE SPECIAL JURY AWARD!

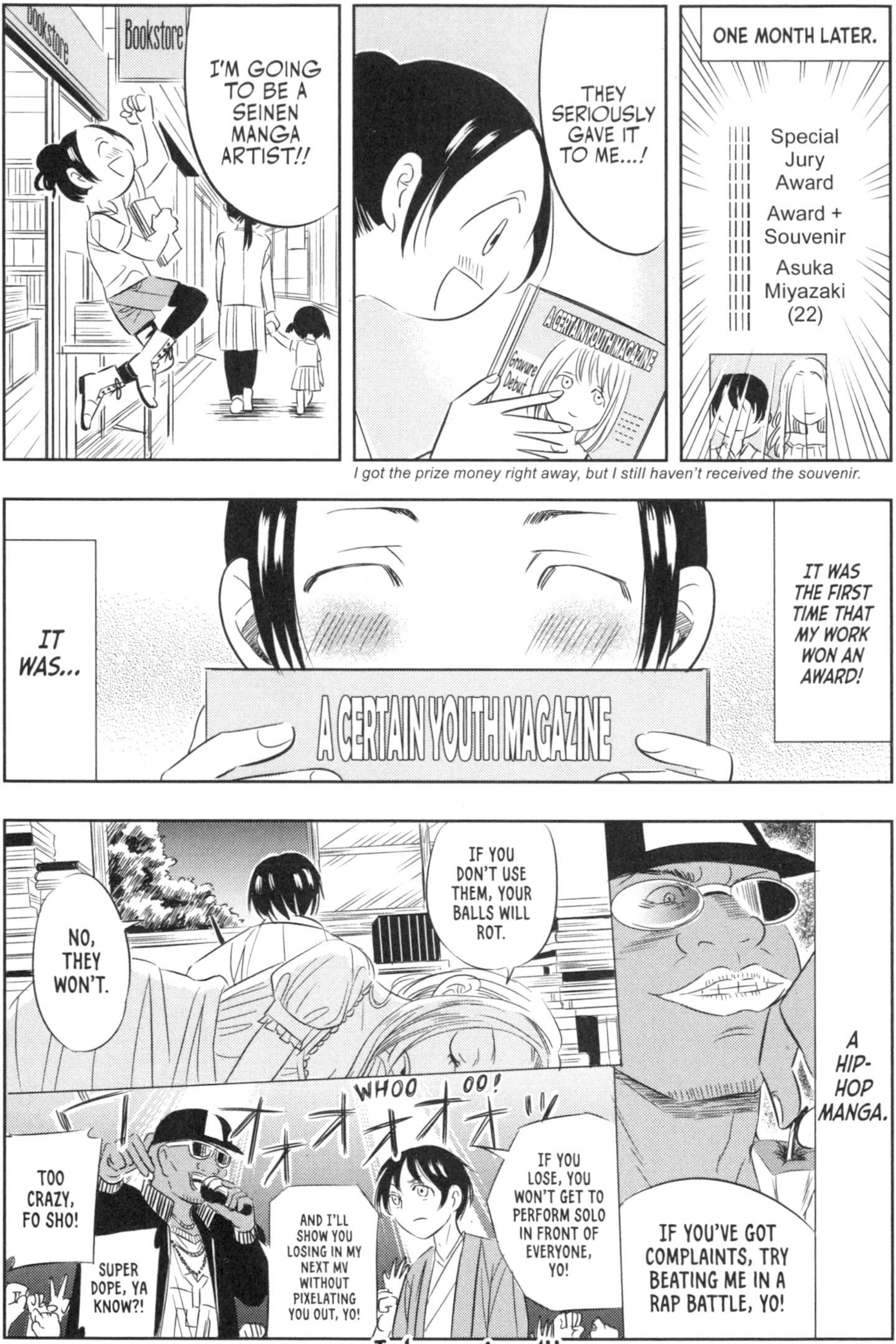
ONE MONTH LATER.
Special Jury Award
Award + Souvenir
Asuka Miyazaki (22)
THEY SERIOUSLY GAVE IT TO ME...!
A CERTAIN YOUTH MAGAZINE
Gravure Debut
Bookstore
Bookstore
I'M GOING TO BE A SEINEN MANGA ARTIST!!
I got the prize money right away, but I still haven't received the souvenir.
IT WAS THE FIRST TIME THAT MY WORK WON AN AWARD!
A CERTAIN YOUTH MAGAZINE
IT WAS...
A HIP-HOP MANGA.
IF YOU DON'T USE THEM, YOUR BALLS WILL ROT.
NO, THEY WON'T.
IF YOU'VE GOT COMPLAINTS, TRY BEATING ME IN A RAP BATTLE, YO!
IF YOU LOSE, YOU WON'T GET TO PERFORM SOLO IN FRONT OF EVERYONE, YO!
AND I'LL SHOW YOU LOSING IN MY NEXT MV WITHOUT PIXELATING YOU OUT, YO!
WHOO OO!
TOO CRAZY, FO SHO!
SUPER DOPE, YA KNOW?!
To be continued!!

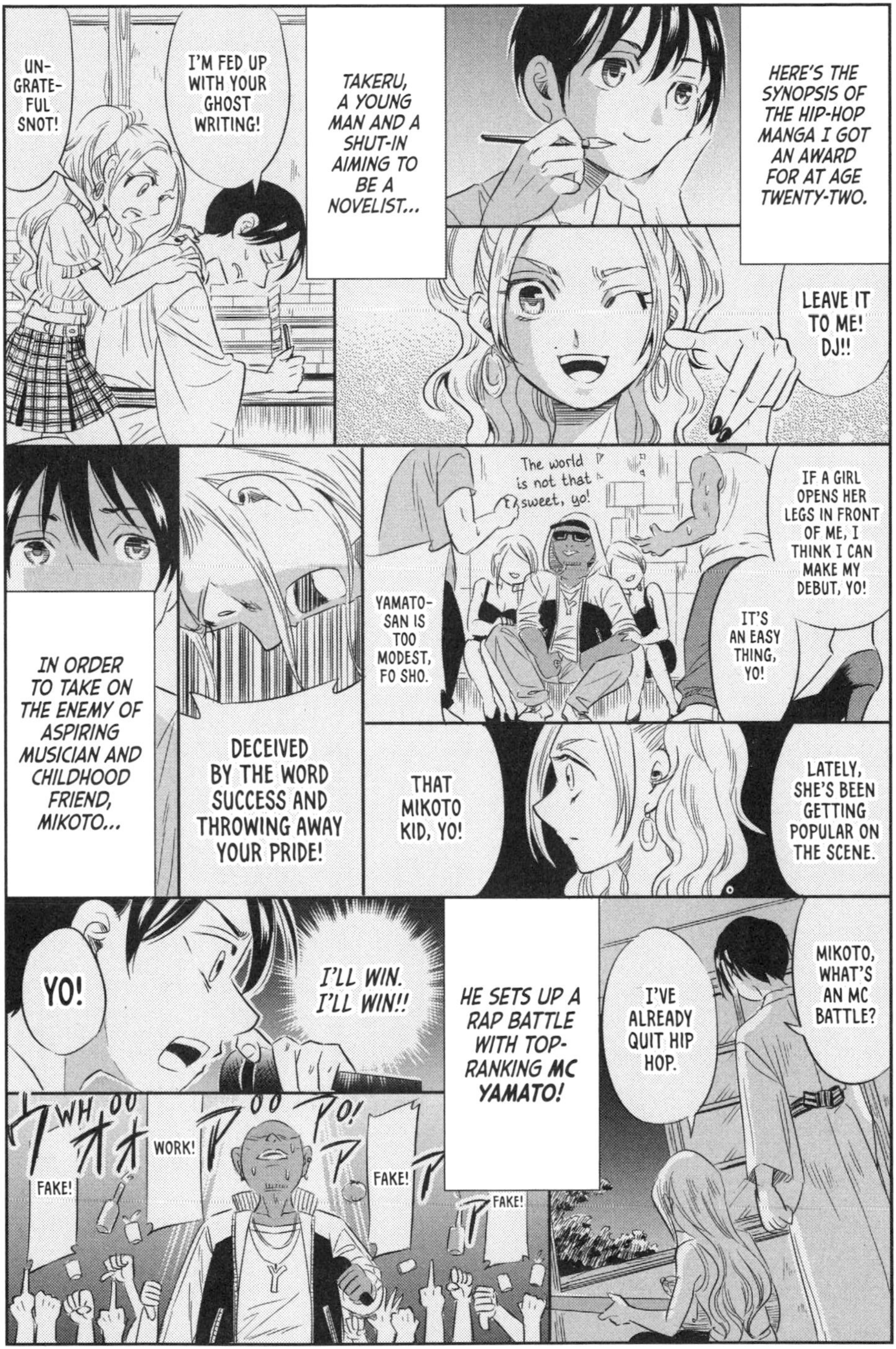
HERE'S THE SYNOPSIS OF THE HIP-HOP MANGA I GOT AN AWARD FOR AT AGE TWENTY-TWO.
LEAVE IT TO ME! DJ!!
TAKERU, A YOUNG MAN AND A SHUT-IN AIMING TO BE A NOVELIST...
I'M FED UP WITH YOUR GHOST WRITING!
UN-GRATEFUL SNOT!
IF A GIRL OPENS HER LEGS IN FRONT OF ME, I THINK I CAN MAKE MY DEBUT, YO!
IT'S AN EASY THING, YO!
The world is not that sweet, yo!
YAMATO-SAN IS TOO MODEST, FO SHO.
LATELY, SHE'S BEEN GETTING POPULAR ON THE SCENE.
THAT MIKOTO KID, YO!
DECEIVED BY THE WORD SUCCESS AND THROWING AWAY YOUR PRIDE!
IN ORDER TO TAKE ON THE ENEMY OF ASPIRING MUSICIAN AND CHILDHOOD FRIEND, MIKOTO...
MIKOTO, WHAT'S AN MC BATTLE?
I'VE ALREADY QUIT HIP HOP.
HE SETS UP A RAP BATTLE WITH TOP-RANKING MC YAMATO!
I'LL WIN. I'LL WIN!!
YO!
WHOOO
PO!
WORK!
FAKE!
FAKE!
FAKE!

Ep. 21: The "Back to My Original Intentions" Story

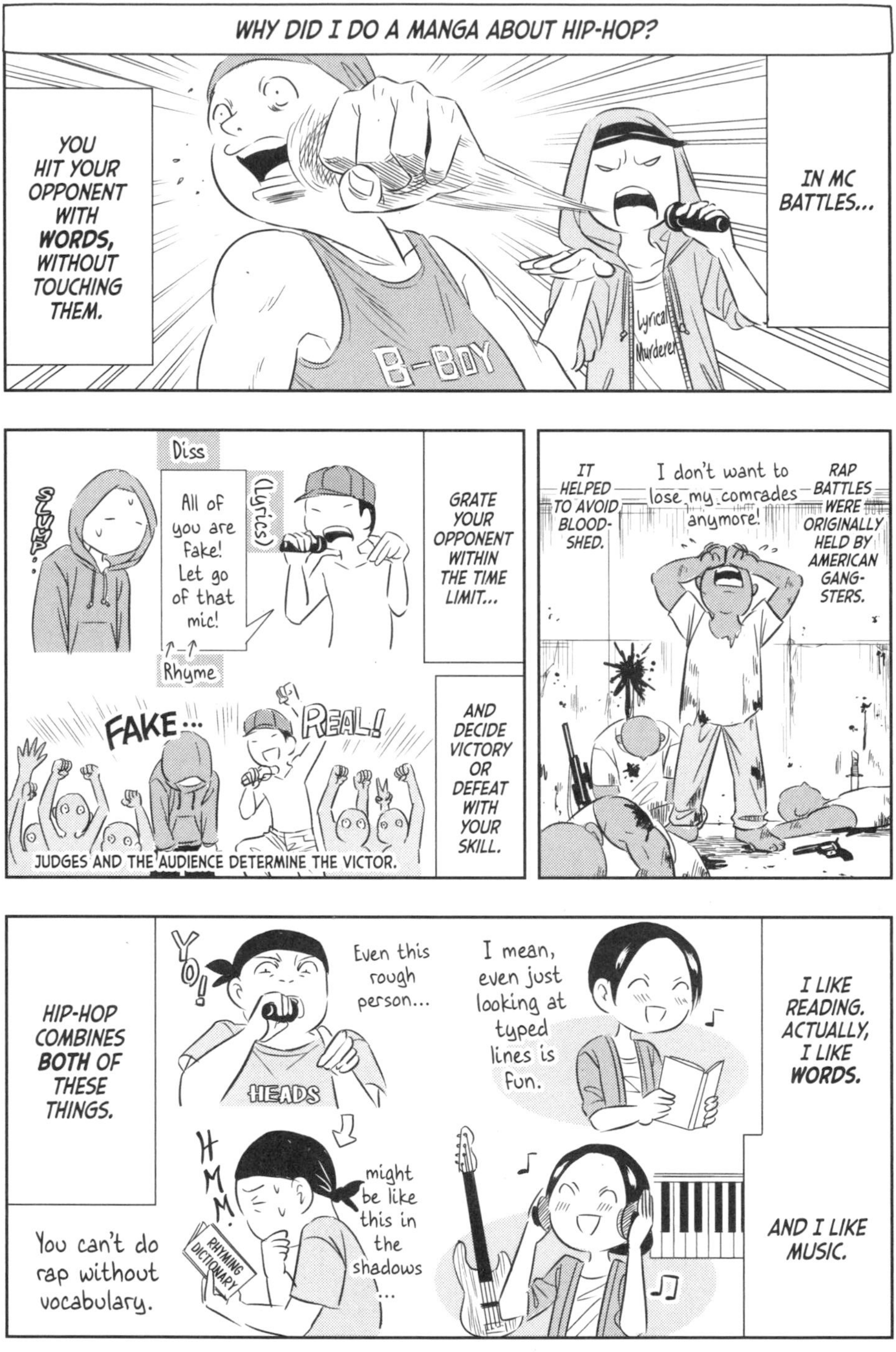
WHY DID I DO A MANGA ABOUT HIP-HOP?
IN MC BATTLES...
YOU HIT YOUR OPPONENT WITH WORDS, WITHOUT TOUCHING THEM.
B-BOY
Lyrical Murderer
RAP BATTLES WERE ORIGINALLY HELD BY AMERICAN GANGSTERS.
I don't want to lose my comrades anymore!
IT HELPED TO AVOID BLOODSHED.
GRATE YOUR OPPONENT WITHIN THE TIME LIMIT...
(Lyrics)
Diss
All of you are fake! Let go of that mic!
Rhyme
SLUMP..
AND DECIDE VICTORY OR DEFEAT WITH YOUR SKILL.
REAL!
FAKE...
JUDGES AND THE AUDIENCE DETERMINE THE VICTOR.
I LIKE READING. ACTUALLY, I LIKE WORDS.
I mean, even just looking at typed lines is fun.
Even this rough person...
YO!
HEADS
AND I LIKE MUSIC.
might be like this in the shadows...
HMM.
RHYMING DICTIONARY
HIP-HOP COMBINES BOTH OF THESE THINGS.
You can't do rap without vocabulary.

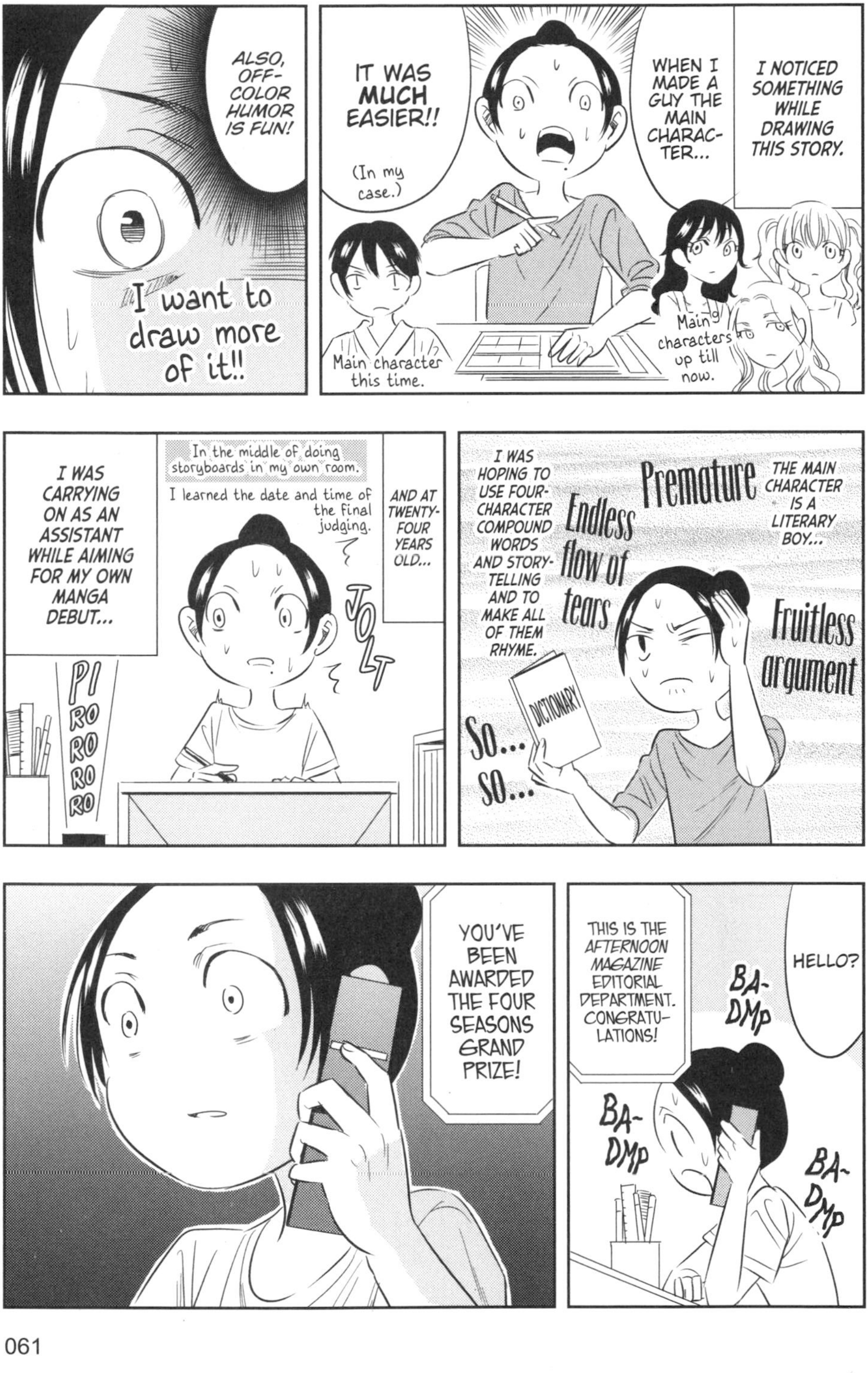
I NOTICED SOMETHING WHILE DRAWING THIS STORY.
WHEN I MADE A GUY THE MAIN CHARACTER...
IT WAS MUCH EASIER!!
(In my case.)
Main characters up till now.
Main character this time.
ALSO, OFF-COLOR HUMOR IS FUN!
I want to draw more of it!!
THE MAIN CHARACTER IS A LITERARY BOY...
Premature
I WAS HOPING TO USE FOUR-CHARACTER COMPOUND WORDS AND STORYTELLING AND TO MAKE ALL OF THEM RHYME.
Endless flow of tears
Fruitless argument
DICTIONARY
So... so...
AND AT TWENTY-FOUR YEARS OLD...
In the middle of doing storyboards in my own room.
I learned the date and time of the final judging.
JOLT
I WAS CARRYING ON AS AN ASSISTANT WHILE AIMING FOR MY OWN MANGA DEBUT...
PIRORORORO
HELLO?
BA-DMP
THIS IS THE AFTERNOON MAGAZINE EDITORIAL DEPARTMENT. CONGRATULATIONS!
BA-DMP
BA-DMP
YOU'VE BEEN AWARDED THE FOUR SEASONS GRAND PRIZE!

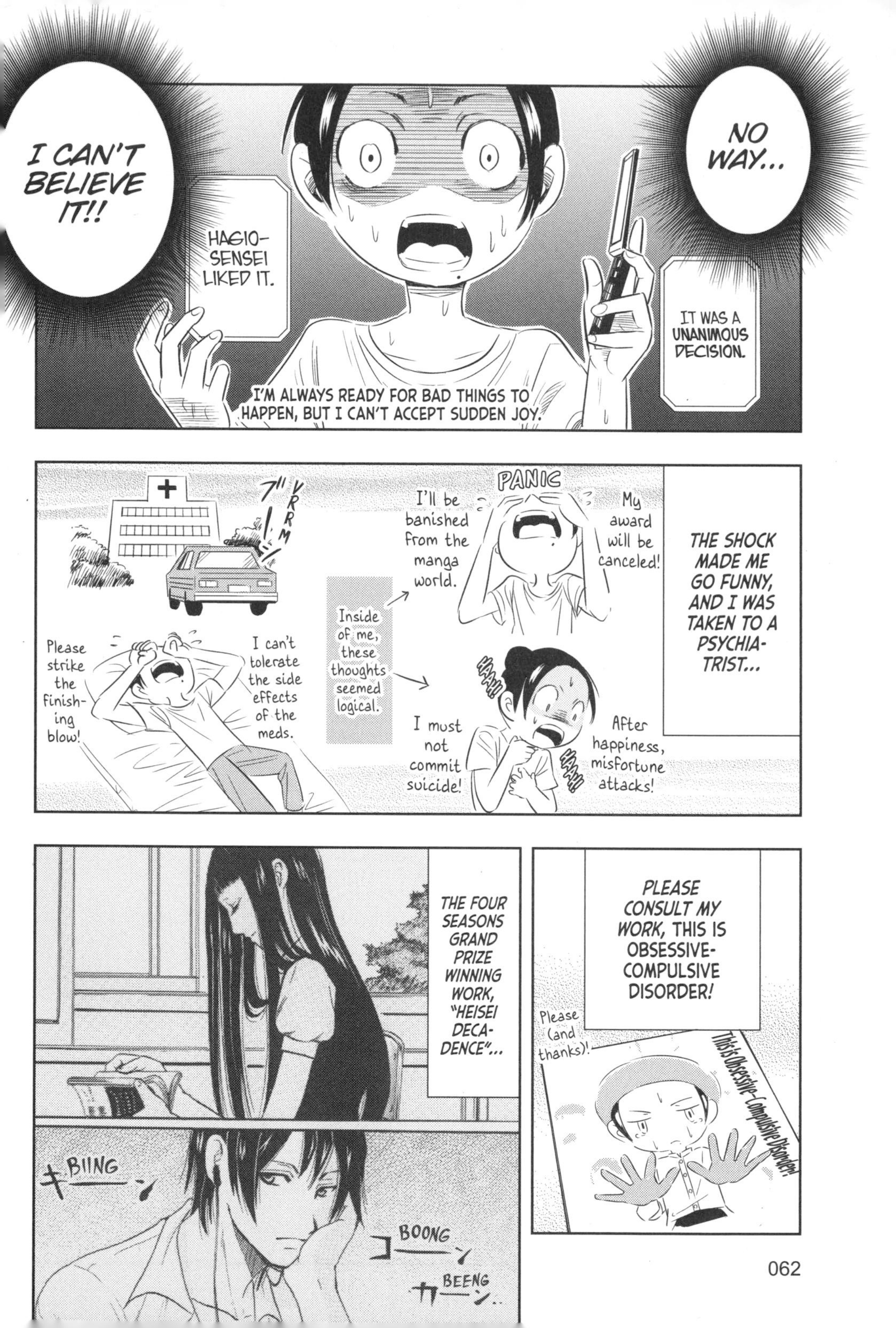
NO WAY...
IT WAS A UNANIMOUS DECISION.
HAGIO-SENSEI LIKED IT.
I CAN'T BELIEVE IT!!
I'M ALWAYS READY FOR BAD THINGS TO HAPPEN, BUT I CAN'T ACCEPT SUDDEN JOY.
THE SHOCK MADE ME GO FUNNY, AND I WAS TAKEN TO A PSYCHIATRIST...
PANIC
My award will be canceled!
I'll be banished from the manga world.
Inside of me, these thoughts seemed logical.
After happiness, misfortune attacks!
HAAH
HAAH
I must not commit suicide!
I can't tolerate the side effects of the meds.
Please strike the finishing blow!
VRRM
PLEASE CONSULT MY WORK, THIS IS OBSESSIVE-COMPULSIVE DISORDER!
This Is Obsessive-Compulsive Disorder!
Please (and thanks)!
THE FOUR SEASONS GRAND PRIZE WINNING WORK, "HEISEI DECADENCE"...
BIING
BOONG
BEENG

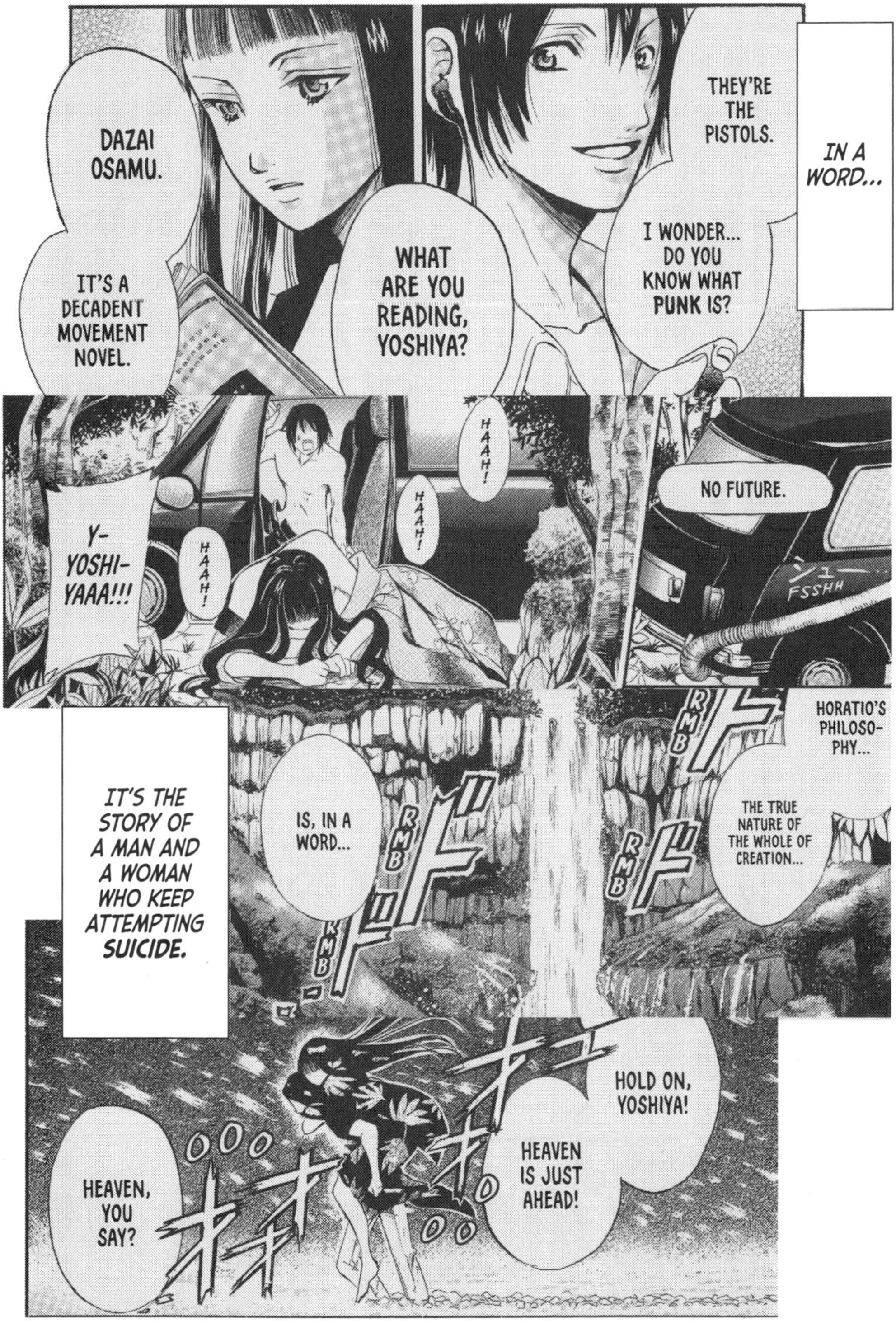
IN A WORD...
THEY'RE THE PISTOLS.
I WONDER... DO YOU KNOW WHAT PUNK IS?
WHAT ARE YOU READING, YOSHIYA?
DAZAI OSAMU.
IT'S A DECADENT MOVEMENT NOVEL.
NO FUTURE.
FSSHH
HAAAH!
HAAAH!
HAAAH!
Y-YOSHI-YAAA!!!
HORATIO'S PHILOSO-PHY...
THE TRUE NATURE OF THE WHOLE OF CREATION...
RMB
RMB
RMB
IS, IN A WORD...
RMB
IT'S THE STORY OF A MAN AND A WOMAN WHO KEEP ATTEMPTING SUICIDE.
HOLD ON, YOSHIYA!
HEAVEN IS JUST AHEAD!
OOO
OOO
HEAVEN, YOU SAY?

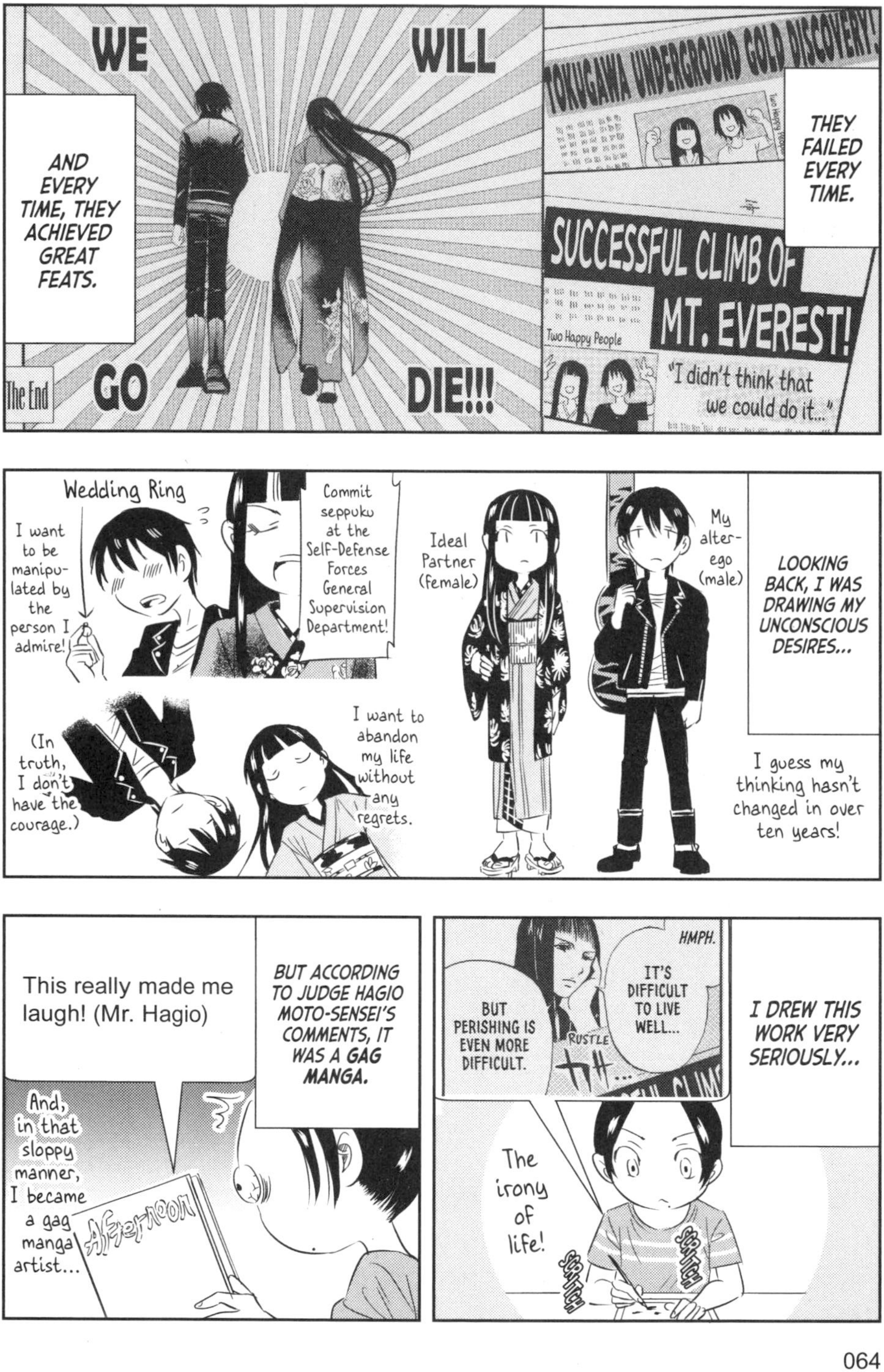
TOKUGAWA UNDERGROUND GOLD DISCOVERY!
THEY FAILED EVERY TIME.
SUCCESSFUL CLIMB OF MT. EVEREST!
Two Happy People
"I didn't think that we could do it..."
AND EVERY TIME, THEY ACHIEVED GREAT FEATS.
WE WILL GO DIE!!!
The End
LOOKING BACK, I WAS DRAWING MY UNCONSCIOUS DESIRES...
I guess my thinking hasn't changed in over ten years!
My alter-ego (male)
Ideal Partner (female)
Commit seppuku at the Self-Defense Forces General Supervision Department!
Wedding Ring
I want to be manipulated by the person I admire!
I want to abandon my life without any regrets.
(In truth, I don't have the courage.)
I DREW THIS WORK VERY SERIOUSLY...
HMPH.
IT'S DIFFICULT TO LIVE WELL...
BUT PERISHING IS EVEN MORE DIFFICULT.
RUSTLE
The irony of life!
SCRITCH
SCRITCH
SCRITCH
BUT ACCORDING TO JUDGE HAGIO MOTO-SENSEI'S COMMENTS, IT WAS A GAG MANGA.
This really made me laugh! (Mr. Hagio)
And, in that sloppy manner, I became a gag manga artist...
Afternoon

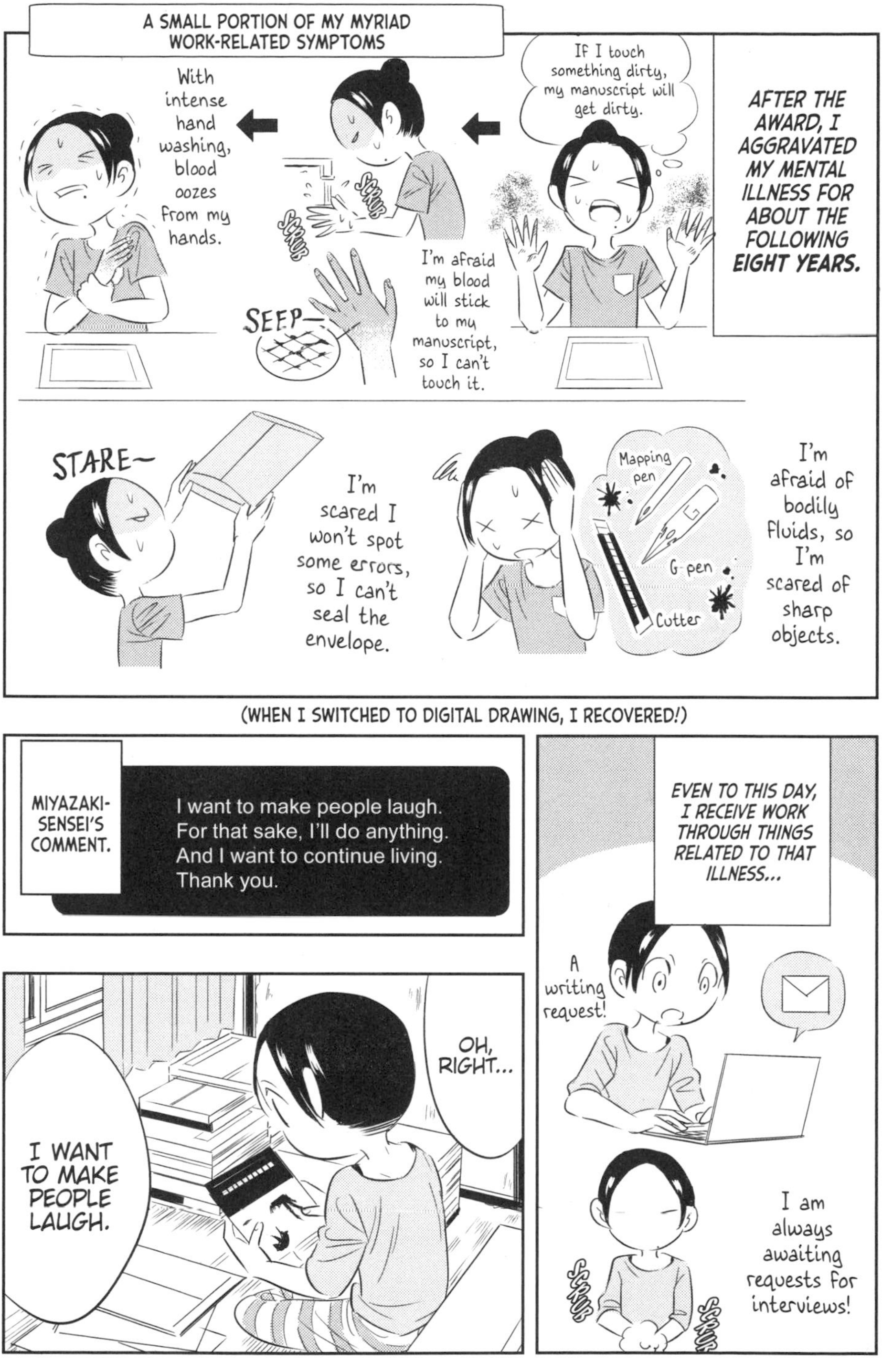

A SMALL PORTION OF MY MYRIAD WORK-RELATED SYMPTOMS
AFTER THE AWARD, I AGGRAVATED MY MENTAL ILLNESS FOR ABOUT THE FOLLOWING EIGHT YEARS.
If I touch something dirty, my manuscript will get dirty.
SCRUB
SCRUB
I'm afraid my blood will stick to my manuscript, so I can't touch it.
SEEP—
With intense hand washing, blood oozes from my hands.
I'm afraid of bodily fluids, so I'm scared of sharp objects.
Mapping pen
G-pen
Cutter
I'm scared I won't spot some errors, so I can't seal the envelope.
STARE~
(WHEN I SWITCHED TO DIGITAL DRAWING, I RECOVERED!)
EVEN TO THIS DAY, I RECEIVE WORK THROUGH THINGS RELATED TO THAT ILLNESS...
A writing request!
I am always awaiting requests for interviews!
SCRUB
SCRUB
MIYAZAKI-SENSEI'S COMMENT.
I want to make people laugh. For that sake, I'll do anything. And I want to continue living. Thank you.
OH, RIGHT...
I WANT TO MAKE PEOPLE LAUGH.

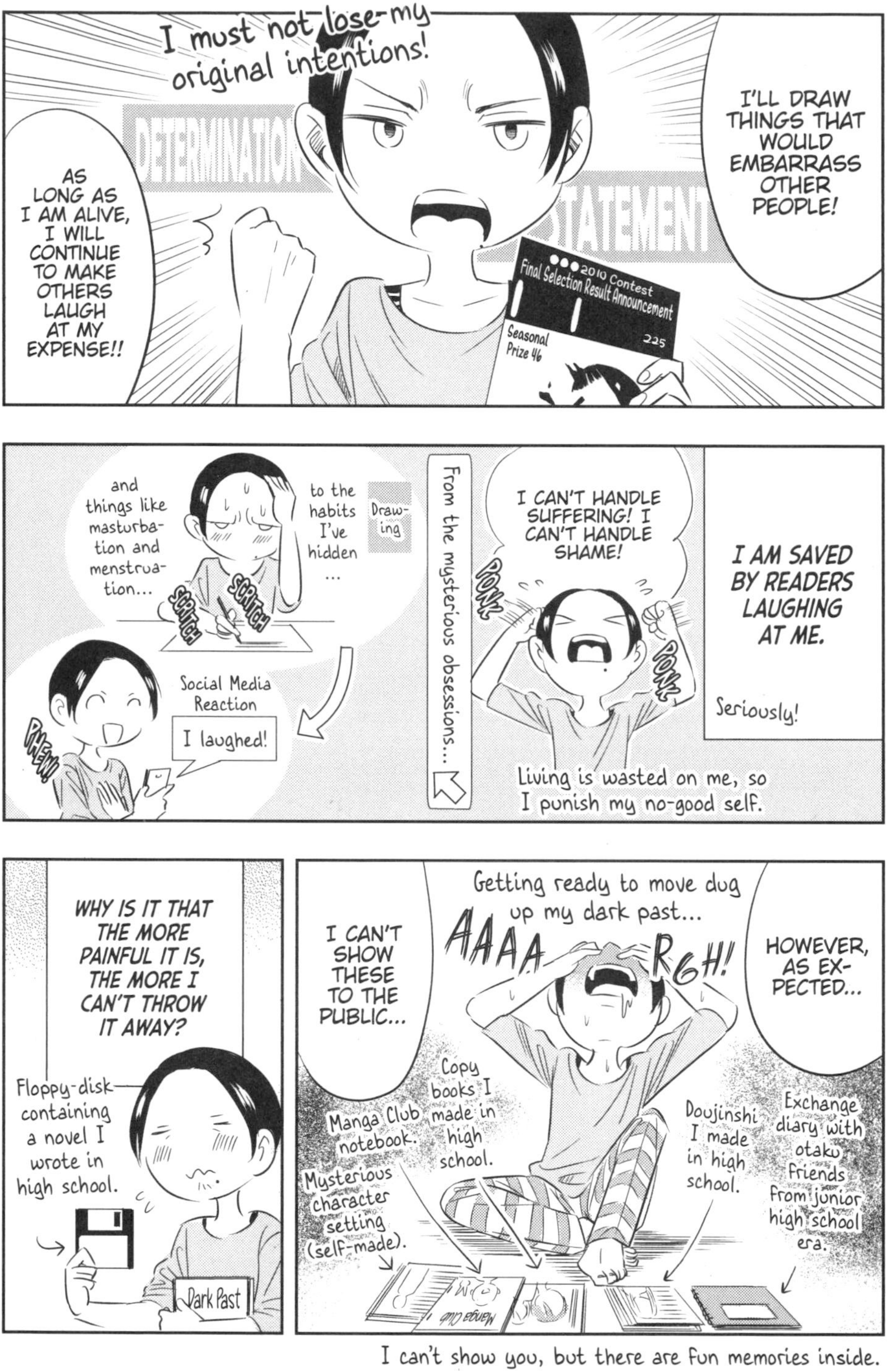
I'LL DRAW THINGS THAT WOULD EMBARRASS OTHER PEOPLE!
I must not lose my original intentions!
DETERMINATION
STATEMENT
2010 Contest
Final Selection Result Announcement
Seasonal Prize 46
225
AS LONG AS I AM ALIVE, I WILL CONTINUE TO MAKE OTHERS LAUGH AT MY EXPENSE!!
I AM SAVED BY READERS LAUGHING AT ME.
Seriously!
I CAN'T HANDLE SUFFERING! I CAN'T HANDLE SHAME!
PONK
PONK
Living is wasted on me, so I punish my no-good self.
From the mysterious obsessions...
Drawing
to the habits I've hidden...
and things like masturbation and menstruation...
SCRITCH
SCRITCH
Social Media Reaction
I laughed!
PHEW!
HOWEVER, AS EXPECTED...
Getting ready to move dug up my dark past...
AAAARGH!
I CAN'T SHOW THESE TO THE PUBLIC...
Exchange diary with otaku friends from junior high school era.
Doujinshi I made in high school.
Copy books I made in high school.
Manga Club notebook.
Mysterious character setting (self-made).
WHY IS IT THAT THE MORE PAINFUL IT IS, THE MORE I CAN'T THROW IT AWAY?
Floppy-disk containing a novel I wrote in high school.
Dark Past

I can't show you, but there are fun memories inside.

Ep. 22: The "I Announce the Theme on the Fourth Page" Story

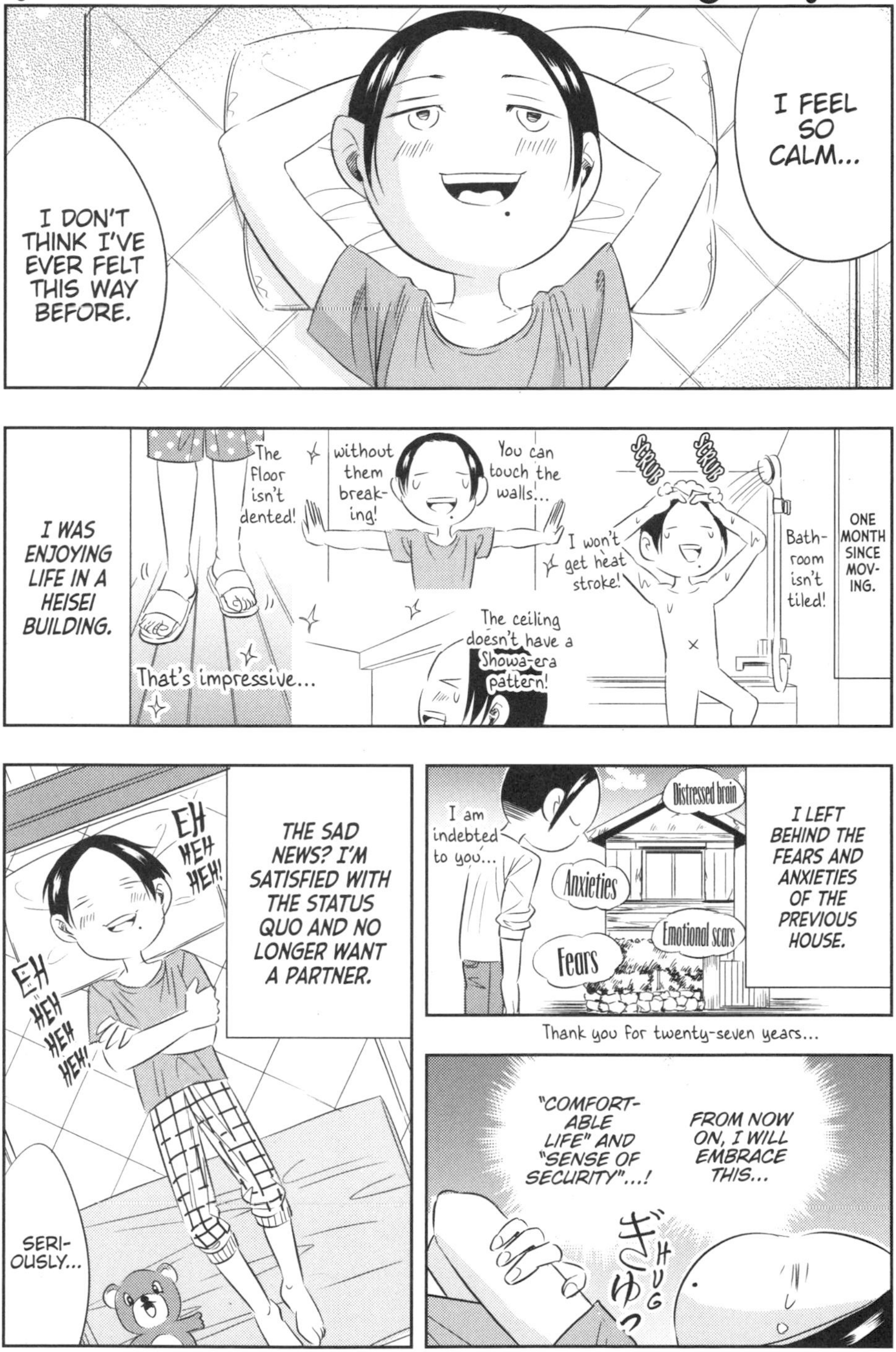
I FEEL SO CALM...
I DON'T THINK I'VE EVER FELT THIS WAY BEFORE.
ONE MONTH SINCE MOVING.
Bathroom isn't tiled!
SCRUB SCRUB
I won't get heat stroke!
The ceiling doesn't have a Showa-era pattern!
You can touch the walls... without them breaking!
The floor isn't dented!
That's impressive...
I WAS ENJOYING LIFE IN A HEISEI BUILDING.
I LEFT BEHIND THE FEARS AND ANXIETIES OF THE PREVIOUS HOUSE.
Distressed brain
Emotional scars
Anxieties
Fears
I am indebted to you...
Thank you for twenty-seven years...
FROM NOW ON, I WILL EMBRACE THIS...
"COMFORTABLE LIFE" AND "SENSE OF SECURITY"...!
ぎゅっ
HUG
THE SAD NEWS? I'M SATISFIED WITH THE STATUS QUO AND NO LONGER WANT A PARTNER.
EH HEH HEH!
EH HEH HEH HEH!
SERIOUSLY...

Although I still live with Ma.

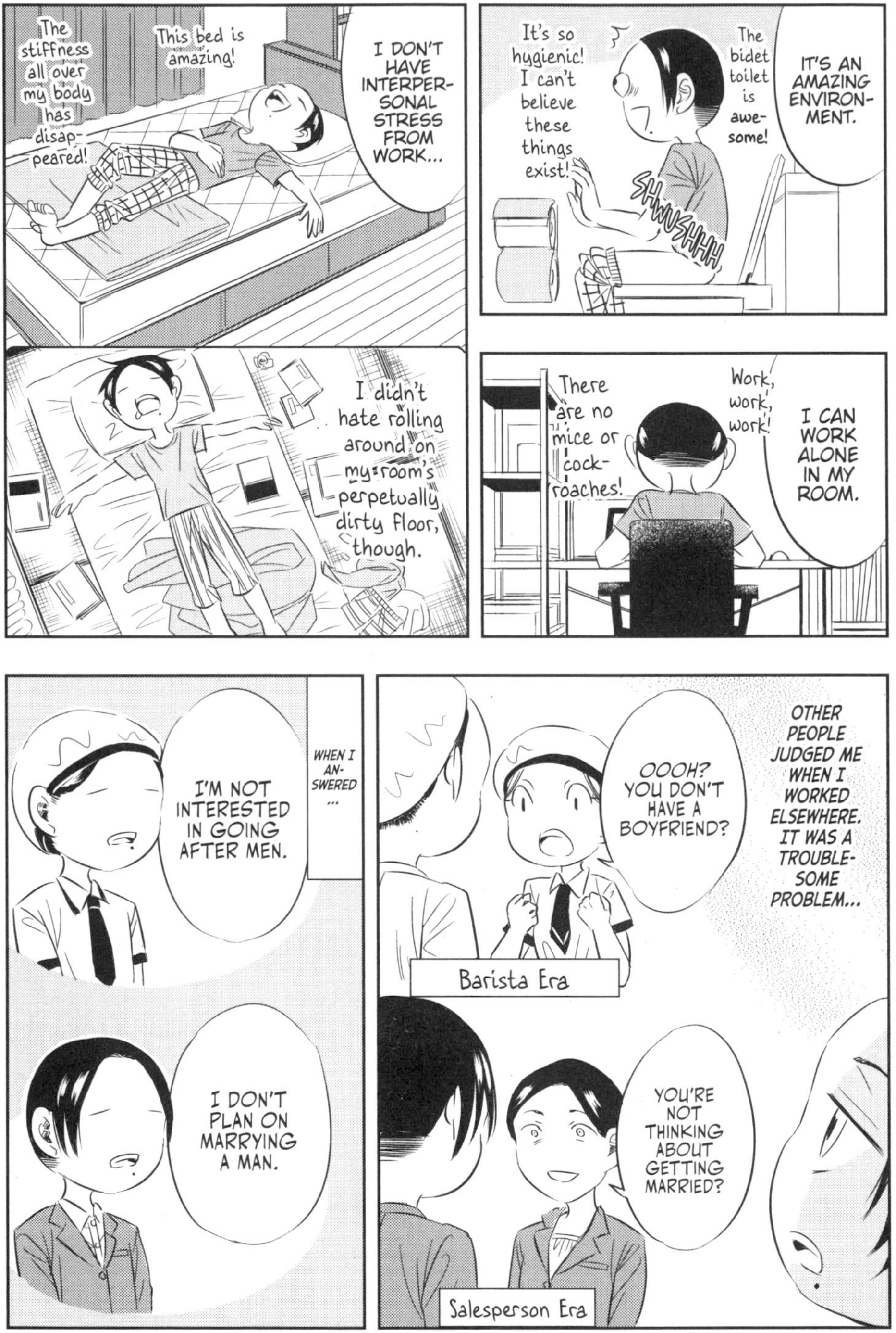
IT'S AN AMAZING ENVIRONMENT.
The bidet toilet is awesome!
It's so hygienic! I can't believe these things exist!
SHWUSHHH
I DON'T HAVE INTERPERSONAL STRESS FROM WORK...
This bed is amazing!
The stiffness all over my body has disappeared!
I CAN WORK ALONE IN MY ROOM.
Work, work, work!
There are no mice or cockroaches!
I didn't hate rolling around on my room's perpetually dirty floor, though.
OTHER PEOPLE JUDGED ME WHEN I WORKED ELSEWHERE. IT WAS A TROUBLESOME PROBLEM...
OOOH? YOU DON'T HAVE A BOYFRIEND?
Barista Era
YOU'RE NOT THINKING ABOUT GETTING MARRIED?
Salesperson Era
WHEN I ANSWERED ...
I'M NOT INTERESTED IN GOING AFTER MEN.
I DON'T PLAN ON MARRYING A MAN.

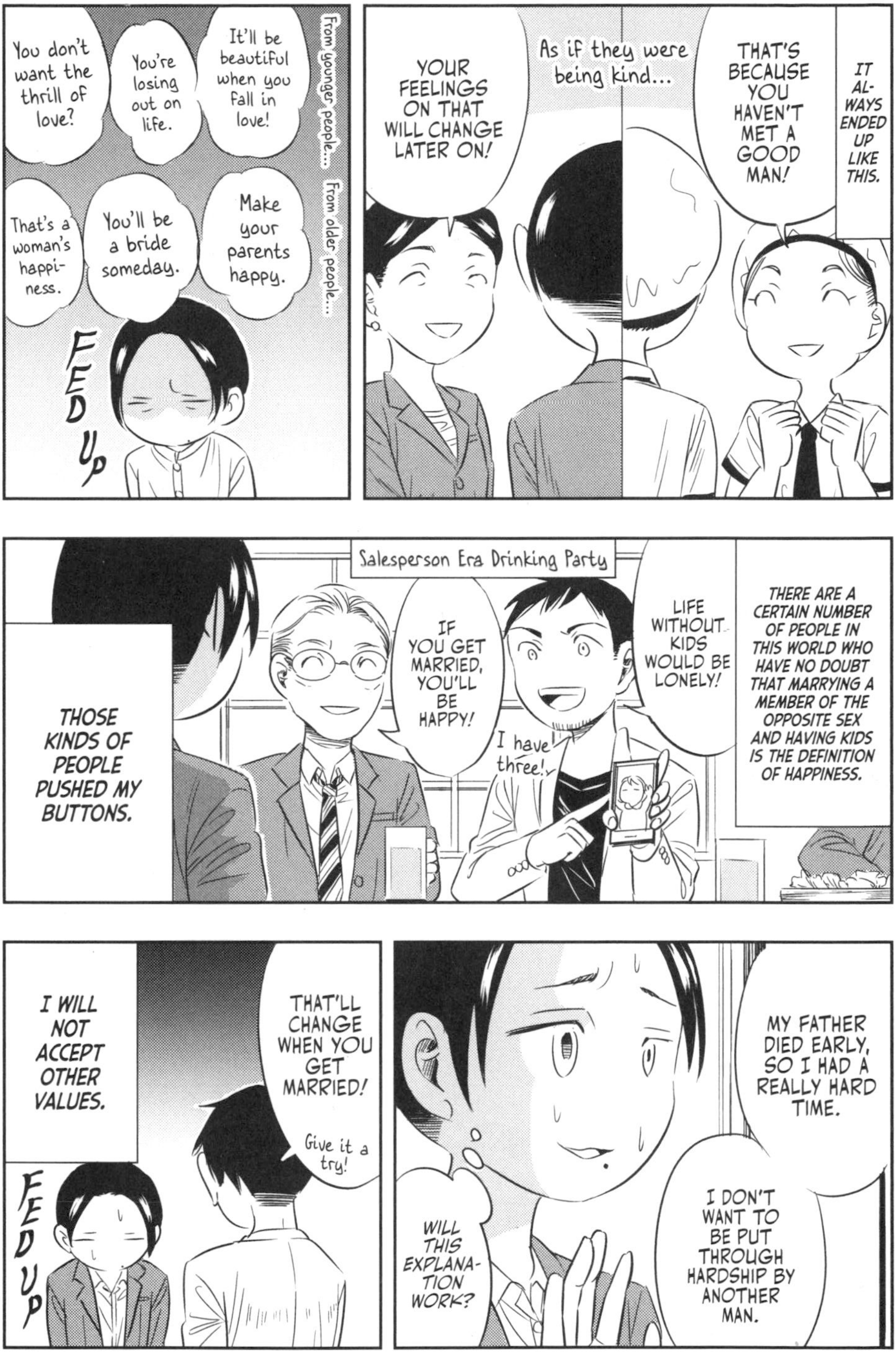
IT ALWAYS ENDED UP LIKE THIS.
THAT'S BECAUSE YOU HAVEN'T MET A GOOD MAN!
As if they were being kind...
YOUR FEELINGS ON THAT WILL CHANGE LATER ON!
From younger people...
It'll be beautiful when you fall in love!
You're losing out on life.
You don't want the thrill of love?
From older people...
Make your parents happy.
You'll be a bride someday.
That's a woman's happiness.
FED UP
Salesperson Era Drinking Party
THERE ARE A CERTAIN NUMBER OF PEOPLE IN THIS WORLD WHO HAVE NO DOUBT THAT MARRYING A MEMBER OF THE OPPOSITE SEX AND HAVING KIDS IS THE DEFINITION OF HAPPINESS.
LIFE WITHOUT KIDS WOULD BE LONELY!
I have three!
IF YOU GET MARRIED, YOU'LL BE HAPPY!
THOSE KINDS OF PEOPLE PUSHED MY BUTTONS.
MY FATHER DIED EARLY, SO I HAD A REALLY HARD TIME.
I DON'T WANT TO BE PUT THROUGH HARDSHIP BY ANOTHER MAN.
WILL THIS EXPLANATION WORK?
THAT'LL CHANGE WHEN YOU GET MARRIED!
Give it a try!
I WILL NOT ACCEPT OTHER VALUES.
FED UP

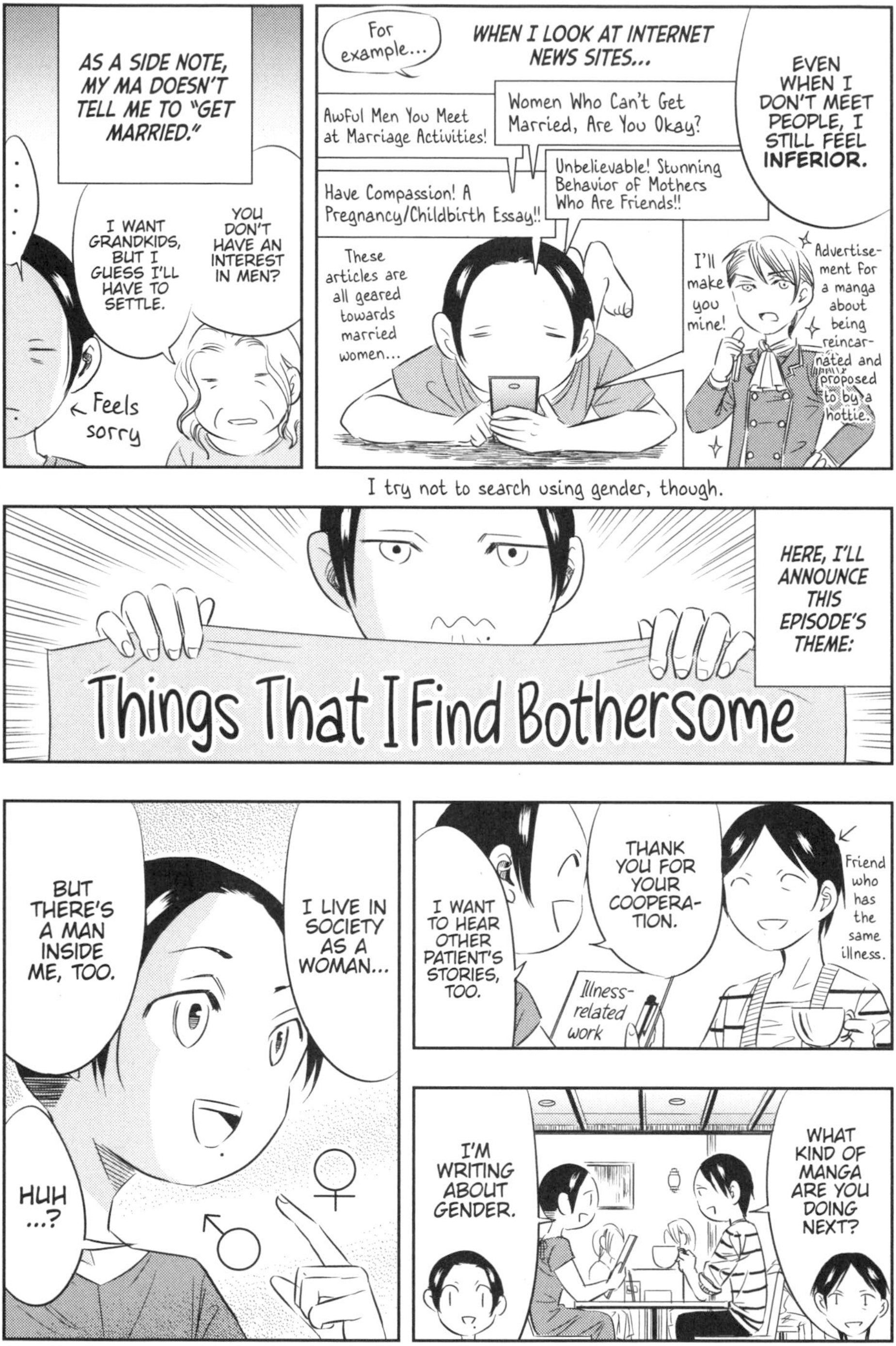
EVEN WHEN I DON'T MEET PEOPLE, I STILL FEEL **INFERIOR.**
WHEN I LOOK AT INTERNET NEWS SITES...
For example...
Women Who Can't Get Married, Are You Okay?
Awful Men You Meet at Marriage Activities!
Unbelievable! Stunning Behavior of Mothers Who Are Friends!!
Have Compassion! A Pregnancy/Childbirth Essay!!
Advertisement for a manga about being reincarnated and proposed to by a hottie.
I'll make you mine!
These articles are all geared towards married women...
AS A SIDE NOTE, MY MA DOESN'T TELL ME TO "GET MARRIED."
YOU DON'T HAVE AN INTEREST IN MEN?
I WANT GRANDKIDS, BUT I GUESS I'LL HAVE TO SETTLE.
......
Feels sorry
I try not to search using gender, though.
HERE, I'LL ANNOUNCE THIS EPISODE'S THEME:
Things That I Find Bothersome
Friend who has the same illness.
THANK YOU FOR YOUR COOPERATION.
I WANT TO HEAR OTHER PATIENT'S STORIES, TOO.
Illness-related work
WHAT KIND OF MANGA ARE YOU DOING NEXT?
I'M WRITING ABOUT GENDER.
I LIVE IN SOCIETY AS A WOMAN...
BUT THERE'S A MAN INSIDE ME, TOO.
HUH...?

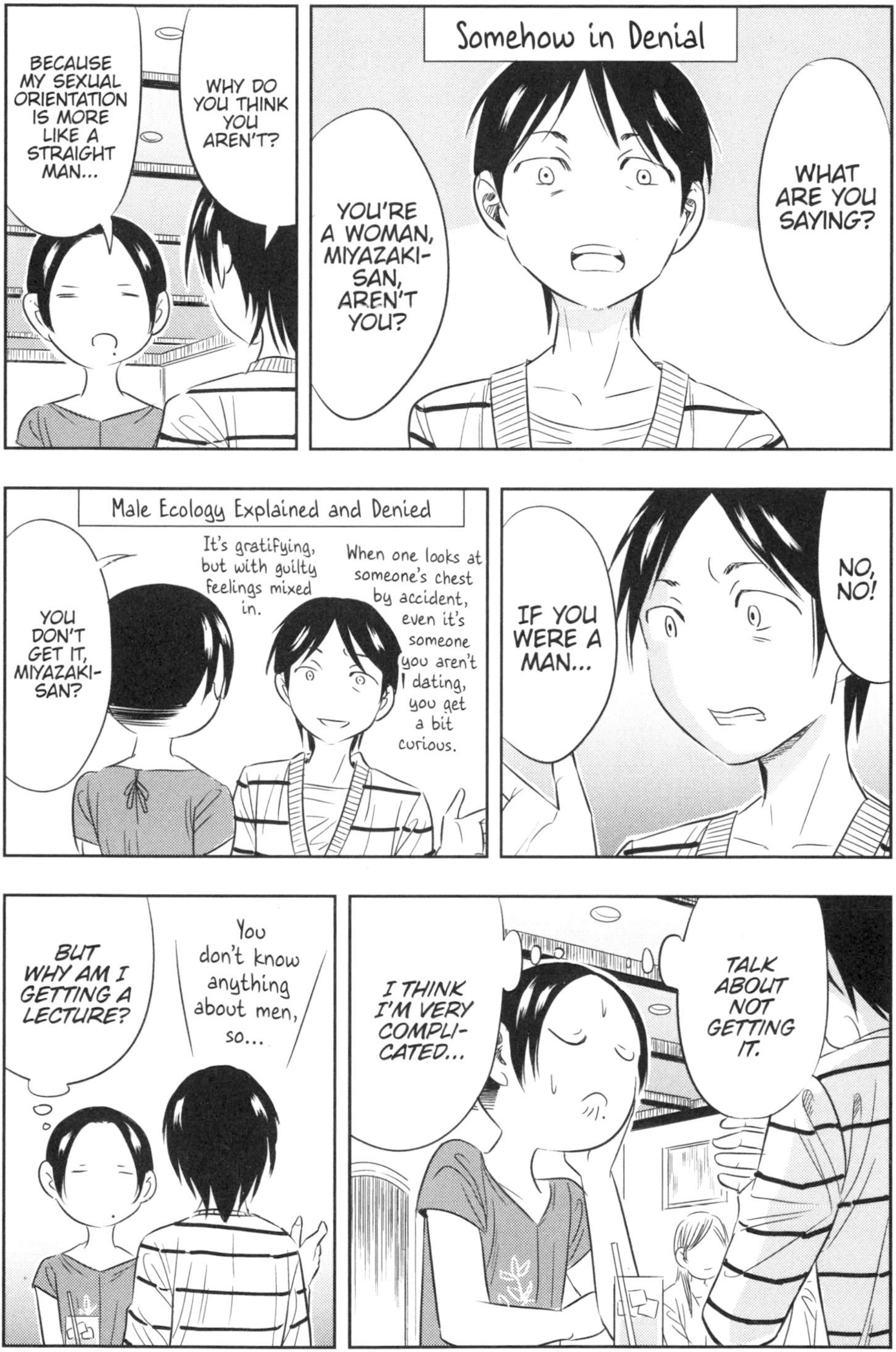
Somehow in Denial
WHAT ARE YOU SAYING?
YOU'RE A WOMAN, MIYAZAKI-SAN, AREN'T YOU?
WHY DO YOU THINK YOU AREN'T?
BECAUSE MY SEXUAL ORIENTATION IS MORE LIKE A STRAIGHT MAN...
NO, NO!
IF YOU WERE A MAN...
Male Ecology Explained and Denied
When one looks at someone's chest by accident, even it's someone you aren't dating, you get a bit curious.
It's gratifying, but with guilty feelings mixed in.
YOU DON'T GET IT, MIYAZAKI-SAN?
TALK ABOUT NOT GETTING IT.
I THINK I'M VERY COMPLI-CATED...
You don't know anything about men, so...
BUT WHY AM I GETTING A LECTURE?

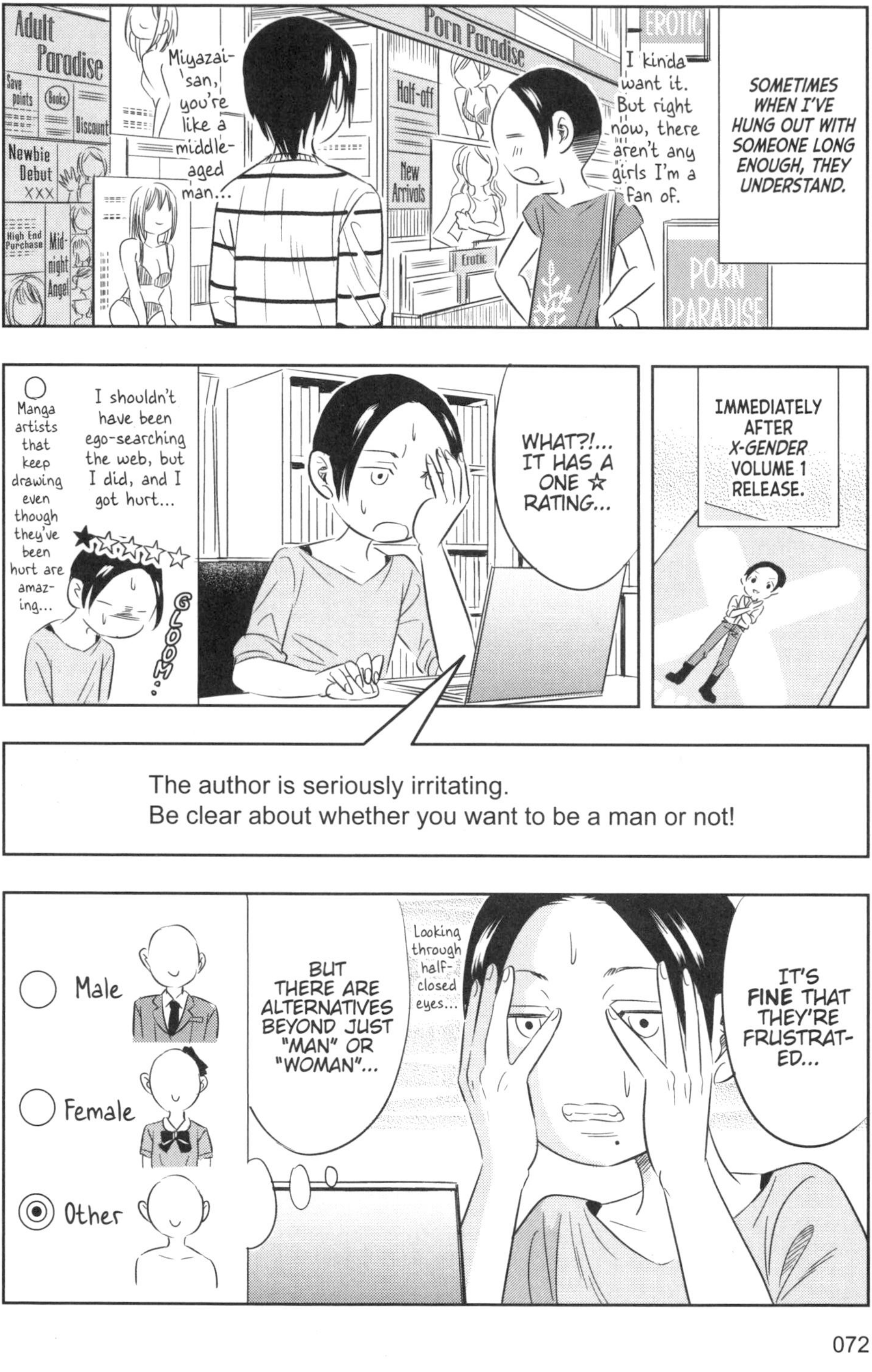
SOMETIMES WHEN I'VE HUNG OUT WITH SOMEONE LONG ENOUGH, THEY UNDERSTAND.
EROTIC
I kinda want it. But right now, there aren't any girls I'm a fan of.
PORN PARADISE
Porn Paradise
Half-off
New Arrivals
Erotic
Miyazai-san, you're like a middle-aged man...
Adult Paradise
Save points
Books
Discount
Newbie Debut XXX
High End Purchase
Mid-night Angel
IMMEDIATELY AFTER X-GENDER VOLUME 1 RELEASE.
WHAT?!... IT HAS A ONE ☆ RATING...
The author is seriously irritating.
Be clear about whether you want to be a man or not!
I shouldn't have been ego-searching the web, but I did, and I got hurt...
Manga artists that keep drawing even though they've been hurt are amazing...
GLOOM...
IT'S FINE THAT THEY'RE FRUSTRATED...
Looking through half-closed eyes...
BUT THERE ARE ALTERNATIVES BEYOND JUST "MAN" OR "WOMAN"...
Male
Female
Other

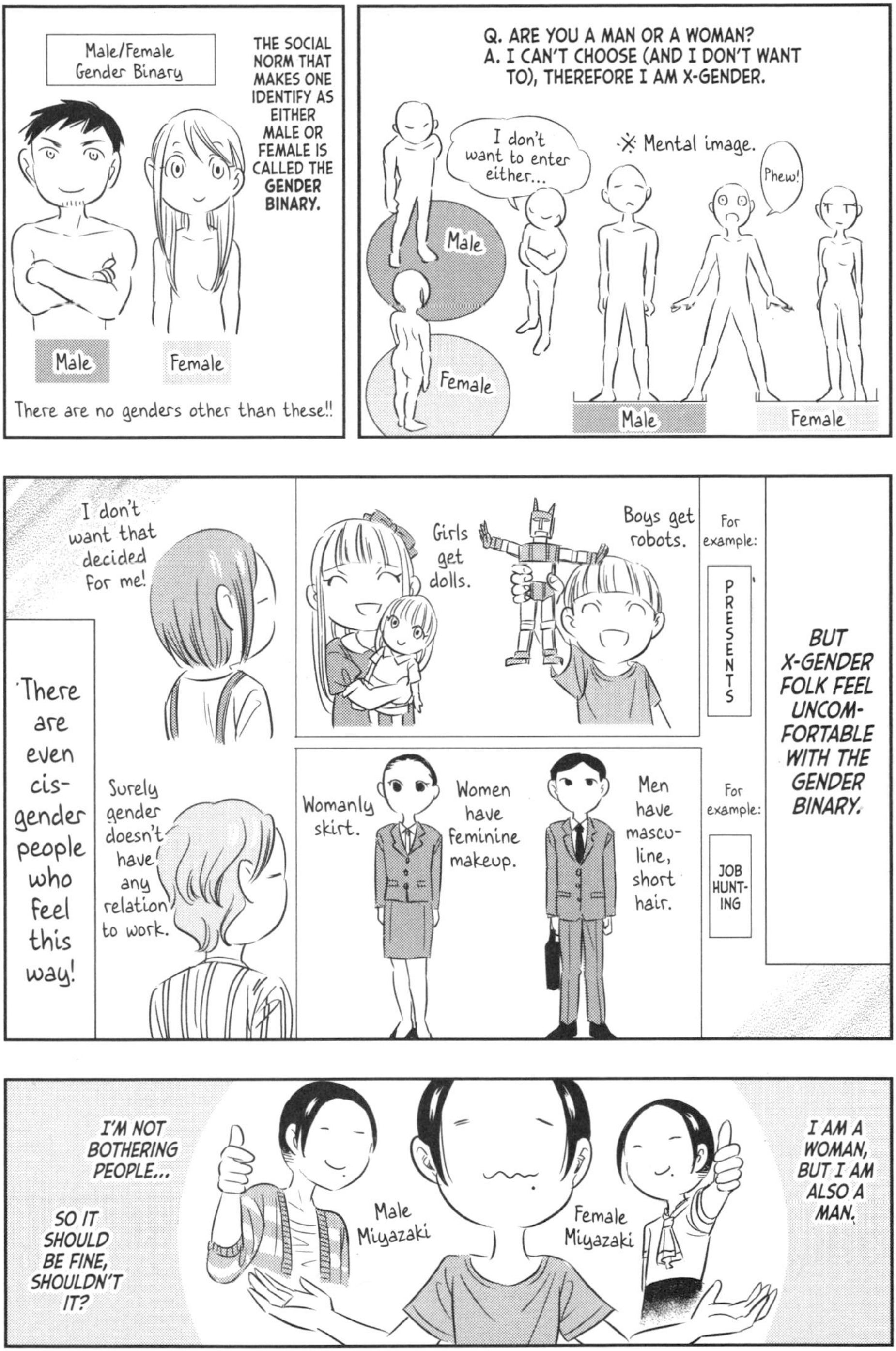

Q. ARE YOU A MAN OR A WOMAN?
A. I CAN'T CHOOSE (AND I DON'T WANT TO), THEREFORE I AM X-GENDER.
※ Mental image.
Phew!
Female
Male
I don't want to enter either...
Male
Female
THE SOCIAL NORM THAT MAKES ONE IDENTIFY AS EITHER MALE OR FEMALE IS CALLED THE GENDER BINARY.
Male/Female Gender Binary
Male
Female
There are no genders other than these!!
BUT X-GENDER FOLK FEEL UNCOMFORTABLE WITH THE GENDER BINARY.
For example:
PRESENTS
Boys get robots.
Girls get dolls.
I don't want that decided for me!
For example:
JOB HUNTING
Men have masculine, short hair.
Women have feminine makeup.
Womanly skirt.
Surely gender doesn't have any relation to work.
There are even cisgender people who feel this way!
I AM A WOMAN, BUT I AM ALSO A MAN.
Female Miyazaki
Male Miyazaki
I'M NOT BOTHERING PEOPLE...
SO IT SHOULD BE FINE, SHOULDN'T IT?

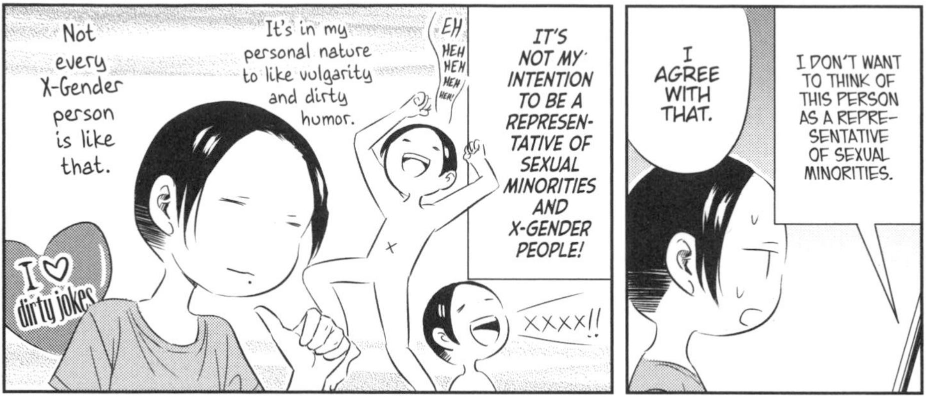
I DON'T WANT TO THINK OF THIS PERSON AS A REPRESENTATIVE OF SEXUAL MINORITIES.
I AGREE WITH THAT.
IT'S NOT MY INTENTION TO BE A REPRESENTATIVE OF SEXUAL MINORITIES AND X-GENDER PEOPLE!
EH HEH HEH HEH HEH!
It's in my personal nature to like vulgarity and dirty humor.
Not every X-Gender person is like that.
I ♡ dirty jokes
XXXX!!

I just want you to know that there are people like me.

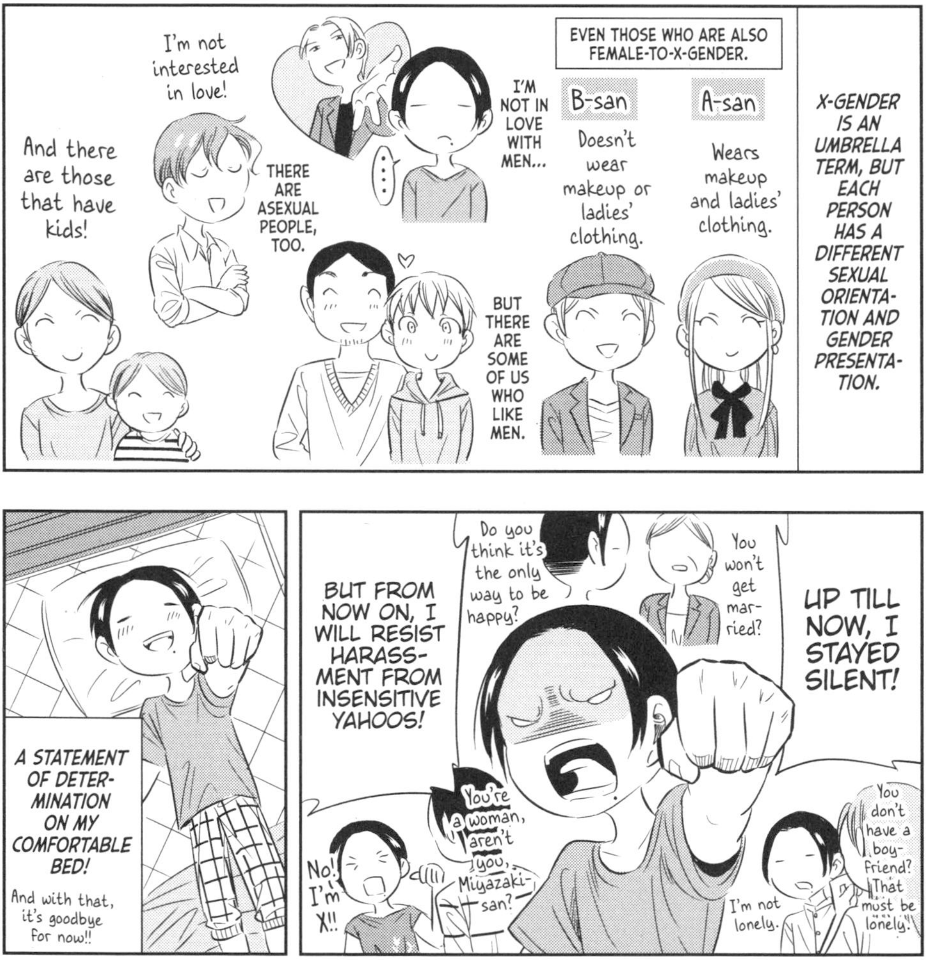
X-GENDER IS AN UMBRELLA TERM, BUT EACH PERSON HAS A DIFFERENT SEXUAL ORIENTATION AND GENDER PRESENTATION.
EVEN THOSE WHO ARE ALSO FEMALE-TO-X-GENDER.
A-san
Wears makeup and ladies' clothing.
B-san
Doesn't wear makeup or ladies' clothing.
I'M NOT IN LOVE WITH MEN...
BUT THERE ARE SOME OF US WHO LIKE MEN.
I'm not interested in love!
THERE ARE ASEXUAL PEOPLE, TOO.
...
And there are those that have kids!
UP TILL NOW, I STAYED SILENT!
You won't get married?
Do you think it's the only way to be happy?
BUT FROM NOW ON, I WILL RESIST HARASSMENT FROM INSENSITIVE YAHOOS!
You don't have a boyfriend? That must be lonely.
I'm not lonely.
You're a woman, aren't you, Miyazaki-san?
No! I'm X!!
A STATEMENT OF DETERMINATION ON MY COMFORTABLE BED!
And with that, it's goodbye for now!!

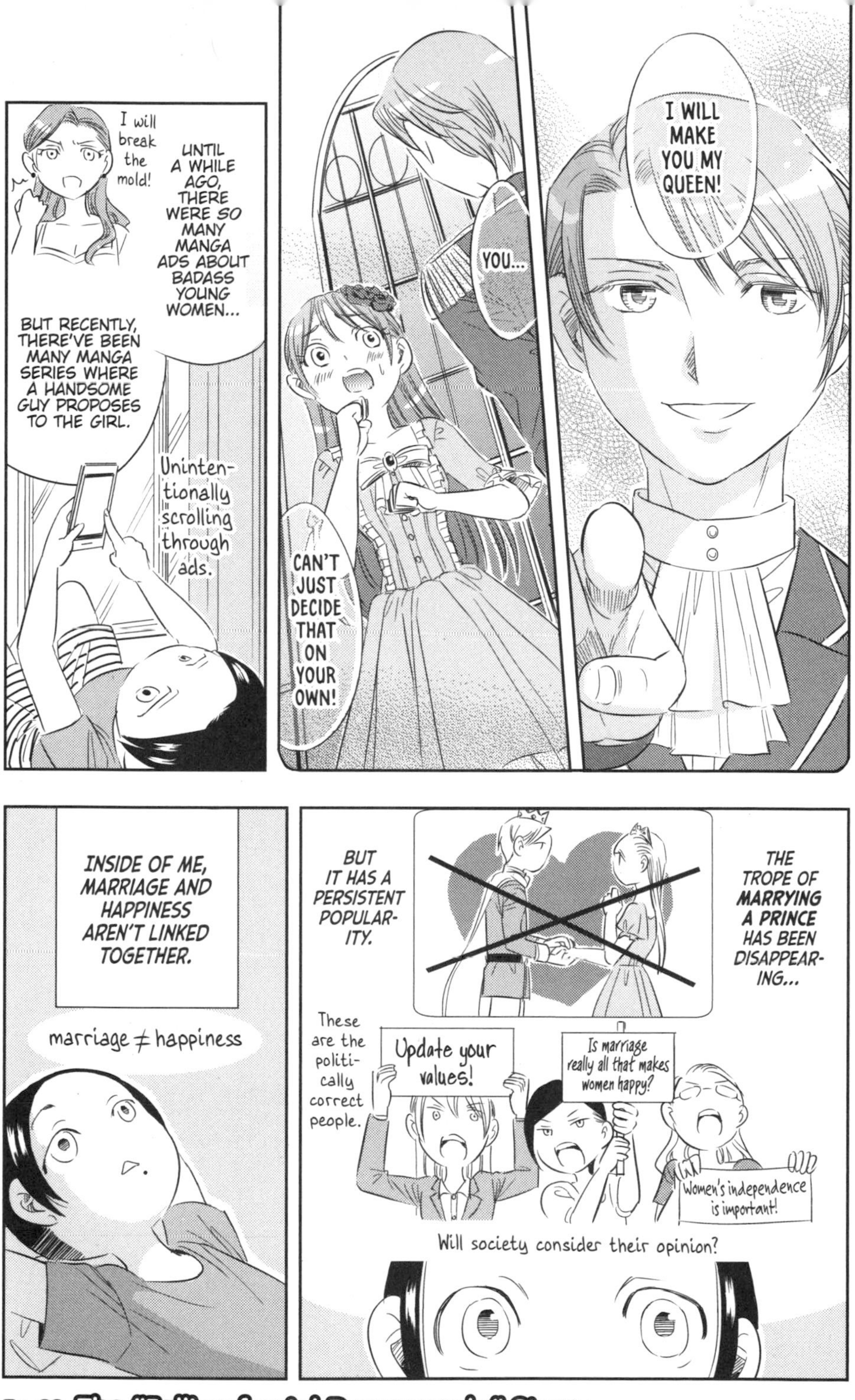
I WILL MAKE YOU MY QUEEN!
YOU...
CAN'T JUST DECIDE THAT ON YOUR OWN!
UNTIL A WHILE AGO, THERE WERE SO MANY MANGA ADS ABOUT BADASS YOUNG WOMEN...
I will break the mold!
BUT RECENTLY, THERE'VE BEEN MANY MANGA SERIES WHERE A HANDSOME GUY PROPOSES TO THE GIRL.
Unintentionally scrolling through ads.
THE TROPE OF MARRYING A PRINCE HAS BEEN DISAPPEARING...
BUT IT HAS A PERSISTENT POPULARITY.
These are the politically correct people.
Update your values!
Is marriage really all that makes women happy?
Women's independence is important!
Will society consider their opinion?
INSIDE OF ME, MARRIAGE AND HAPPINESS AREN'T LINKED TOGETHER.
marriage ≠ happiness

Ep. 23: The "Falling for Ad Propaganda" Story

It was a rather old Japanese house.

WE CLEANED UP THE ABANDONED HOUSE THAT BELONGED TO MY FATHER'S PARENTS.

Album

Ma?!

THAT WAS WHEN I WAS A DEPARTMENT STORE CLERK.

Café You're of Today

THE LIFE OF THE MA I KNOW...

1999	1998	1994
MID-40S		LATE 30S

Husband went to eternal sleep at age forty-two.

Her husband got cancer, and she stayed over every night in the hospital to nurse him.

Get out and go.

Left husband's parents' home together.

Dog

Older Brother

Me

Ma Chronology

2010 - 2018	2000 - 2010
MID-50S - MID-60S	MID-40S - MID-50S

Child (me) has severe mental illness...

Document preparation at night.

Long-term care work. Works hard to raise two kids.

SHAKE SHAKE

I see... We only lived four years as a four-person, one-dog family...

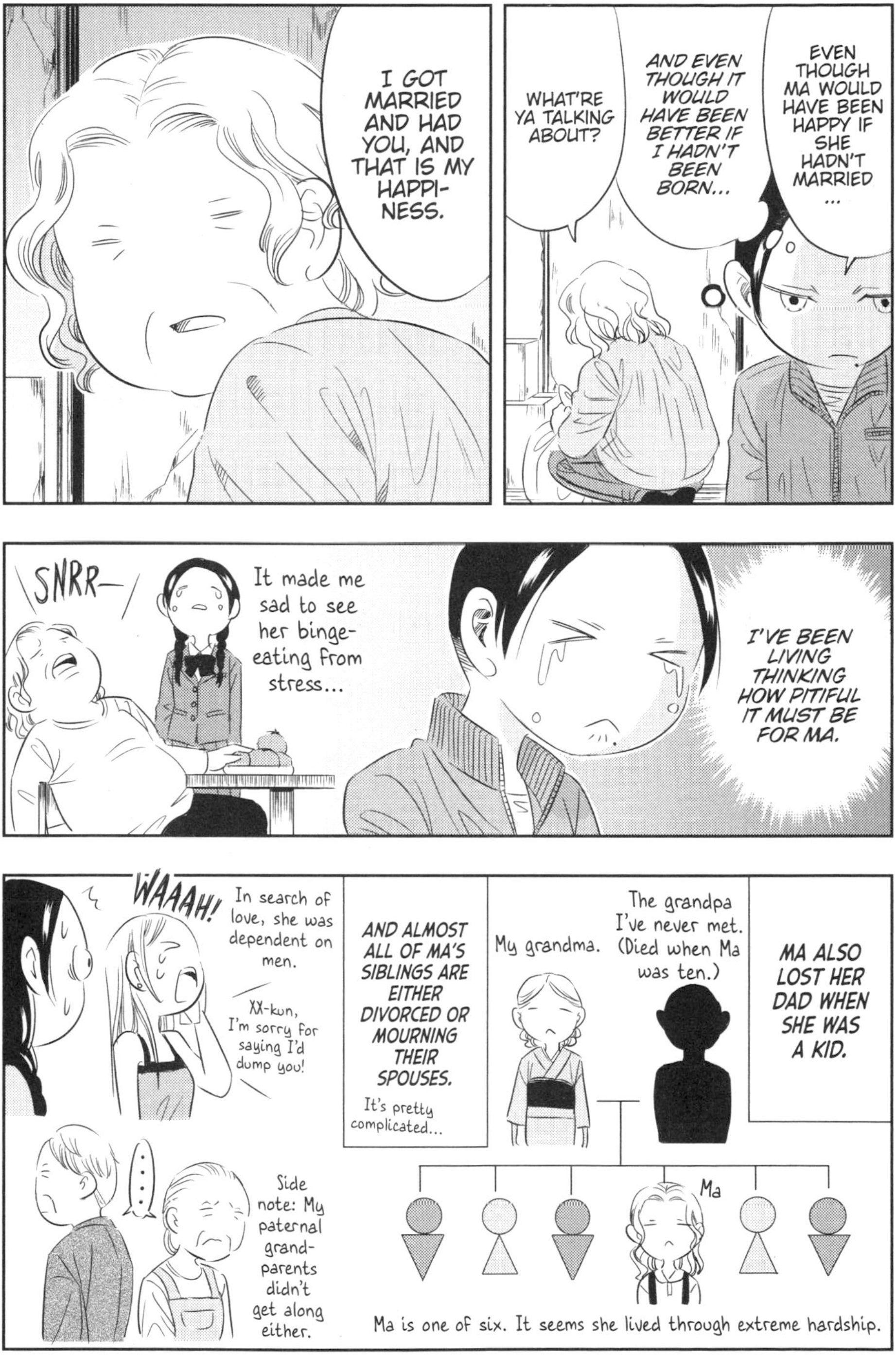

EVEN THOUGH MA WOULD HAVE BEEN HAPPY IF SHE HADN'T MARRIED ...
AND EVEN THOUGH IT WOULD HAVE BEEN BETTER IF I HADN'T BEEN BORN...
WHAT'RE YA TALKING ABOUT?
I GOT MARRIED AND HAD YOU, AND THAT IS MY HAPPI-NESS.
I'VE BEEN LIVING THINKING HOW PITIFUL IT MUST BE FOR MA.
It made me sad to see her binge-eating from stress...
SNRR—
MA ALSO LOST HER DAD WHEN SHE WAS A KID.
The grandpa I've never met. (Died when Ma was ten.)
My grandma.
Ma
Ma is one of six. It seems she lived through extreme hardship.
AND ALMOST ALL OF MA'S SIBLINGS ARE EITHER DIVORCED OR MOURNING THEIR SPOUSES.
It's pretty complicated...
In search of love, she was dependent on men.
WAAAH!
XX-kun, I'm sorry for saying I'd dump you!
Side note: My paternal grand-parents didn't get along either.

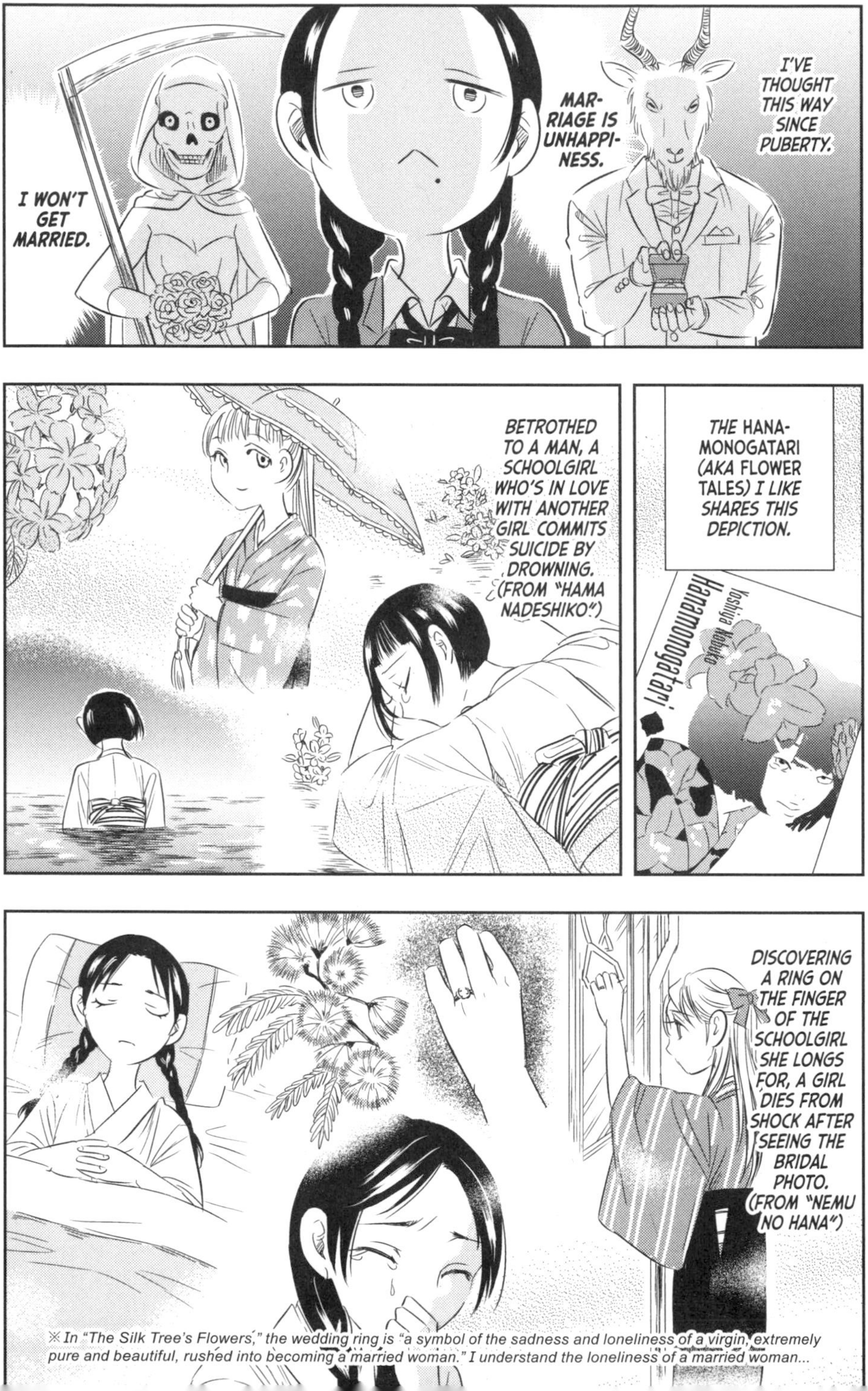
I'VE THOUGHT THIS WAY SINCE PUBERTY.
MAR-RIAGE IS UNHAPPI-NESS.
I WON'T GET MARRIED.
THE HANA-MONOGATARI (AKA FLOWER TALES) I LIKE SHARES THIS DEPICTION.
Yoshiya Nobuko
Hanamonogatari
BETROTHED TO A MAN, A SCHOOLGIRL WHO'S IN LOVE WITH ANOTHER GIRL COMMITS SUICIDE BY DROWNING. (FROM "HAMA NADESHIKO")
DISCOVERING A RING ON THE FINGER OF THE SCHOOLGIRL SHE LONGS FOR, A GIRL DIES FROM SHOCK AFTER SEEING THE BRIDAL PHOTO. (FROM "NEMU NO HANA")

※In "The Silk Tree's Flowers," the wedding ring is "a symbol of the sadness and loneliness of a virgin, extremely pure and beautiful, rushed into becoming a married woman." I understand the loneliness of a married woman...

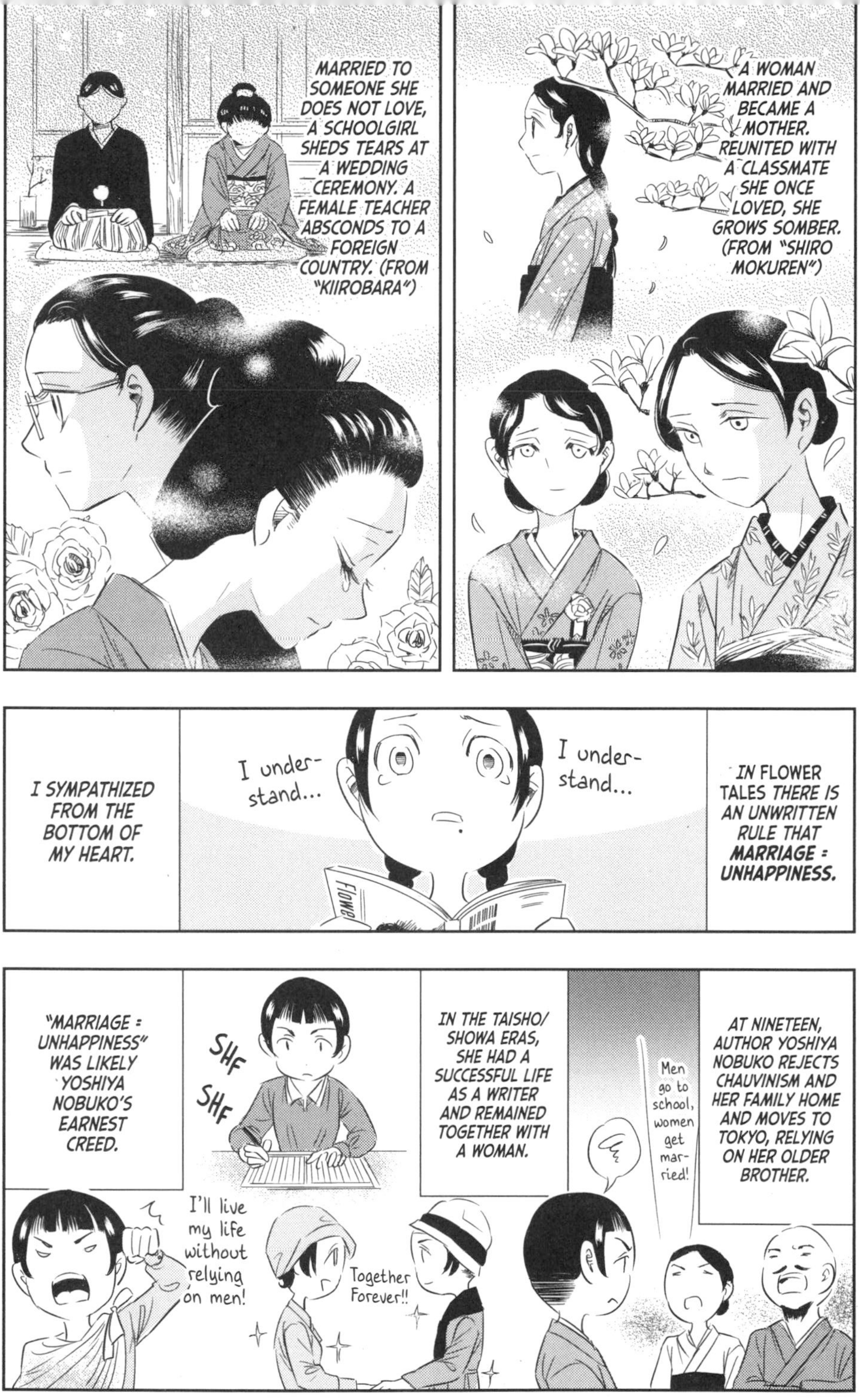
A WOMAN MARRIED AND BECAME A MOTHER. REUNITED WITH A CLASSMATE SHE ONCE LOVED, SHE GROWS SOMBER. (FROM "SHIRO MOKUREN")
MARRIED TO SOMEONE SHE DOES NOT LOVE, A SCHOOLGIRL SHEDS TEARS AT A WEDDING CEREMONY. A FEMALE TEACHER ABSCONDS TO A FOREIGN COUNTRY. (FROM "KIIROBARA")
IN FLOWER TALES THERE IS AN UNWRITTEN RULE THAT MARRIAGE = UNHAPPINESS.
I understand...
I understand...
I SYMPATHIZED FROM THE BOTTOM OF MY HEART.
AT NINETEEN, AUTHOR YOSHIYA NOBUKO REJECTS CHAUVINISM AND HER FAMILY HOME AND MOVES TO TOKYO, RELYING ON HER OLDER BROTHER.
Men go to school, women get married!
IN THE TAISHO/SHOWA ERAS, SHE HAD A SUCCESSFUL LIFE AS A WRITER AND REMAINED TOGETHER WITH A WOMAN.
SHF
SHF
"MARRIAGE = UNHAPPINESS" WAS LIKELY YOSHIYA NOBUKO'S EARNEST CREED.
Together Forever!!
I'll live my life without relying on men!

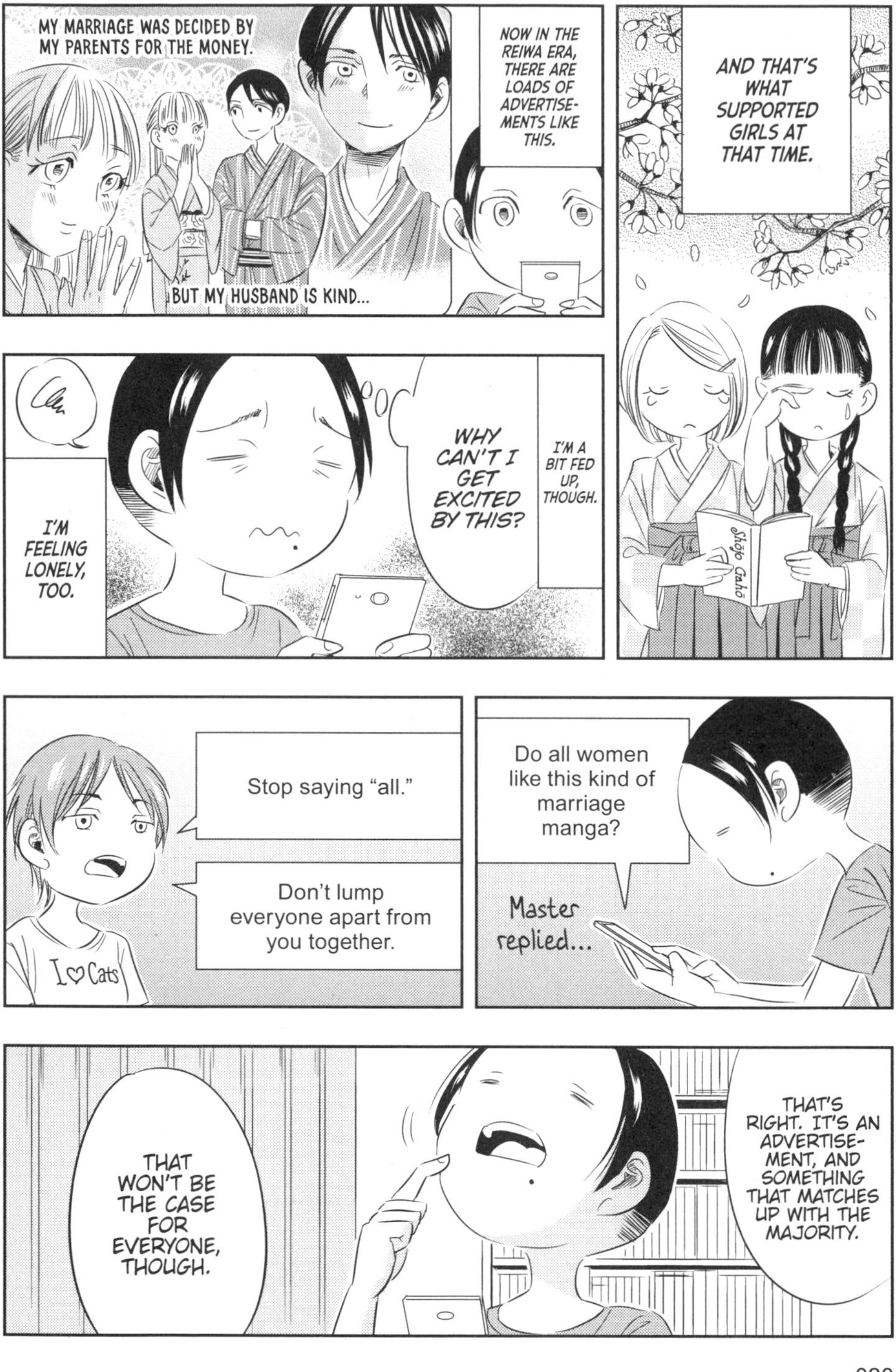
AND THAT'S WHAT SUPPORTED GIRLS AT THAT TIME.
Shojo Gahō
NOW IN THE REIWA ERA, THERE ARE LOADS OF ADVERTISEMENTS LIKE THIS.
MY MARRIAGE WAS DECIDED BY MY PARENTS FOR THE MONEY.
BUT MY HUSBAND IS KIND...
I'M A BIT FED UP, THOUGH.
WHY CAN'T I GET EXCITED BY THIS?
I'M FEELING LONELY, TOO.
Do all women like this kind of marriage manga?
Master replied...
Stop saying "all."
Don't lump everyone apart from you together.
I ♡ Cats
THAT'S RIGHT. IT'S AN ADVERTISEMENT, AND SOMETHING THAT MATCHES UP WITH THE MAJORITY.
THAT WON'T BE THE CASE FOR EVERYONE, THOUGH.

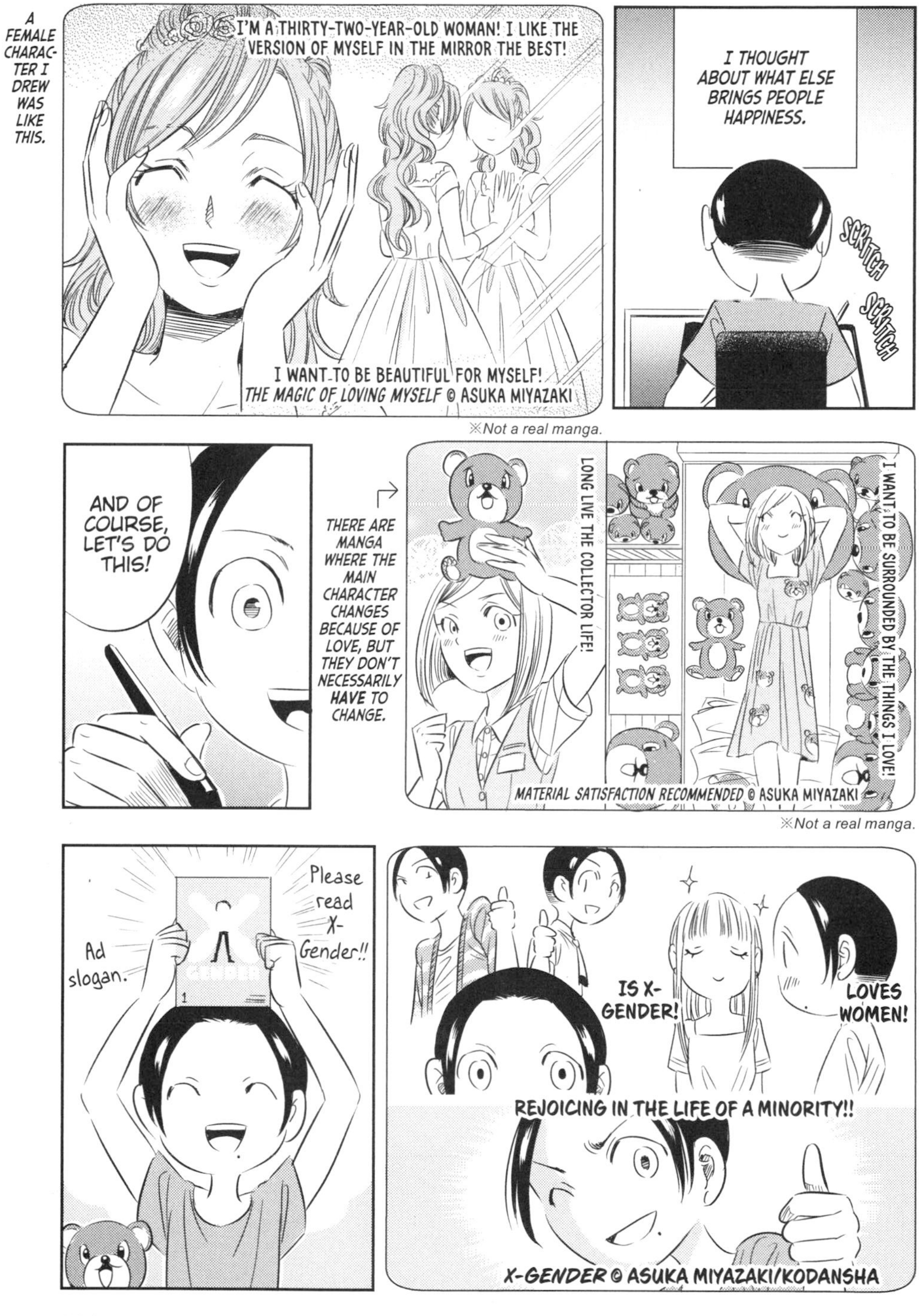
I THOUGHT ABOUT WHAT ELSE BRINGS PEOPLE HAPPINESS.
SCRITCH
SCRITCH
A FEMALE CHARACTER I DREW WAS LIKE THIS.
I'M A THIRTY-TWO-YEAR-OLD WOMAN! I LIKE THE VERSION OF MYSELF IN THE MIRROR THE BEST!
I WANT TO BE BEAUTIFUL FOR MYSELF!
THE MAGIC OF LOVING MYSELF © ASUKA MIYAZAKI
※Not a real manga.
I WANT TO BE SURROUNDED BY THE THINGS I LOVE!
LONG LIVE THE COLLECTOR LIFE!
MATERIAL SATISFACTION RECOMMENDED © ASUKA MIYAZAKI
THERE ARE MANGA WHERE THE MAIN CHARACTER CHANGES BECAUSE OF LOVE, BUT THEY DON'T NECESSARILY **HAVE** TO CHANGE.
※Not a real manga.
AND OF COURSE, LET'S DO THIS!
LOVES WOMEN!
IS X-GENDER!
REJOICING IN THE LIFE OF A MINORITY!!
X-GENDER © ASUKA MIYAZAKI/KODANSHA
Please read X-Gender!!
Ad slogan.

Ep. 24: The "Gay World" Story

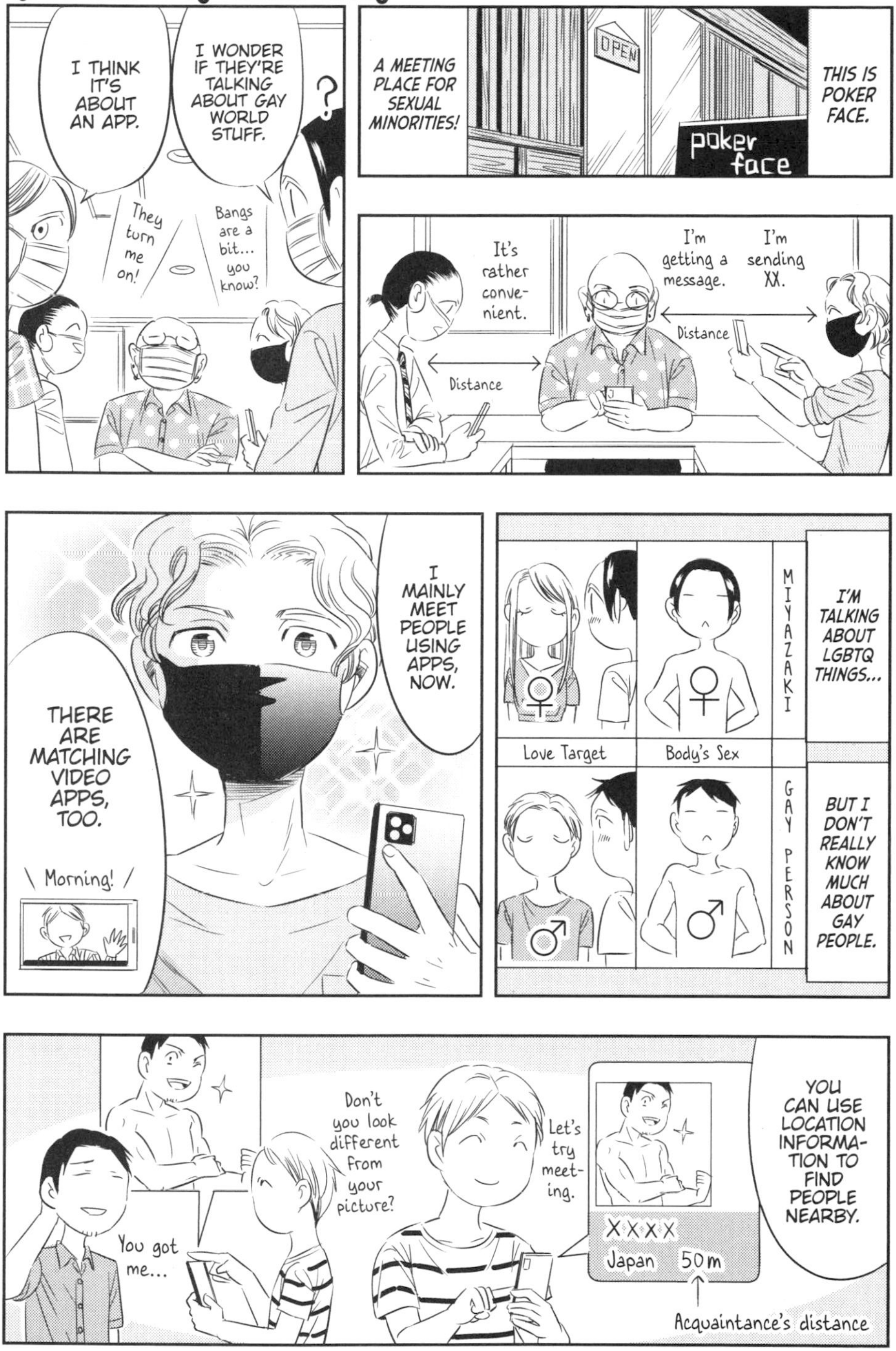
THIS IS POKER FACE.
OPEN
poker face
A MEETING PLACE FOR SEXUAL MINORITIES!
I'm sending XX.
I'm getting a message.
Distance
It's rather convenient.
Distance
I WONDER IF THEY'RE TALKING ABOUT GAY WORLD STUFF.
I THINK IT'S ABOUT AN APP.
Bangs are a bit… you know?
They turn me on!
I'M TALKING ABOUT LGBTQ THINGS…
MIYAZAKI
Body's Sex
Love Target
BUT I DON'T REALLY KNOW MUCH ABOUT GAY PEOPLE.
GAY PERSON
I MAINLY MEET PEOPLE USING APPS, NOW.
THERE ARE MATCHING VIDEO APPS, TOO.
Morning!
YOU CAN USE LOCATION INFORMATION TO FIND PEOPLE NEARBY.
XXXX
Japan 50m
Acquaintance's distance
Let's try meeting.
Don't you look different from your picture?
You got me…

Sometimes I meet extremely beautiful gay and trans people.

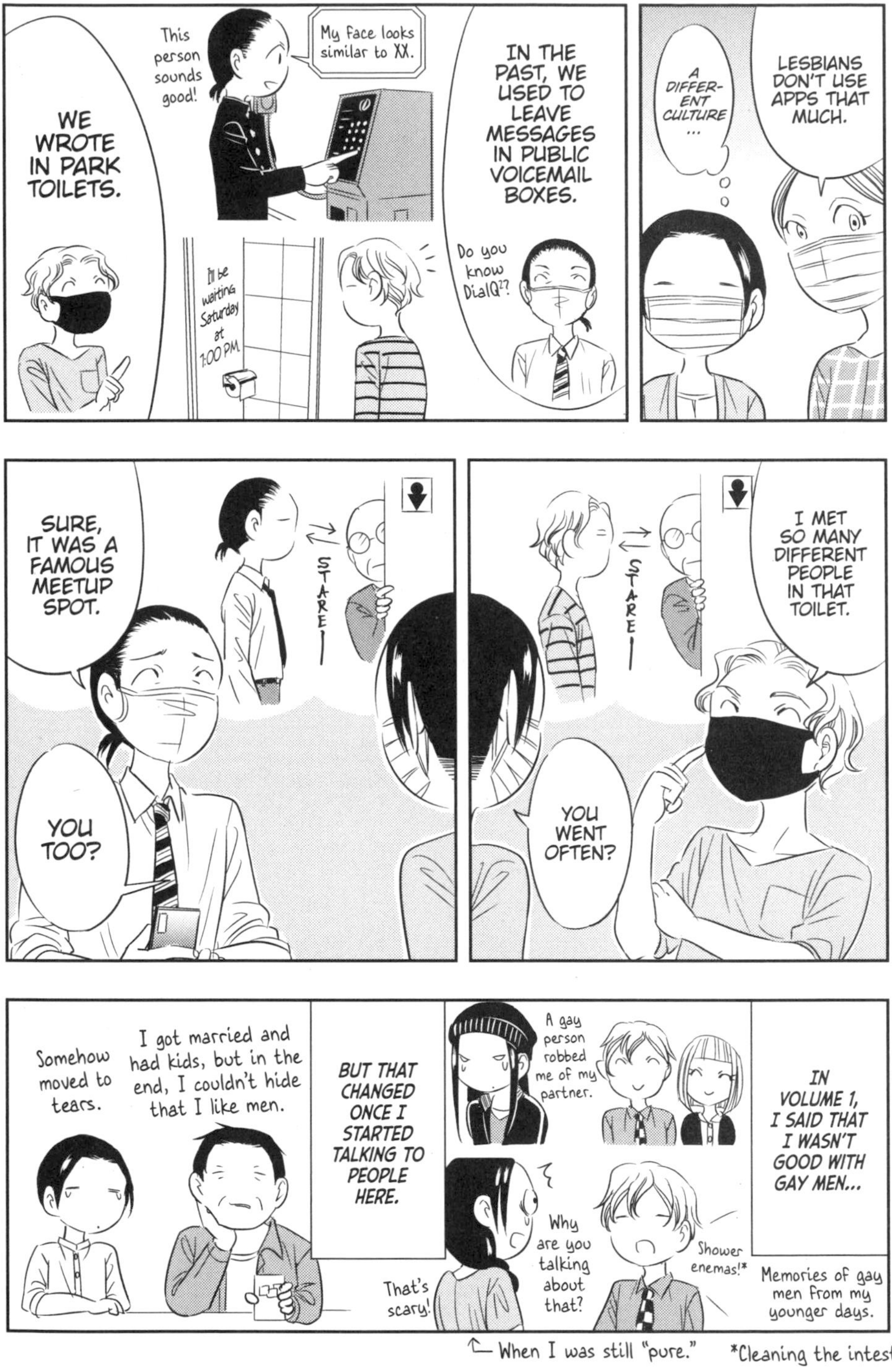
LESBIANS DON'T USE APPS THAT MUCH.
A DIFFERENT CULTURE...
IN THE PAST, WE USED TO LEAVE MESSAGES IN PUBLIC VOICEMAIL BOXES.
My face looks similar to XX.
This person sounds good!
Do you know DialQ2?
WE WROTE IN PARK TOILETS.
I'll be waiting Saturday at 1:00 PM.
I MET SO MANY DIFFERENT PEOPLE IN THAT TOILET.
STARE—
YOU WENT OFTEN?
SURE, IT WAS A FAMOUS MEETUP SPOT.
STARE—
YOU TOO?
IN VOLUME 1, I SAID THAT I WASN'T GOOD WITH GAY MEN...
Memories of gay men from my younger days.
A gay person robbed me of my partner.
Shower enemas!*
Why are you talking about that?
That's scary!
BUT THAT CHANGED ONCE I STARTED TALKING TO PEOPLE HERE.
I got married and had kids, but in the end, I couldn't hide that I like men.
Somehow moved to tears.

↖ When I was still "pure."

*Cleaning the intestines.

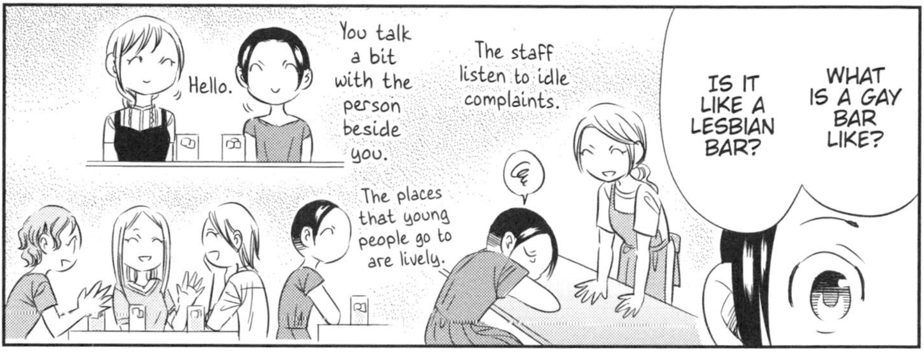
WHAT IS A GAY BAR LIKE?
IS IT LIKE A LESBIAN BAR?
The staff listen to idle complaints.
You talk a bit with the person beside you.
Hello.
The places that young people go to are lively.

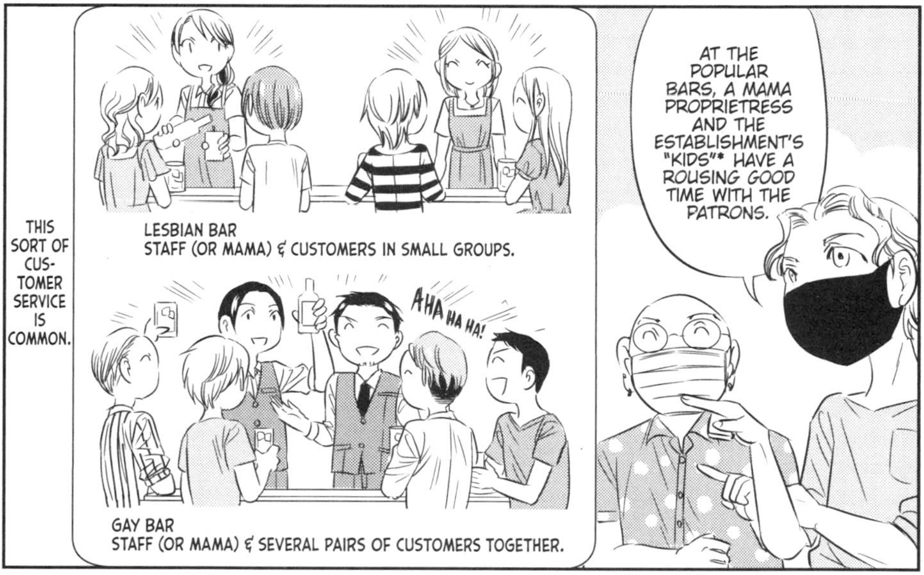
AT THE POPULAR BARS, A MAMA PROPRIETRESS AND THE ESTABLISHMENT'S "KIDS"* HAVE A ROUSING GOOD TIME WITH THE PATRONS.
LESBIAN BAR
STAFF (OR MAMA) & CUSTOMERS IN SMALL GROUPS.
AHA HA HA!
GAY BAR
STAFF (OR MAMA) & SEVERAL PAIRS OF CUSTOMERS TOGETHER.
THIS SORT OF CUSTOMER SERVICE IS COMMON.

*The establishment's employees.

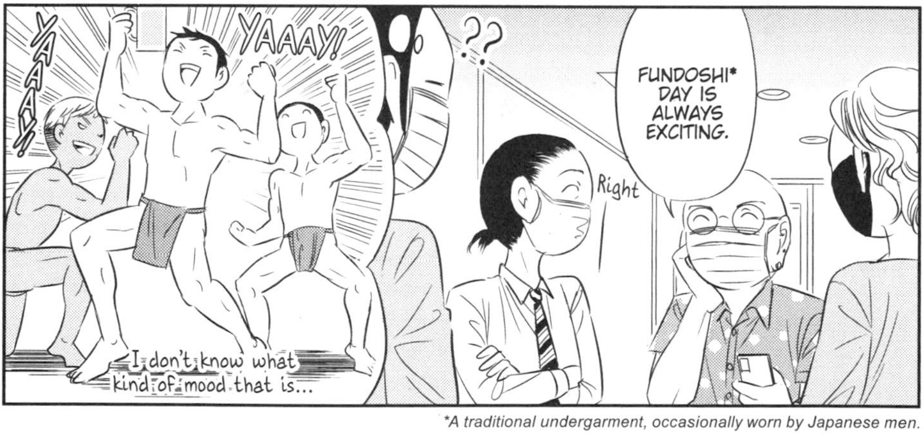
FUNDOSHI* DAY IS ALWAYS EXCITING.
Right
??
YAAAY!
YAAAAY!
I don't know what kind of mood that is...

I imagine it's like boys at high school cultural festivals.

*A traditional undergarment, occasionally worn by Japanese men.

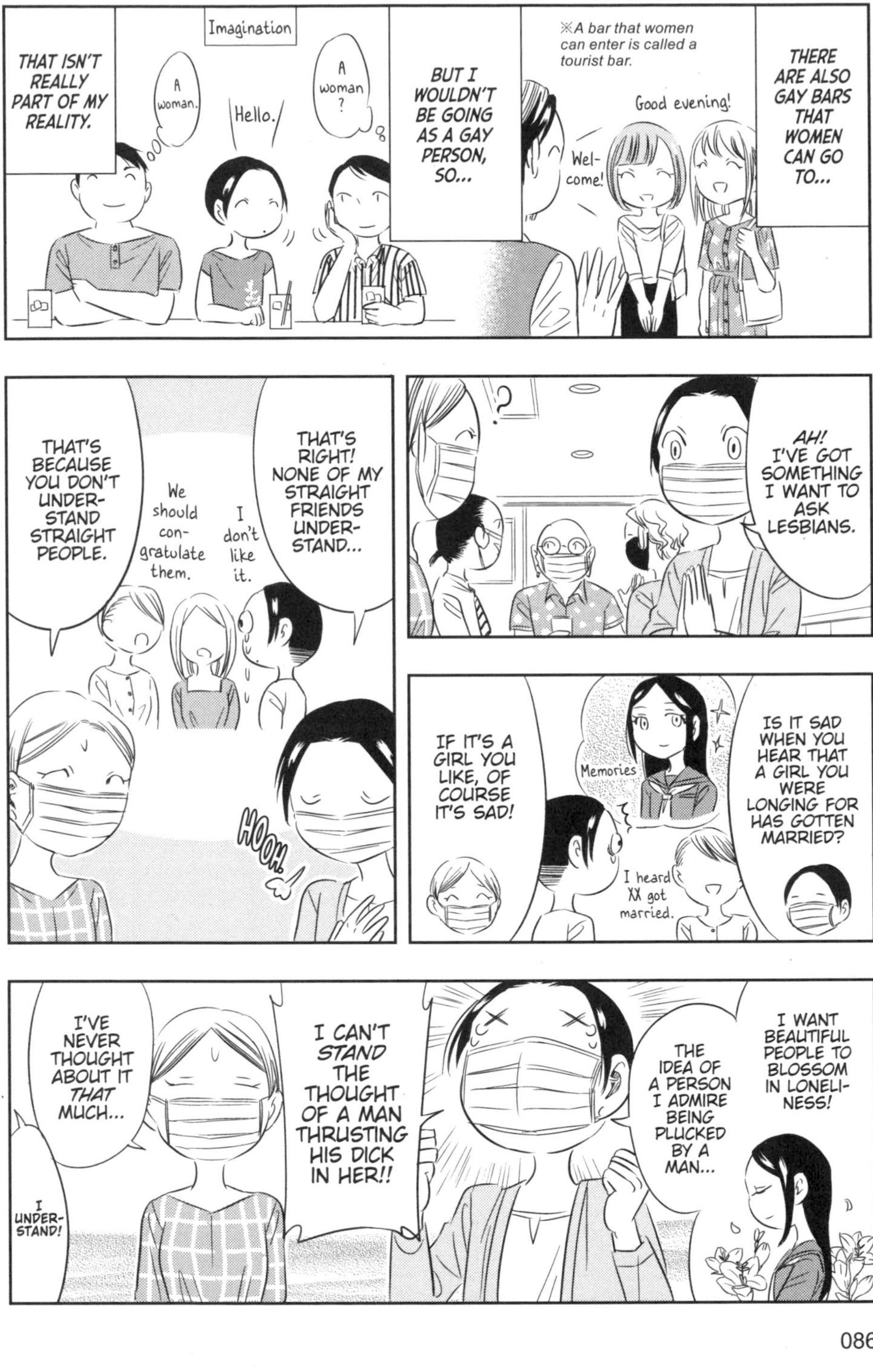
THERE ARE ALSO GAY BARS THAT WOMEN CAN GO TO...
※A bar that women can enter is called a tourist bar.
Good evening!
Wel-come!
BUT I WOULDN'T BE GOING AS A GAY PERSON, SO...
THAT ISN'T REALLY PART OF MY REALITY.
Imagination
A woman?
Hello.
A woman.
AH! I'VE GOT SOMETHING I WANT TO ASK LESBIANS.
IS IT SAD WHEN YOU HEAR THAT A GIRL YOU WERE LONGING FOR HAS GOTTEN MARRIED?
Memories
IF IT'S A GIRL YOU LIKE, OF COURSE IT'S SAD!
I heard XX got married.
THAT'S RIGHT! NONE OF MY STRAIGHT FRIENDS UNDER-STAND...
I don't like it.
We should con-gratulate them.
THAT'S BECAUSE YOU DON'T UNDER-STAND STRAIGHT PEOPLE.
HOOH
I WANT BEAUTIFUL PEOPLE TO BLOSSOM IN LONELI-NESS!
THE IDEA OF A PERSON I ADMIRE BEING PLUCKED BY A MAN...
I CAN'T *STAND* THE THOUGHT OF A MAN THRUSTING HIS DICK IN HER!!
I'VE NEVER THOUGHT ABOUT IT *THAT* MUCH...
I UNDER-STAND!

※A place with LGBT staff and customers of various genders and sexualities is called a "mix bar."

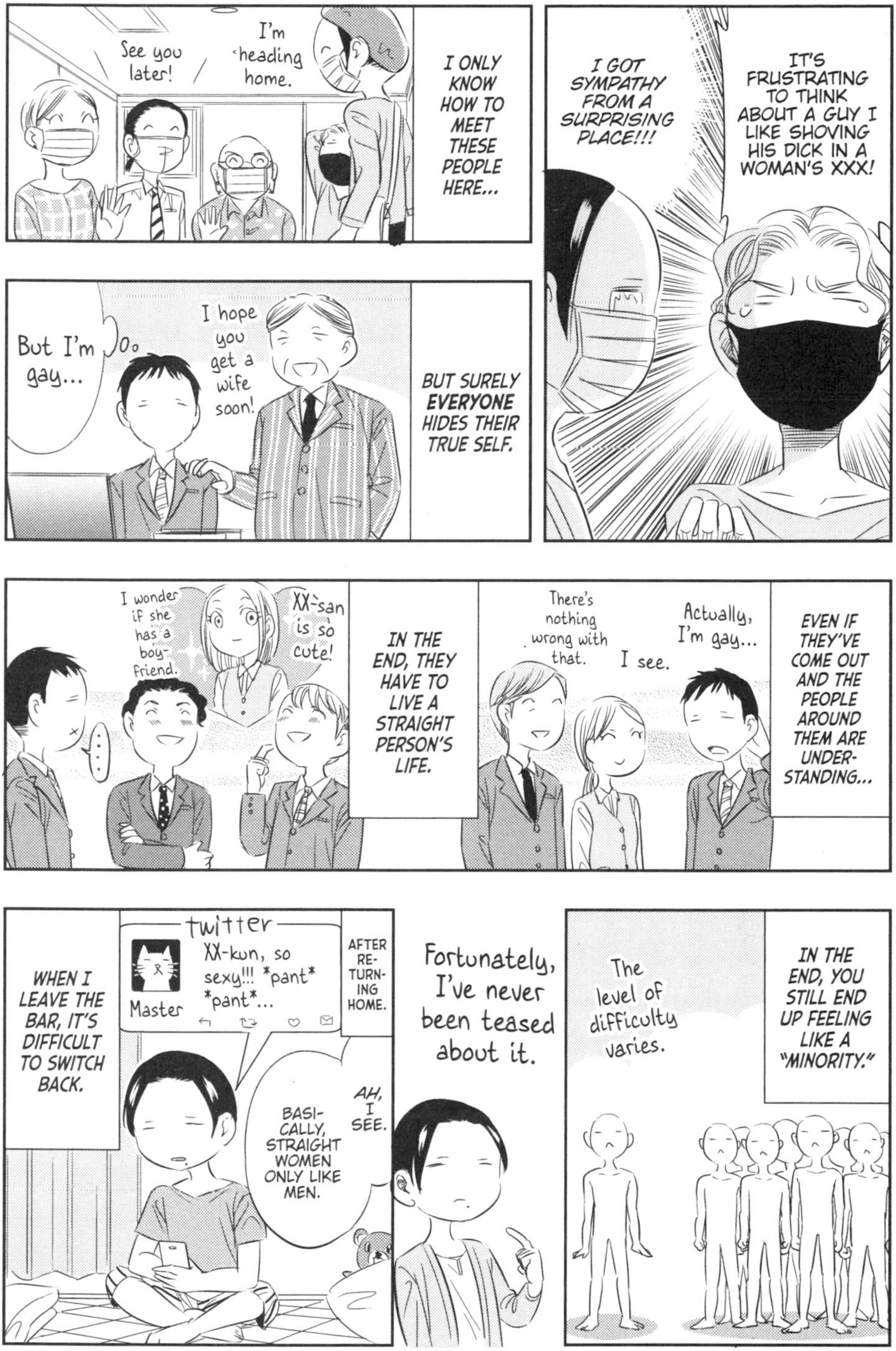
IT'S FRUSTRATING TO THINK ABOUT A GUY I LIKE SHOVING HIS DICK IN A WOMAN'S XXX!
I GOT SYMPATHY FROM A SURPRISING PLACE!!!
I ONLY KNOW HOW TO MEET THESE PEOPLE HERE...
I'm heading home.
See you later!
BUT SURELY EVERYONE HIDES THEIR TRUE SELF.
I hope you get a wife soon!
But I'm gay...
EVEN IF THEY'VE COME OUT AND THE PEOPLE AROUND THEM ARE UNDER-STANDING...
Actually, I'm gay...
I see.
There's nothing wrong with that.
IN THE END, THEY HAVE TO LIVE A STRAIGHT PERSON'S LIFE.
XX-san is so cute!
I wonder if she has a boy-friend.
...
IN THE END, YOU STILL END UP FEELING LIKE A "MINORITY."
The level of difficulty varies.
Fortunately, I've never been teased about it.
AFTER RE-TURN-ING HOME.
twitter
XX-kun, so sexy!!! *pant* *pant*...
Master
WHEN I LEAVE THE BAR, IT'S DIFFICULT TO SWITCH BACK.
AH, I SEE.
BASI-CALLY, STRAIGHT WOMEN ONLY LIKE MEN.

I've drawn manga essays on mental illness since the beginning, so this time, I will draw with that tension!

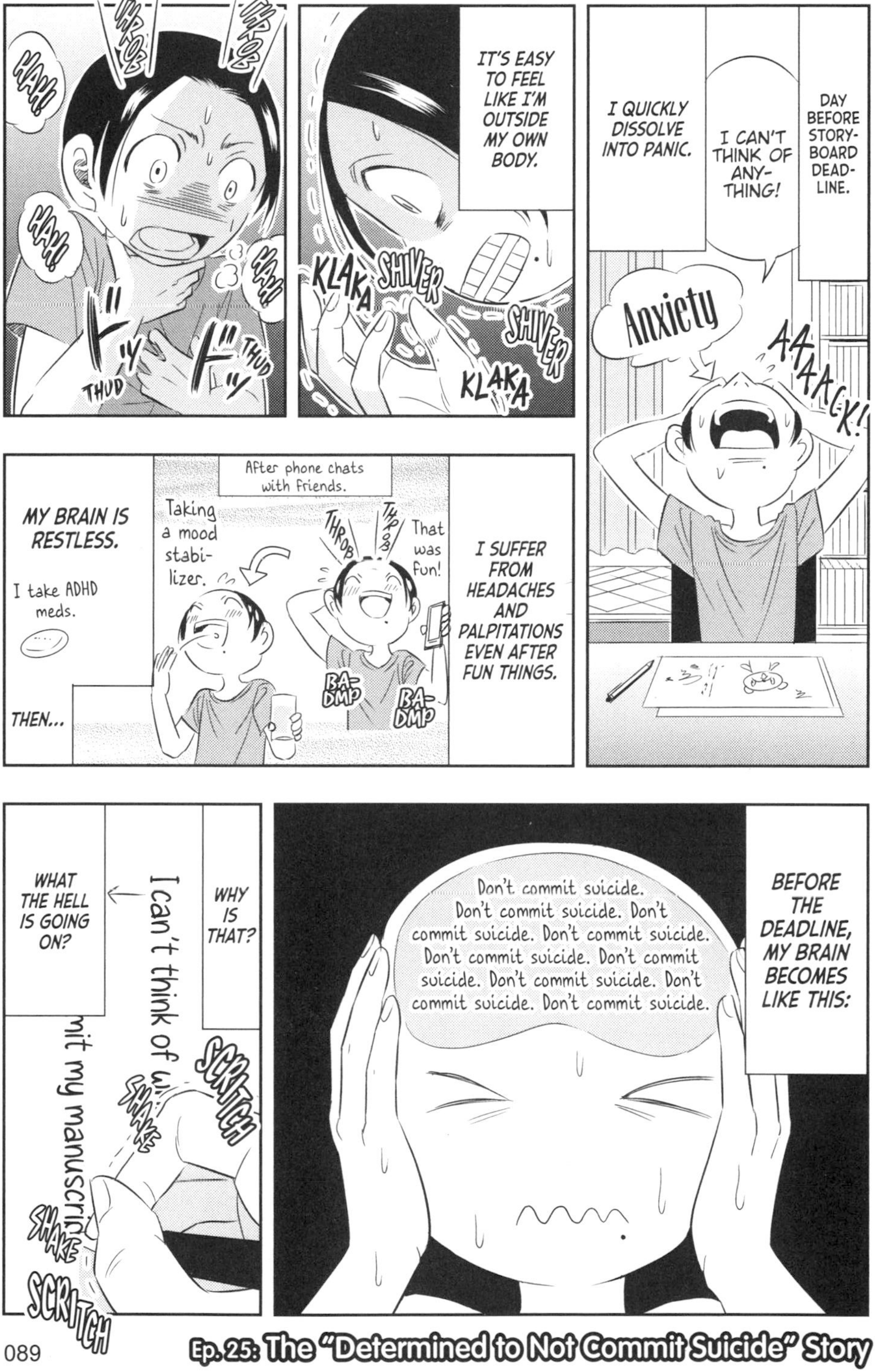

DAY BEFORE STORY-BOARD DEAD-LINE.
I CAN'T THINK OF ANY-THING!
I QUICKLY DISSOLVE INTO PANIC.
Anxiety
AAAACK!
IT'S EASY TO FEEL LIKE I'M OUTSIDE MY OWN BODY.
SHIVER
KLAKA
SHIVER
KLAKA
THROB
THROB
HAH!
HAH!
HAH!
THUD
THUD
I SUFFER FROM HEADACHES AND PALPITATIONS EVEN AFTER FUN THINGS.
After phone chats with friends.
THROB
THROB
That was fun!
BA-DMP
BA-DMP
Taking a mood stabi-lizer.
MY BRAIN IS RESTLESS.
I take ADHD meds.
THEN...
BEFORE THE DEADLINE, MY BRAIN BECOMES LIKE THIS:
Don't commit suicide. Don't commit suicide. Don't commit suicide. Don't commit suicide. Don't commit suicide. Don't commit suicide. Don't commit suicide. Don't commit suicide.
WHY IS THAT?
I can't think of
mit my manuscri
SCRITCH
SHAKE
SHAKE
SCRITCH
WHAT THE HELL IS GOING ON?

Ep. 25: The "Determined to Not Commit Suicide" Story

Reference literature: When Panic Attacks by David D. Barns (Seiwa Shoten)

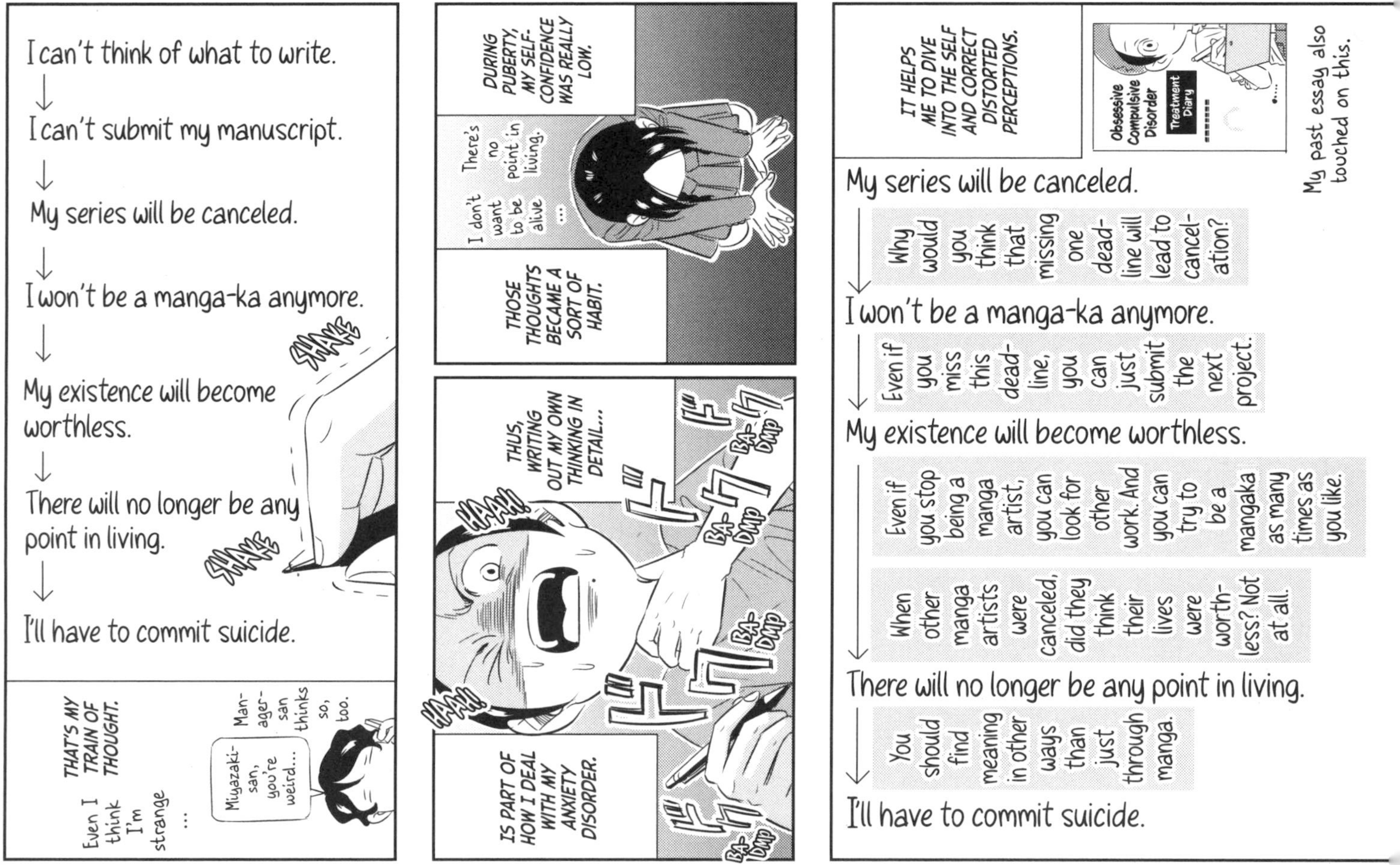

I can't think of what to write.
↓
I can't submit my manuscript.
↓
My series will be canceled.
↓
I won't be a manga-ka anymore.
↓
My existence will become worthless.
↓
There will no longer be any point in living.
↓
I'll have to commit suicide.
SHAKE
SHAKE
THAT'S MY TRAIN OF THOUGHT.
Even I think I'm strange ...
Man-ager-san thinks so, too.
Miyazaki-san, you're weird...
DURING PUBERTY, MY SELF-CONFIDENCE WAS REALLY LOW.
There's no point in living.
I don't want to be alive ...
THOSE THOUGHTS BECAME A SORT OF HABIT.
THUS, WRITING OUT MY OWN THINKING IN DETAIL...
HAAH
HAAH
BA-DMP
BA-DMP
BA-DMP
BA-DMP
IS PART OF HOW I DEAL WITH MY ANXIETY DISORDER.
IT HELPS ME TO DIVE INTO THE SELF AND CORRECT DISTORTED PERCEPTIONS.
Obsessive Compulsive Disorder
Treatment Diary
My past essay also touched on this.
My series will be canceled.
Why would you think that missing one dead-line will lead to cancel-ation?
I won't be a manga-ka anymore.
Even if you miss this dead-line, you can just submit the next project.
My existence will become worthless.
Even if you stop being a manga artist, you can look for other work. And you can try to be a mangaka as many times as you like.
When other manga artists were canceled, did they think their lives were worth-less? Not at all.
There will no longer be any point in living.
You should find meaning in other ways than just through manga.
I'll have to commit suicide.

IN THEORY, THIS WILL BEAT MY FEELINGS OF SELF-DENIAL.
AN-OTHER BREATH...
AND I'LL STOP WANTING TO COMMIT SUICIDE.
THROB THROB
HAAH!
SHAKE
SHAKE
HAAH!
IF I JUMP...
Line Stoppage due to Personal Injury
Shit!
KA-SNAP
The worst!
I'LL ANNOY TONS OF PEOPLE.
MY FAMILY WILL GET A LARGE BILL FROM THE RAILROAD COMPANY.
Billing Amount
¥100000000
JUMPING...
POTENTIALLY INVOLVES OTHER PEOPLE.
IF I FAIL, THERE'S A POSSIBILITY I'LL HAVE TO LIVE WITH SEVERE INJURIES.
IF I HANG MYSELF...
Psychologically Defective Property
IT WILL BE TREATED AS AN ON-SITE PROPERTY ACCIDENT AND CAUSE TROUBLE TO BOTH THE OWNER AND MY FAMILY.
Billing Amount
¥10000000
AN OVERDOSE...
IS THE SAME AS JUMPING. THE CERTAINTY OF DYING IS LOW.
It seems that my body refuses the medicine.
BESIDES, THERE ARE LOTS OF RISKS TO SUICIDE.
URF!
All the knowledge on how to die that I learned in my teens is still here...
← Perfect Suicide Manual
Suicide Methods
KLAKA KLAKA
AND ABOVE ALL ELSE...
I'M SCARED.

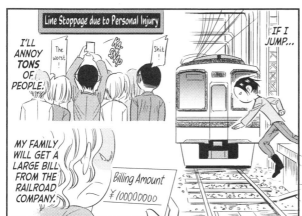

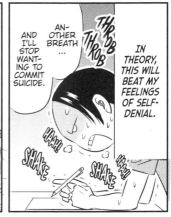

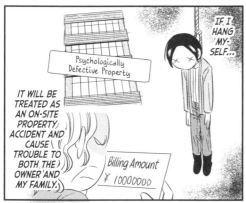

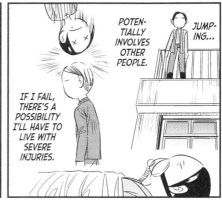

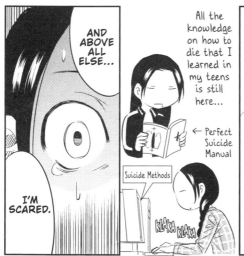

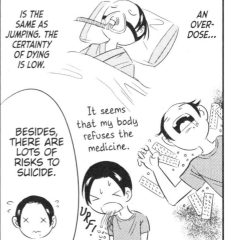

SORRY FOR THE MELANCHOLY...

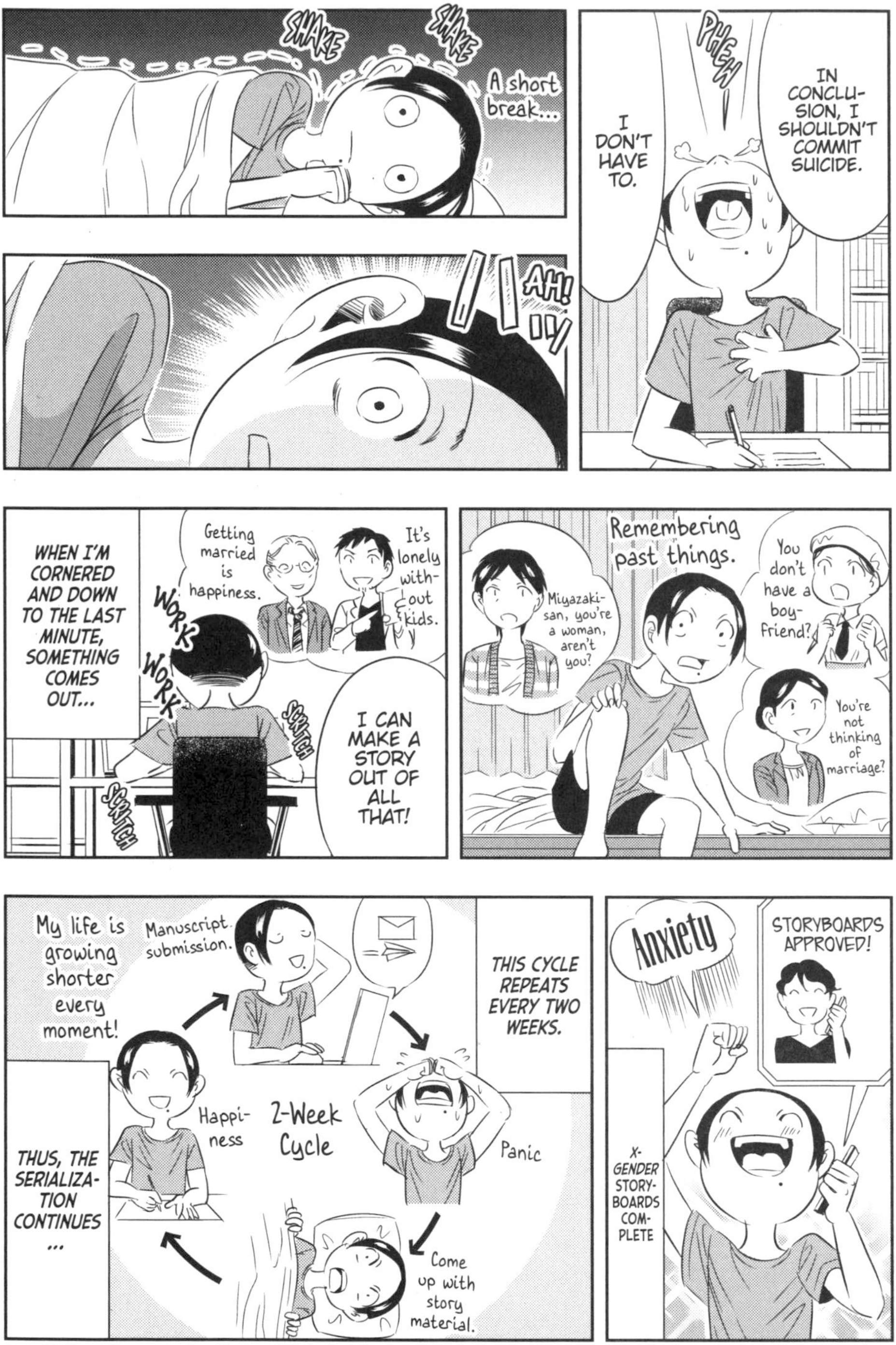
PHEW
IN CONCLUSION, I SHOULDN'T COMMIT SUICIDE.
I DON'T HAVE TO.
SHAKE
SHAKE
A short break...
AH!
Remembering past things.
You don't have a boyfriend?
You're not thinking of marriage?
Miyazaki-san, you're a woman, aren't you?
WHEN I'M CORNERED AND DOWN TO THE LAST MINUTE, SOMETHING COMES OUT...
It's lonely without kids.
Getting married is happiness.
WORK
WORK
SCRITCH
SCRITCH
I CAN MAKE A STORY OUT OF ALL THAT!
STORYBOARDS APPROVED!
Anxiety
X-GENDER STORYBOARDS COMPLETE
THIS CYCLE REPEATS EVERY TWO WEEKS.
Manuscript submission.
My life is growing shorter every moment!
2-Week Cycle
Happiness
Panic
Come up with story material.
THUS, THE SERIALIZATION CONTINUES...

One day, I want to create a funny work about my random tendency to think about death. I'm looking forward to what it will be like.

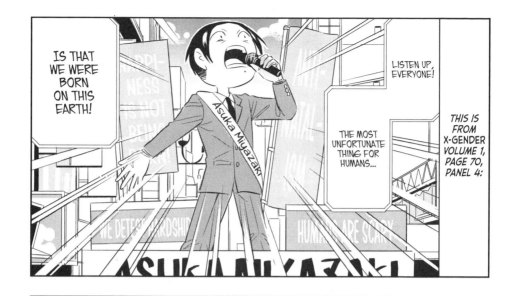

THIS IS FROM X-GENDER VOLUME 1, PAGE 70, PANEL 4:
LISTEN UP, EVERYONE!
THE MOST UNFORTUNATE THING FOR HUMANS...
IS THAT WE WERE BORN ON THIS EARTH!
Asuka Miyazaki
"ANTINATALISM" IS A GREAT WORD, BUT...
LATELY, IT HAS BEEN PICKED UP BY A CERTAIN ONLINE PROGRAM, AND...
Is it true that it's getting atten-tion?
XX-san is somewhat positive about it...
I wanted to partici-pate, too!
I WANT TO INTRODUCE X-GENDER TO THEM, TOO!
I THOUGHT.
ROUGHLY EXPLAINED, "ANTINATALISM" IS THINKING THAT THINGS WOULD BE BETTER IF HUMANS WERE NOT BORN.
Anti-natalism
Anti-natalism

Ep. 26: The "Antinatalism" Story

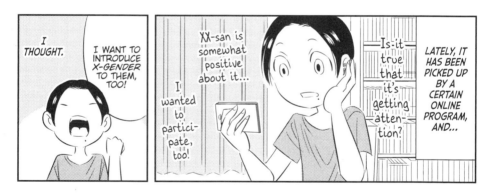

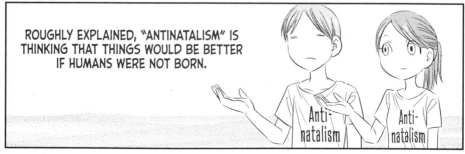

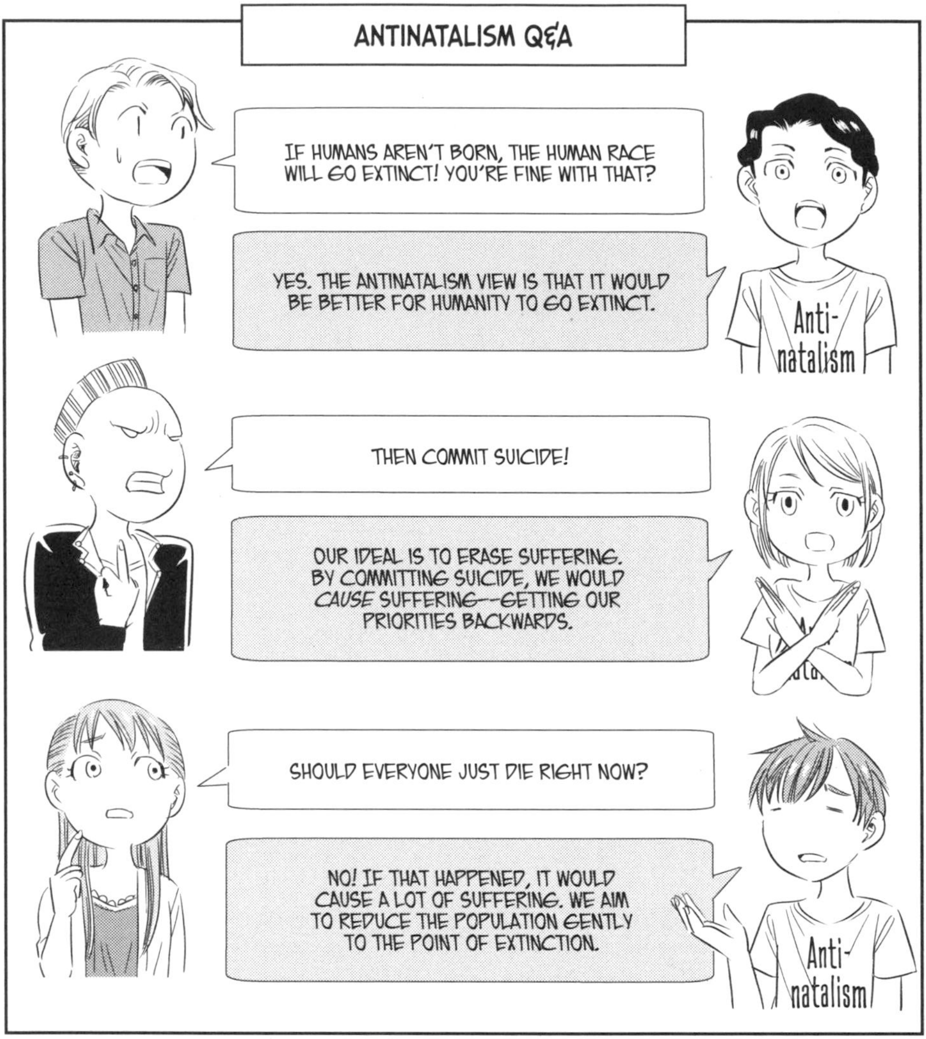
ANTINATALISM Q&A
IF HUMANS AREN'T BORN, THE HUMAN RACE WILL GO EXTINCT! YOU'RE FINE WITH THAT?
YES. THE ANTINATALISM VIEW IS THAT IT WOULD BE BETTER FOR HUMANITY TO GO EXTINCT.
Anti-natalism
THEN COMMIT SUICIDE!
OUR IDEAL IS TO ERASE SUFFERING. BY COMMITTING SUICIDE, WE WOULD *CAUSE* SUFFERING--GETTING OUR PRIORITIES BACKWARDS.
SHOULD EVERYONE JUST DIE RIGHT NOW?
NO! IF THAT HAPPENED, IT WOULD CAUSE A LOT OF SUFFERING. WE AIM TO REDUCE THE POPULATION GENTLY TO THE POINT OF EXTINCTION.
Anti-natalism

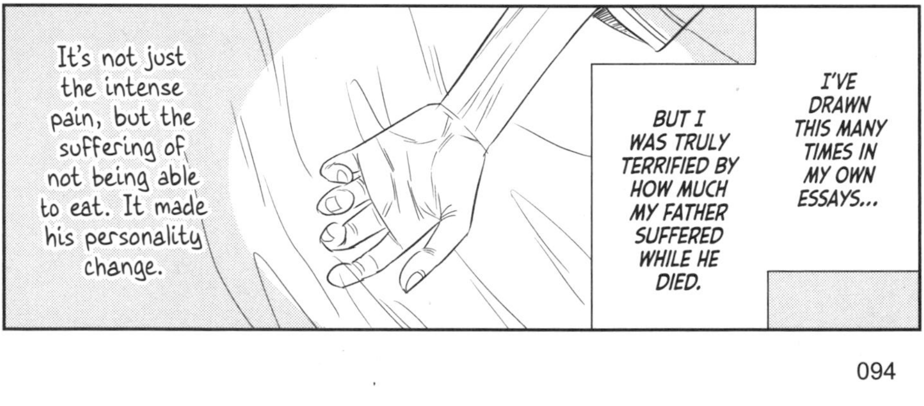
I'VE DRAWN THIS MANY TIMES IN MY OWN ESSAYS...
BUT I WAS TRULY TERRIFIED BY HOW MUCH MY FATHER SUFFERED WHILE HE DIED.
It's not just the intense pain, but the suffering of not being able to eat. It made his personality change.

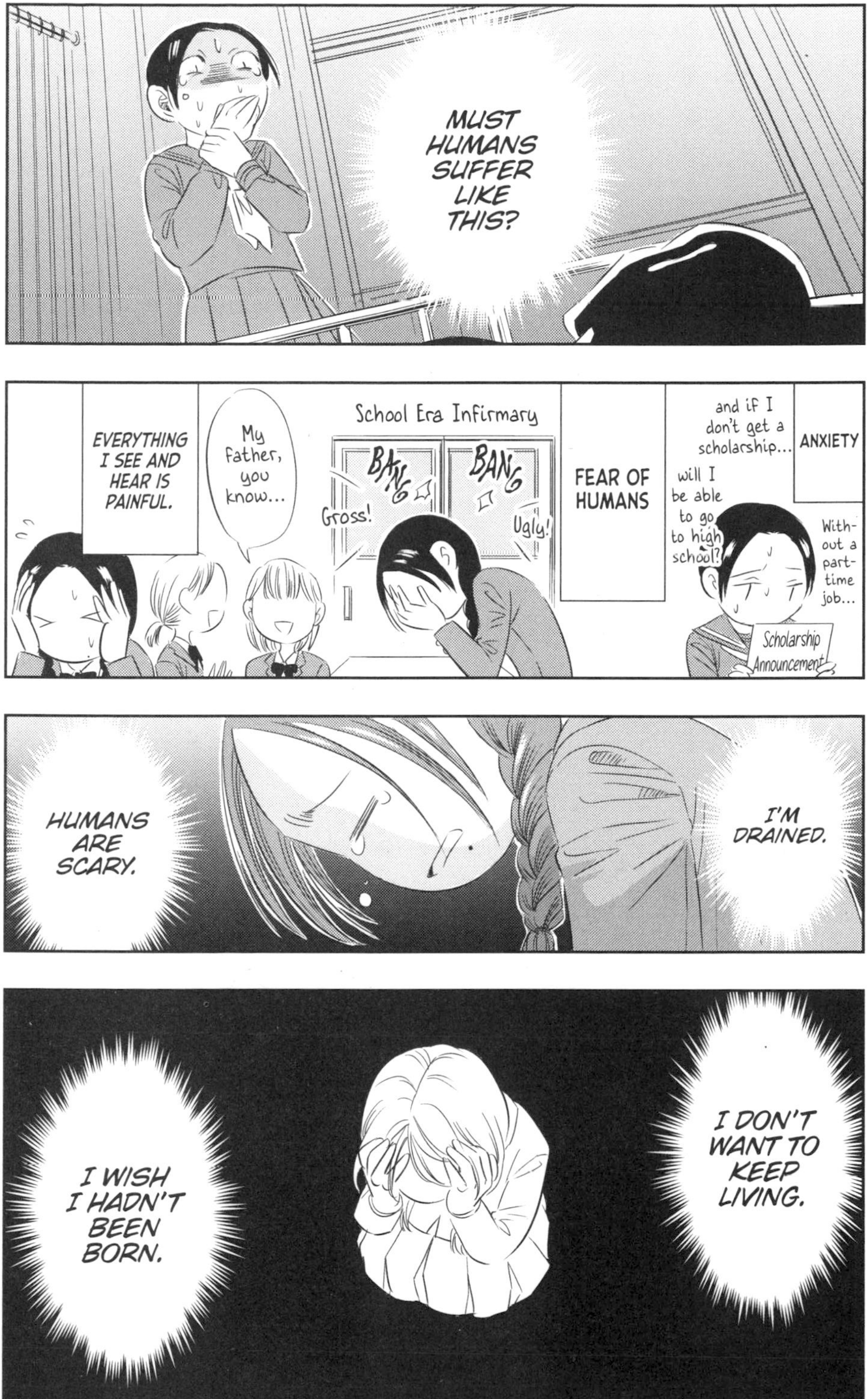
MUST HUMANS SUFFER LIKE THIS?
ANXIETY
and if I don't get a scholarship...
Without a part-time job...
will I be able to go to high school?
Scholarship Announcement
FEAR OF HUMANS
Ugly!
BANG
BANG
Gross!
School Era Infirmary
My father, you know...
EVERYTHING I SEE AND HEAR IS PAINFUL.
I'M DRAINED.
HUMANS ARE SCARY.
I DON'T WANT TO KEEP LIVING.
I WISH I HADN'T BEEN BORN.

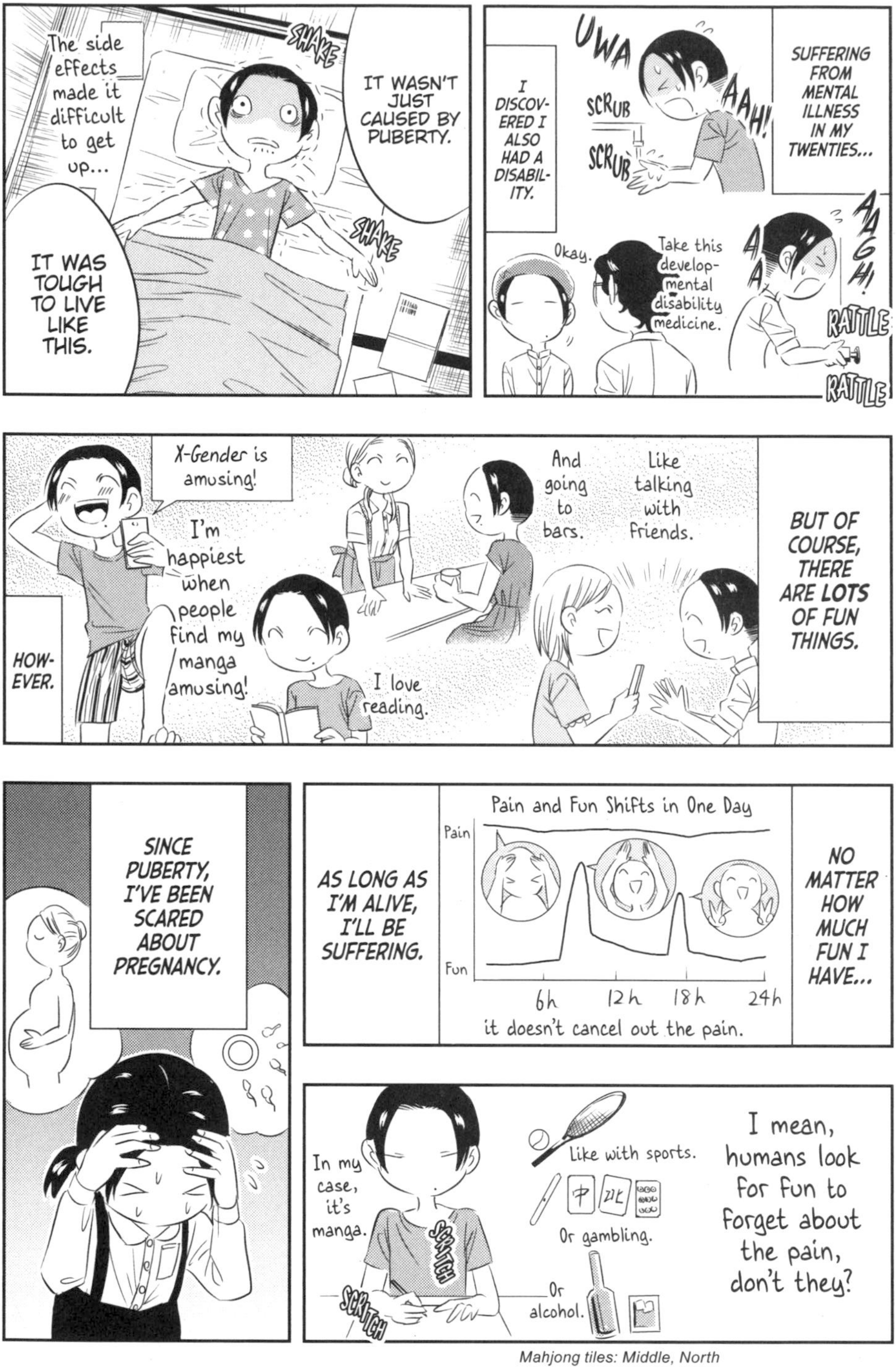
SUFFERING FROM MENTAL ILLNESS IN MY TWENTIES...
UWA
AAH!
SCRUB
SCRUB
I DISCOVERED I ALSO HAD A DISABILITY.
AAAGH!
Take this developmental disability medicine.
Okay.
RATTLE
RATTLE
IT WASN'T JUST CAUSED BY PUBERTY.
SHAKE
The side effects made it difficult to get up...
SHAKE
IT WAS TOUGH TO LIVE LIKE THIS.
BUT OF COURSE, THERE ARE LOTS OF FUN THINGS.
Like talking with friends.
And going to bars.
I love reading.
X-Gender is amusing!
I'm happiest when people find my manga amusing!
HOW-EVER.
NO MATTER HOW MUCH FUN I HAVE...
Pain and Fun Shifts in One Day
Pain
Fun
6h
12h
18h
24h
it doesn't cancel out the pain.
AS LONG AS I'M ALIVE, I'LL BE SUFFERING.
I mean, humans look for fun to forget about the pain, don't they?
Like with sports.
Or gambling.
Or alcohol.
In my case, it's manga.
SCRITCH
SCRITCH
SINCE PUBERTY, I'VE BEEN SCARED ABOUT PREGNANCY.

Mahjong tiles: Middle, North

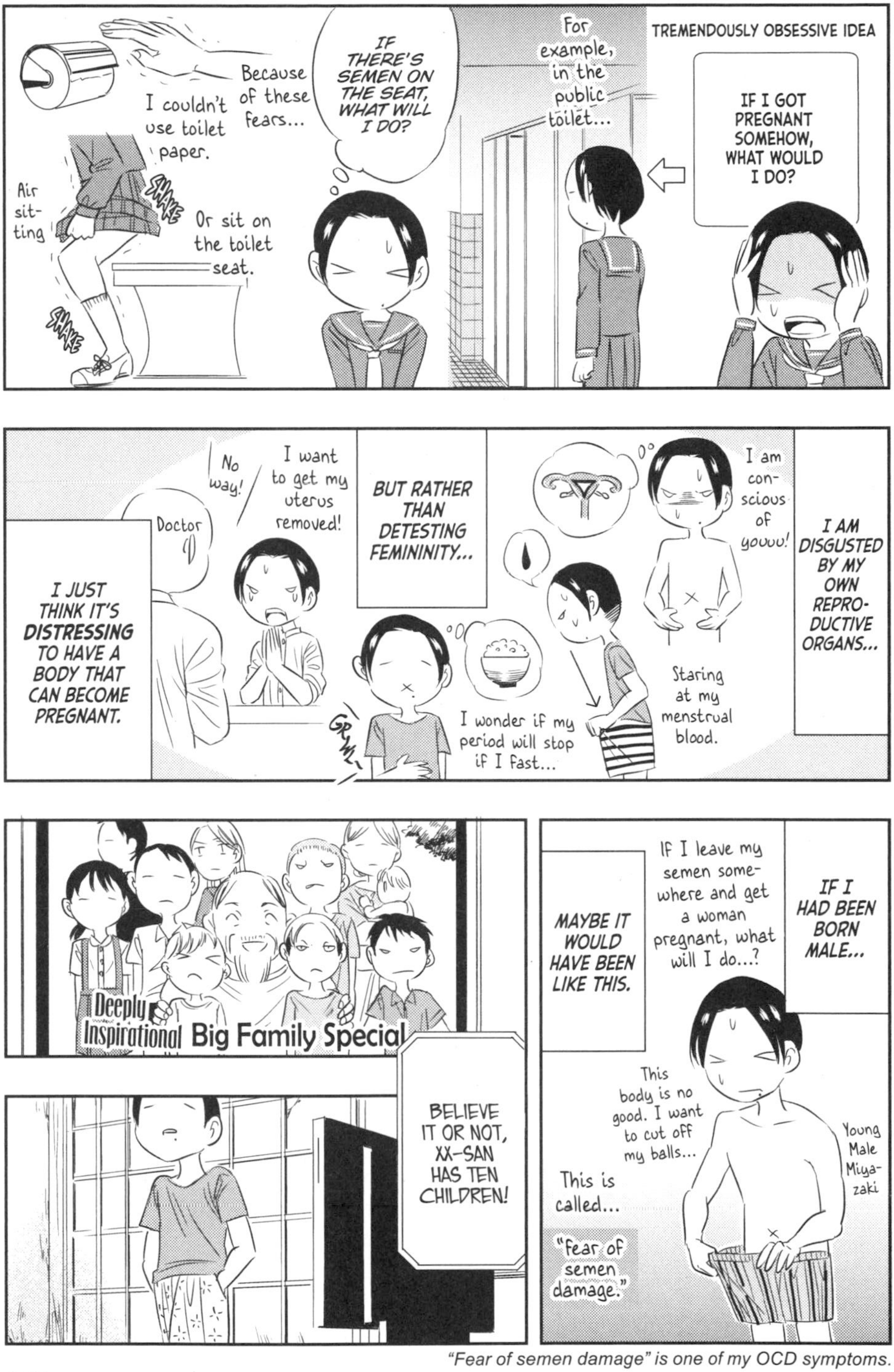
TREMENDOUSLY OBSESSIVE IDEA
IF I GOT PREGNANT SOMEHOW, WHAT WOULD I DO?
For example, in the public toilet...
IF THERE'S SEMEN ON THE SEAT, WHAT WILL I DO?
Because of these fears...
I couldn't use toilet paper.
SHAKE
Or sit on the toilet seat.
Air sitting
SHAKE
I AM DISGUSTED BY MY OWN REPRODUCTIVE ORGANS...
I am conscious of youuu!
Staring at my menstrual blood.
I wonder if my period will stop if I fast...
GRWL
BUT RATHER THAN DETESTING FEMININITY...
I want to get my uterus removed!
No way!
Doctor
I JUST THINK IT'S DISTRESSING TO HAVE A BODY THAT CAN BECOME PREGNANT.
IF I HAD BEEN BORN MALE...
If I leave my semen somewhere and get a woman pregnant, what will I do...?
MAYBE IT WOULD HAVE BEEN LIKE THIS.
This body is no good. I want to cut off my balls...
Young Male Miyazaki
This is called...
"Fear of semen damage."
Deeply Inspirational Big Family Special
BELIEVE IT OR NOT, XX-SAN HAS TEN CHILDREN!

"Fear of semen damage" is one of my OCD symptoms.

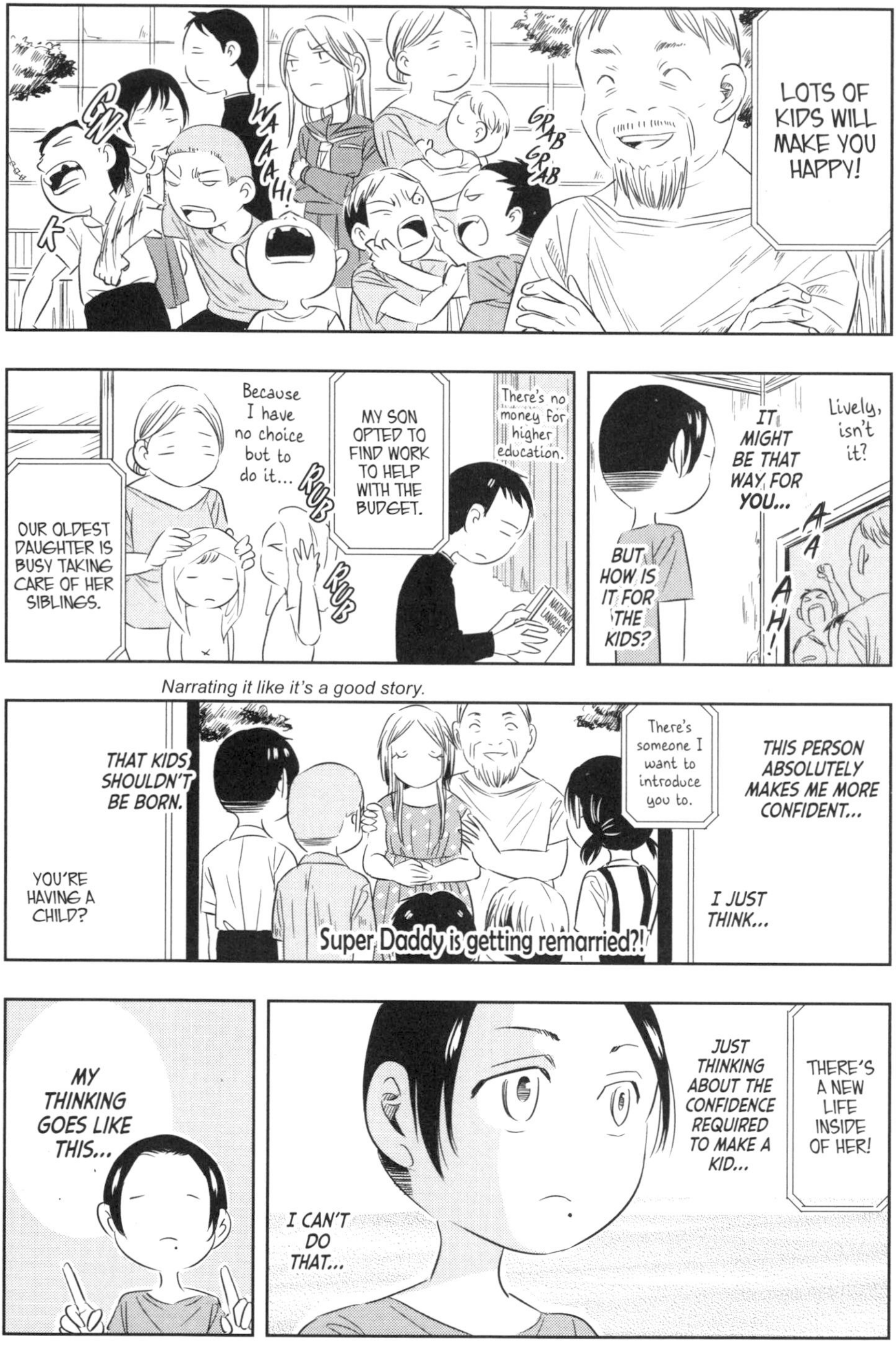
LOTS OF KIDS WILL MAKE YOU HAPPY!
GRAB GRAB
WAAAAH!
GN K
Lively, isn't it?
IT MIGHT BE THAT WAY FOR YOU...
BUT HOW IS IT FOR THE KIDS?
AAAAH!
There's no money for higher education.
MY SON OPTED TO FIND WORK TO HELP WITH THE BUDGET.
Because I have no choice but to do it...
RUB RUB
OUR OLDEST DAUGHTER IS BUSY TAKING CARE OF HER SIBLINGS.
NATIONAL LANGUAGE
Narrating it like it's a good story.
THIS PERSON ABSOLUTELY MAKES ME MORE CONFIDENT...
There's someone I want to introduce you to.
I JUST THINK...
THAT KIDS SHOULDN'T BE BORN.
YOU'RE HAVING A CHILD?
Super Daddy is getting remarried?!
THERE'S A NEW LIFE INSIDE OF HER!
JUST THINKING ABOUT THE CONFIDENCE REQUIRED TO MAKE A KID...
I CAN'T DO THAT...
MY THINKING GOES LIKE THIS...

I've drawn this very simply. If you are interested, please look these things up!

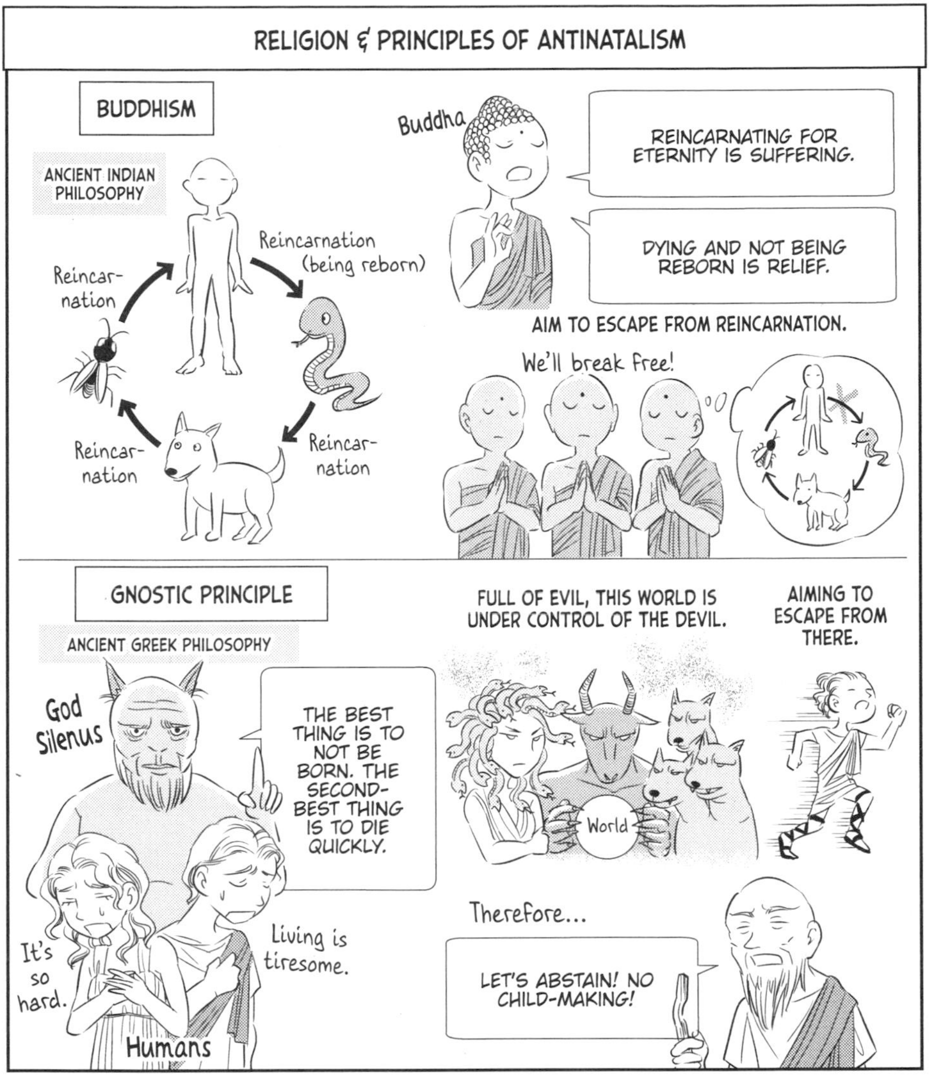
RELIGION & PRINCIPLES OF ANTINATALISM
Buddha
REINCARNATING FOR ETERNITY IS SUFFERING.
DYING AND NOT BEING REBORN IS RELIEF.
AIM TO ESCAPE FROM REINCARNATION.
We'll break free!
BUDDHISM
ANCIENT INDIAN PHILOSOPHY
Reincarnation (being reborn)
Reincar-nation
Reincar-nation
Reincar-nation
AIMING TO ESCAPE FROM THERE.
FULL OF EVIL, THIS WORLD IS UNDER CONTROL OF THE DEVIL.
World
Therefore...
LET'S ABSTAIN! NO CHILD-MAKING!
GNOSTIC PRINCIPLE
ANCIENT GREEK PHILOSOPHY
God Silenus
THE BEST THING IS TO NOT BE BORN. THE SECOND-BEST THING IS TO DIE QUICKLY.
Living is tiresome.
It's so hard.
Humans

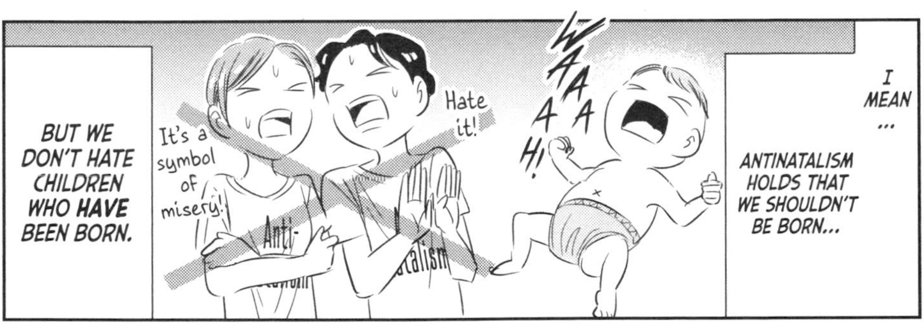
I MEAN ...
ANTINATALISM HOLDS THAT WE SHOULDN'T BE BORN...
WAAAAH!
Hate it!
It's a symbol of misery!
Anti-
BUT WE DON'T HATE CHILDREN WHO **HAVE** BEEN BORN.

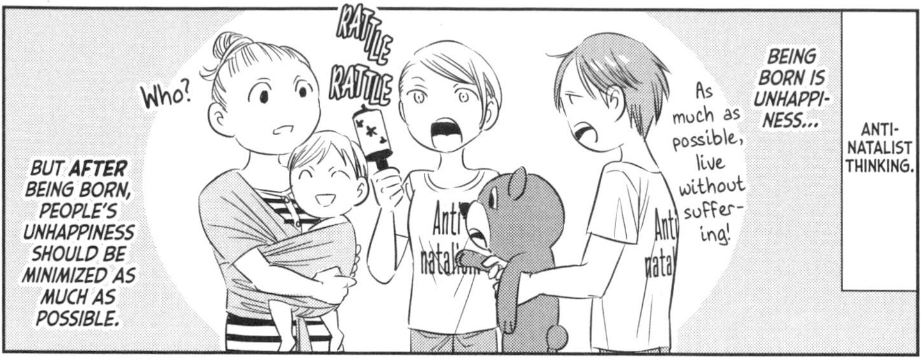
ANTI-NATALIST THINKING.
BEING BORN IS UNHAPPINESS...
As much as possible, live without suffering!
RATTLE RATTLE
Antinatalism
Who?
BUT **AFTER** BEING BORN, PEOPLE'S UNHAPPINESS SHOULD BE MINIMIZED AS MUCH AS POSSIBLE.

※ *There are various ways of antinatalist thinking. This is one lasting example.*

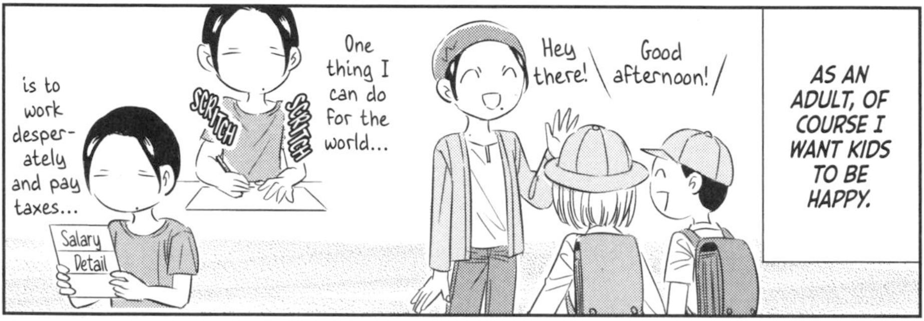
AS AN ADULT, OF COURSE I WANT KIDS TO BE HAPPY.
Good afternoon!
Hey there!
One thing I can do for the world...
SCRITCH SCRITCH
is to work desperately and pay taxes...
Salary Detail

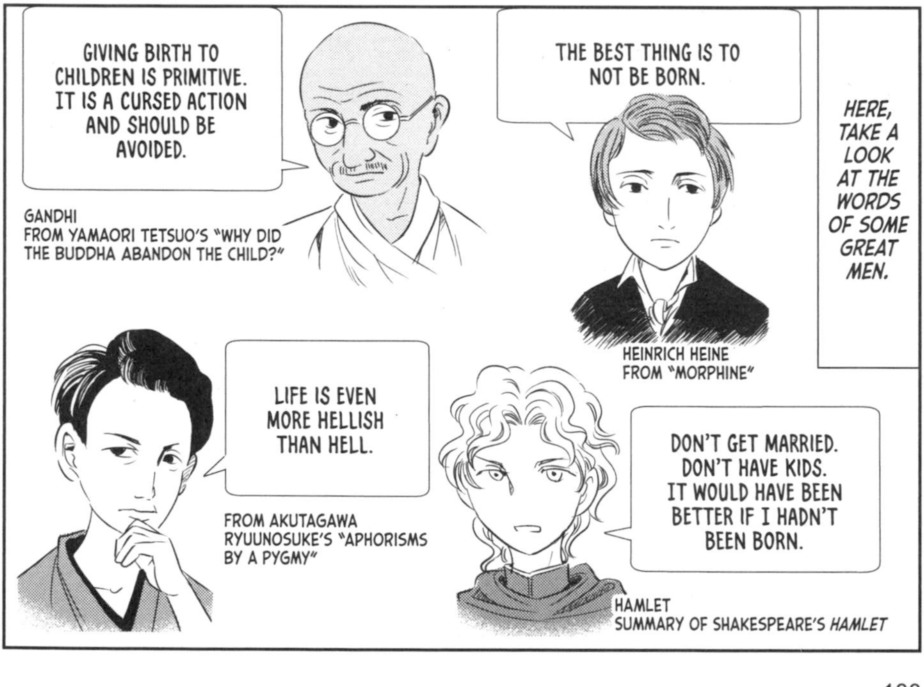
HERE, TAKE A LOOK AT THE WORDS OF SOME GREAT MEN.
THE BEST THING IS TO NOT BE BORN.
HEINRICH HEINE FROM "MORPHINE"
GIVING BIRTH TO CHILDREN IS PRIMITIVE. IT IS A CURSED ACTION AND SHOULD BE AVOIDED.
GANDHI FROM YAMAORI TETSUO'S "WHY DID THE BUDDHA ABANDON THE CHILD?"
DON'T GET MARRIED. DON'T HAVE KIDS. IT WOULD HAVE BEEN BETTER IF I HADN'T BEEN BORN.
HAMLET SUMMARY OF SHAKESPEARE'S *HAMLET*
LIFE IS EVEN MORE HELLISH THAN HELL.
FROM AKUTAGAWA RYUUNOSUKE'S "APHORISMS BY A PYGMY"

Dazai-sensei made four suicide attempts. On the fifth attempt, he finally succeeded. He's a hardcore pessimist, isn't he? He thinks one should die alone, without a companion...

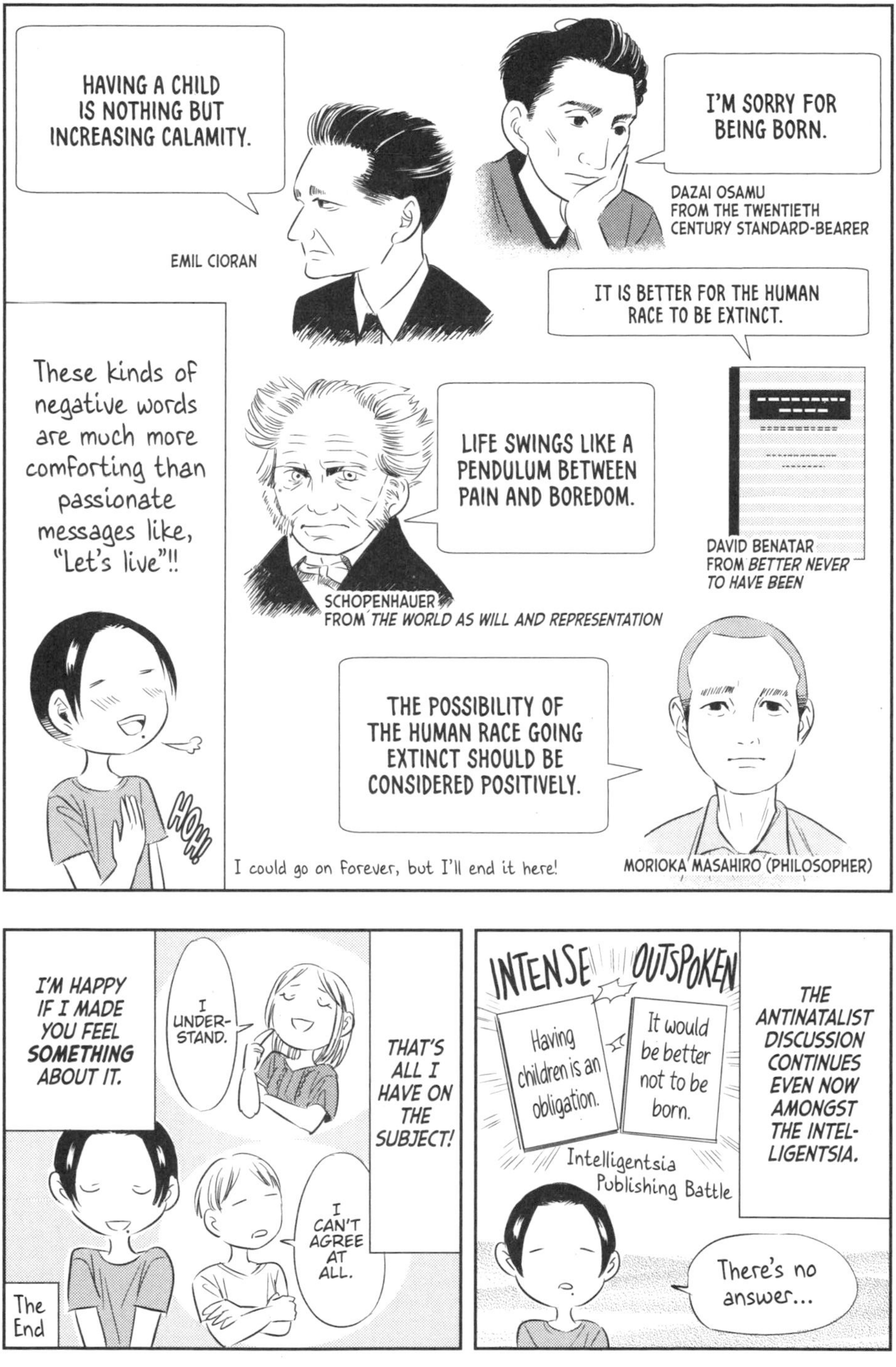

I'M SORRY FOR BEING BORN.
DAZAI OSAMU FROM THE TWENTIETH CENTURY STANDARD-BEARER
HAVING A CHILD IS NOTHING BUT INCREASING CALAMITY.
EMIL CIORAN
IT IS BETTER FOR THE HUMAN RACE TO BE EXTINCT.
DAVID BENATAR FROM BETTER NEVER TO HAVE BEEN
LIFE SWINGS LIKE A PENDULUM BETWEEN PAIN AND BOREDOM.
SCHOPENHAUER FROM THE WORLD AS WILL AND REPRESENTATION
THE POSSIBILITY OF THE HUMAN RACE GOING EXTINCT SHOULD BE CONSIDERED POSITIVELY.
MORIOKA MASAHIRO (PHILOSOPHER)
These kinds of negative words are much more comforting than passionate messages like, "Let's live"!!
HOH!
I could go on forever, but I'll end it here!
THE ANTINATALIST DISCUSSION CONTINUES EVEN NOW AMONGST THE INTELLIGENTSIA.
INTENSE
OUTSPOKEN
It would be better not to be born.
Having children is an obligation.
Intelligentsia Publishing Battle
There's no answer...
THAT'S ALL I HAVE ON THE SUBJECT!
I UNDERSTAND.
I'M HAPPY IF I MADE YOU FEEL SOMETHING ABOUT IT.
I CAN'T AGREE AT ALL.
The End

Reference Material: *Contemporary Thought*, November 2019 issue, Special Feature: Thinking About Antinatalism (Seidosha)

ACCORDING TO THE PHILOSOPHER MORIOKA MASAHIRO-SENSEI, THERE ARE VARIOUS FACTIONS WITHIN ANTINATALISM. THERE ARE PEOPLE WHO THINK, "I DON'T KNOW ABOUT OTHERS, BUT I WON'T GIVE BIRTH," AND PEOPLE WHO THINK, "NO HUMAN SHOULD GIVE BIRTH." MY THOUGHTS ARE "BECAUSE I WISH I WASN'T BORN, I WON'T GIVE BIRTH. I WANT MY PARTNER (IF I OBTAIN ONE) TO THINK THAT AS WELL." SO MY THOUGHTS DON'T EXTEND TO OTHER PEOPLE.

Ep. 27: The "Lookism" Story

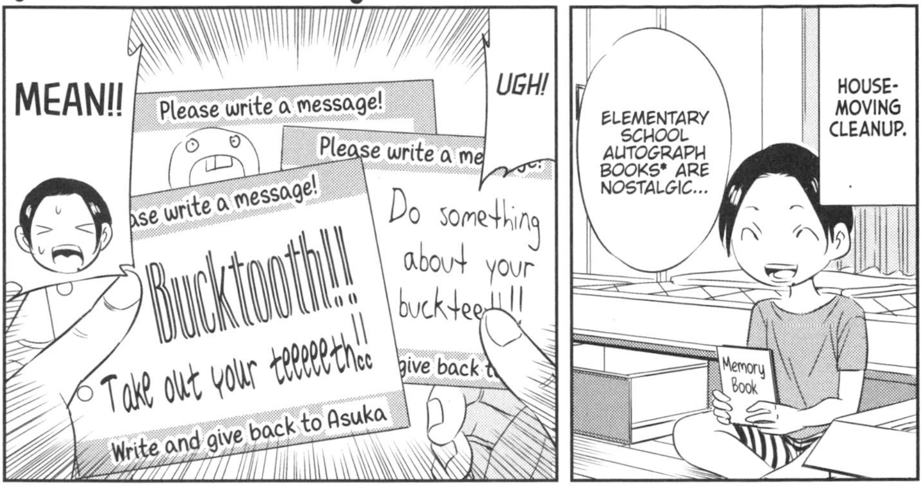
HOUSE-MOVING CLEANUP.
ELEMENTARY SCHOOL AUTOGRAPH BOOKS* ARE NOSTALGIC...
Memory Book
UGH!
Please write a message!
Do something about your bucktee!!!!
Bucktooth!!
Take out your teeeeeth!!
Write and give back to Asuka
MEAN!!

*A book where ex-elementary/junior high students write profiles of their friends.

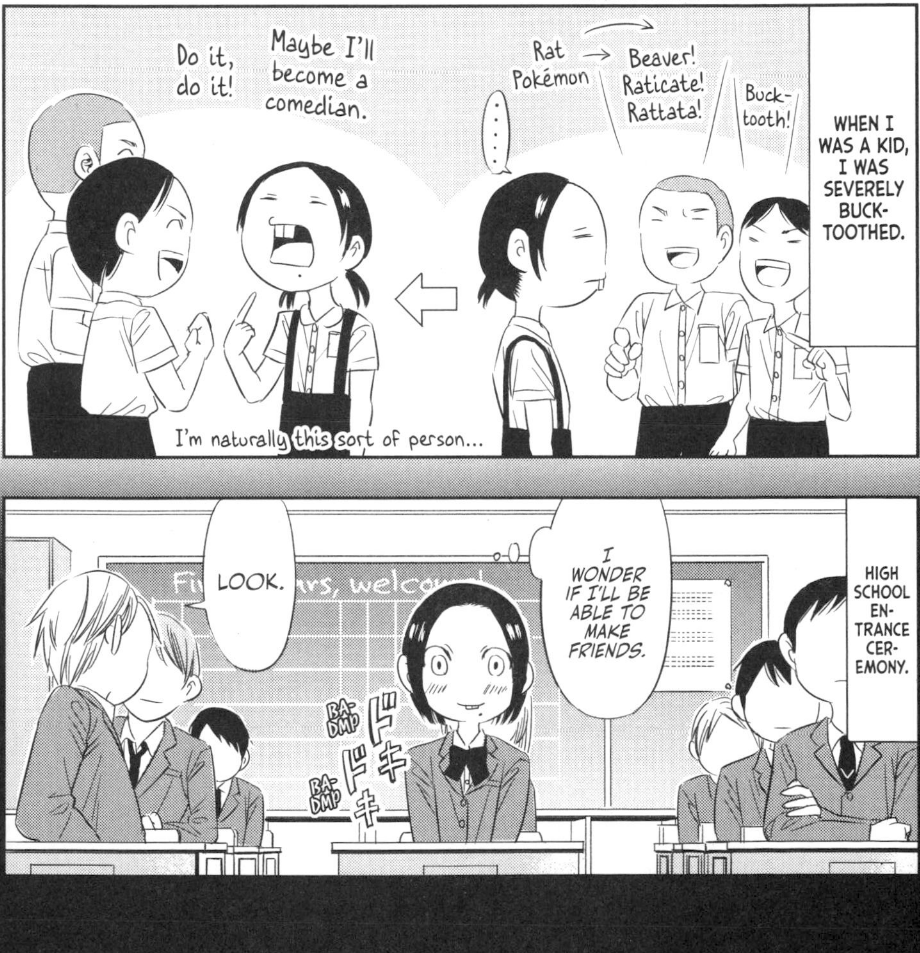
WHEN I WAS A KID, I WAS SEVERELY BUCK-TOOTHED.
Buck-tooth!
Beaver! Raticate! Rattata!
Rat → Pokémon
...
Maybe I'll become a comedian.
Do it, do it!
I'm naturally this sort of person...
HIGH SCHOOL EN-TRANCE CER-EMONY.
I WONDER IF I'LL BE ABLE TO MAKE FRIENDS.
BA-DMP BA-DMP
LOOK.

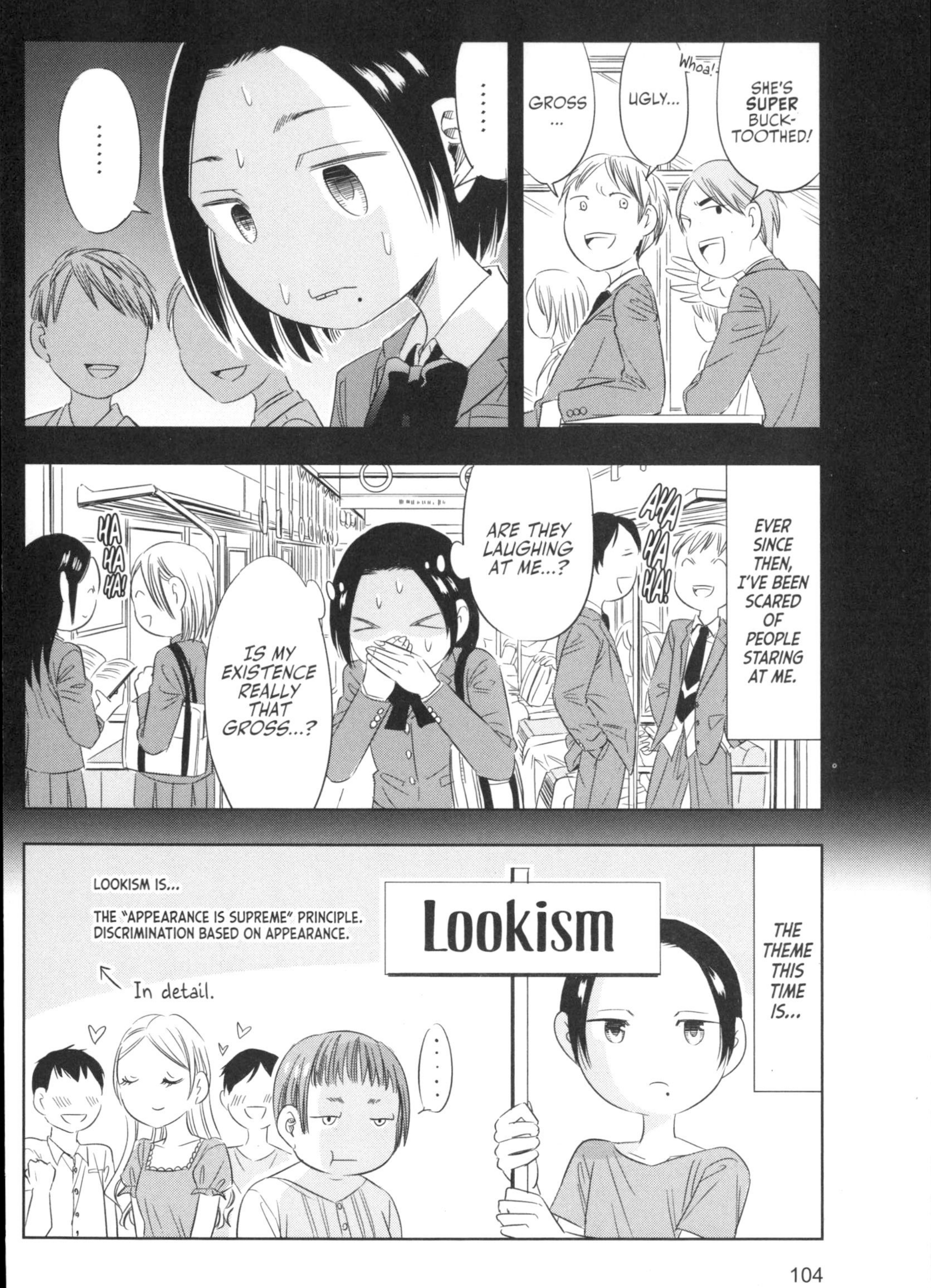
Whoa!
SHE'S SUPER BUCK-TOOTHED!
UGLY...
GROSS ...
......
......
EVER SINCE THEN, I'VE BEEN SCARED OF PEOPLE STARING AT ME.
AHA HA HA HA!
ARE THEY LAUGHING AT ME...?
IS MY EXISTENCE REALLY THAT GROSS...?
HA HA HA!
THE THEME THIS TIME IS...
Lookism
LOOKISM IS...
THE "APPEARANCE IS SUPREME" PRINCIPLE. DISCRIMINATION BASED ON APPEARANCE.
In detail.
......

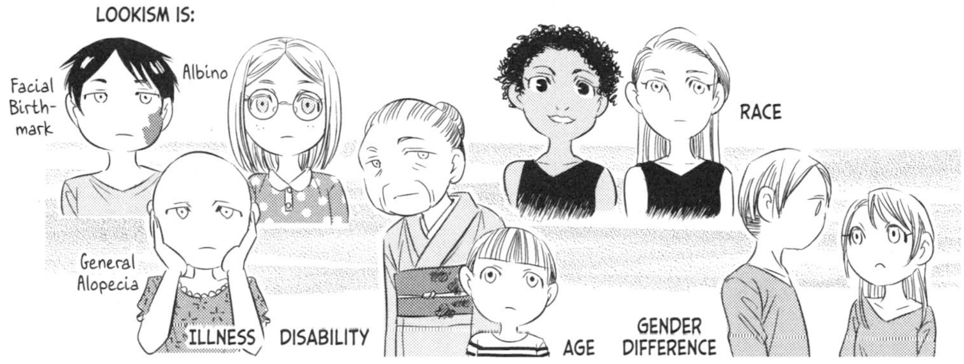
LOOKISM IS:
Facial Birth-mark
Albino
General Alopecia
ILLNESS
DISABILITY
RACE
AGE
GENDER DIFFERENCE

IT COVERS A WIDE RANGE OF THEMES RELATED TO PEOPLES' APPEARANCE.

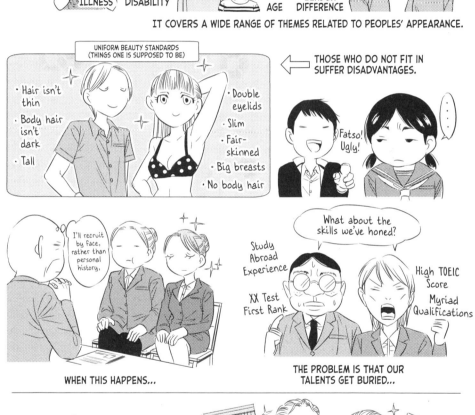

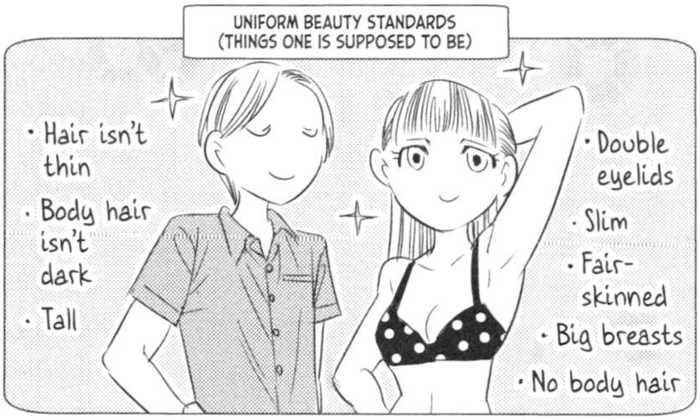
UNIFORM BEAUTY STANDARDS (THINGS ONE IS SUPPOSED TO BE)
· Hair isn't thin
· Body hair isn't dark
· Tall
· Double eyelids
· Slim
· Fair-skinned
· Big breasts
· No body hair

THOSE WHO DO NOT FIT IN SUFFER DISADVANTAGES.

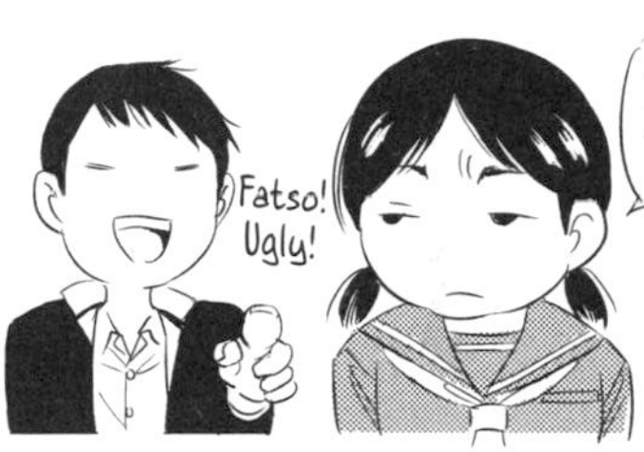
Fatso! Ugly!
· · · ·

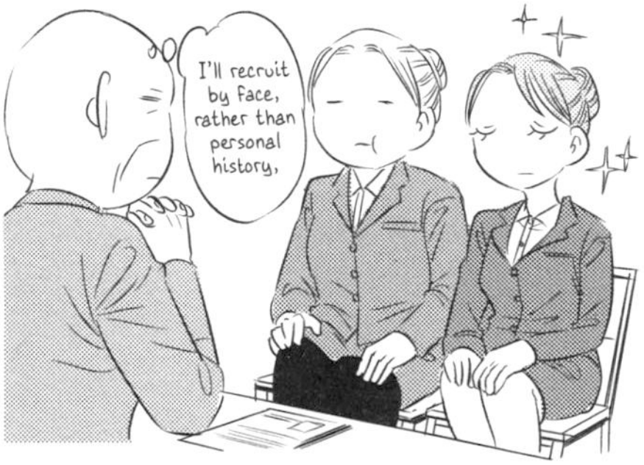
I'll recruit by face, rather than personal history,

WHEN THIS HAPPENS...

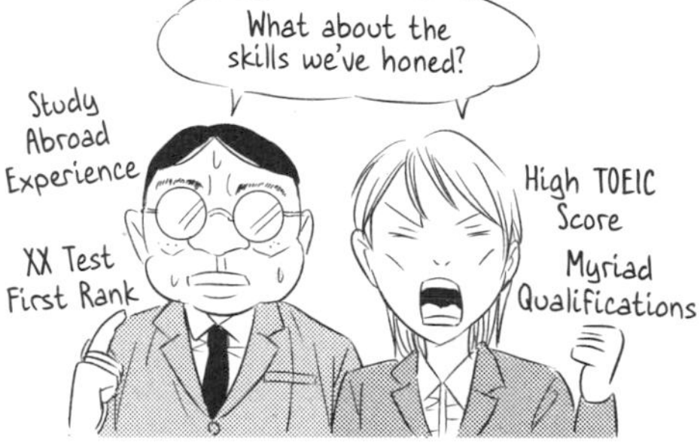
What about the skills we've honed?
Study Abroad Experience
XX Test First Rank
High TOEIC Score
Myriad Qualifications

THE PROBLEM IS THAT OUR TALENTS GET BURIED...

Incidentally...

ACCORDING TO OVERSEAS RESEARCH, THE BETTER-LOOKING THE PERSON, THE EASIER IT IS FOR THEM TO SUCCEED WITH OTHERS.

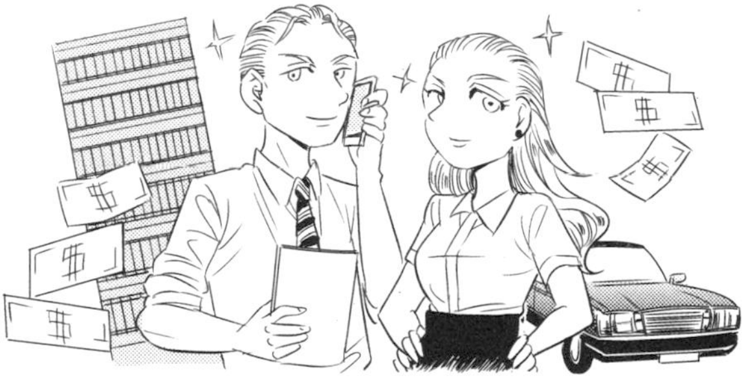

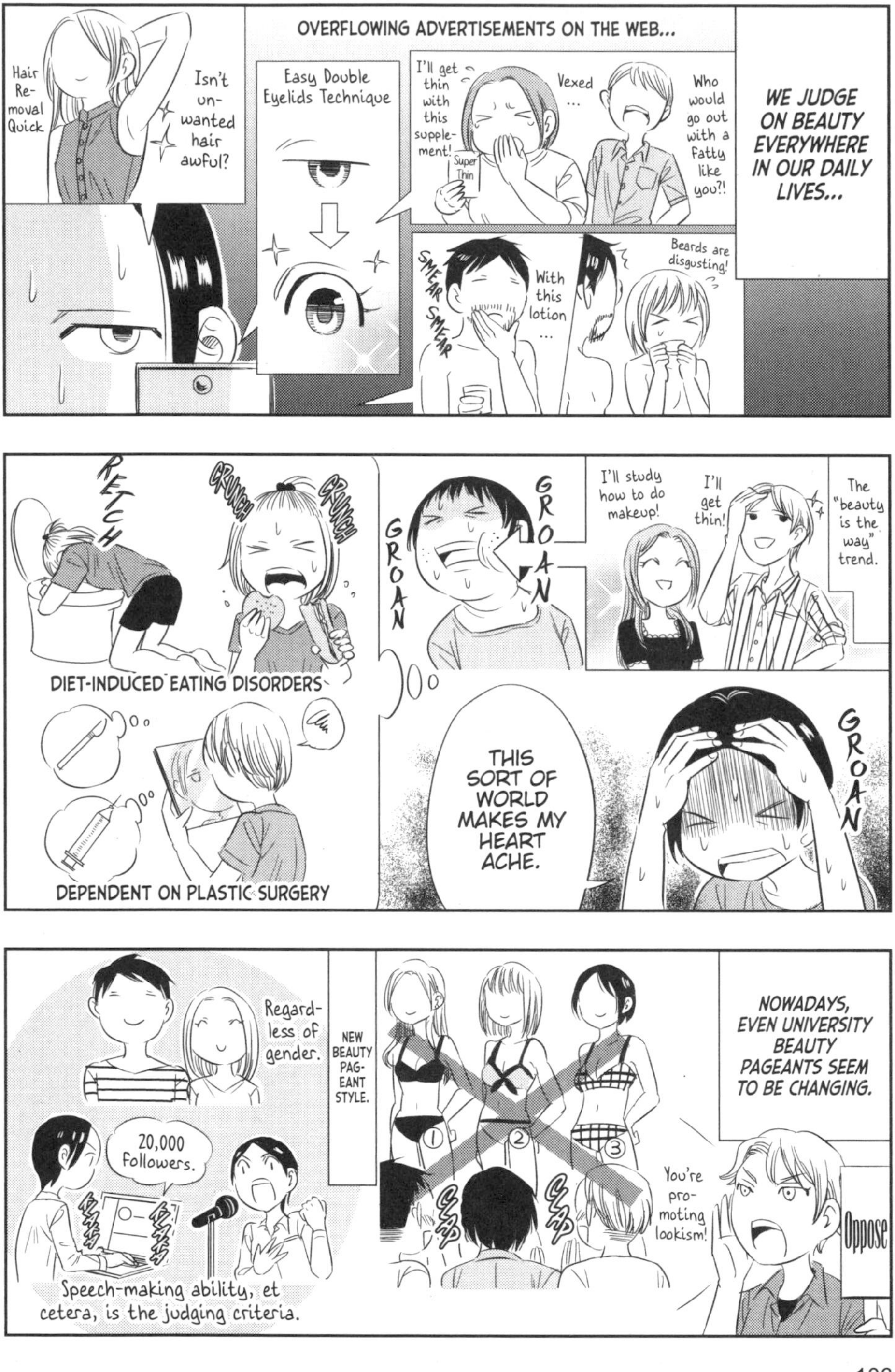
WE JUDGE ON BEAUTY EVERYWHERE IN OUR DAILY LIVES...
OVERFLOWING ADVERTISEMENTS ON THE WEB...
Who would go out with a Fatty like you?!
Vexed ...
I'll get thin with this supplement!
Super Thin
Beards are disgusting!
With this lotion ...
SMEAR SMEAR
Easy Double Eyelids Technique
Isn't unwanted hair awful?
Hair Removal Quick
The "beauty is the way" trend.
I'll get thin!
I'll study how to do makeup!
GROAN GROAN
RETCH
CRUNCH CRUNCH
DIET-INDUCED EATING DISORDERS
DEPENDENT ON PLASTIC SURGERY
THIS SORT OF WORLD MAKES MY HEART ACHE.
GROAN
NOWADAYS, EVEN UNIVERSITY BEAUTY PAGEANTS SEEM TO BE CHANGING.
Oppose
You're promoting lookism!
CLAP CLAP
NEW BEAUTY PAGEANT STYLE.
Regardless of gender.
20,000 followers.
Speech-making ability, et cetera, is the judging criteria.

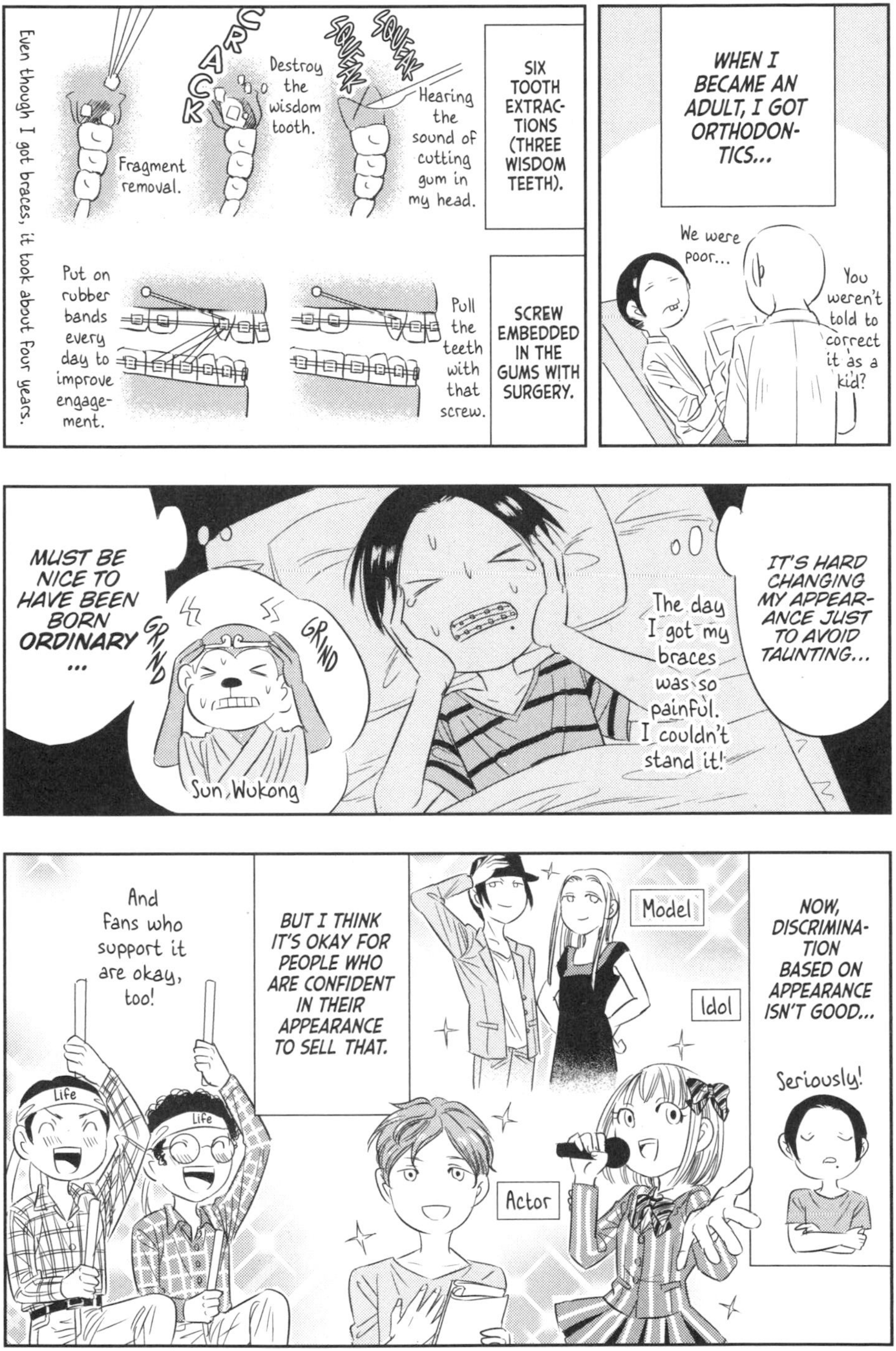
WHEN I BECAME AN ADULT, I GOT ORTHODONTICS...
You weren't told to correct it as a kid?
We were poor...
SIX TOOTH EXTRACTIONS (THREE WISDOM TEETH).
Hearing the sound of cutting gum in my head.
SQUEAK SQUEAK
Destroy the wisdom tooth.
CRACK
Fragment removal.
SCREW EMBEDDED IN THE GUMS WITH SURGERY.
Pull the teeth with that screw.
Put on rubber bands every day to improve engagement.
Even though I got braces, it took about four years.
IT'S HARD CHANGING MY APPEARANCE JUST TO AVOID TAUNTING...
The day I got my braces was so painful. I couldn't stand it!
GRIND GRIND
Sun Wukong
MUST BE NICE TO HAVE BEEN BORN ORDINARY...
NOW, DISCRIMINATION BASED ON APPEARANCE ISN'T GOOD...
Seriously!
Model
Idol
Actor
BUT I THINK IT'S OKAY FOR PEOPLE WHO ARE CONFIDENT IN THEIR APPEARANCE TO SELL THAT.
And fans who support it are okay, too!
Life
Life

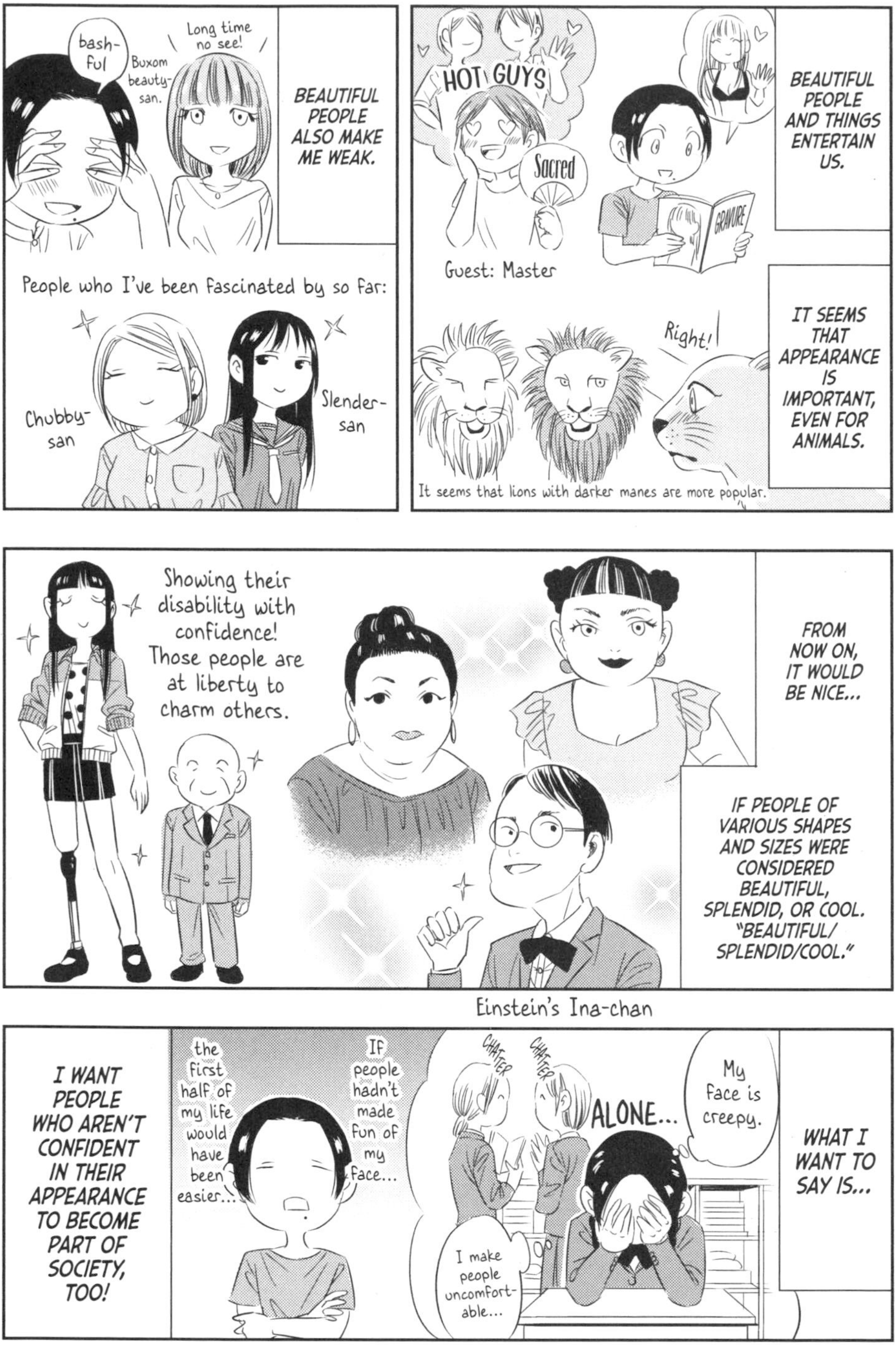
BEAUTIFUL PEOPLE AND THINGS ENTERTAIN US.
HOT GUYS
Sacred
GRAVURE
Guest: Master
IT SEEMS THAT APPEARANCE IS IMPORTANT, EVEN FOR ANIMALS.
Right!
It seems that lions with darker manes are more popular.
BEAUTIFUL PEOPLE ALSO MAKE ME WEAK.
Long time no see!
Buxom beauty-san.
bash-ful
People who I've been fascinated by so far:
Slender-san
Chubby-san
FROM NOW ON, IT WOULD BE NICE...
IF PEOPLE OF VARIOUS SHAPES AND SIZES WERE CONSIDERED BEAUTIFUL, SPLENDID, OR COOL. "BEAUTIFUL/ SPLENDID/COOL."
Showing their disability with confidence! Those people are at liberty to charm others.
Einstein's Ina-chan
WHAT I WANT TO SAY IS...
My face is creepy.
ALONE...
CHATTER
CHATTER
I make people uncomfort-able...
If people hadn't made fun of my face...
the first half of my life would have been easier...
I WANT PEOPLE WHO AREN'T CONFIDENT IN THEIR APPEARANCE TO BECOME PART OF SOCIETY, TOO!

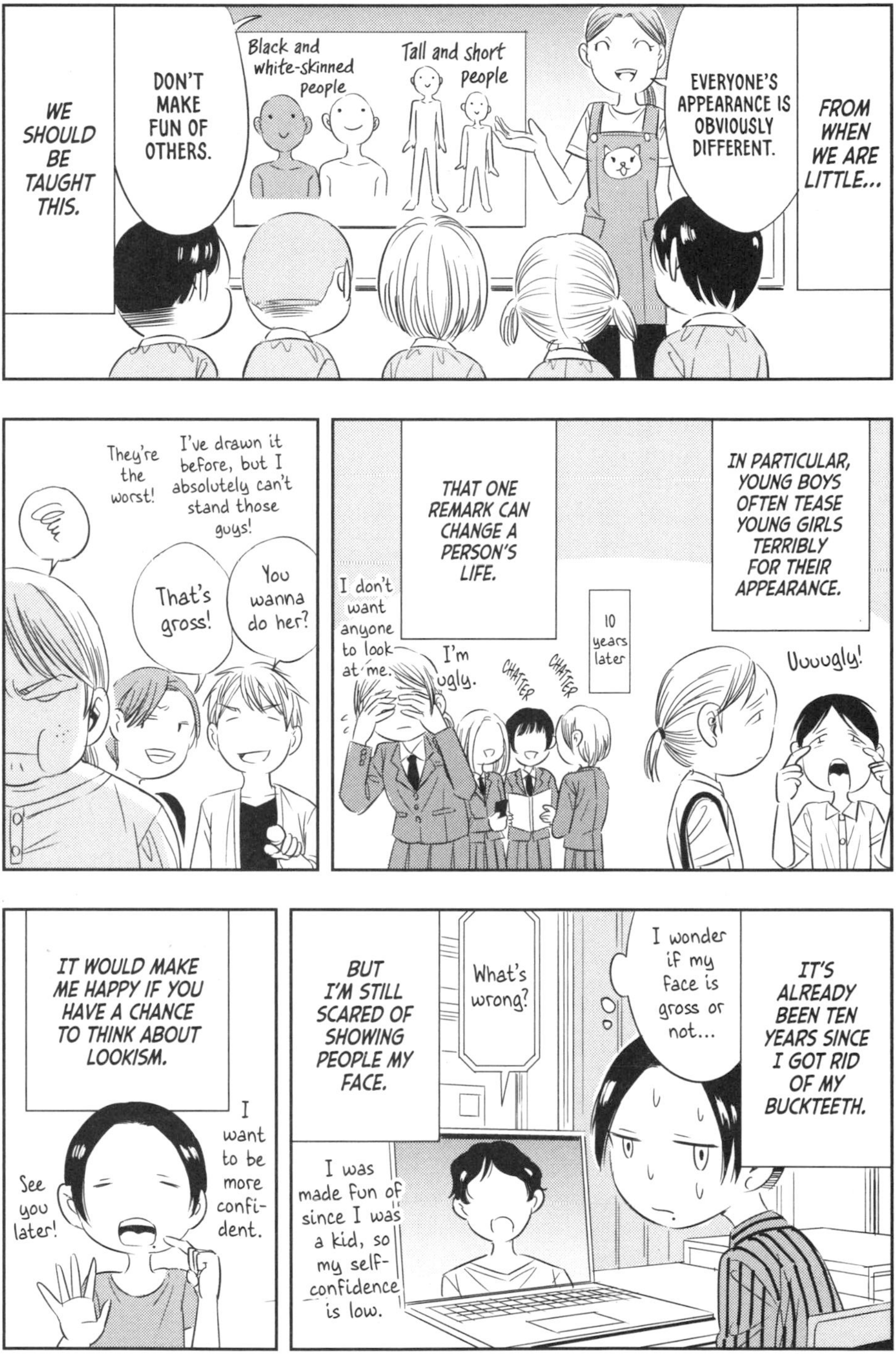
FROM WHEN WE ARE LITTLE...
EVERYONE'S APPEARANCE IS OBVIOUSLY DIFFERENT.
Tall and short people
Black and white-skinned people
DON'T MAKE FUN OF OTHERS.
WE SHOULD BE TAUGHT THIS.
IN PARTICULAR, YOUNG BOYS OFTEN TEASE YOUNG GIRLS TERRIBLY FOR THEIR APPEARANCE.
Uuuugly!
10 years later
CHATTER
CHATTER
THAT ONE REMARK CAN CHANGE A PERSON'S LIFE.
I'm ugly.
I don't want anyone to look at me.
I've drawn it before, but I absolutely can't stand those guys!
They're the worst!
You wanna do her?
That's gross!
IT'S ALREADY BEEN TEN YEARS SINCE I GOT RID OF MY BUCKTEETH.
I wonder if my face is gross or not...
What's wrong?
BUT I'M STILL SCARED OF SHOWING PEOPLE MY FACE.
I was made fun of since I was a kid, so my self-confidence is low.
IT WOULD MAKE ME HAPPY IF YOU HAVE A CHANCE TO THINK ABOUT LOOKISM.
I want to be more confident.
See you later!

Ep.28: The "It's Hopeless, So Let's Talk about *Kokoro*" Story

**Stage Four: Explosive infection spread.*

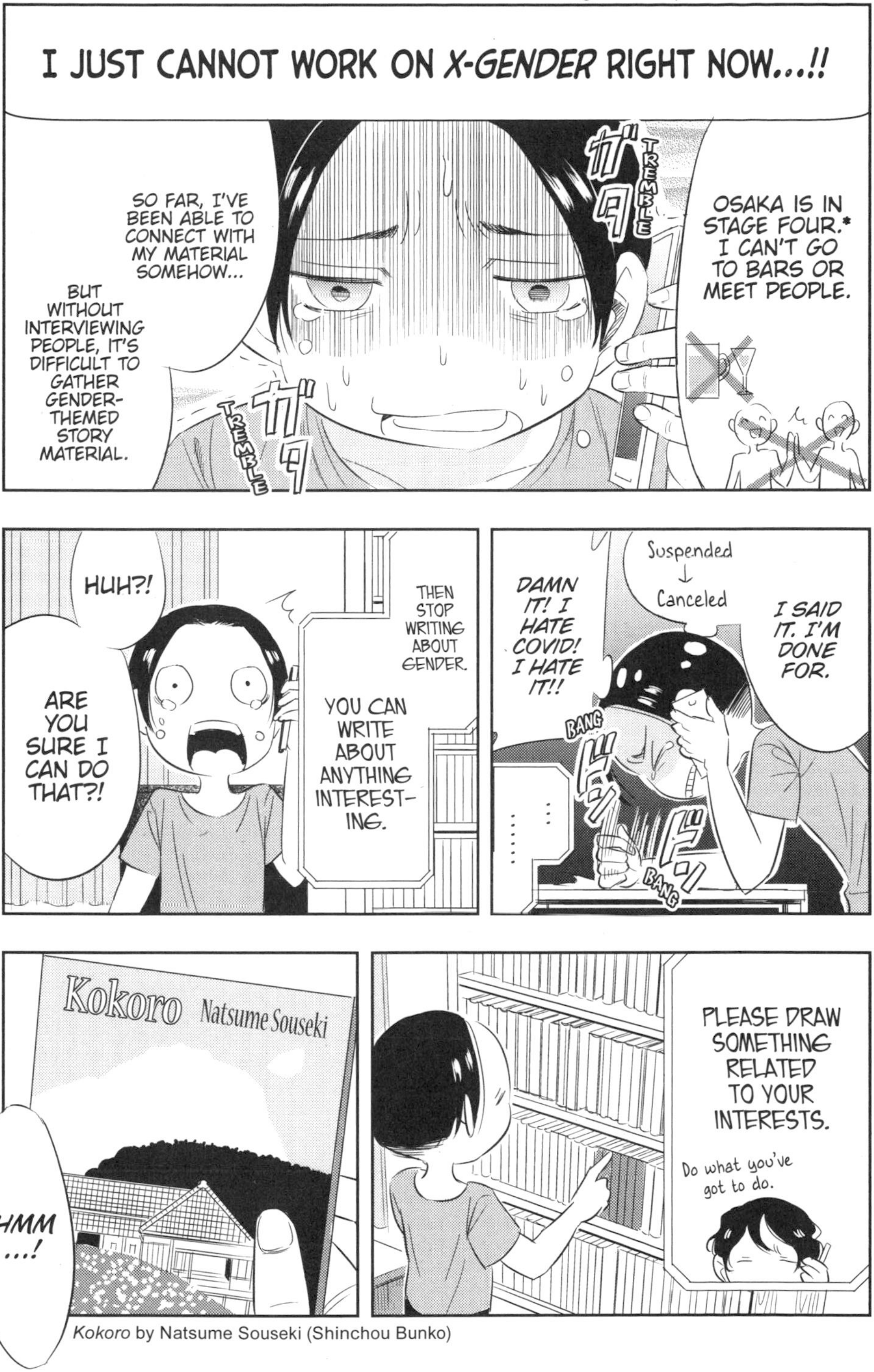

I JUST CANNOT WORK ON *X-GENDER* RIGHT NOW...!!
OSAKA IS IN STAGE FOUR.* I CAN'T GO TO BARS OR MEET PEOPLE.
TREMBLE
SO FAR, I'VE BEEN ABLE TO CONNECT WITH MY MATERIAL SOMEHOW...
BUT WITHOUT INTERVIEWING PEOPLE, IT'S DIFFICULT TO GATHER GENDER-THEMED STORY MATERIAL.
TREMBLE
Suspended ↓ Canceled
I SAID IT. I'M DONE FOR.
DAMN IT! I HATE COVID! I HATE IT!!
BANG
BANG
THEN STOP WRITING ABOUT GENDER.
YOU CAN WRITE ABOUT ANYTHING INTERESTING.
HUH?!
ARE YOU SURE I CAN DO THAT?!
PLEASE DRAW SOMETHING RELATED TO YOUR INTERESTS.
Do what you've got to do.
Kokoro Natsume Souseki
HMM ...!

Kokoro by Natsume Souseki (Shinchou Bunko)

Asuka Miyazaki's Introduction to Literature

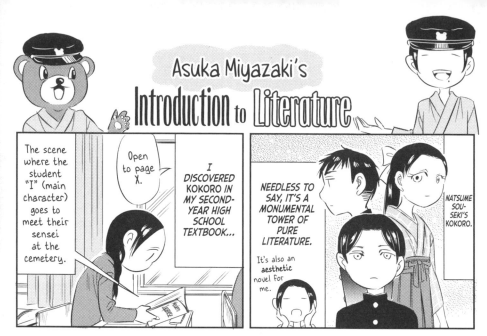

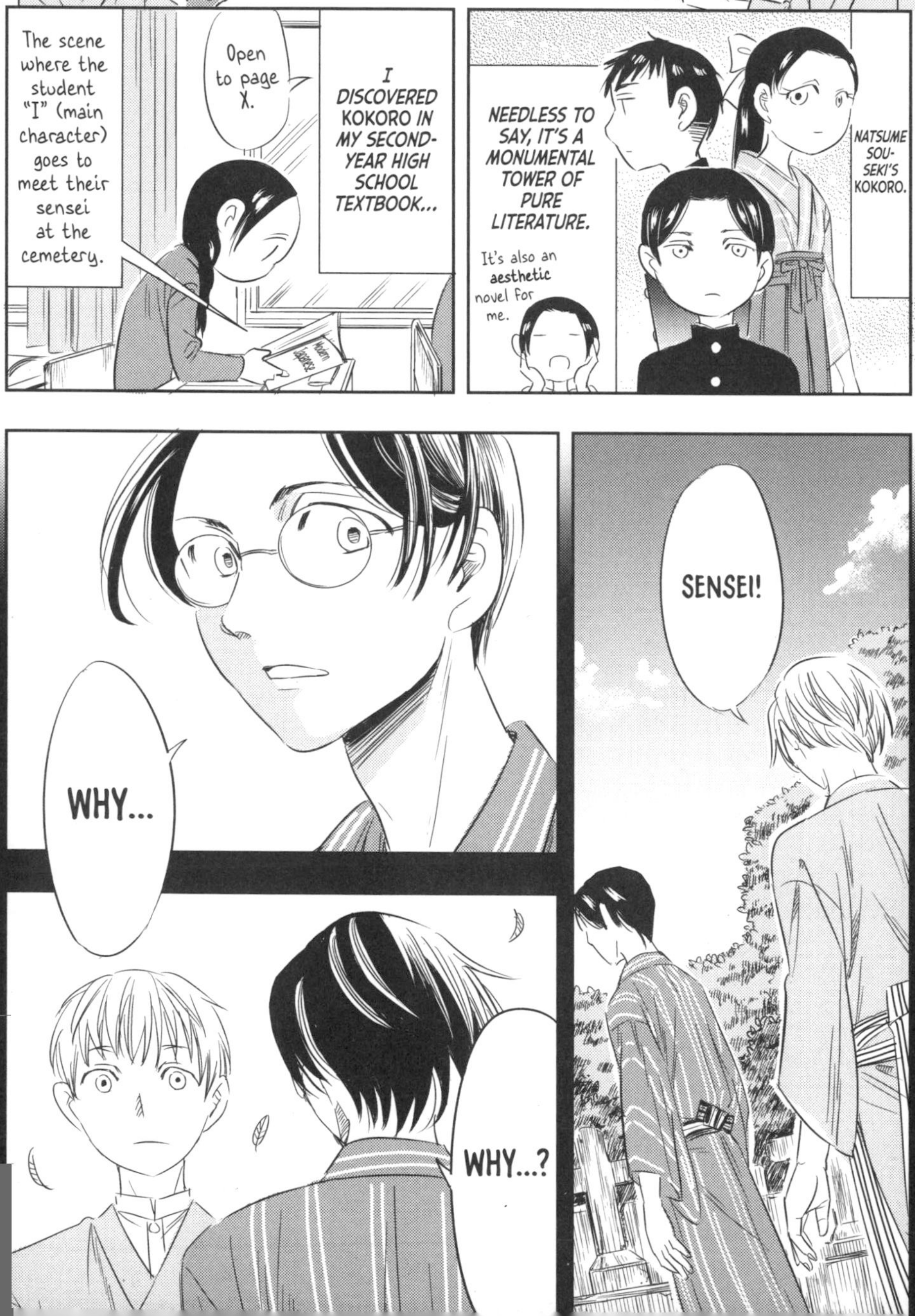
NATSUME SOU-SEKI'S KOKORO.
NEEDLESS TO SAY, IT'S A MONUMENTAL TOWER OF PURE LITERATURE.
It's also an aesthetic novel for me.
I DISCOVERED KOKORO IN MY SECOND-YEAR HIGH SCHOOL TEXTBOOK...
Open to page X.
The scene where the student "I" (main character) goes to meet their sensei at the cemetery.
SENSEI!
WHY...
WHY...?

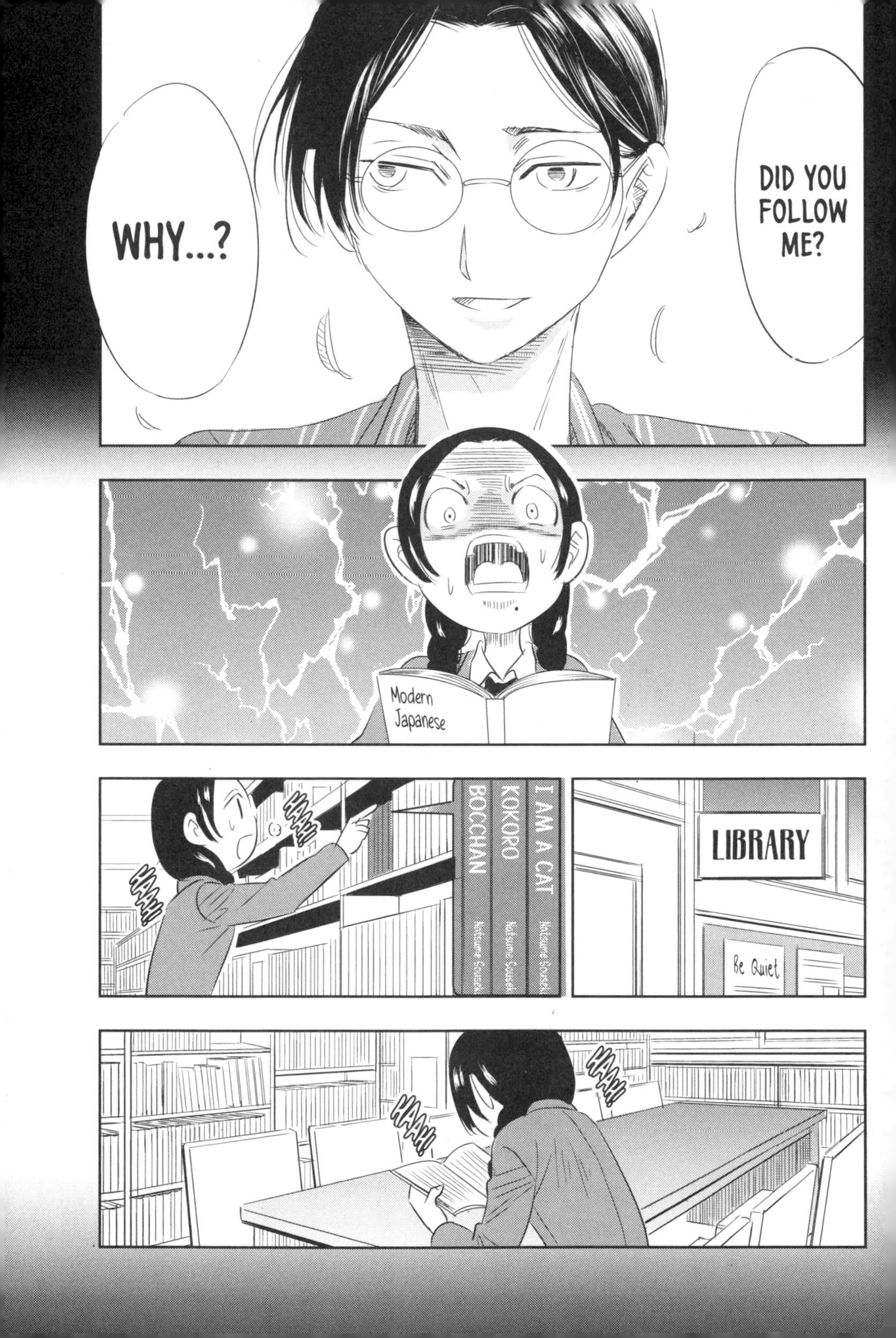
DID YOU FOLLOW ME?
WHY...?
Modern Japanese
LIBRARY
Be Quiet
I AM A CAT Natsume Souseki
KOKORO Natsume Souseki
BOCCHAN Natsume Souseki
HAAH!
HAAH!
HAAH!
HAAH!

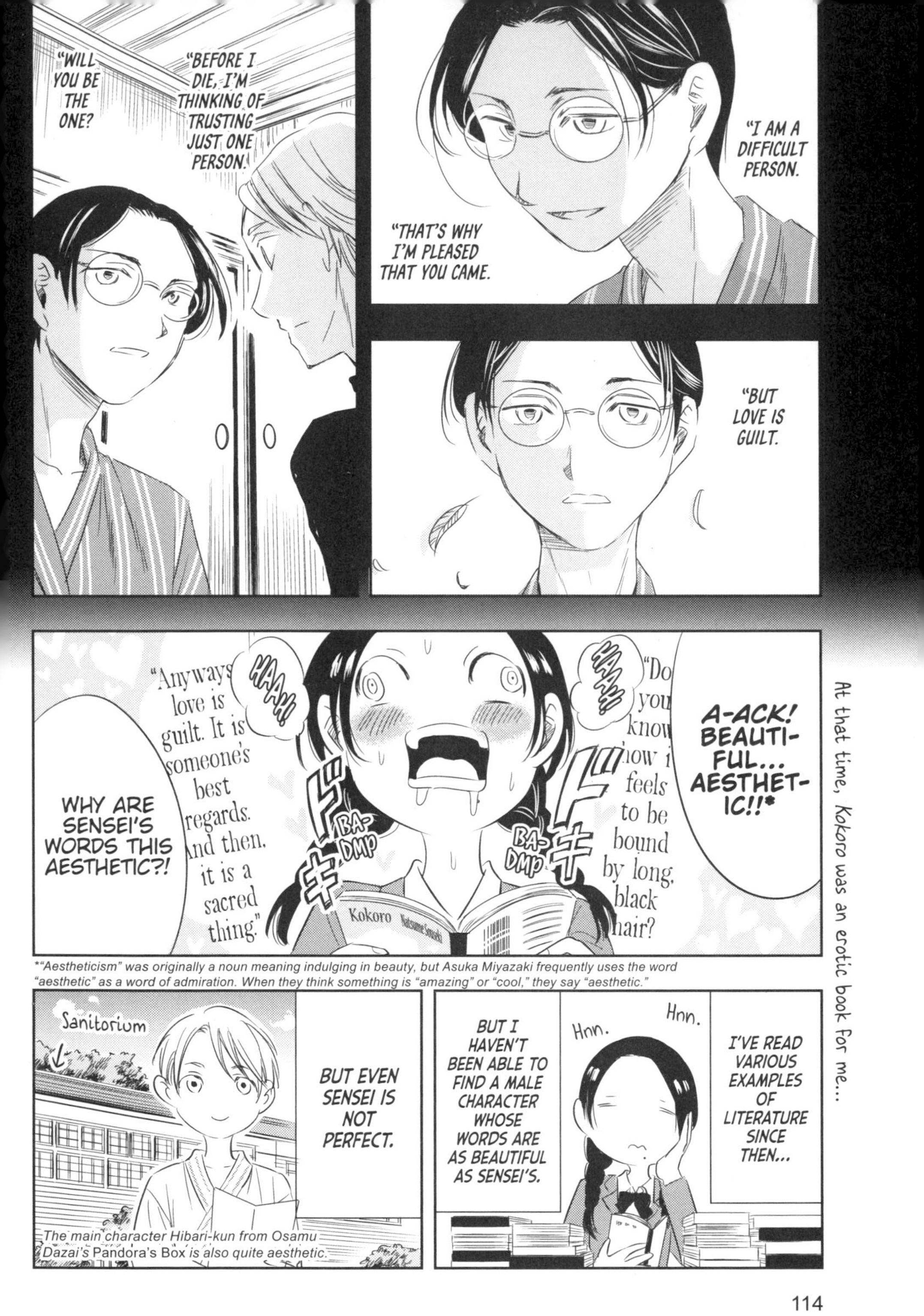
"I AM A DIFFICULT PERSON.
"THAT'S WHY I'M PLEASED THAT YOU CAME.
"BUT LOVE IS GUILT.
"BEFORE I DIE, I'M THINKING OF TRUSTING JUST ONE PERSON.
"WILL YOU BE THE ONE?
A-ACK! BEAUTIFUL... AESTHETIC!!*
"Do you know how it feels to be bound by long, black hair?
HAAH!
ドキ
BA-DMP
HAAH!
ドキ
BA-DMP
Kokoro Natsume Soseki
"Anyways love is guilt. It is someone's best regards. And then, it is a sacred thing."
WHY ARE SENSEI'S WORDS THIS AESTHETIC?!
I'VE READ VARIOUS EXAMPLES OF LITERATURE SINCE THEN...
Hnn.
Hnn.
BUT I HAVEN'T BEEN ABLE TO FIND A MALE CHARACTER WHOSE WORDS ARE AS BEAUTIFUL AS SENSEI'S.
BUT EVEN SENSEI IS NOT PERFECT.
Sanitorium

*"Aestheticism" was originally a noun meaning indulging in beauty, but Asuka Miyazaki frequently uses the word "aesthetic" as a word of admiration. When they think something is "amazing" or "cool," they say "aesthetic."

The main character Hibari-kun from Osamu Dazai's Pandora's Box is also quite aesthetic.

At that time, Kokoro was an erotic book for me...

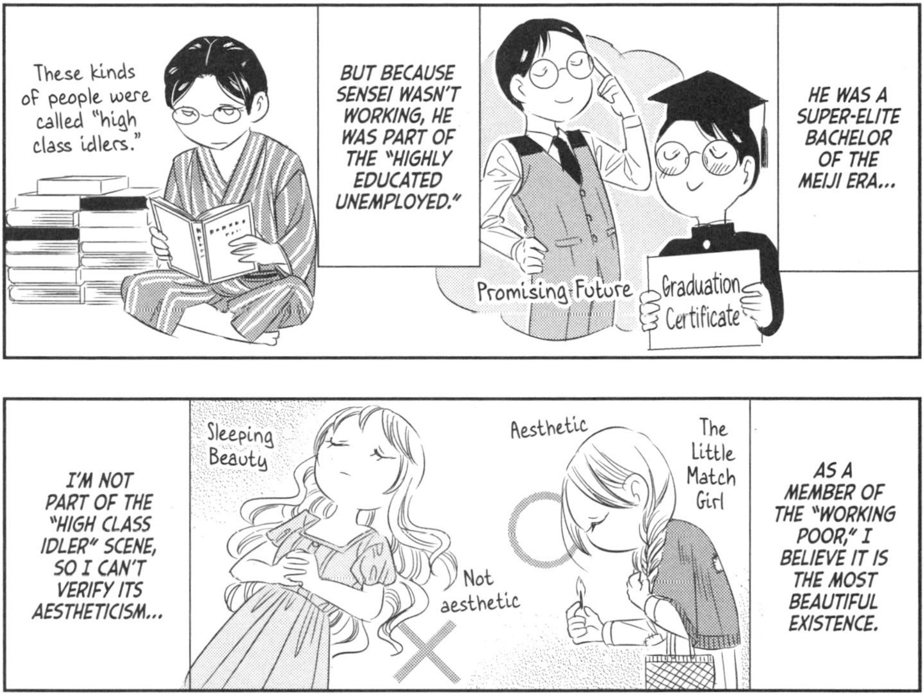
HE WAS A SUPER-ELITE BACHELOR OF THE MEIJI ERA...
Graduation Certificate
Promising Future
BUT BECAUSE SENSEI WASN'T WORKING, HE WAS PART OF THE "HIGHLY EDUCATED UNEMPLOYED."
These kinds of people were called "high class idlers."
AS A MEMBER OF THE "WORKING POOR," I BELIEVE IT IS THE MOST BEAUTIFUL EXISTENCE.
The Little Match Girl
Aesthetic
Not aesthetic
Sleeping Beauty
I'M NOT PART OF THE "HIGH CLASS IDLER" SCENE, SO I CAN'T VERIFY ITS AESTHETICISM...

• Home environment wasn't good. • Low education history.
• Not having a solid job. • Poor. • Living is hard. • Ephemeral thinking.
People for whom four or more of these are applicable are aesthetic, aren't they?

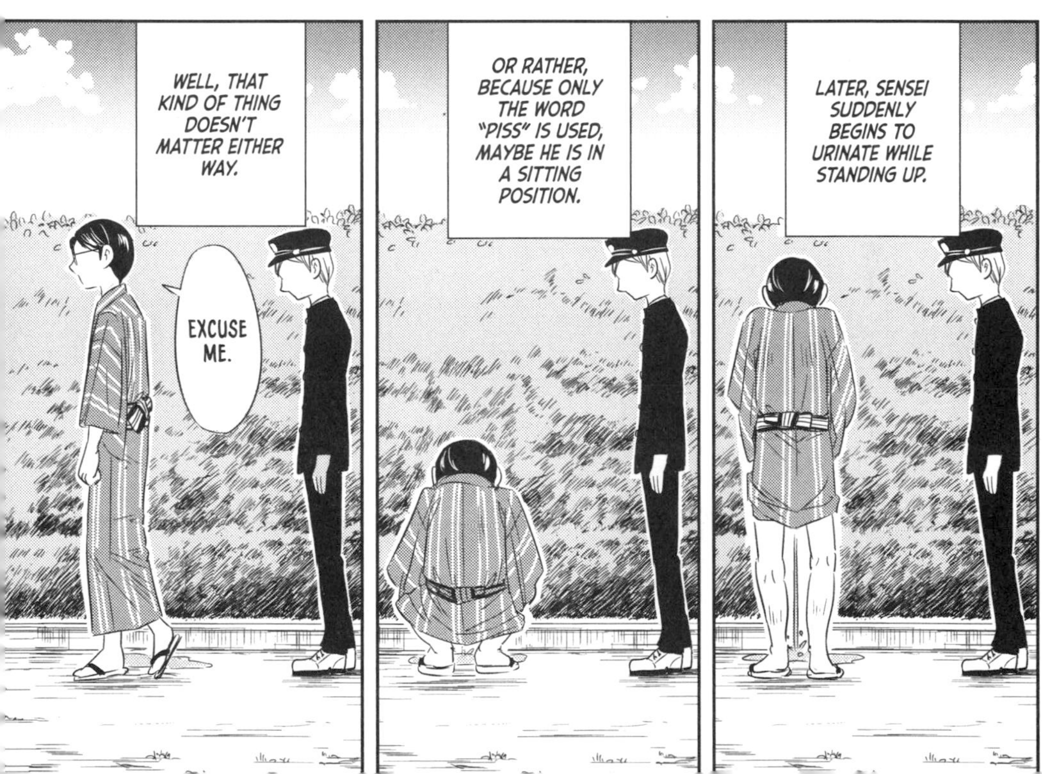
LATER, SENSEI SUDDENLY BEGINS TO URINATE WHILE STANDING UP.
OR RATHER, BECAUSE ONLY THE WORD "PISS" IS USED, MAYBE HE IS IN A SITTING POSITION.
WELL, THAT KIND OF THING DOESN'T MATTER EITHER WAY.
EXCUSE ME.

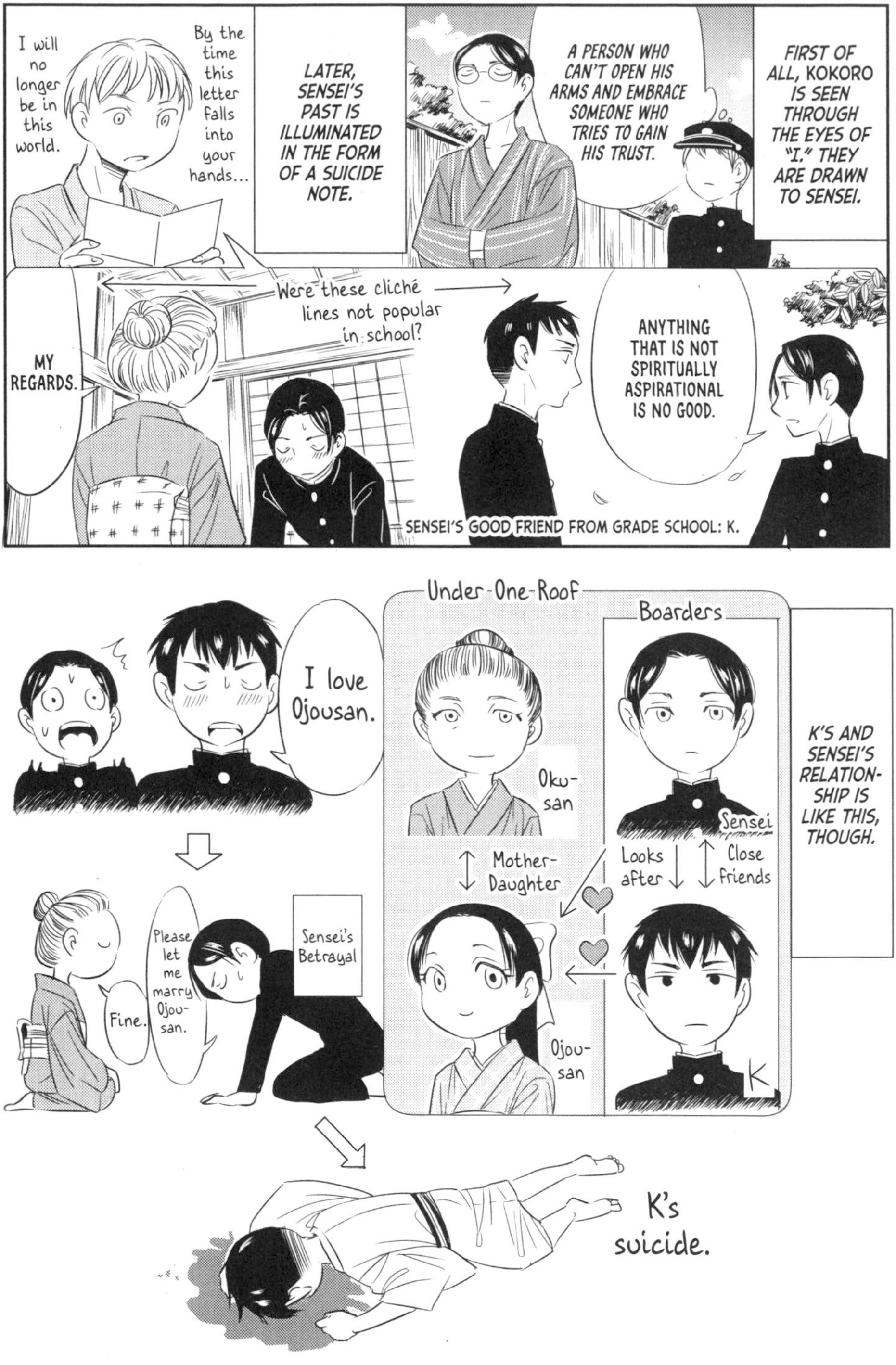
FIRST OF ALL, KOKORO IS SEEN THROUGH THE EYES OF "I." THEY ARE DRAWN TO SENSEI.
A PERSON WHO CAN'T OPEN HIS ARMS AND EMBRACE SOMEONE WHO TRIES TO GAIN HIS TRUST.
LATER, SENSEI'S PAST IS ILLUMINATED IN THE FORM OF A SUICIDE NOTE.
By the time this letter falls into your hands...
I will no longer be in this world.
ANYTHING THAT IS NOT SPIRITUALLY ASPIRATIONAL IS NO GOOD.
SENSEI'S GOOD FRIEND FROM GRADE SCHOOL: K.
Were these cliché lines not popular in school?
MY REGARDS.
K'S AND SENSEI'S RELATIONSHIP IS LIKE THIS, THOUGH.
Under-One-Roof
Boarders
Sensei
Okusan
Looks after
Close friends
Mother-Daughter
Ojousan
K
I love Ojousan.
Sensei's Betrayal
Please let me marry Ojousan.
Fine.
K's suicide.

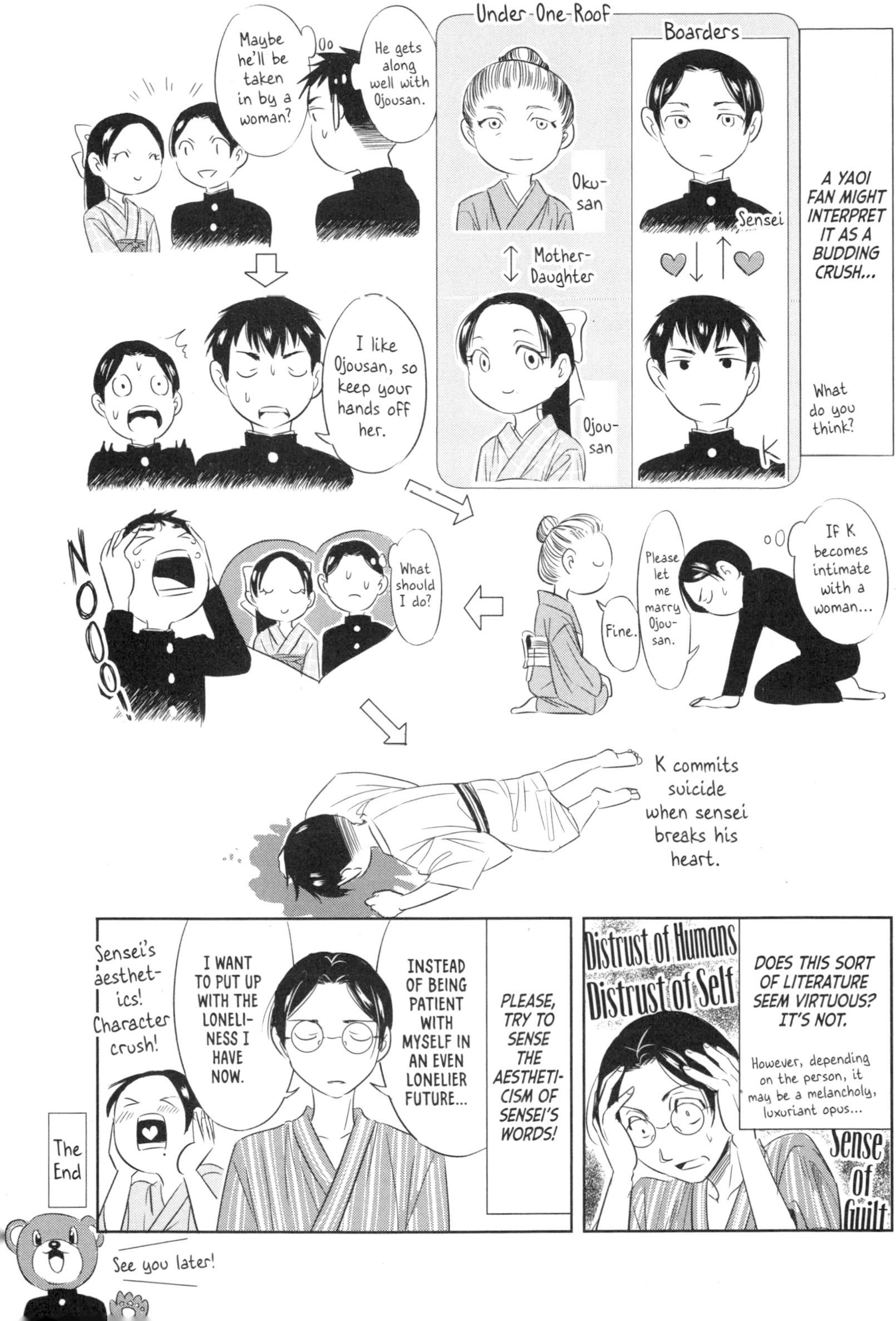
A YAOI FAN MIGHT INTERPRET IT AS A BUDDING CRUSH...
What do you think?
Under-One-Roof
Boarders
Sensei
K
Oku-san
Mother-Daughter
Ojou-san
He gets along well with Ojousan.
Maybe he'll be taken in by a woman?
I like Ojousan, so keep your hands off her.
If K becomes intimate with a woman...
Please let me marry Ojou-san.
Fine.
What should I do?
NOOOO
K commits suicide when sensei breaks his heart.
Distrust of Humans
Distrust of Self
DOES THIS SORT OF LITERATURE SEEM VIRTUOUS? IT'S NOT.
However, depending on the person, it may be a melancholy, luxuriant opus...
Sense of Guilt
PLEASE, TRY TO SENSE THE AESTHETICISM OF SENSEI'S WORDS!
INSTEAD OF BEING PATIENT WITH MYSELF IN AN EVEN LONELIER FUTURE...
I WANT TO PUT UP WITH THE LONELINESS I HAVE NOW.
Sensei's aesthetics! Character crush!
The End
See you later!

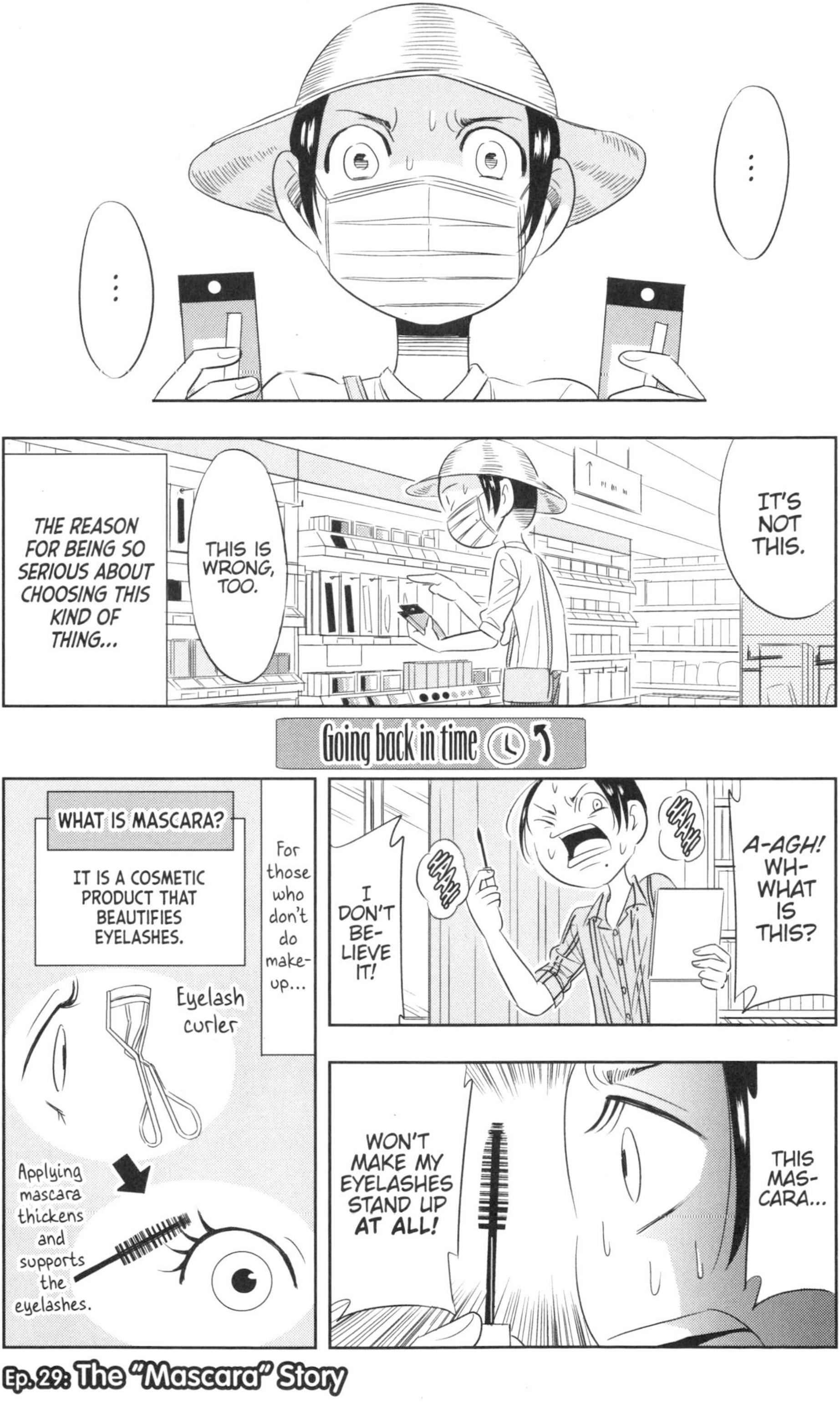
…
…
IT'S NOT THIS.
THIS IS WRONG, TOO.
THE REASON FOR BEING SO SERIOUS ABOUT CHOOSING THIS KIND OF THING...
Going back in time
A-AGH! WH-WHAT IS THIS?
HAAH
HAAH
I DON'T BE-LIEVE IT!
THIS MAS-CARA...
WON'T MAKE MY EYELASHES STAND UP AT ALL!
For those who don't do make-up...
WHAT IS MASCARA?
IT IS A COSMETIC PRODUCT THAT BEAUTIFIES EYELASHES.
Eyelash curler
Applying mascara thickens and supports the eyelashes.

Ep. 29: The "Mascara" Story

Makeup companies change their stock frequently, so suddenly your "usual" one will disappear.

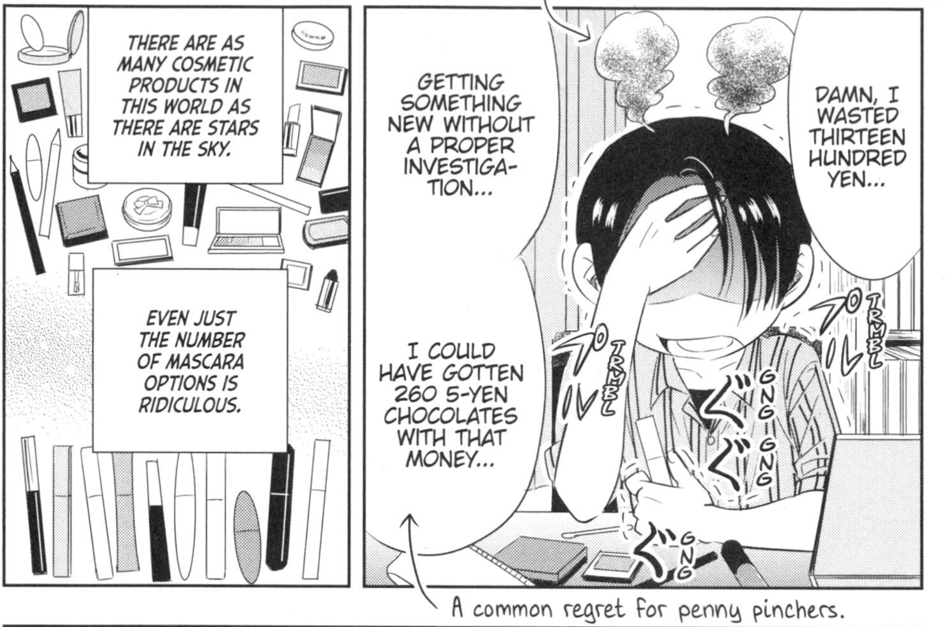
Intense resentment for elusive mascara.
DAMN, I WASTED THIRTEEN HUNDRED YEN...
GETTING SOMETHING NEW WITHOUT A PROPER INVESTIGATION...
I COULD HAVE GOTTEN 260 5-YEN CHOCOLATES WITH THAT MONEY...
TREMBL
TREMBL
GNG GNG
GNG
A common regret for penny pinchers.
THERE ARE AS MANY COSMETIC PRODUCTS IN THIS WORLD AS THERE ARE STARS IN THE SKY.
EVEN JUST THE NUMBER OF MASCARA OPTIONS IS RIDICULOUS.

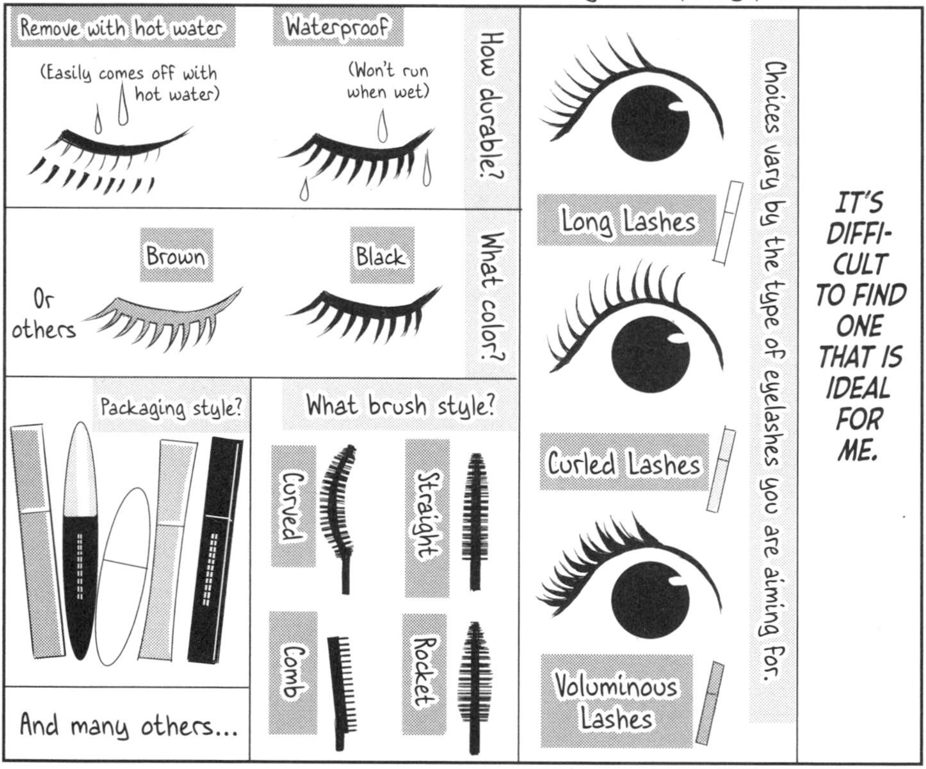
IT'S DIFFICULT TO FIND ONE THAT IS IDEAL FOR ME.
Choices vary by the type of eyelashes you are aiming for.
Long Lashes
Curled Lashes
Voluminous Lashes
How durable?
Waterproof
(Won't run when wet)
Remove with hot water
(Easily comes off with hot water)
What color?
Black
Brown
Or others
What brush style?
Straight
Curved
Rocket
Comb
Packaging style?
And many others...

Information that doesn't matter:
Miyazaki is, in general, looking for black, waterproof, curling mascara!

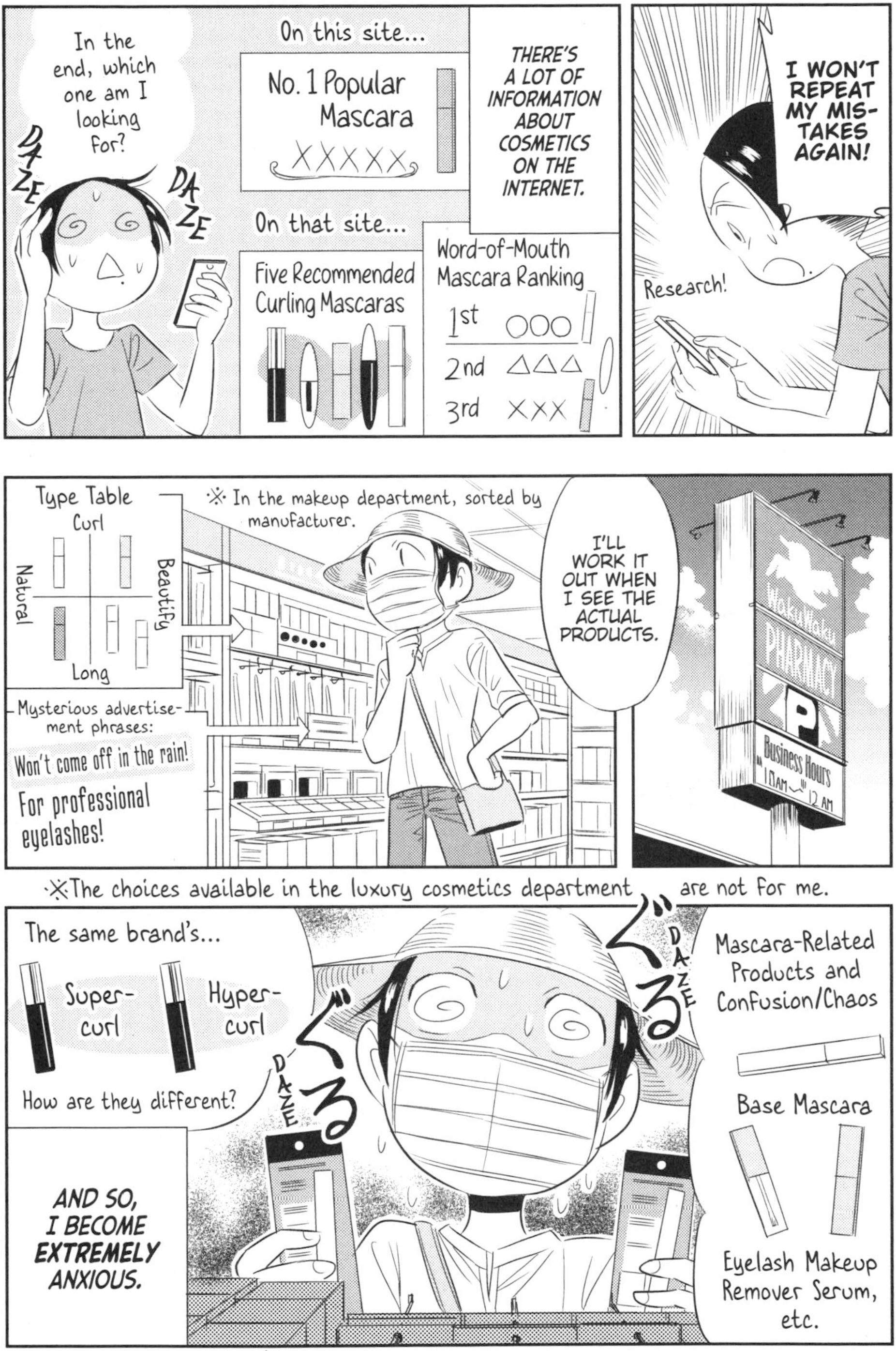
I WON'T REPEAT MY MISTAKES AGAIN!
Research!
In the end, which one am I looking for?
DAZE
DAZE
On this site...
No. 1 Popular Mascara
XXXXX
THERE'S A LOT OF INFORMATION ABOUT COSMETICS ON THE INTERNET.
On that site...
Five Recommended Curling Mascaras
Word-of-Mouth Mascara Ranking
1st ○○○
2nd △△△
3rd ×××
WakuWaku PHARMACY
P
Business Hours 11 AM ~ 12 AM
I'LL WORK IT OUT WHEN I SEE THE ACTUAL PRODUCTS.
※ In the makeup department, sorted by manufacturer.
Type Table
Curl
Natural
Beautify
Long
Mysterious advertisement phrases:
Won't come off in the rain!
For professional eyelashes!
※The choices available in the luxury cosmetics department are not for me.
Mascara-Related Products and Confusion/Chaos
Base Mascara
Eyelash Makeup Remover Serum, etc.
DAZE
DAZE
The same brand's...
Super-curl
Hyper-curl
How are they different?
AND SO, I BECOME EXTREMELY ANXIOUS.

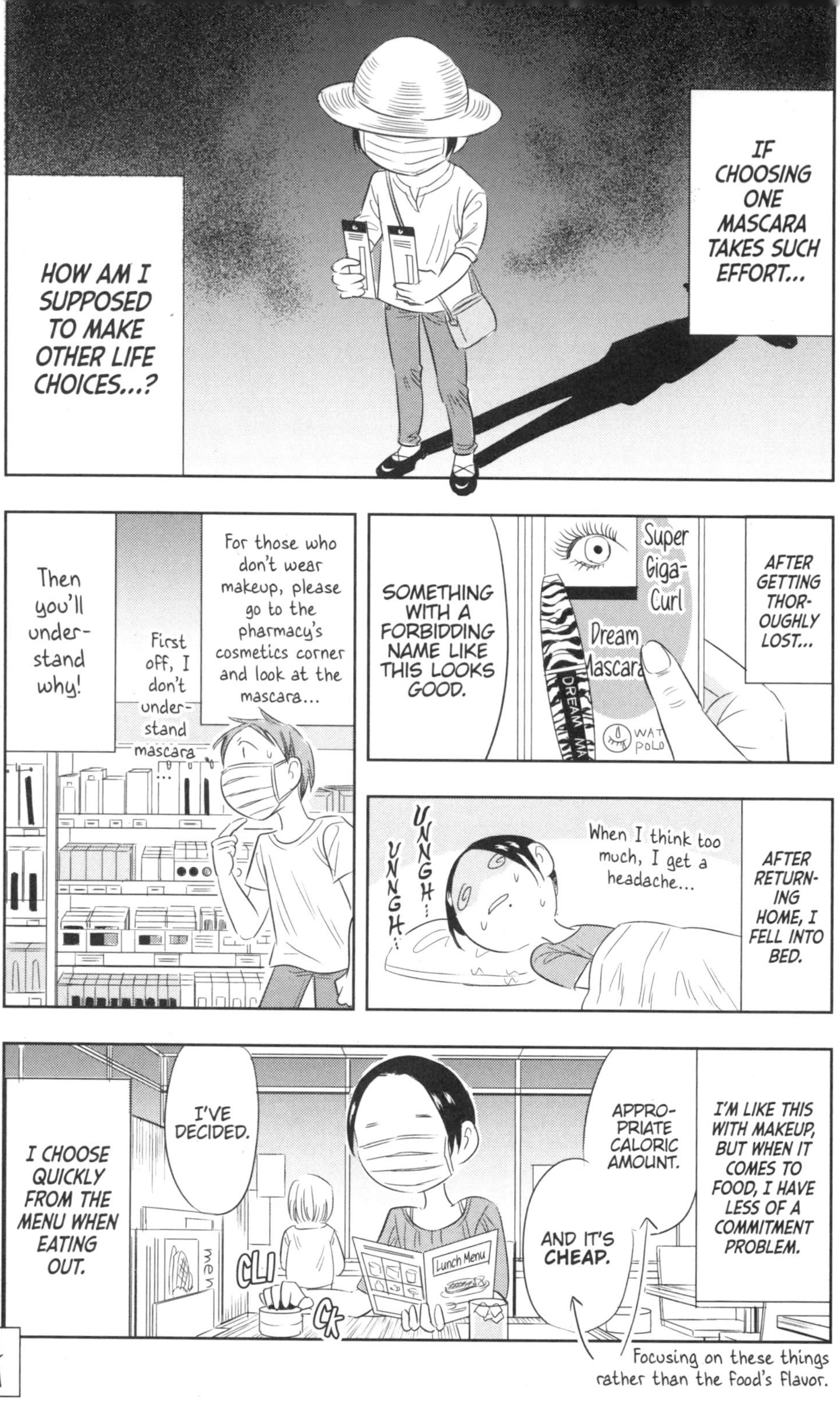

IF CHOOSING ONE MASCARA TAKES SUCH EFFORT...
HOW AM I SUPPOSED TO MAKE OTHER LIFE CHOICES...?
AFTER GETTING THOROUGHLY LOST...
Super Giga-Curl
Dream Mascara
SOMETHING WITH A FORBIDDING NAME LIKE THIS LOOKS GOOD.
AFTER RETURNING HOME, I FELL INTO BED.
When I think too much, I get a headache...
UNNGH...
UNNGH...
For those who don't wear makeup, please go to the pharmacy's cosmetics corner and look at the mascara...
First off, I don't understand mascara
Then you'll understand why!
I'M LIKE THIS WITH MAKEUP, BUT WHEN IT COMES TO FOOD, I HAVE LESS OF A COMMITMENT PROBLEM.
APPROPRIATE CALORIC AMOUNT.
I'VE DECIDED.
AND IT'S CHEAP.
Lunch Menu
I CHOOSE QUICKLY FROM THE MENU WHEN EATING OUT.
CLI
CK
Focusing on these things rather than the food's flavor.

Ep. 30: The "Refresh!" Story

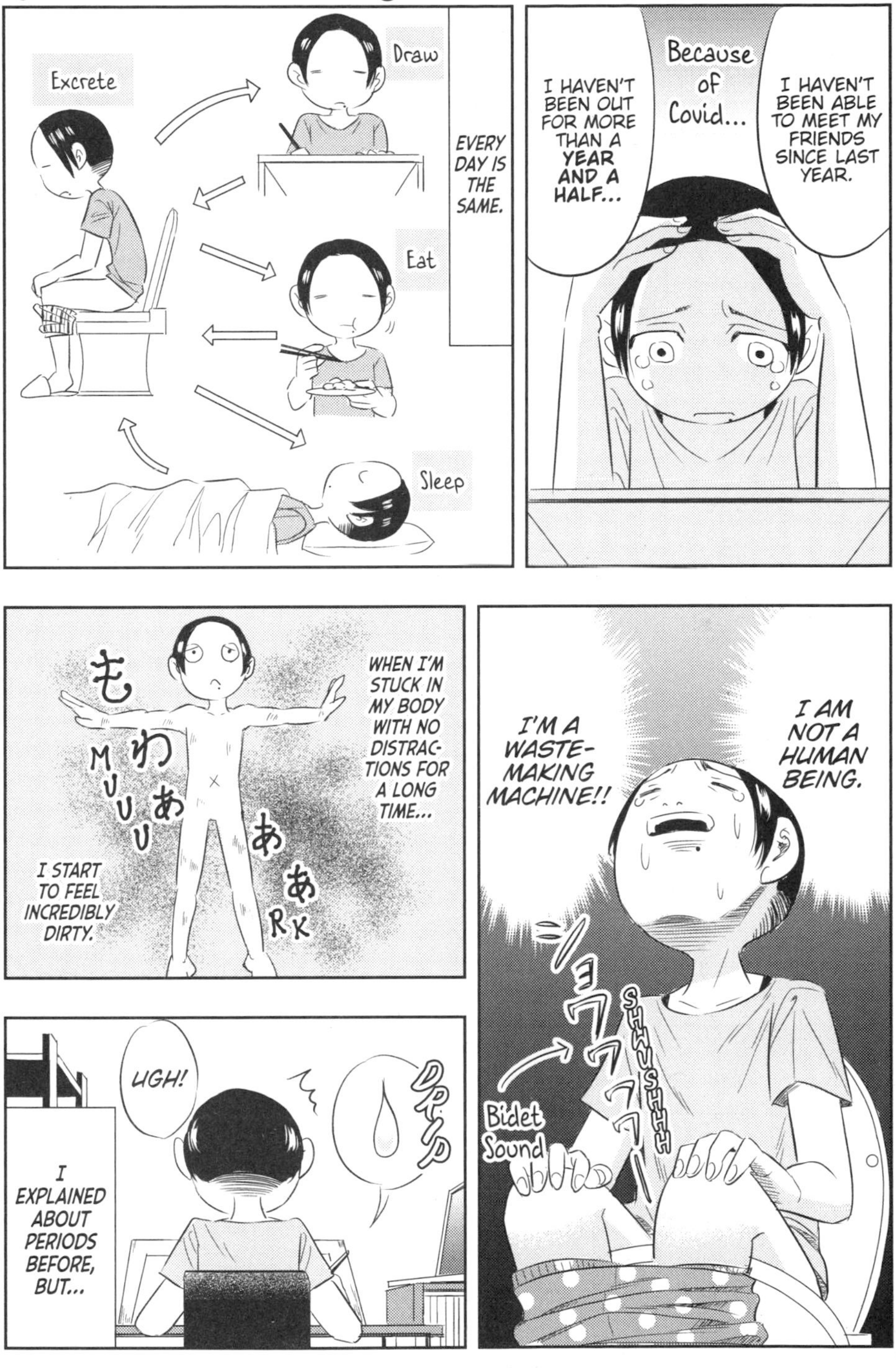
I HAVEN'T BEEN ABLE TO MEET MY FRIENDS SINCE LAST YEAR.
Because of Covid...
I HAVEN'T BEEN OUT FOR MORE THAN A YEAR AND A HALF...
EVERY DAY IS THE SAME.
Draw
Excrete
Eat
Sleep
I AM NOT A HUMAN BEING.
I'M A WASTE-MAKING MACHINE!!
SHWUSHHH
ショワワワー
Bidet Sound
WHEN I'M STUCK IN MY BODY WITH NO DISTRACTIONS FOR A LONG TIME...
もわあああ
MUUURK
I START TO FEEL INCREDIBLY DIRTY.
DRIP
UGH!
I EXPLAINED ABOUT PERIODS BEFORE, BUT...

Reference: X-Gender Volume 1, Episode 8, "The 'I Want to Teach You About Periods' Story"

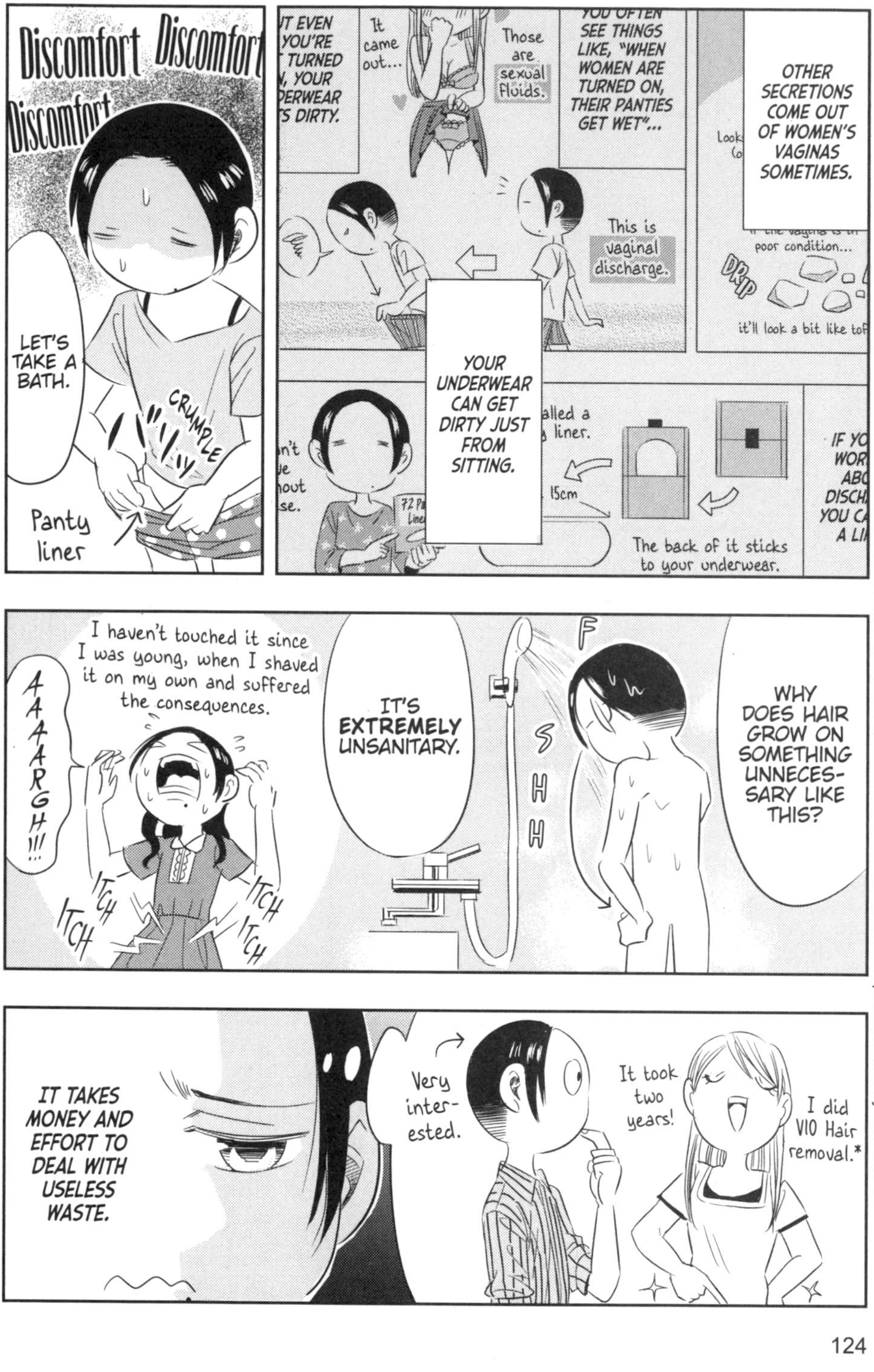

OTHER SECRETIONS COME OUT OF WOMEN'S VAGINAS SOMETIMES.
poor condition...
DRIP
it'll look a bit like tof
YOU OFTEN SEE THINGS LIKE, "WHEN WOMEN ARE TURNED ON, THEIR PANTIES GET WET"...
Those are sexual fluids.
It came out...
This is vaginal discharge.
YOUR UNDERWEAR CAN GET DIRTY JUST FROM SITTING.
The back of it sticks to your underwear.
15cm
Discomfort Discomfort Discomfort
LET'S TAKE A BATH.
CRUMPLE
Panty liner
WHY DOES HAIR GROW ON SOMETHING UNNECES-SARY LIKE THIS?
F SHH
IT'S EXTREMELY UNSANITARY.
I haven't touched it since I was young, when I shaved it on my own and suffered the consequences.
AAAARGH!!!
ITCH ITCH ITCH ITCH
I did VIO Hair removal.*
It took two years!
Very inter-ested.
IT TAKES MONEY AND EFFORT TO DEAL WITH USELESS WASTE.

*V-line/I-line/O-line. In other words, hair removal from the parts hidden by underwear.

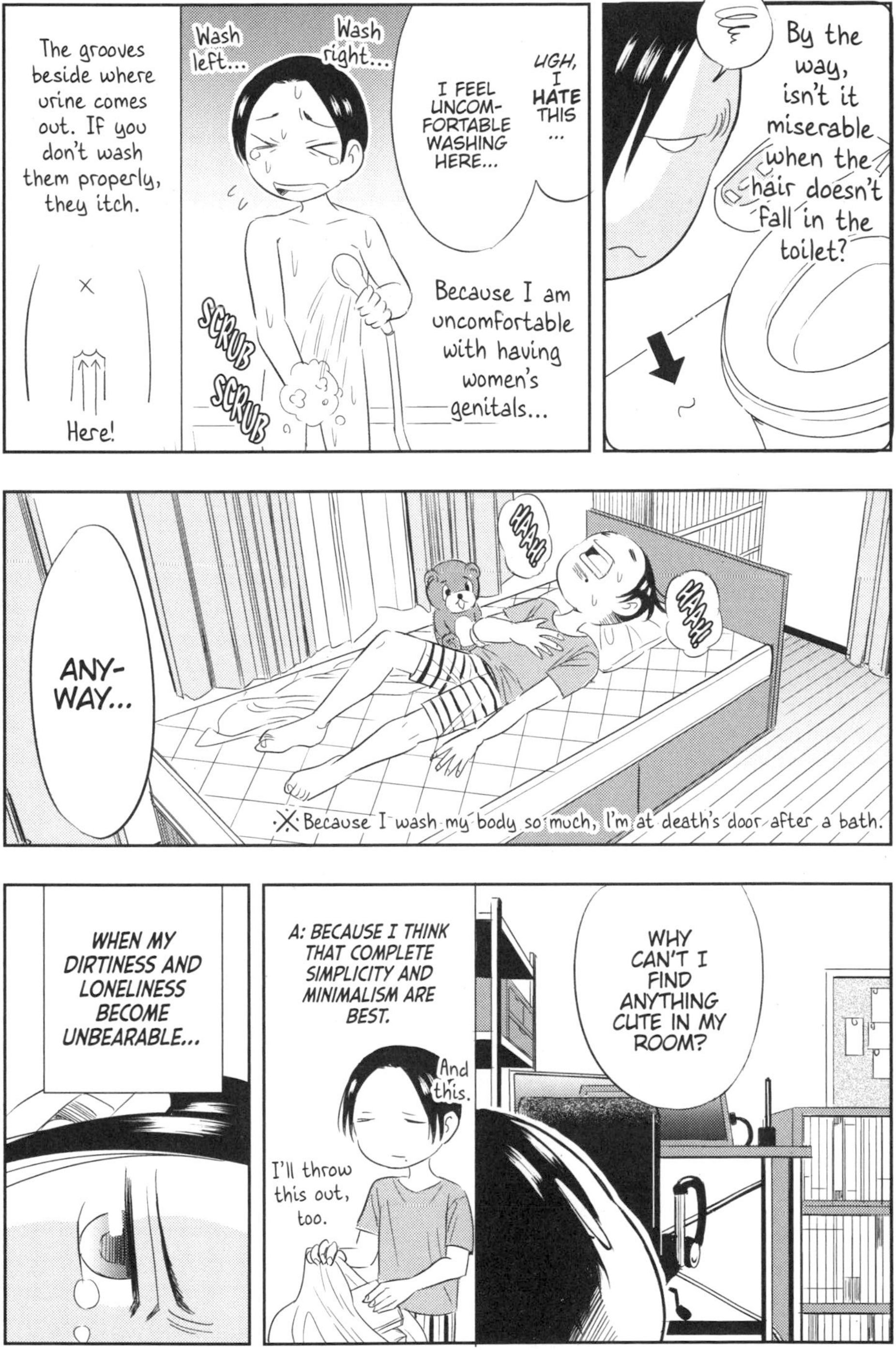

By the way, isn't it miserable when the hair doesn't fall in the toilet?
UGH, I HATE THIS...
I FEEL UNCOMFORTABLE WASHING HERE...
Wash right...
Wash left...
SCRUB SCRUB
Because I am uncomfortable with having women's genitals...
The grooves beside where urine comes out. If you don't wash them properly, they itch.
Here!
HAAH!
HAAH!
ANY-WAY...
※Because I wash my body so much, I'm at death's door after a bath.
WHY CAN'T I FIND ANYTHING CUTE IN MY ROOM?
A: BECAUSE I THINK THAT COMPLETE SIMPLICITY AND MINIMALISM ARE BEST.
And this.
I'll throw this out, too.
WHEN MY DIRTINESS AND LONELINESS BECOME UNBEARABLE...

It seems that men have difficulty washing, too...

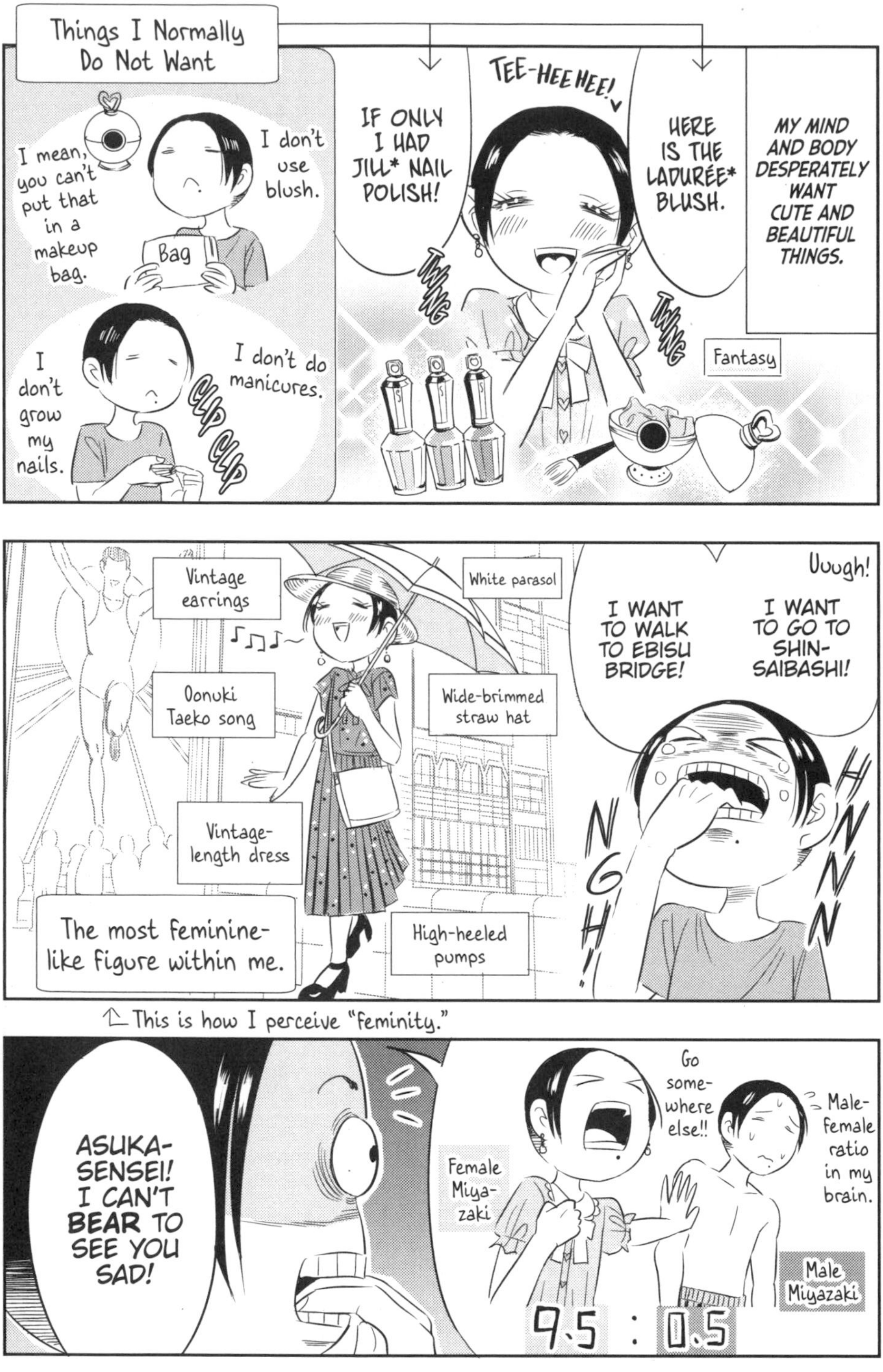

MY MIND AND BODY DESPERATELY WANT CUTE AND BEAUTIFUL THINGS.
TEE-HEE HEE!
HERE IS THE LADURÉE* BLUSH.
IF ONLY I HAD JILL* NAIL POLISH!
TWING
TWING
Fantasy
Things I Normally Do Not Want
I don't use blush.
I mean, you can't put that in a makeup bag.
Bag
I don't do manicures.
I don't grow my nails.
CLIP CLIP
Uuugh!
I WANT TO GO TO SHIN-SAIBASHI!
I WANT TO WALK TO EBISU BRIDGE!
HNNNN
NGH!!
White parasol
Vintage earrings
♪♫♪~
Wide-brimmed straw hat
Oonuki Taeko song
Vintage-length dress
High-heeled pumps
The most feminine-like figure within me.
This is how I perceive "feminity."
Male-female ratio in my brain.
Go somewhere else!!
Female Miyazaki
Male Miyazaki
9.5 : 0.5
ASUKA-SENSEI! I CAN'T BEAR TO SEE YOU SAD!

※Les Merveilleuses Ladurée. A French cosmetics brand. Their blush is the cutest in the world. Probably.

※Jill Stuart. Cosmetics brand. The cutest nail polish bottle in the world. Probably.

Note: When I can't stand the loneliness, I begin to have conversations with my stuffed animals.

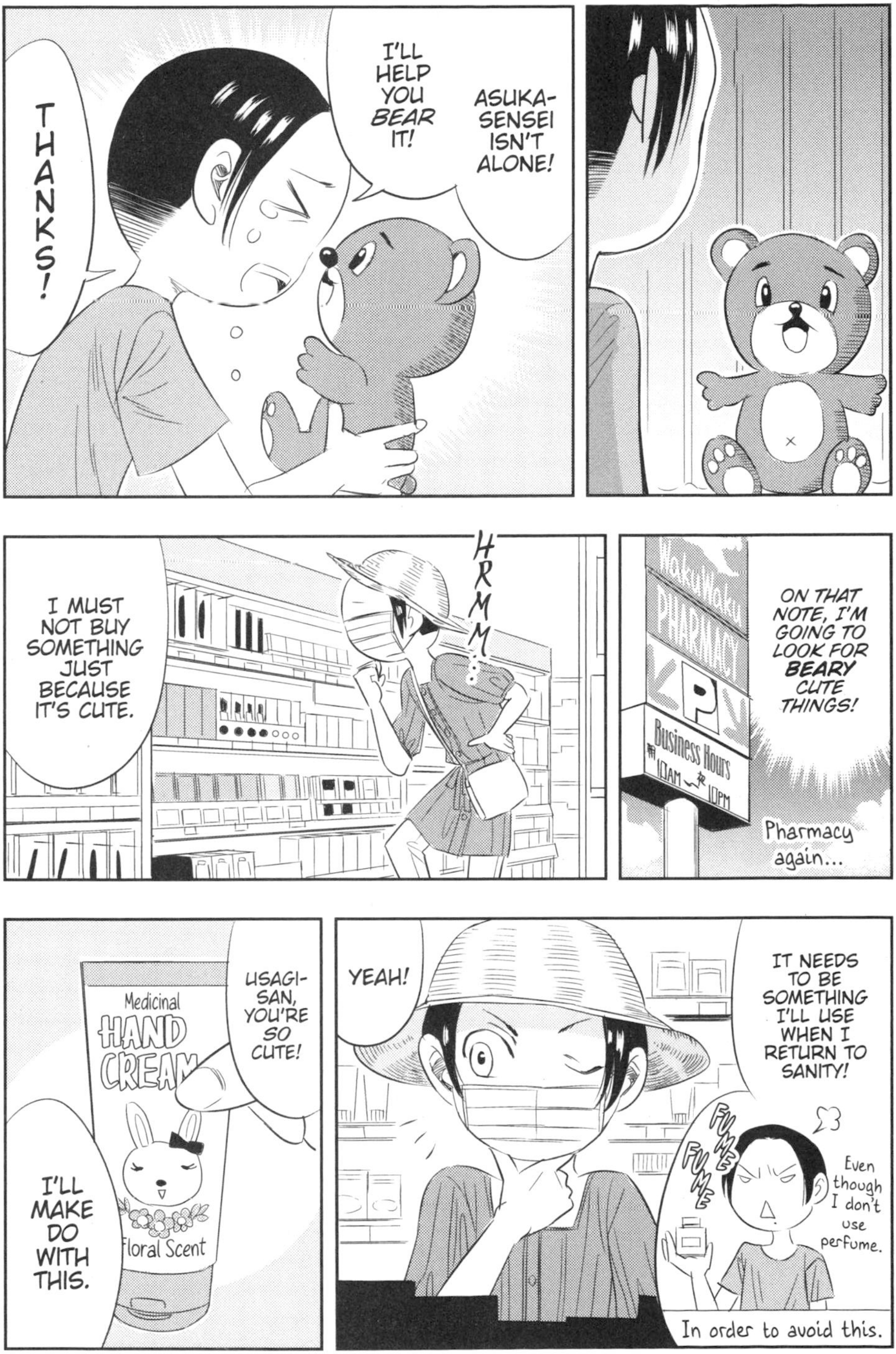
ASUKA-SENSEI ISN'T ALONE!
I'LL HELP YOU BEAR IT!
THANKS!
ON THAT NOTE, I'M GOING TO LOOK FOR **BEARY** CUTE THINGS!
WakuWaku PHARMACY
Business Hours
10AM 10PM
Pharmacy again...
HRMM...
I MUST NOT BUY SOMETHING JUST BECAUSE IT'S CUTE.
IT NEEDS TO BE SOMETHING I'LL USE WHEN I RETURN TO SANITY!
FUME FUME
Even though I don't use perfume.
In order to avoid this.
YEAH!
USAGI-SAN, YOU'RE SO CUTE!
Medicinal HAND CREAM
Floral Scent
I'LL MAKE DO WITH THIS.

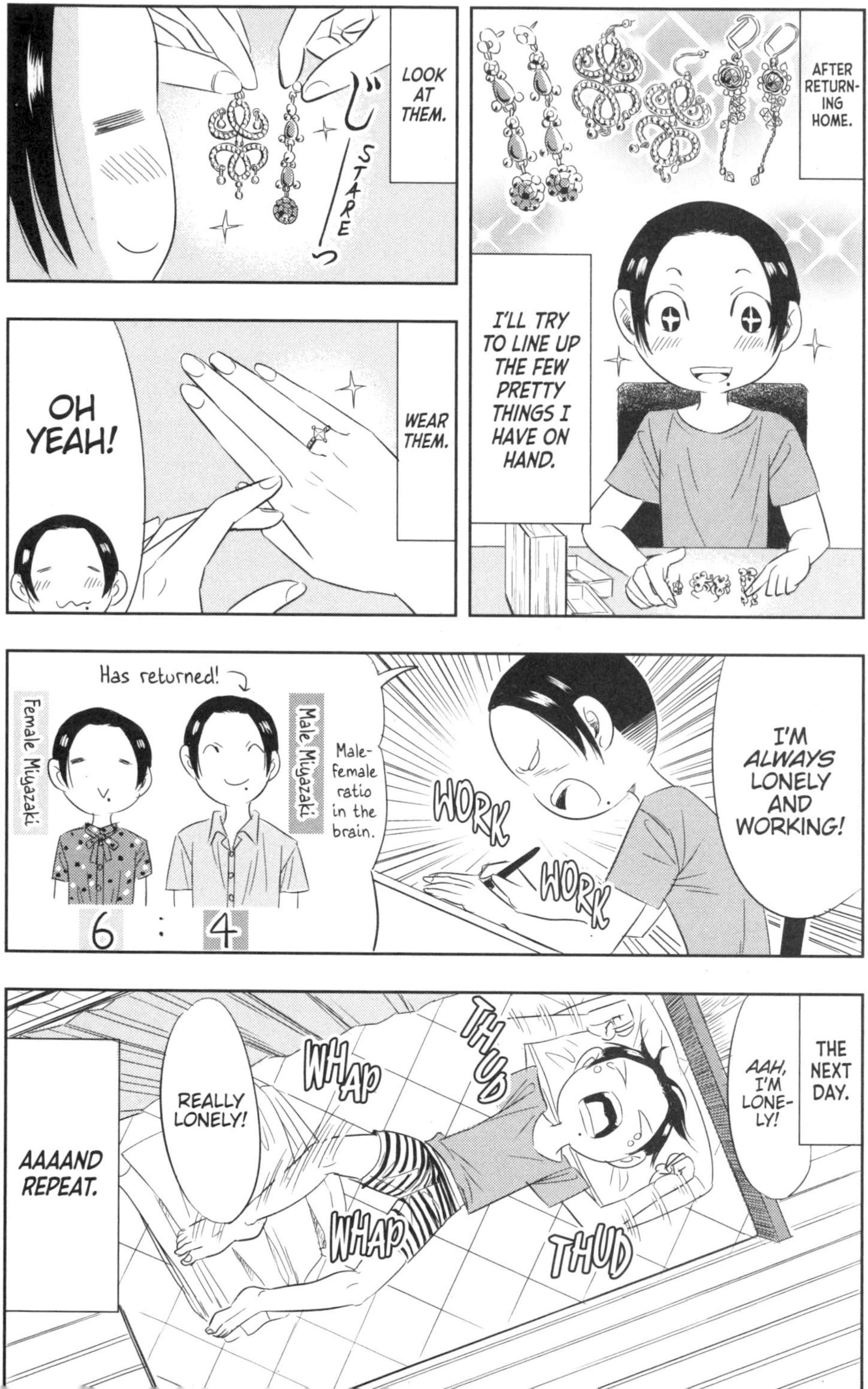
AFTER RETURNING HOME.
I'LL TRY TO LINE UP THE FEW PRETTY THINGS I HAVE ON HAND.
LOOK AT THEM.
STARE
WEAR THEM.
OH YEAH!
I'M ALWAYS LONELY AND WORKING!
WORK
WORK
Male-female ratio in the brain.
Male Miyazaki
Has returned!
Female Miyazaki
6 : 4
THE NEXT DAY.
AAH, I'M LONELY!
THUD
WHAP
REALLY LONELY!
THUD
WHAP
AAAAND REPEAT.

Ep. 31: The "Sleeping" Story

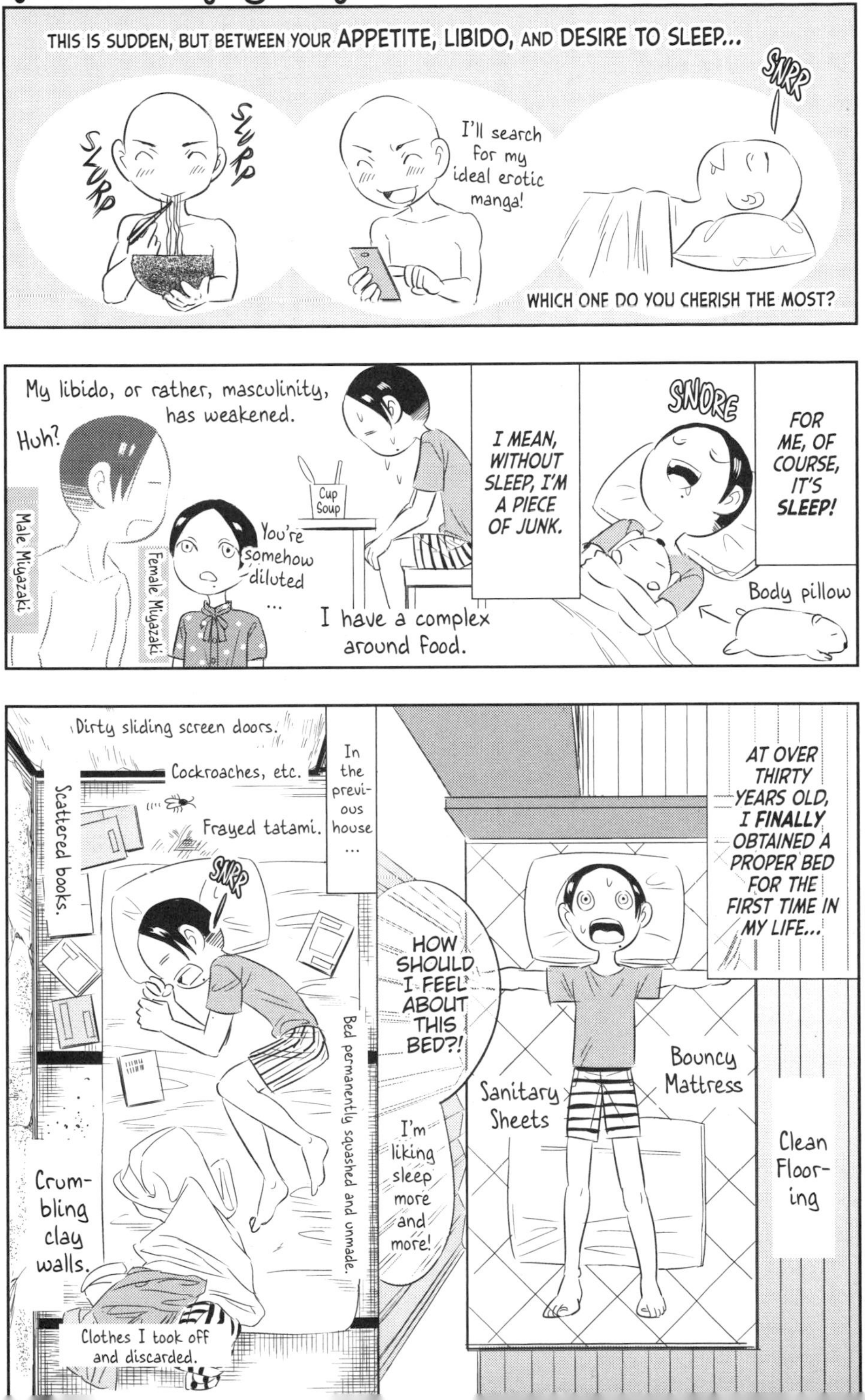
THIS IS SUDDEN, BUT BETWEEN YOUR APPETITE, LIBIDO, AND DESIRE TO SLEEP...
SNRR
I'll search for my ideal erotic manga!
SLURP
SLURP
WHICH ONE DO YOU CHERISH THE MOST?
SNORE
FOR ME, OF COURSE, IT'S SLEEP!
Body pillow
I MEAN, WITHOUT SLEEP, I'M A PIECE OF JUNK.
My libido, or rather, masculinity, has weakened.
Huh?
Cup Soup
Male Miyazaki
Female Miyazaki
You're somehow diluted ...
I have a complex around food.
AT OVER THIRTY YEARS OLD, I FINALLY OBTAINED A PROPER BED FOR THE FIRST TIME IN MY LIFE...
HOW SHOULD I FEEL ABOUT THIS BED?!
Bouncy Mattress
Sanitary Sheets
Clean Flooring
I'm liking sleep more and more!
In the previous house ...
Dirty sliding screen doors.
Cockroaches, etc.
Frayed tatami.
Scattered books.
SNRR
Bed permanently squashed and unmade.
Crumbling clay walls.
Clothes I took off and discarded.

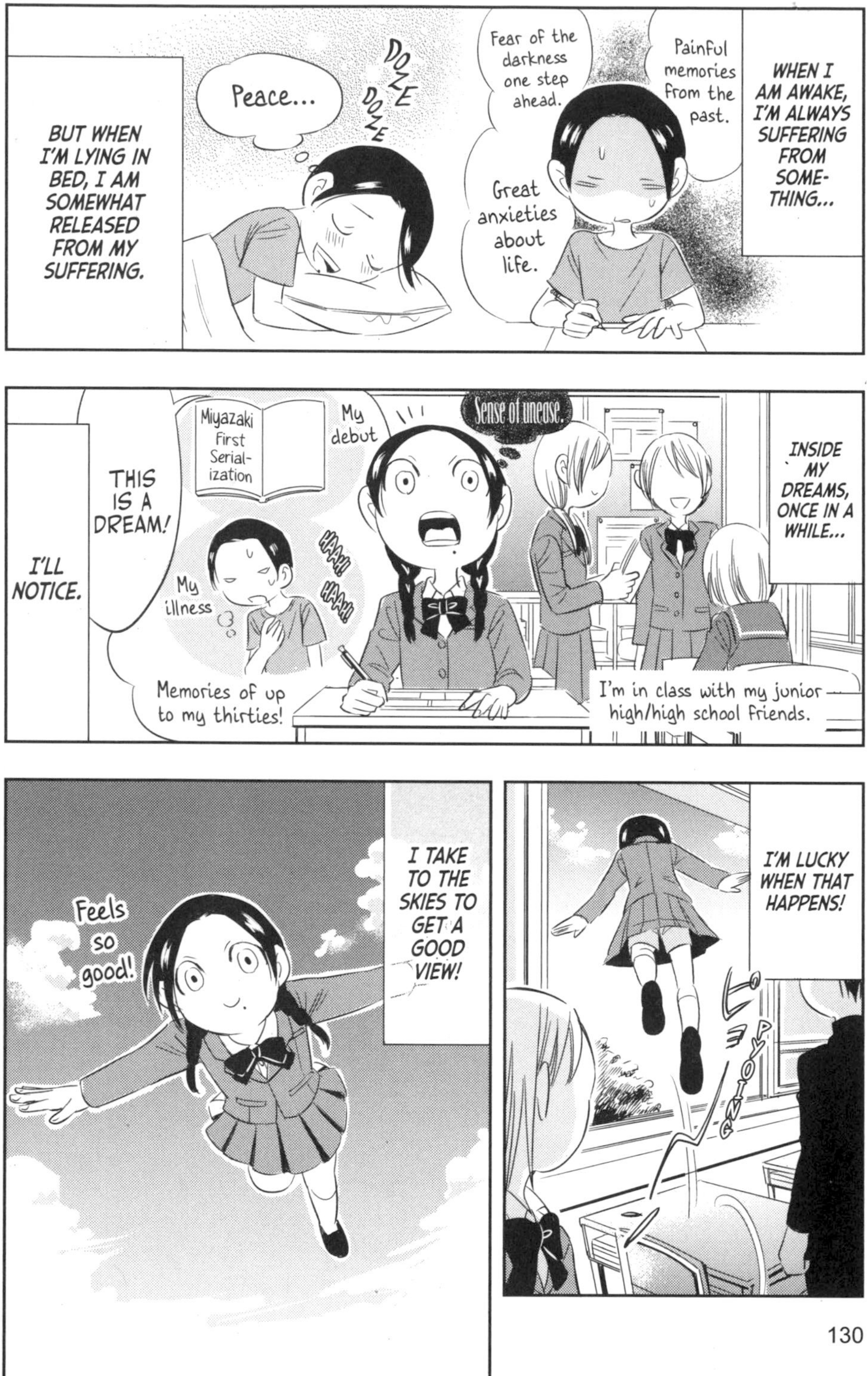
WHEN I AM AWAKE, I'M ALWAYS SUFFERING FROM SOME-THING...
Painful memories from the past.
Fear of the darkness one step ahead.
Great anxieties about life.
DOZE DOZE
Peace...
BUT WHEN I'M LYING IN BED, I AM SOMEWHAT RELEASED FROM MY SUFFERING.
INSIDE MY DREAMS, ONCE IN A WHILE...
Sense of unease.
I'm in class with my junior high/high school friends.
My debut
Miyazaki First Serial-ization
HAAH HAAH
My illness
Memories of up to my thirties!
THIS IS A DREAM!
I'LL NOTICE.
I'M LUCKY WHEN THAT HAPPENS!
PYOING
I TAKE TO THE SKIES TO GET A GOOD VIEW!
Feels so good!

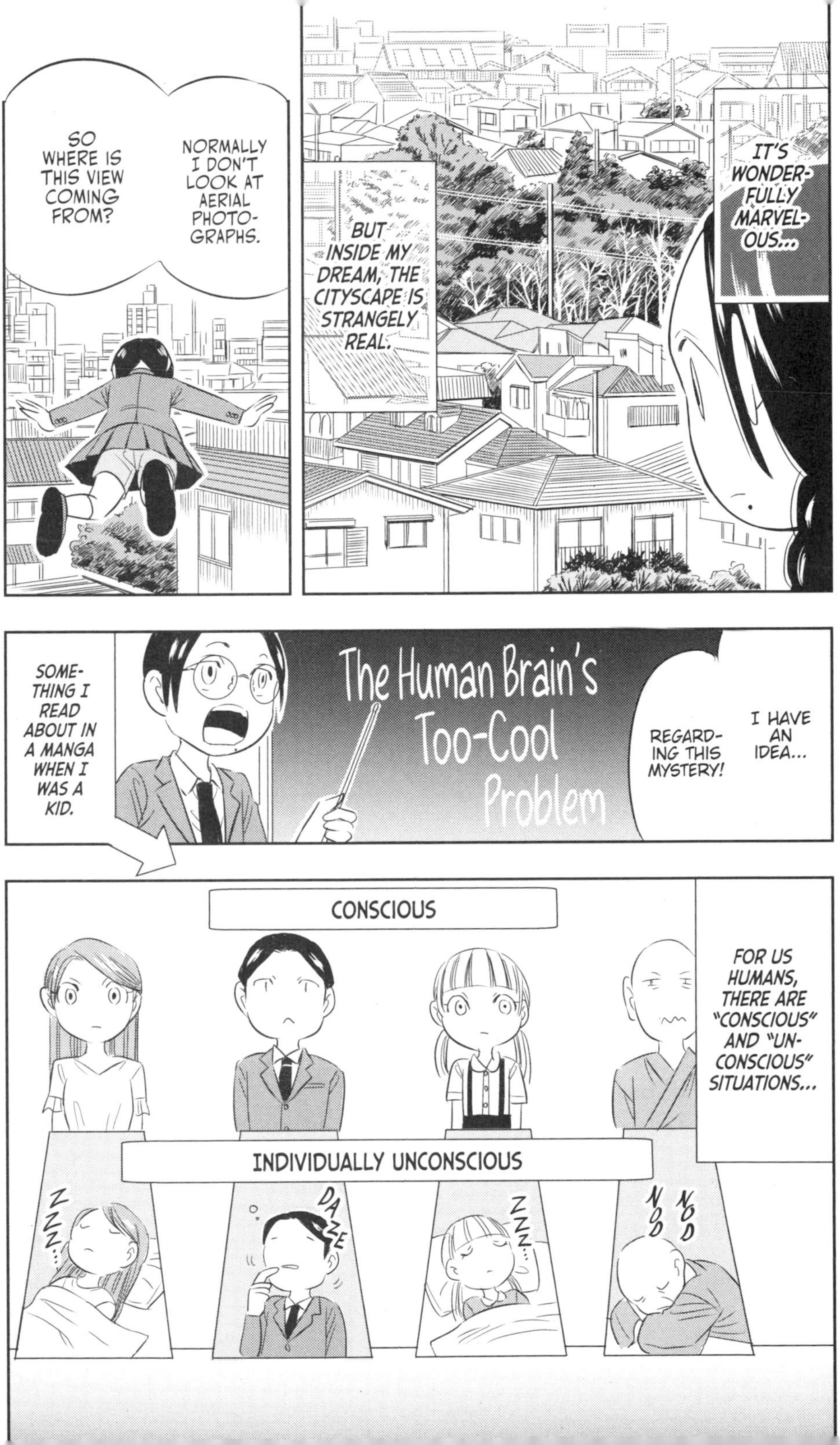
IT'S WONDERFULLY MARVELOUS...
BUT INSIDE MY DREAM, THE CITYSCAPE IS STRANGELY REAL.
NORMALLY I DON'T LOOK AT AERIAL PHOTOGRAPHS.
SO WHERE IS THIS VIEW COMING FROM?
I HAVE AN IDEA...
REGARDING THIS MYSTERY!
The Human Brain's Too-Cool Problem
SOMETHING I READ ABOUT IN A MANGA WHEN I WAS A KID.
FOR US HUMANS, THERE ARE "CONSCIOUS" AND "UNCONSCIOUS" SITUATIONS...
CONSCIOUS
INDIVIDUALLY UNCONSCIOUS
NOD NOD
ZZZ...
DAZE
ZZZ...

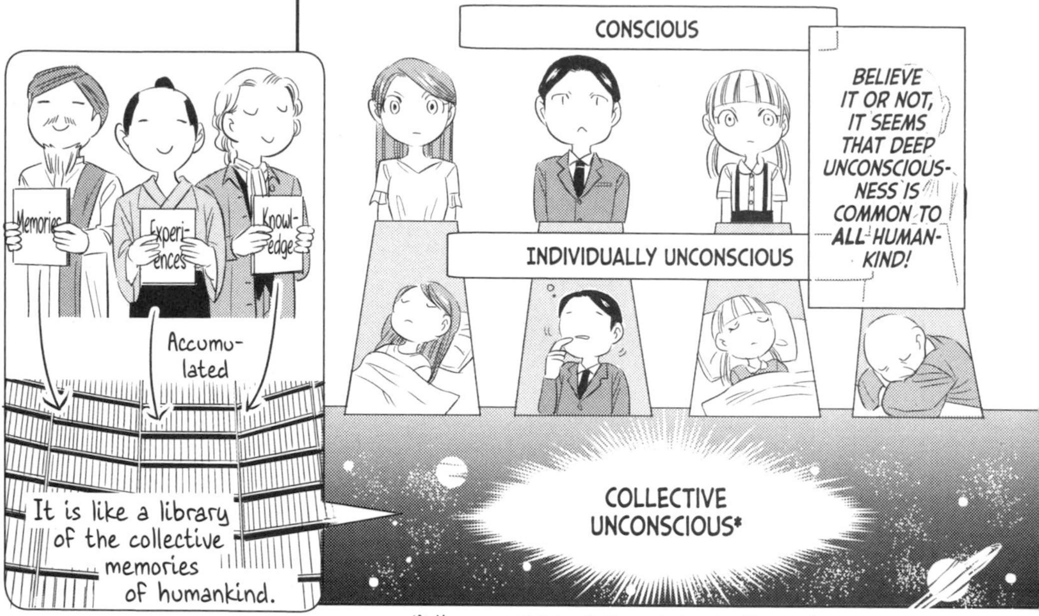
CONSCIOUS
BELIEVE IT OR NOT, IT SEEMS THAT DEEP UNCONSCIOUSNESS IS COMMON TO ALL HUMANKIND!
INDIVIDUALLY UNCONSCIOUS
COLLECTIVE UNCONSCIOUS*
Memories
Experiences
Knowledge
Accumulated
It is like a library of the collective memories of humankind.

·※ You can think of it as being half-occult.

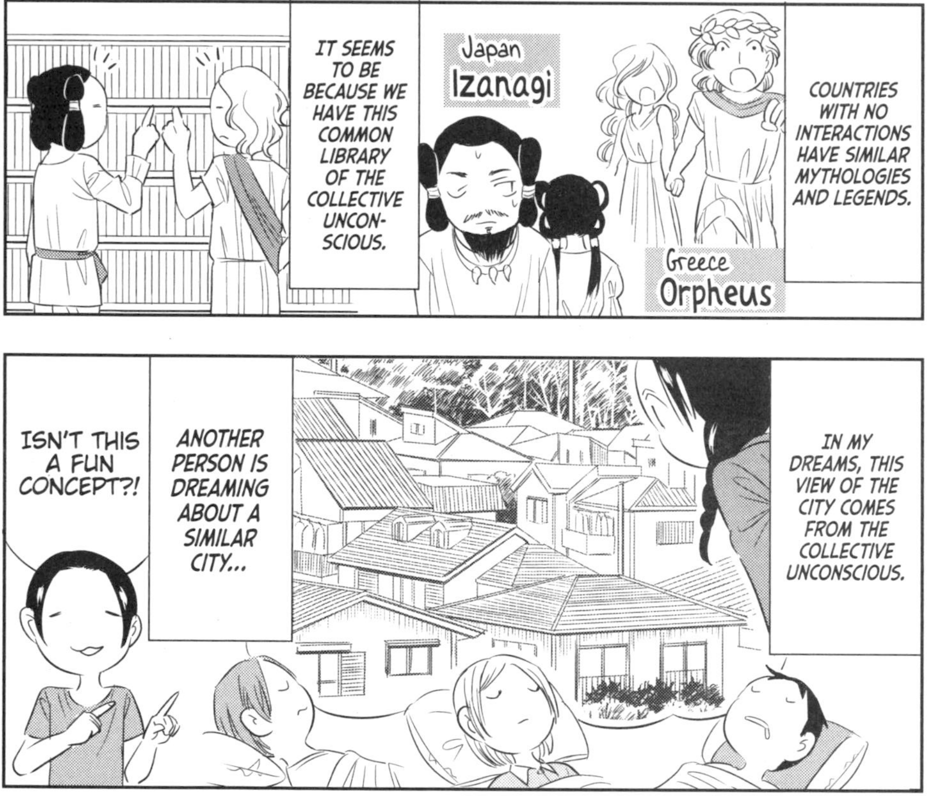
COUNTRIES WITH NO INTERACTIONS HAVE SIMILAR MYTHOLOGIES AND LEGENDS.
Greece Orpheus
Japan Izanagi
IT SEEMS TO BE BECAUSE WE HAVE THIS COMMON LIBRARY OF THE COLLECTIVE UNCONSCIOUS.
IN MY DREAMS, THIS VIEW OF THE CITY COMES FROM THE COLLECTIVE UNCONSCIOUS.
ANOTHER PERSON IS DREAMING ABOUT A SIMILAR CITY...
ISN'T THIS A FUN CONCEPT?!

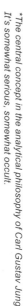

*The central concept in the analytical philosophy of Carl Gustav Jung. It's somewhat serious, somewhat occult.

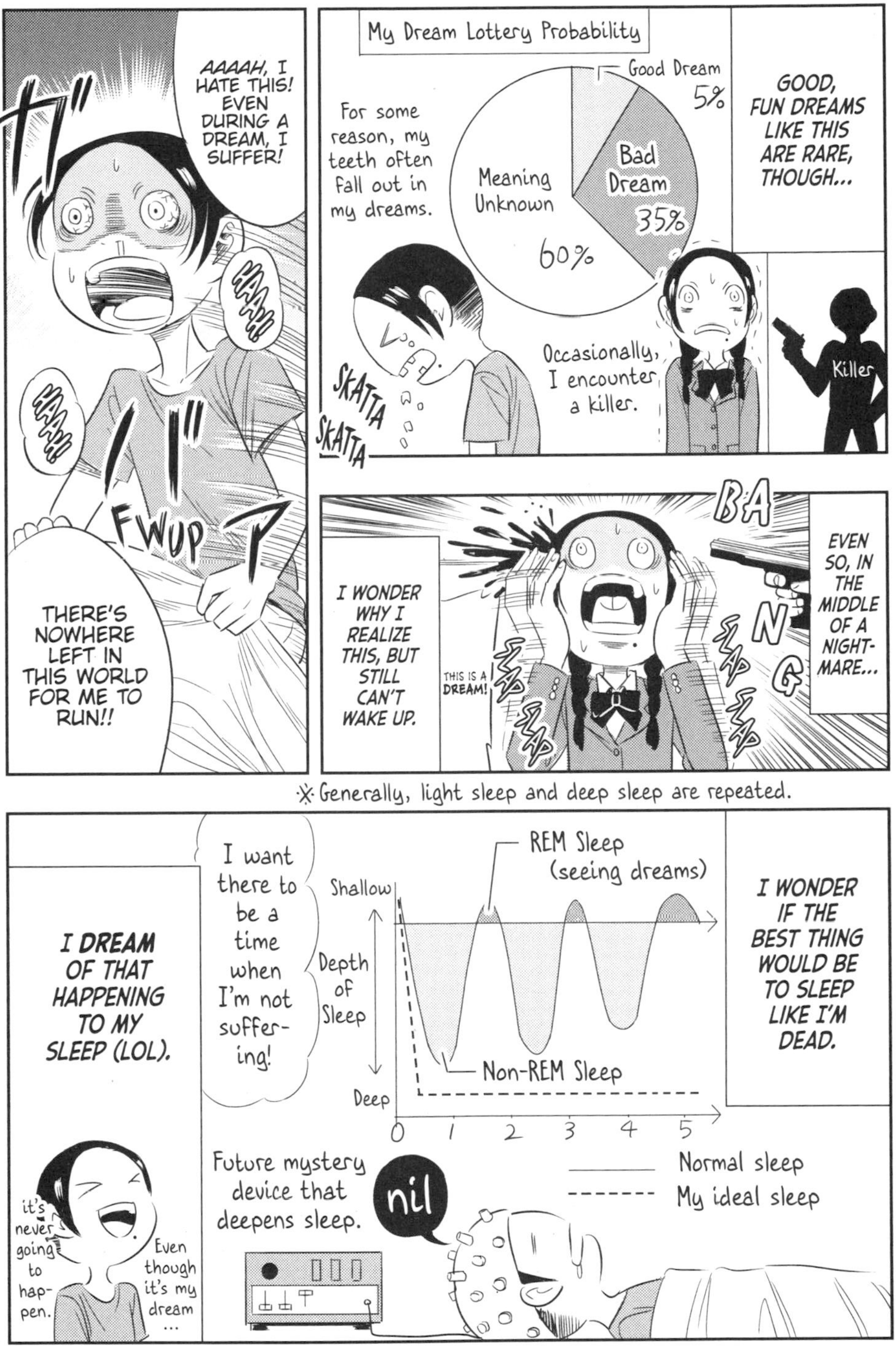
GOOD, FUN DREAMS LIKE THIS ARE RARE, THOUGH...
My Dream Lottery Probability
Good Dream 5%
Bad Dream 35%
Meaning Unknown 60%
Occasionally, I encounter a killer.
Killer
For some reason, my teeth often fall out in my dreams.
SKATTA
SKATTA
EVEN SO, IN THE MIDDLE OF A NIGHT-MARE...
BANG
SLAP SLAP
SLAP SLAP
THIS IS A DREAM!
I WONDER WHY I REALIZE THIS, BUT STILL CAN'T WAKE UP.
AAAAH, I HATE THIS! EVEN DURING A DREAM, I SUFFER!
FWUP
THERE'S NOWHERE LEFT IN THIS WORLD FOR ME TO RUN!!
※Generally, light sleep and deep sleep are repeated.
I WONDER IF THE BEST THING WOULD BE TO SLEEP LIKE I'M DEAD.
REM Sleep (seeing dreams)
Shallow
Depth of Sleep
Deep
Non-REM Sleep
0 1 2 3 4 5
Normal sleep
My ideal sleep
I want there to be a time when I'm not suffer-ing!
I DREAM OF THAT HAPPENING TO MY SLEEP (LOL).
nil
Future mystery device that deepens sleep.
Even though it's my dream...
it's never going to hap-pen.

That's all! Occult-loving Miyazaki, signing off!

Ep. 32: The "In Order to Die Peacefully" Story

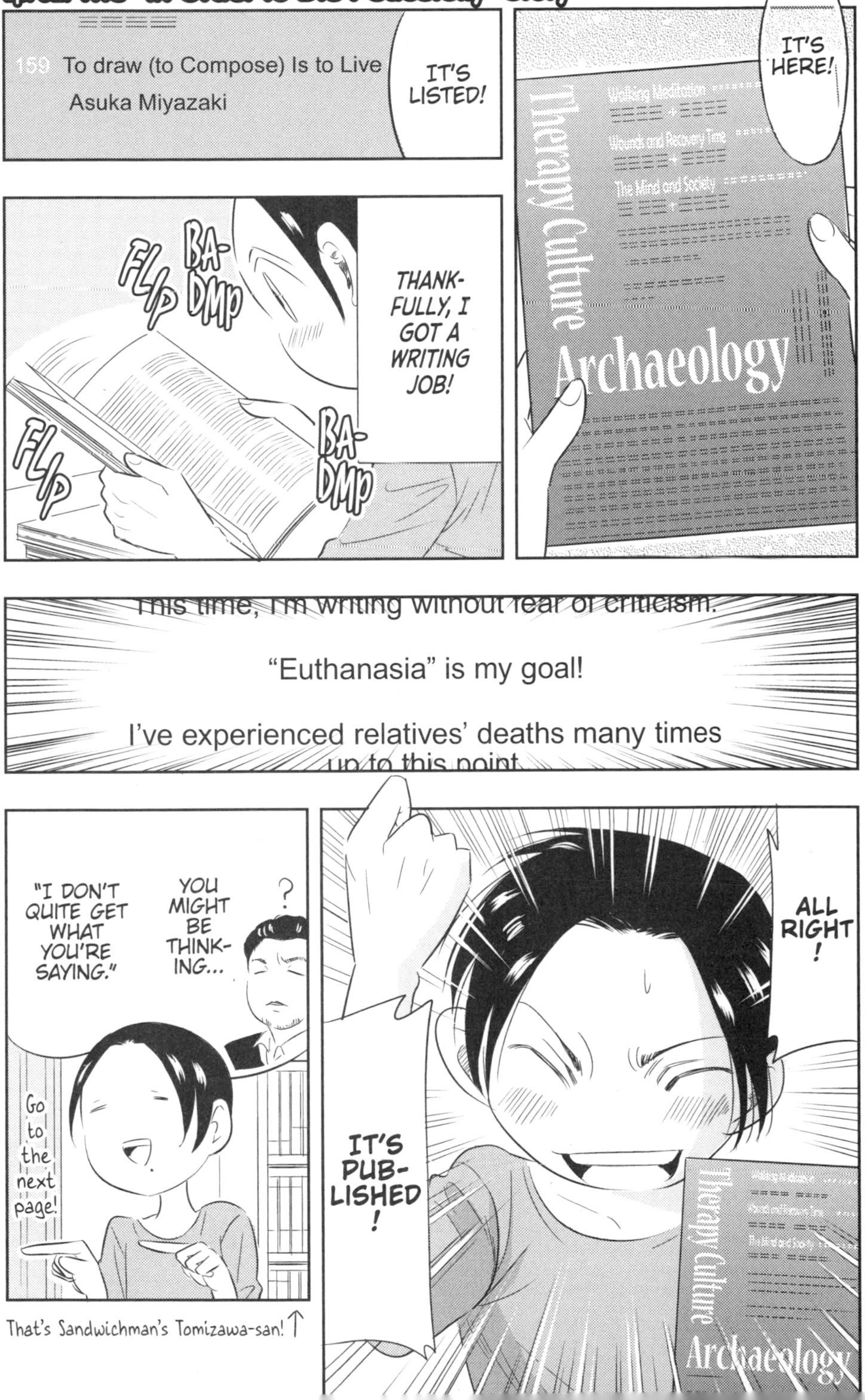
IT'S HERE!
Therapy Culture Archaeology
Walking Meditation
Wounds and Recovery Time
The Mind and Society
159 To draw (to Compose) Is to Live
Asuka Miyazaki
IT'S LISTED!
FLIP
BA-DMP
THANKFULLY, I GOT A WRITING JOB!
FLIP
BA-DMP
This time, I'm writing without fear of criticism.
"Euthanasia" is my goal!
I've experienced relatives' deaths many times up to this point.
ALL RIGHT!
IT'S PUBLISHED!
Therapy Culture Archaeology
YOU MIGHT BE THINKING...
?
"I DON'T QUITE GET WHAT YOU'RE SAYING."
Go to the next page!
That's Sandwichman's Tomizawa-san!

Clinical Psychology, Special Issue No. 13, "Therapy Culture Archaeology" (Kongo Publishing)

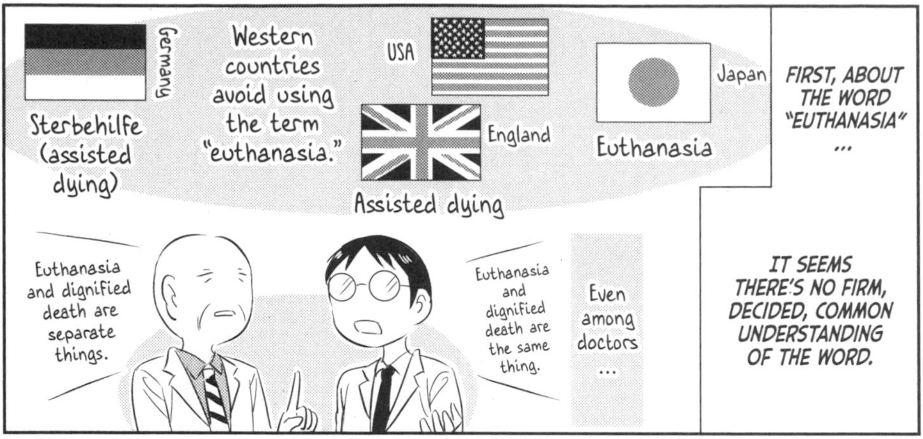
FIRST, ABOUT THE WORD "EUTHANASIA"...
Japan
Euthanasia
England
Assisted dying
USA
Western countries avoid using the term "euthanasia."
Germany
Sterbehilfe (assisted dying)
IT SEEMS THERE'S NO FIRM, DECIDED, COMMON UNDERSTANDING OF THE WORD.
Even among doctors...
Euthanasia and dignified death are the same thing.
Euthanasia and dignified death are separate things.

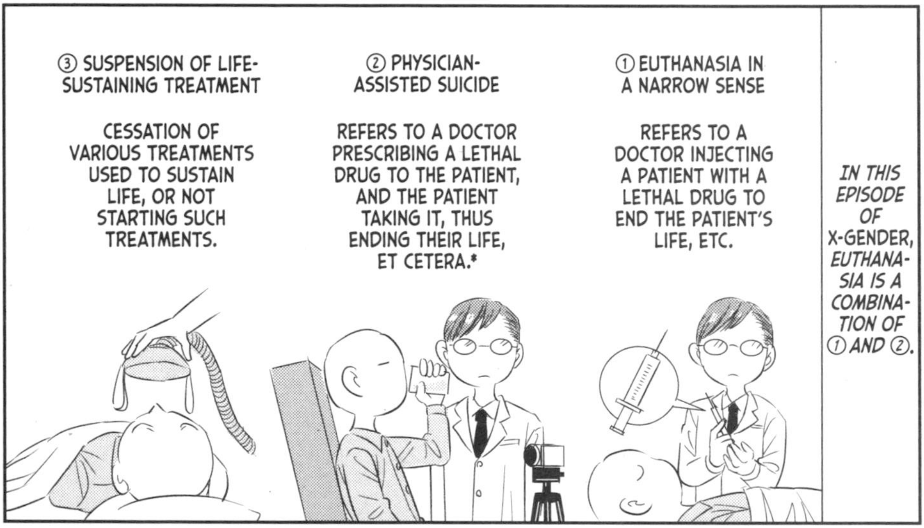
IN THIS EPISODE OF X-GENDER, EUTHANASIA IS A COMBINATION OF ① AND ②.
① EUTHANASIA IN A NARROW SENSE
REFERS TO A DOCTOR INJECTING A PATIENT WITH A LETHAL DRUG TO END THE PATIENT'S LIFE, ETC.
② PHYSICIAN-ASSISTED SUICIDE
REFERS TO A DOCTOR PRESCRIBING A LETHAL DRUG TO THE PATIENT, AND THE PATIENT TAKING IT, THUS ENDING THEIR LIFE, ET CETERA.*
③ SUSPENSION OF LIFE-SUSTAINING TREATMENT
CESSATION OF VARIOUS TREATMENTS USED TO SUSTAIN LIFE, OR NOT STARTING SUCH TREATMENTS.

I will use *Current Status of Euthanasia and Dying with Dignity* by Matsuda Jun (Chuuko Shinso) as a reference.

**The reason I wrote "et cetera" was because some forms of the drug aren't "taken."*

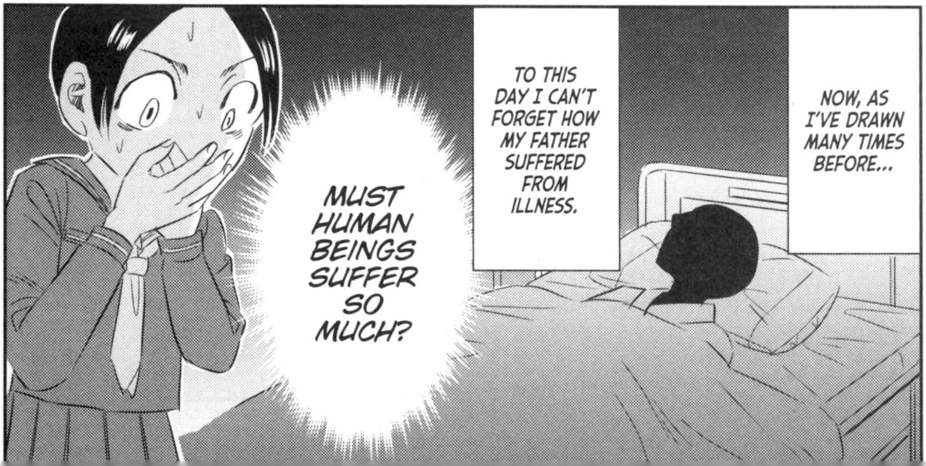
NOW, AS I'VE DRAWN MANY TIMES BEFORE...
TO THIS DAY I CAN'T FORGET HOW MY FATHER SUFFERED FROM ILLNESS.
MUST HUMAN BEINGS SUFFER SO MUCH?

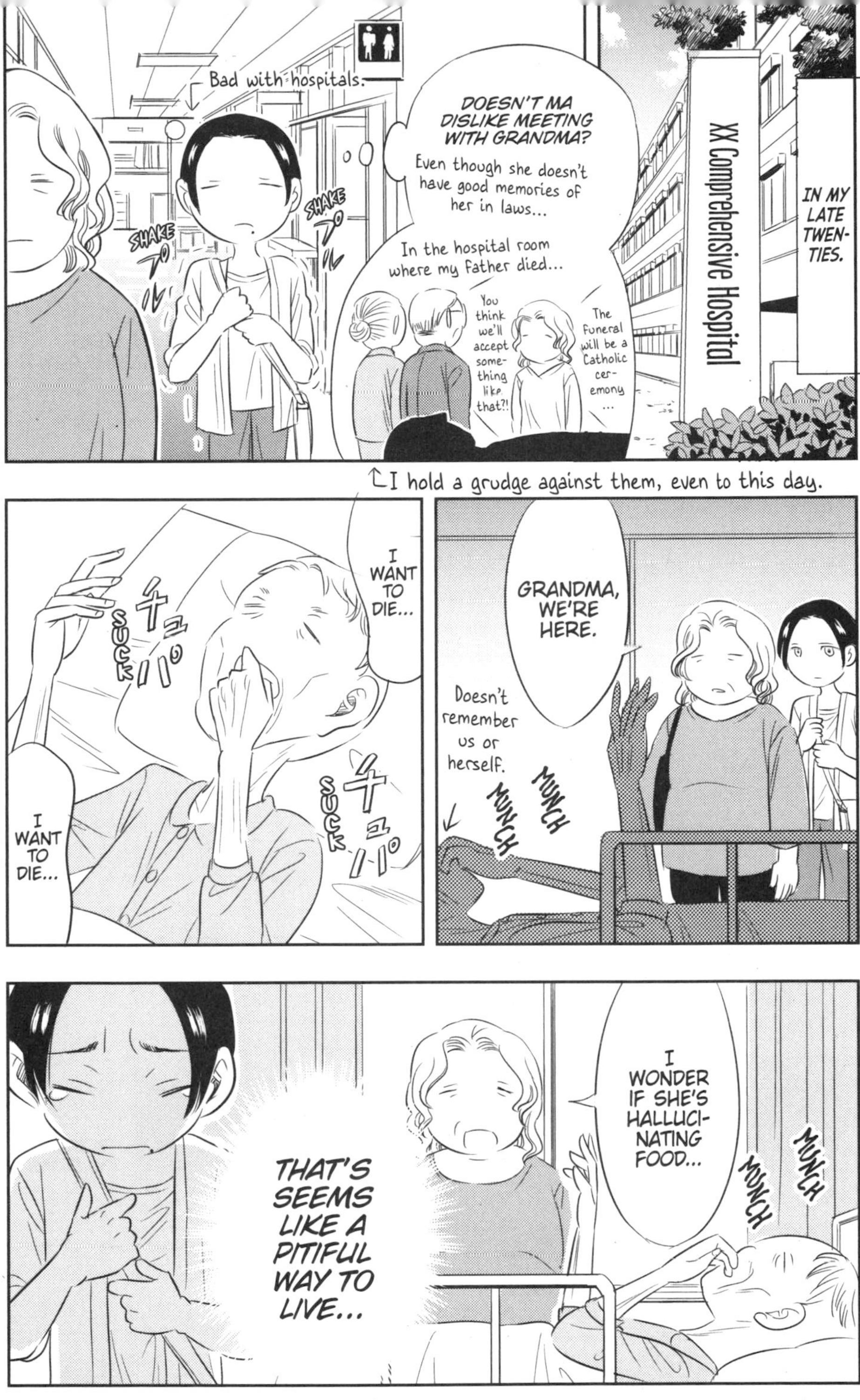
IN MY LATE TWENTIES.
XX Comprehensive Hospital
DOESN'T MA DISLIKE MEETING WITH GRANDMA?
Even though she doesn't have good memories of her in laws...
In the hospital room where my father died...
The funeral will be a Catholic ceremony...
You think we'll accept something like that?!
Bad with hospitals.
SHAKE
SHAKE
I hold a grudge against them, even to this day.
GRANDMA, WE'RE HERE.
Doesn't remember us or herself.
MUNCH
MUNCH
I WANT TO DIE...
SUCK
SUCK
I WANT TO DIE...
I WONDER IF SHE'S HALLUCINATING FOOD...
MUNCH
MUNCH
THAT'S SEEMS LIKE A PITIFUL WAY TO LIVE...

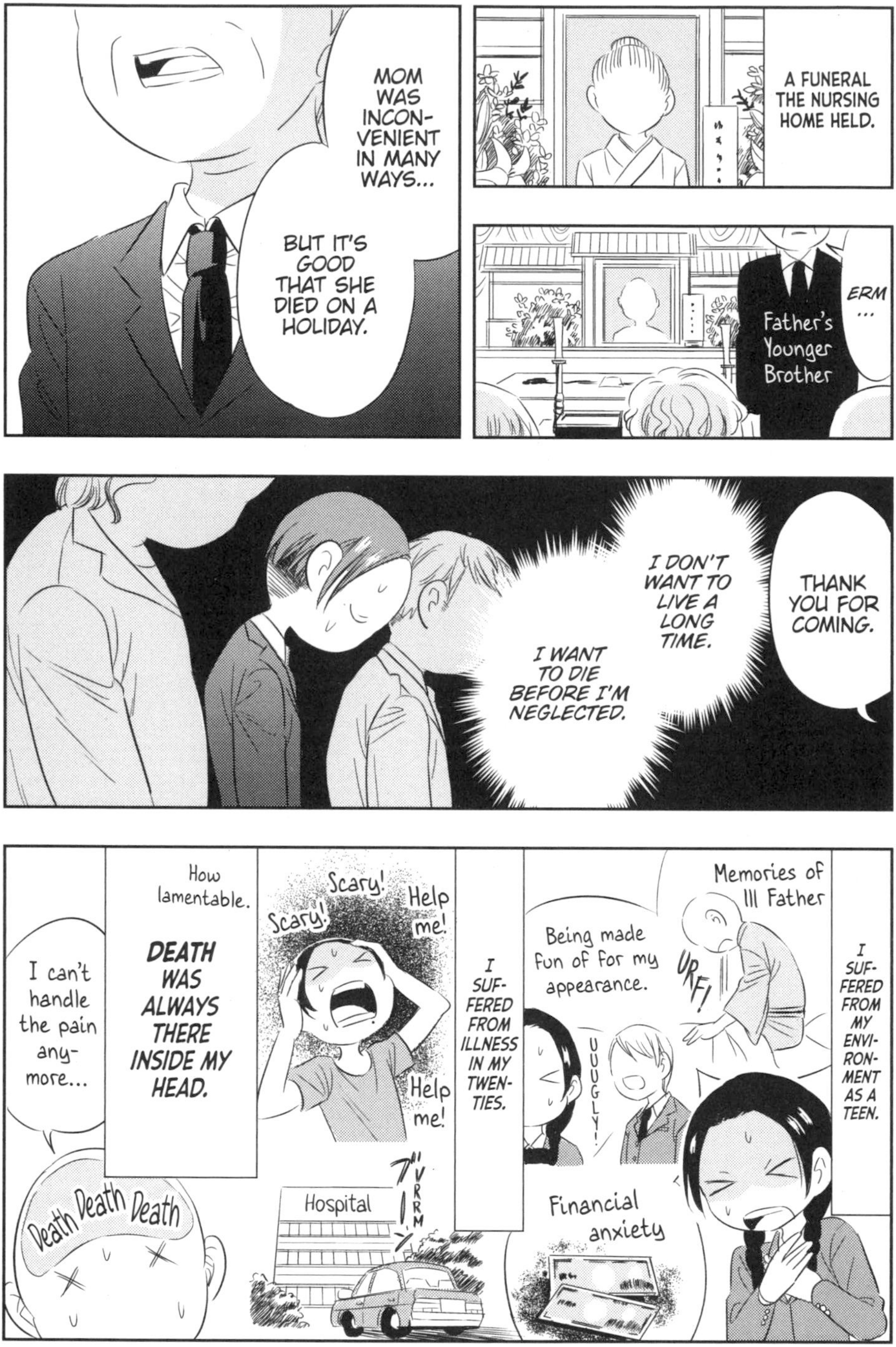
A FUNERAL THE NURSING HOME HELD.
ERM ...
Father's Younger Brother
MOM WAS INCON-VENIENT IN MANY WAYS...
BUT IT'S GOOD THAT SHE DIED ON A HOLIDAY.
THANK YOU FOR COMING.
I DON'T WANT TO LIVE A LONG TIME.
I WANT TO DIE BEFORE I'M NEGLECTED.
Memories of Ill Father
I SUF-FERED FROM MY ENVI-RON-MENT AS A TEEN.
URF!
Being made fun of for my appearance.
UUUGLY!
Financial anxiety
I SUF-FERED FROM ILLNESS IN MY TWEN-TIES.
Help me!
Scary!
Scary!
Help me!
VRRM
Hospital
How lamentable.
DEATH WAS ALWAYS THERE INSIDE MY HEAD.
I can't handle the pain any-more...
Death Death Death

It seems that my paternal grandpa also suffered a long time, poor thing. Every time his breath returned, the gathered relatives would ask, "He's still alive?" It was truly a draining atmosphere.

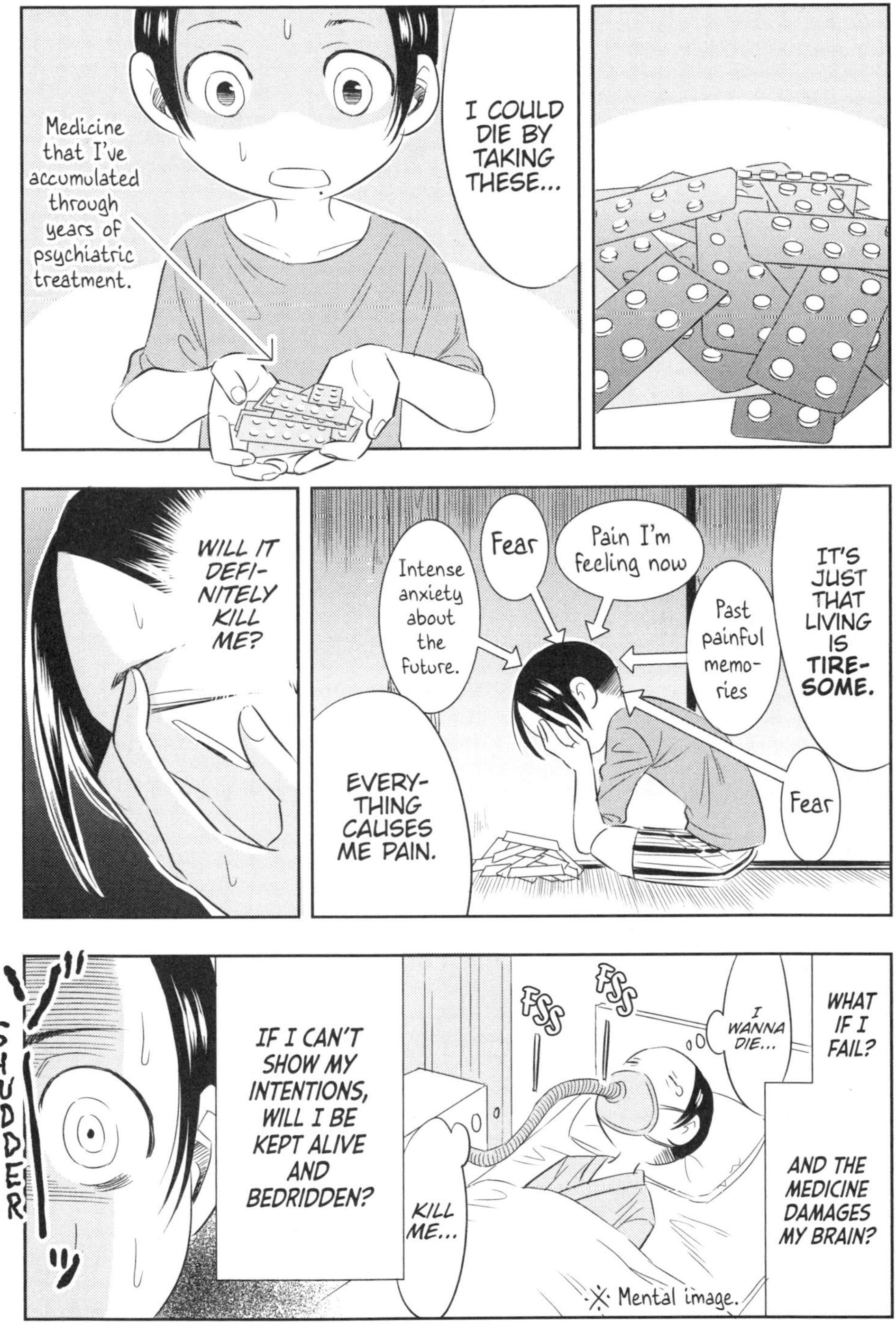
I COULD DIE BY TAKING THESE...
Medicine that I've accumulated through years of psychiatric treatment.
IT'S JUST THAT LIVING IS TIRESOME.
Past painful memories
Pain I'm feeling now
Fear
Intense anxiety about the future.
Fear
EVERYTHING CAUSES ME PAIN.
WILL IT DEFINITELY KILL ME?
WHAT IF I FAIL?
AND THE MEDICINE DAMAGES MY BRAIN?
I WANNA DIE...
FSS
FSS
KILL ME...
※ Mental image.
IF I CAN'T SHOW MY INTENTIONS, WILL I BE KEPT ALIVE AND BEDRIDDEN?
SHUDDER

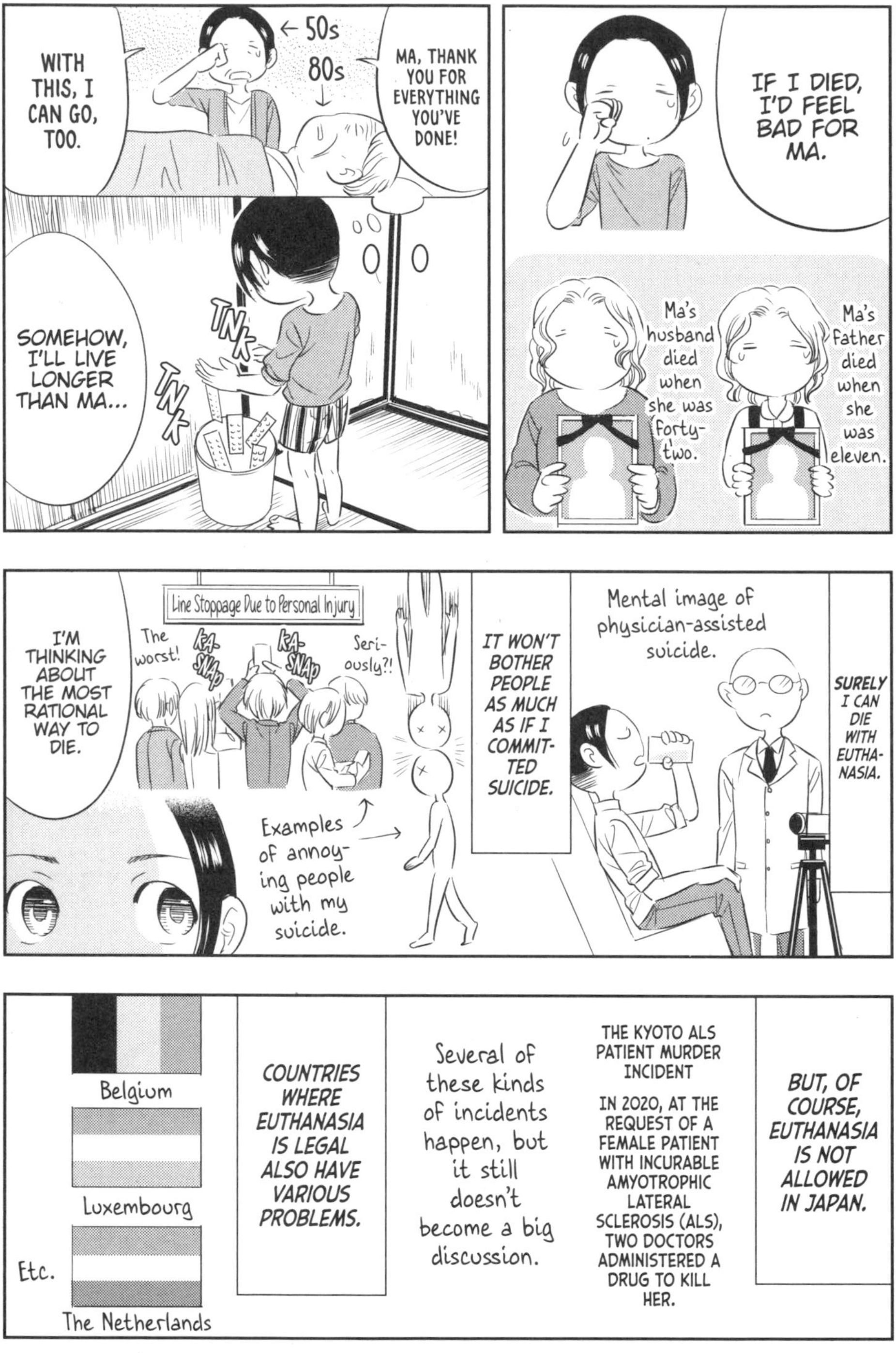
IF I DIED, I'D FEEL BAD FOR MA.
Ma's Father died when she was eleven.
Ma's husband died when she was forty-two.
MA, THANK YOU FOR EVERYTHING YOU'VE DONE!
80s
← 50s
WITH THIS, I CAN GO, TOO.
TNK
TNK
SOMEHOW, I'LL LIVE LONGER THAN MA...
SURELY I CAN DIE WITH EUTHANASIA.
Mental image of physician-assisted suicide.
IT WON'T BOTHER PEOPLE AS MUCH AS IF I COMMITTED SUICIDE.
Line Stoppage Due to Personal Injury
Seri-ously?!
KA-SNAP
KA-SNAP
The worst!
I'M THINKING ABOUT THE MOST RATIONAL WAY TO DIE.
Examples of annoying people with my suicide.
BUT, OF COURSE, EUTHANASIA IS NOT ALLOWED IN JAPAN.
THE KYOTO ALS PATIENT MURDER INCIDENT
IN 2020, AT THE REQUEST OF A FEMALE PATIENT WITH INCURABLE AMYOTROPHIC LATERAL SCLEROSIS (ALS), TWO DOCTORS ADMINISTERED A DRUG TO KILL HER.
Several of these kinds of incidents happen, but it still doesn't become a big discussion.
COUNTRIES WHERE EUTHANASIA IS LEGAL ALSO HAVE VARIOUS PROBLEMS.
Belgium
Luxembourg
The Netherlands
Etc.

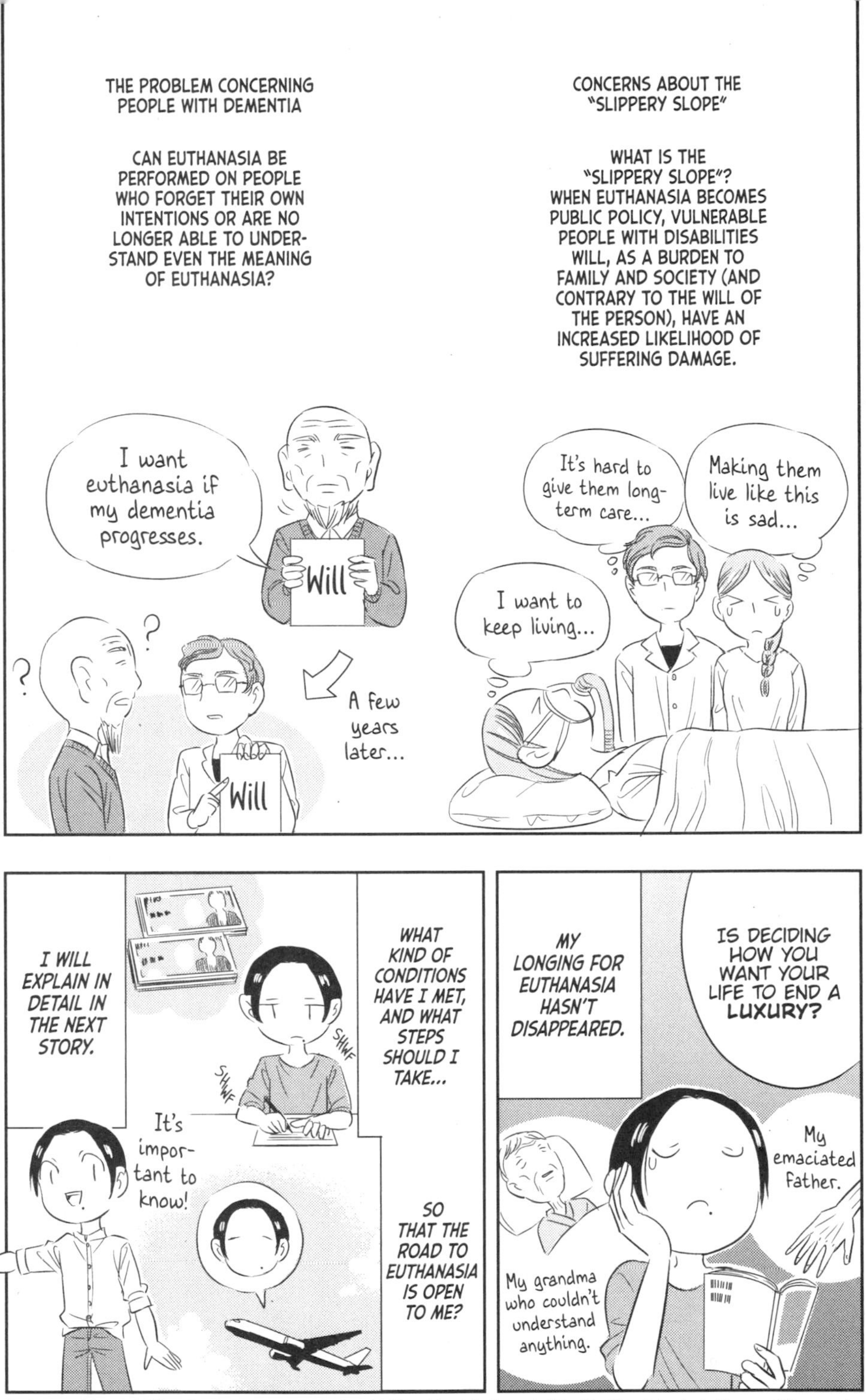
CONCERNS ABOUT THE "SLIPPERY SLOPE"
WHAT IS THE "SLIPPERY SLOPE"? WHEN EUTHANASIA BECOMES PUBLIC POLICY, VULNERABLE PEOPLE WITH DISABILITIES WILL, AS A BURDEN TO FAMILY AND SOCIETY (AND CONTRARY TO THE WILL OF THE PERSON), HAVE AN INCREASED LIKELIHOOD OF SUFFERING DAMAGE.
Making them live like this is sad...
It's hard to give them long-term care...
I want to keep living...
THE PROBLEM CONCERNING PEOPLE WITH DEMENTIA
CAN EUTHANASIA BE PERFORMED ON PEOPLE WHO FORGET THEIR OWN INTENTIONS OR ARE NO LONGER ABLE TO UNDERSTAND EVEN THE MEANING OF EUTHANASIA?
I want euthanasia if my dementia progresses.
Will
A few years later...
Will
IS DECIDING HOW YOU WANT YOUR LIFE TO END A **LUXURY?**
MY LONGING FOR EUTHANASIA HASN'T DISAPPEARED.
My emaciated father.
My grandma who couldn't understand anything.
WHAT KIND OF CONDITIONS HAVE I MET, AND WHAT STEPS SHOULD I TAKE...
SHWF
SHWF
SO THAT THE ROAD TO EUTHANASIA IS OPEN TO ME?
I WILL EXPLAIN IN DETAIL IN THE NEXT STORY.
It's important to know!

Reference Material: *What You Need to Know Before Talking About Euthanasia/Dignified Death* by Ando Yasunori (Iwanami Booklet), *The Road to Euthanasia* (Shogakukan), and *The Japanese People Who Achieved Euthanasia* (Shogakukan Bunko) by Miyashita Youichi

Ep. 33: The "Euthanasia" Story

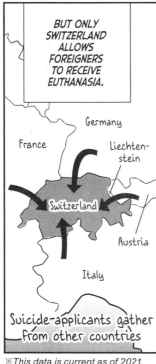

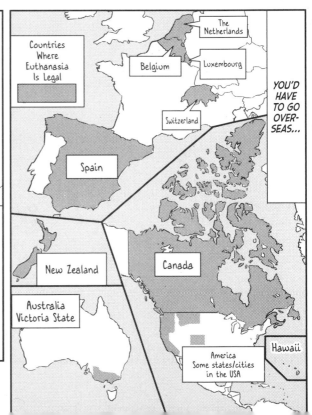

CONTINUATION FROM BEFORE.
HOW CAN YOU BE EUTHANIZED?
I'LL SAY IT FROM THE GET-GO.
IT'S REEEALLY DIFFICULT.
OF COURSE, BECAUSE EUTHANASIA ISN'T RECOGNIZED IN JAPAN...
THE JAPAN SOCIETY FOR DYING WITH DIGNITY
Kuramoto Soh is the association's advisor.
ITS PURPOSE IS TO POPULARIZE MAKING A "LIVING WILL" TO SHOW YOUR INTENTIONS.
IT IS OPPOSED TO EUTHANASIA WHICH "ACTIVELY ACCELERATES A PATIENT'S DEATH."
YOU'D HAVE TO GO OVERSEAS...
Countries Where Euthanasia Is Legal
The Netherlands
Belgium
Luxembourg
Switzerland
Spain
Canada
New Zealand
Australia Victoria State
Hawaii
America Some states/cities in the USA
BUT ONLY SWITZERLAND ALLOWS FOREIGNERS TO RECEIVE EUTHANASIA.
Germany
France
Liechtenstein
Switzerland
Austria
Italy
Suicide-applicants gather from other countries

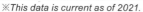

※This data is current as of 2021.

AND OF COURSE, IT'S NOT AS SIMPLE AS JUST PAYING MONEY AND RECEIVING THE EUTHANASIA.
FOUR CONDITIONS FOR DYING
① YOU HAVE UNBEARABLE PAIN.
② THERE IS NO EXPECTED RECOVERY.
③ YOU CAN CLEARLY EXPRESS YOUR INTENTIONS.
④ THERE IS NO TREATMENT METHOD THE PATIENT DESIRES.
THROB THROB
FSS FSS
YOU NEED TO CLEAR ALL OF THESE CONDITIONS.
EUTHANASIA DUE TO MENTAL ILLNESS IS RECOGNIZED IN THESE COUNTRIES:
The Netherlands
Belgium
Canada
THE FOUR CONDITIONS BECOME AS SUCH:
① YOU HAVE UNBEARABLE PAIN-- PHYSICALLY OR MENTALLY.
② THERE IS NO EXPECTED RECOVERY.
③ YOU CAN CLEARLY EXPRESS YOUR INTENTIONS.
④ THERE IS NO TREATMENT METHOD THE PATIENT DESIRES.
IN THAT CASE, I COULD DO IT!
Why?
YOU'RE DRAWING MANGA AND ARE DOING WELL!
YOU MIGHT THINK SO...
AND ACTUALLY, I AM DOING WELL NOW, BUT...
Doesn't really mean anything in particular.
WOOF!
DANCE
Dancing
DANCE
Drawing
WORK WORK

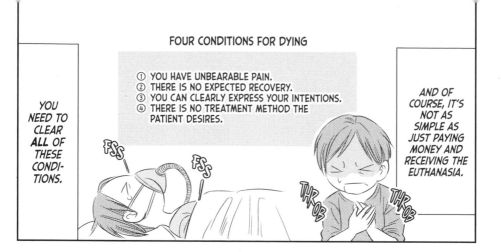

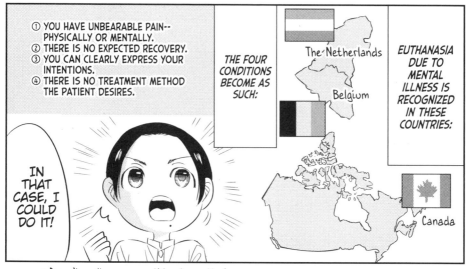

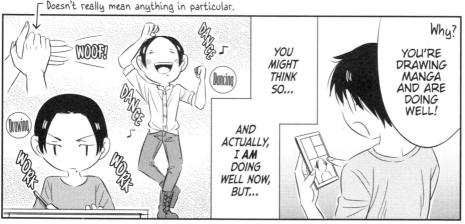

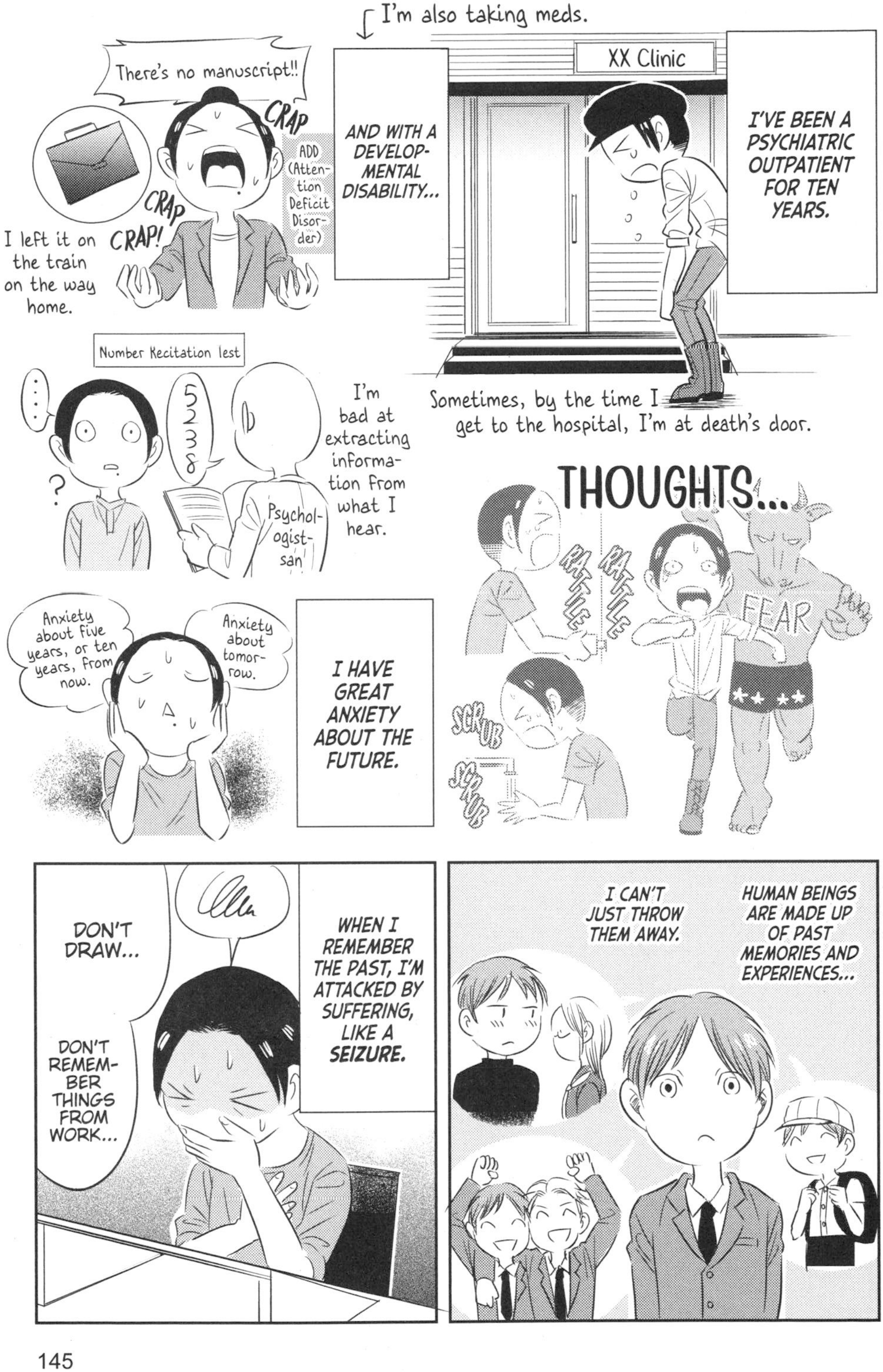

I'VE BEEN A PSYCHIATRIC OUTPATIENT FOR TEN YEARS.
XX Clinic
I'm also taking meds.
AND WITH A DEVELOP-MENTAL DISABILITY...
Sometimes, by the time I get to the hospital, I'm at death's door.
There's no manuscript!!
CRAP
CRAP
CRAP!
ADD (Atten-tion Deficit Disor-der)
I left it on the train on the way home.
THOUGHTS...
RATTLE
RATTLE
FEAR
SCRUB
SCRUB
I'm bad at extracting informa-tion from what I hear.
Number Recitation Test
5238
Psychol-ogist-san
...
?
I HAVE GREAT ANXIETY ABOUT THE FUTURE.
Anxiety about tomor-row.
Anxiety about five years, or ten years, from now.
HUMAN BEINGS ARE MADE UP OF PAST MEMORIES AND EXPERIENCES...
I CAN'T JUST THROW THEM AWAY.
WHEN I REMEMBER THE PAST, I'M ATTACKED BY SUFFERING, LIKE A SEIZURE.
DON'T DRAW...
DON'T REMEM-BER THINGS FROM WORK...

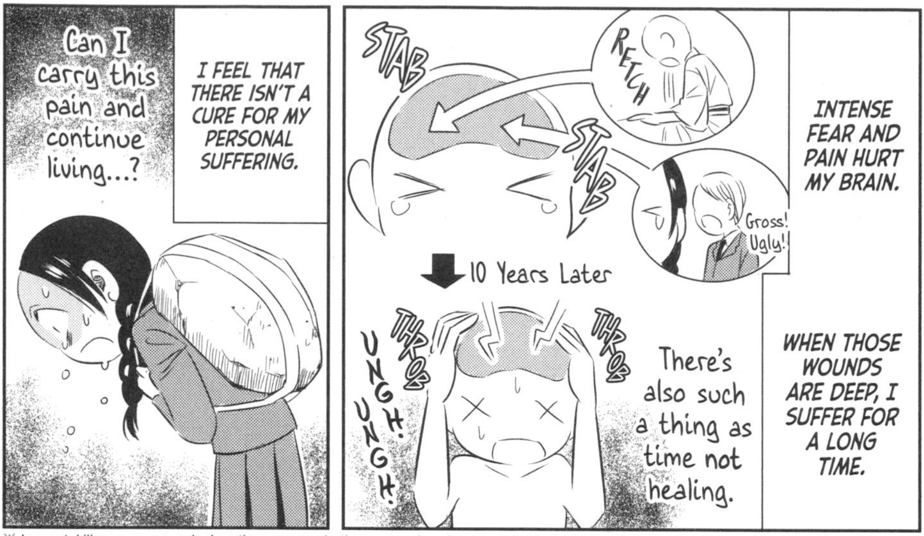
INTENSE FEAR AND PAIN HURT MY BRAIN.
STAB
RETCH
STAB
Gross! Ugly!!
10 Years Later
THROB
THROB
UNGH! UNGH!
There's also such a thing as time not healing.
WHEN THOSE WOUNDS ARE DEEP, I SUFFER FOR A LONG TIME.
I FEEL THAT THERE ISN'T A CURE FOR MY PERSONAL SUFFERING.
Can I carry this pain and continue living...?

※ *In mental illness, you can do drug therapy, psychotherapy, and environmental adjustment treatment methods, et cetera. Many people improve.*

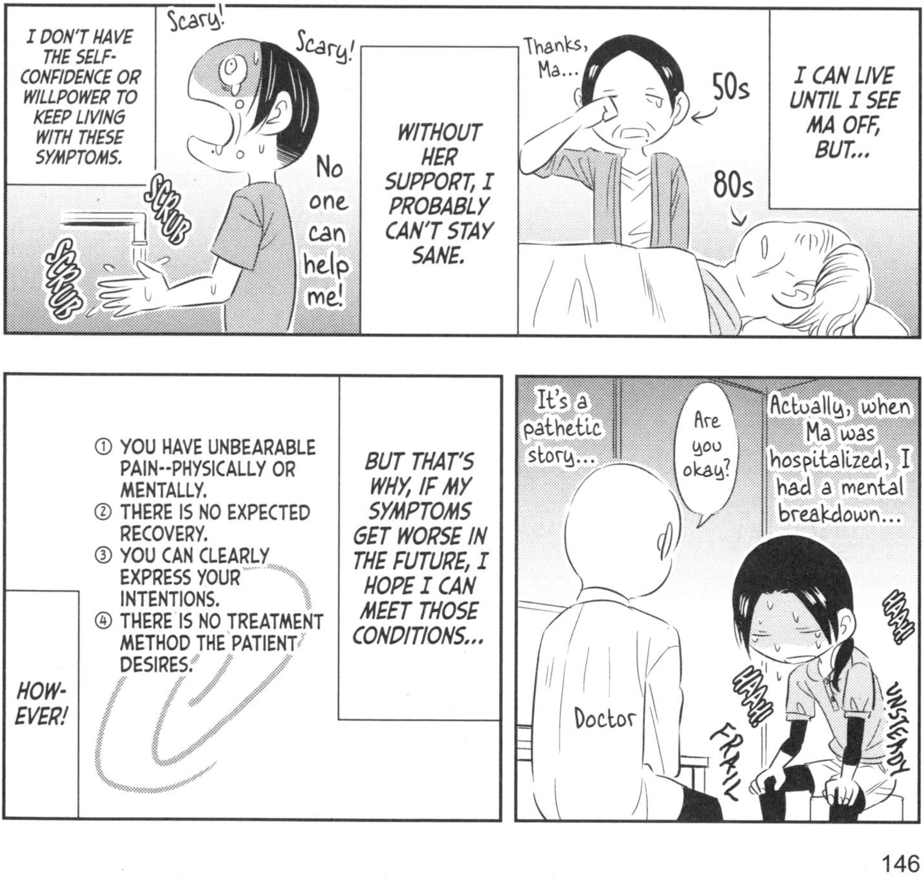
I CAN LIVE UNTIL I SEE MA OFF, BUT...
Thanks, Ma...
50s
80s
WITHOUT HER SUPPORT, I PROBABLY CAN'T STAY SANE.
Scary!
Scary!
No one can help me!
I DON'T HAVE THE SELF-CONFIDENCE OR WILLPOWER TO KEEP LIVING WITH THESE SYMPTOMS.
SCRUB
SCRUB
Actually, when Ma was hospitalized, I had a mental breakdown...
Are you okay?
It's a pathetic story...
HAAH
UNSTEADY
HAAH
FRAIL
Doctor
BUT THAT'S WHY, IF MY SYMPTOMS GET WORSE IN THE FUTURE, I HOPE I CAN MEET THOSE CONDITIONS...
① YOU HAVE UNBEARABLE PAIN--PHYSICALLY OR MENTALLY.
② THERE IS NO EXPECTED RECOVERY.
③ YOU CAN CLEARLY EXPRESS YOUR INTENTIONS.
④ THERE IS NO TREATMENT METHOD THE PATIENT DESIRES.
HOW-EVER!

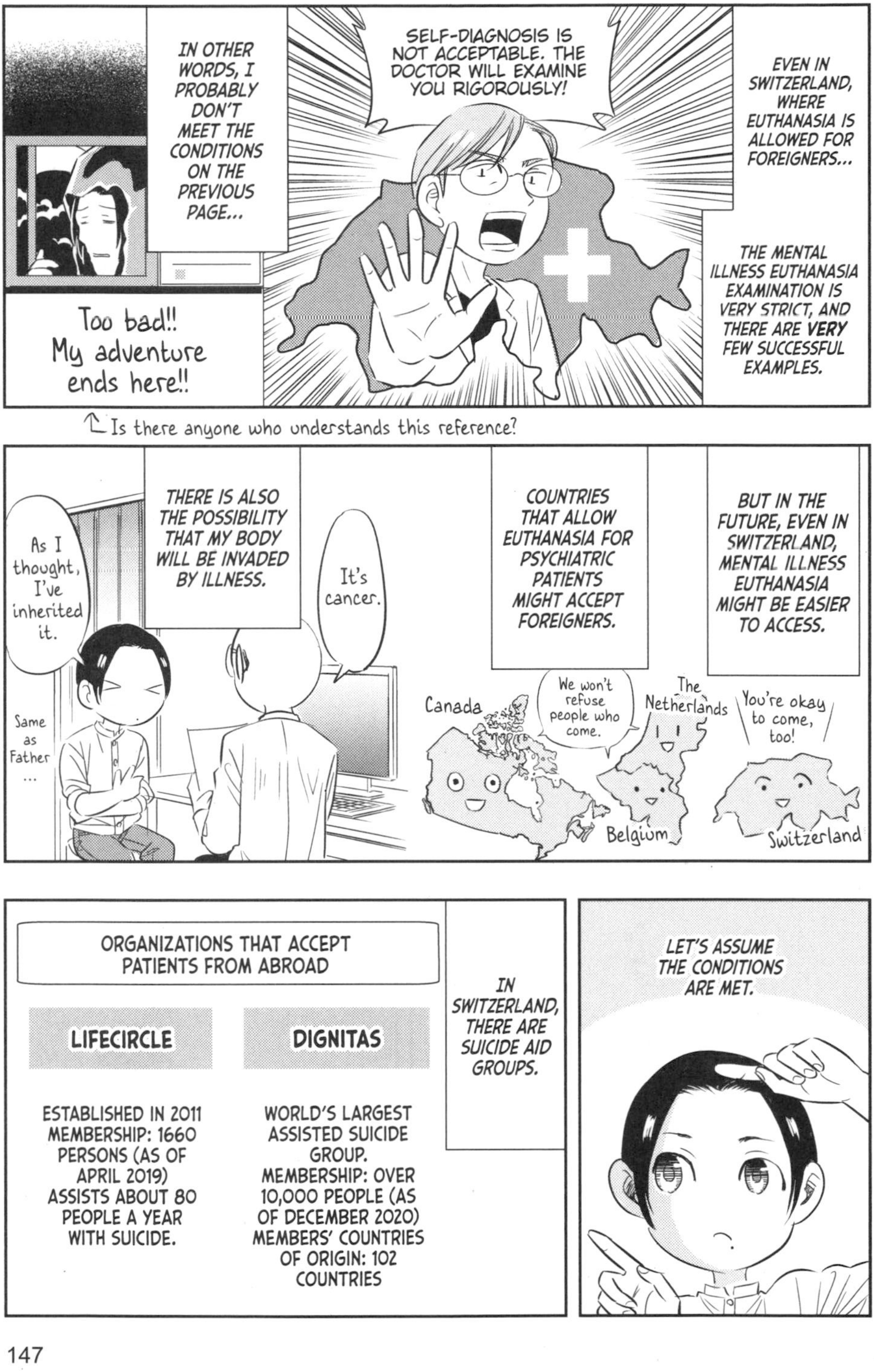
EVEN IN SWITZERLAND, WHERE EUTHANASIA IS ALLOWED FOR FOREIGNERS...
THE MENTAL ILLNESS EUTHANASIA EXAMINATION IS VERY STRICT, AND THERE ARE VERY FEW SUCCESSFUL EXAMPLES.
SELF-DIAGNOSIS IS NOT ACCEPTABLE. THE DOCTOR WILL EXAMINE YOU RIGOROUSLY!
IN OTHER WORDS, I PROBABLY DON'T MEET THE CONDITIONS ON THE PREVIOUS PAGE...
Too bad!! My adventure ends here!!
Is there anyone who understands this reference?
BUT IN THE FUTURE, EVEN IN SWITZERLAND, MENTAL ILLNESS EUTHANASIA MIGHT BE EASIER TO ACCESS.
COUNTRIES THAT ALLOW EUTHANASIA FOR PSYCHIATRIC PATIENTS MIGHT ACCEPT FOREIGNERS.
You're okay to come, too!
Switzerland
The Netherlands
We won't refuse people who come.
Belgium
Canada
THERE IS ALSO THE POSSIBILITY THAT MY BODY WILL BE INVADED BY ILLNESS.
It's cancer.
As I thought, I've inherited it.
Same as Father ...
LET'S ASSUME THE CONDITIONS ARE MET.
IN SWITZERLAND, THERE ARE SUICIDE AID GROUPS.
ORGANIZATIONS THAT ACCEPT PATIENTS FROM ABROAD
LIFECIRCLE
ESTABLISHED IN 2011 MEMBERSHIP: 1660 PERSONS (AS OF APRIL 2019) ASSISTS ABOUT 80 PEOPLE A YEAR WITH SUICIDE.
DIGNITAS
WORLD'S LARGEST ASSISTED SUICIDE GROUP. MEMBERSHIP: OVER 10,000 PEOPLE (AS OF DECEMBER 2020) MEMBERS' COUNTRIES OF ORIGIN: 102 COUNTRIES

IN THE CASE OF LIFECIRCLE

※This illustration is just my mental image.

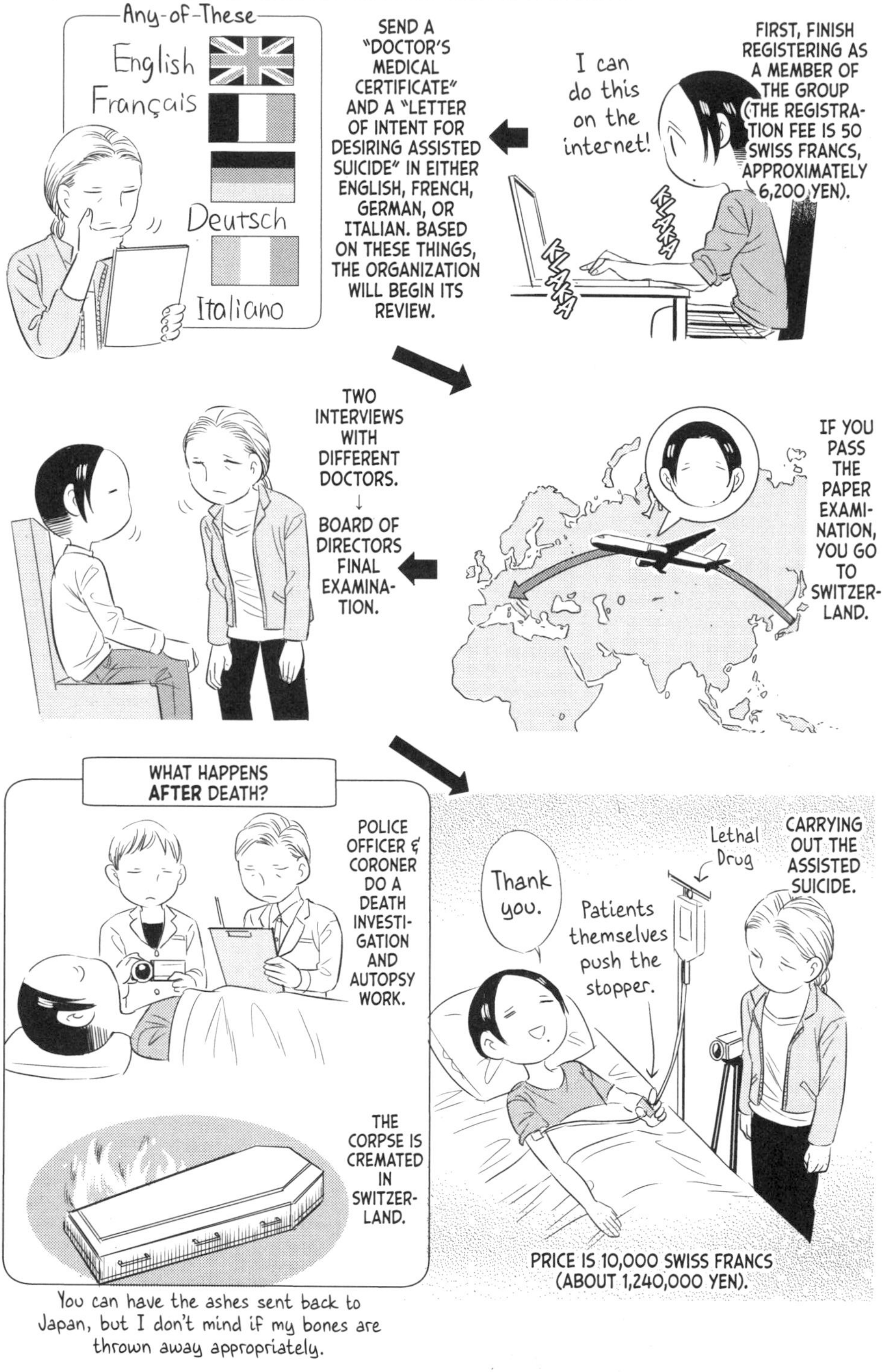
FIRST, FINISH REGISTERING AS A MEMBER OF THE GROUP (THE REGISTRATION FEE IS 50 SWISS FRANCS, APPROXIMATELY 6,200 YEN).
I can do this on the internet!
KLAKA
KLAKA
SEND A "DOCTOR'S MEDICAL CERTIFICATE" AND A "LETTER OF INTENT FOR DESIRING ASSISTED SUICIDE" IN EITHER ENGLISH, FRENCH, GERMAN, OR ITALIAN. BASED ON THESE THINGS, THE ORGANIZATION WILL BEGIN ITS REVIEW.
Any-of-These
English
Français
Deutsch
Italiano
IF YOU PASS THE PAPER EXAMINATION, YOU GO TO SWITZERLAND.
TWO INTERVIEWS WITH DIFFERENT DOCTORS.
↓
BOARD OF DIRECTORS FINAL EXAMINATION.
CARRYING OUT THE ASSISTED SUICIDE.
Lethal Drug
Thank you.
Patients themselves push the stopper.
PRICE IS 10,000 SWISS FRANCS (ABOUT 1,240,000 YEN).
WHAT HAPPENS AFTER DEATH?
POLICE OFFICER & CORONER DO A DEATH INVESTIGATION AND AUTOPSY WORK.
THE CORPSE IS CREMATED IN SWITZERLAND.
You can have the ashes sent back to Japan, but I don't mind if my bones are thrown away appropriately.

Lifecircle's membership is over 1,500 people, with about 80 cases of assisted suicide a year. It's difficult to get selected early.

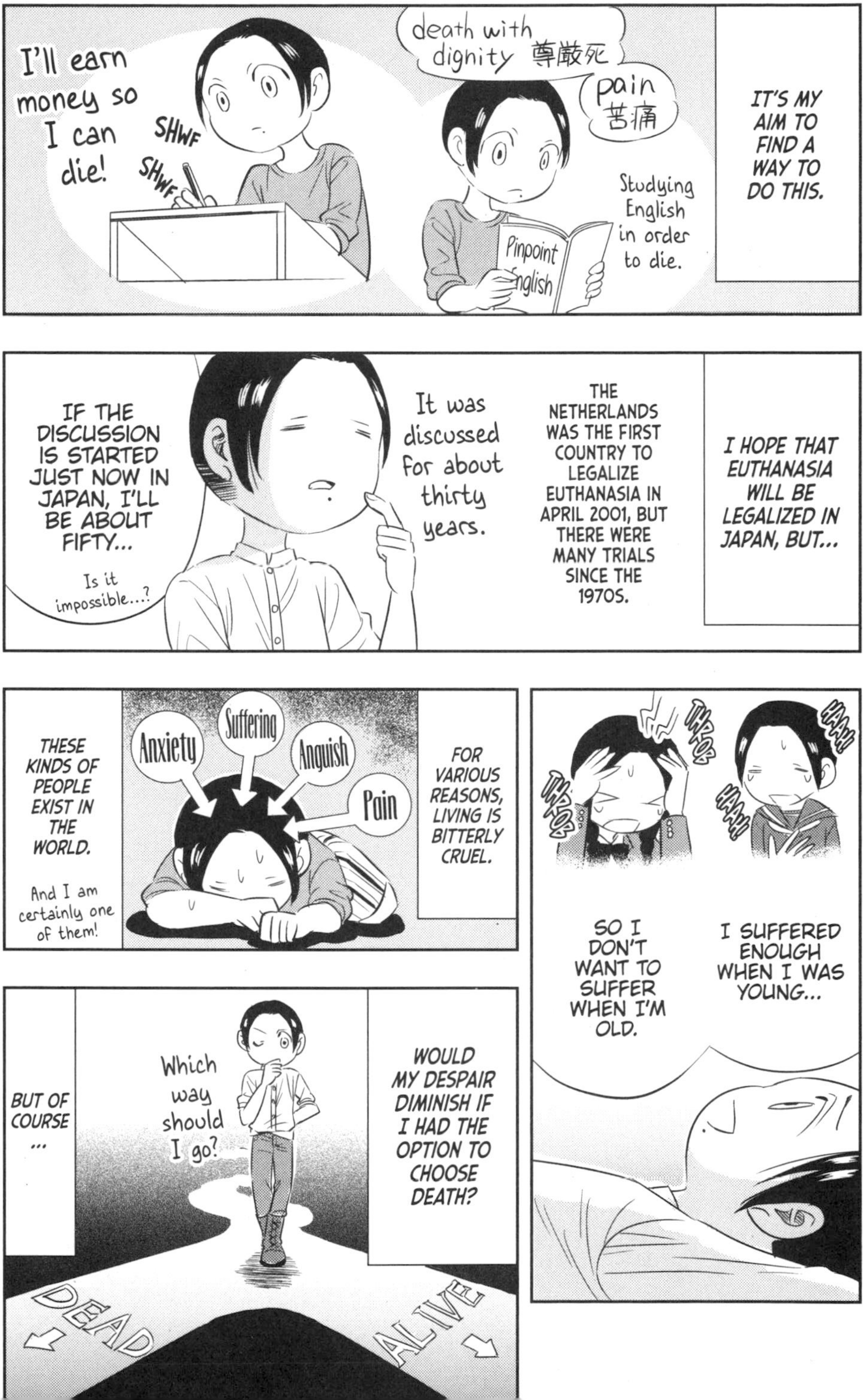
IT'S MY AIM TO FIND A WAY TO DO THIS.
death with dignity 尊厳死
pain 苦痛
Studying English in order to die.
Pinpoint English
I'll earn money so I can die!
SHWF
SHWF
I HOPE THAT EUTHANASIA WILL BE LEGALIZED IN JAPAN, BUT...
THE NETHERLANDS WAS THE FIRST COUNTRY TO LEGALIZE EUTHANASIA IN APRIL 2001, BUT THERE WERE MANY TRIALS SINCE THE 1970S.
It was discussed for about thirty years.
IF THE DISCUSSION IS STARTED JUST NOW IN JAPAN, I'LL BE ABOUT FIFTY...
Is it impossible...?
HAAH
HAAH
THROB
THROB
I SUFFERED ENOUGH WHEN I WAS YOUNG...
SO I DON'T WANT TO SUFFER WHEN I'M OLD.
FOR VARIOUS REASONS, LIVING IS BITTERLY CRUEL.
Suffering
Anguish
Anxiety
Pain
THESE KINDS OF PEOPLE EXIST IN THE WORLD.
And I am certainly one of them!
WOULD MY DESPAIR DIMINISH IF I HAD THE OPTION TO CHOOSE DEATH?
Which way should I go?
BUT OF COURSE ...
ALIVE
DEAD

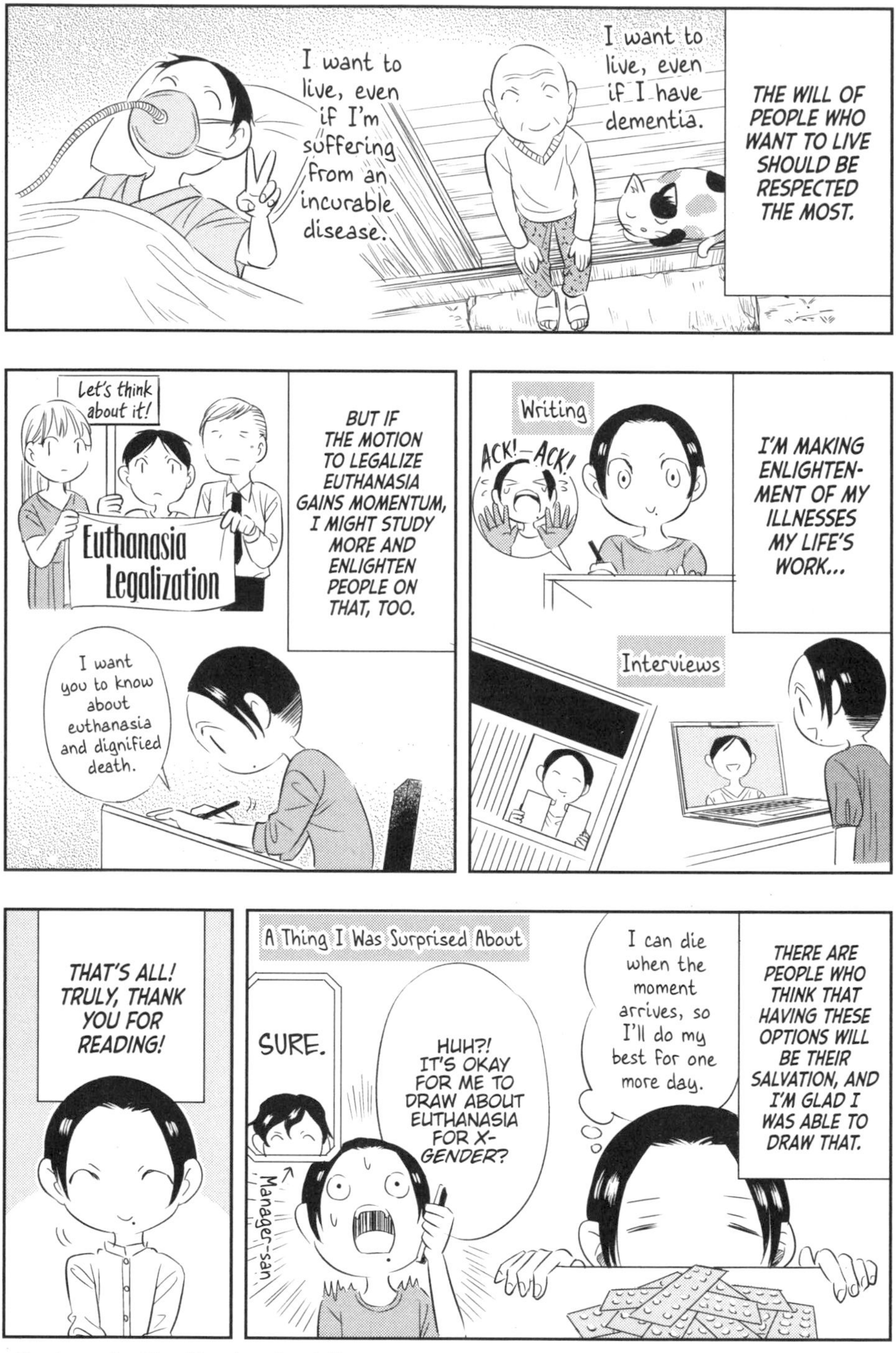
THE WILL OF PEOPLE WHO WANT TO LIVE SHOULD BE RESPECTED THE MOST.
I want to live, even if I have dementia.
I want to live, even if I'm suffering from an incurable disease.
I'M MAKING ENLIGHTENMENT OF MY ILLNESSES MY LIFE'S WORK...
Writing
ACK! ACK!
Interviews
BUT IF THE MOTION TO LEGALIZE EUTHANASIA GAINS MOMENTUM, I MIGHT STUDY MORE AND ENLIGHTEN PEOPLE ON THAT, TOO.
Let's think about it!
Euthanasia Legalization
I want you to know about euthanasia and dignified death.
THERE ARE PEOPLE WHO THINK THAT HAVING THESE OPTIONS WILL BE THEIR SALVATION, AND I'M GLAD I WAS ABLE TO DRAW THAT.
I can die when the moment arrives, so I'll do my best for one more day.
A Thing I Was Surprised About
HUH?! IT'S OKAY FOR ME TO DRAW ABOUT EUTHANASIA FOR X-GENDER?
SURE.
Manager-san
THAT'S ALL! TRULY, THANK YOU FOR READING!

Next up is the final episode!!

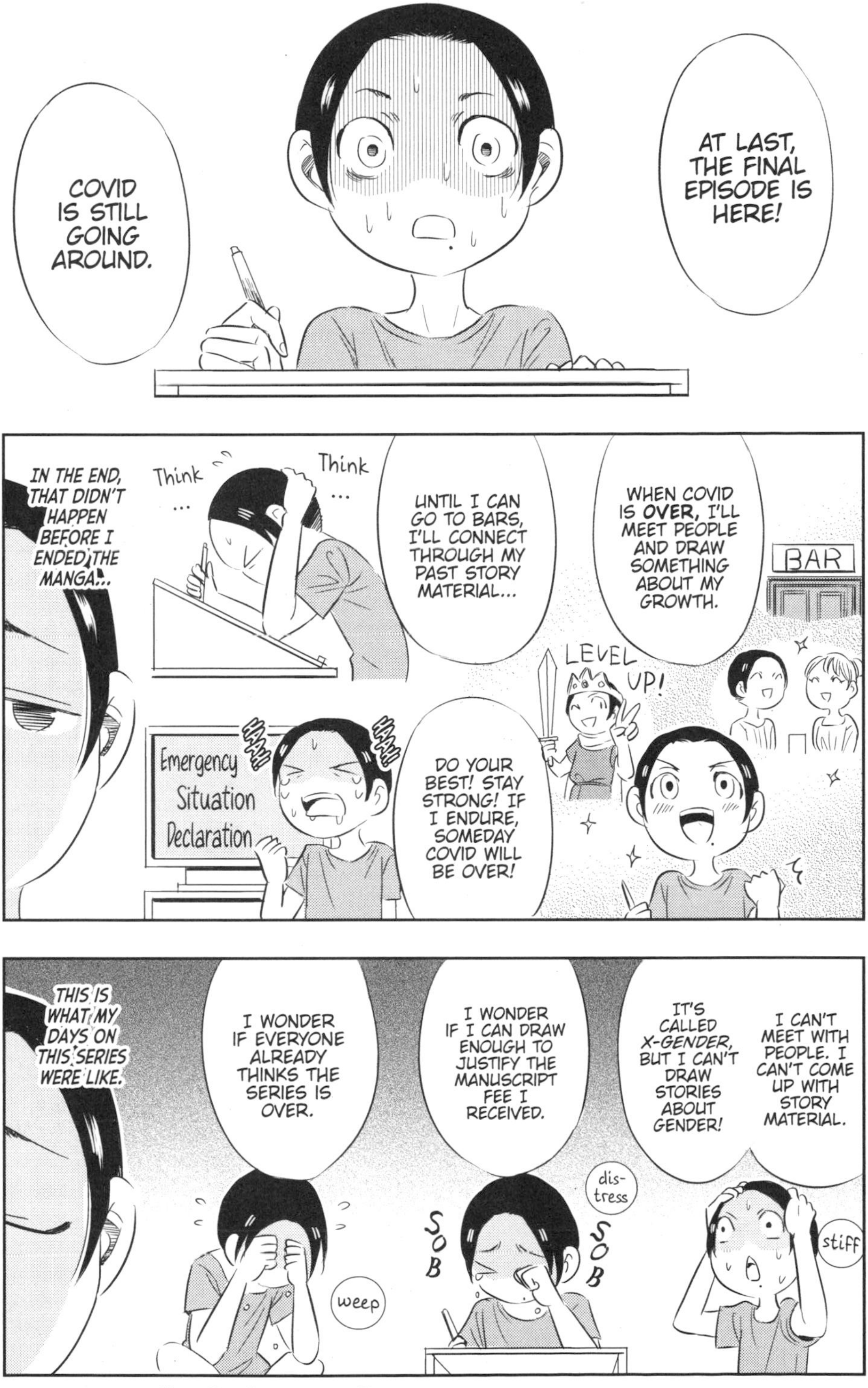
AT LAST, THE FINAL EPISODE IS HERE!
COVID IS STILL GOING AROUND.
WHEN COVID IS OVER, I'LL MEET PEOPLE AND DRAW SOMETHING ABOUT MY GROWTH.
BAR
LEVEL UP!
UNTIL I CAN GO TO BARS, I'LL CONNECT THROUGH MY PAST STORY MATERIAL...
Think ...
Think ...
IN THE END, THAT DIDN'T HAPPEN BEFORE I ENDED THE MANGA...
DO YOUR BEST! STAY STRONG! IF I ENDURE, SOMEDAY COVID WILL BE OVER!
Emergency Situation Declaration
I CAN'T MEET WITH PEOPLE. I CAN'T COME UP WITH STORY MATERIAL.
IT'S CALLED X-GENDER, BUT I CAN'T DRAW STORIES ABOUT GENDER!
stiff
I WONDER IF I CAN DRAW ENOUGH TO JUSTIFY THE MANUSCRIPT FEE I RECEIVED.
dis-tress
SOB
SOB
I WONDER IF EVERYONE ALREADY THINKS THE SERIES IS OVER.
weep
THIS IS WHAT MY DAYS ON THIS SERIES WERE LIKE.

Final Episode: The "Adventure" Story

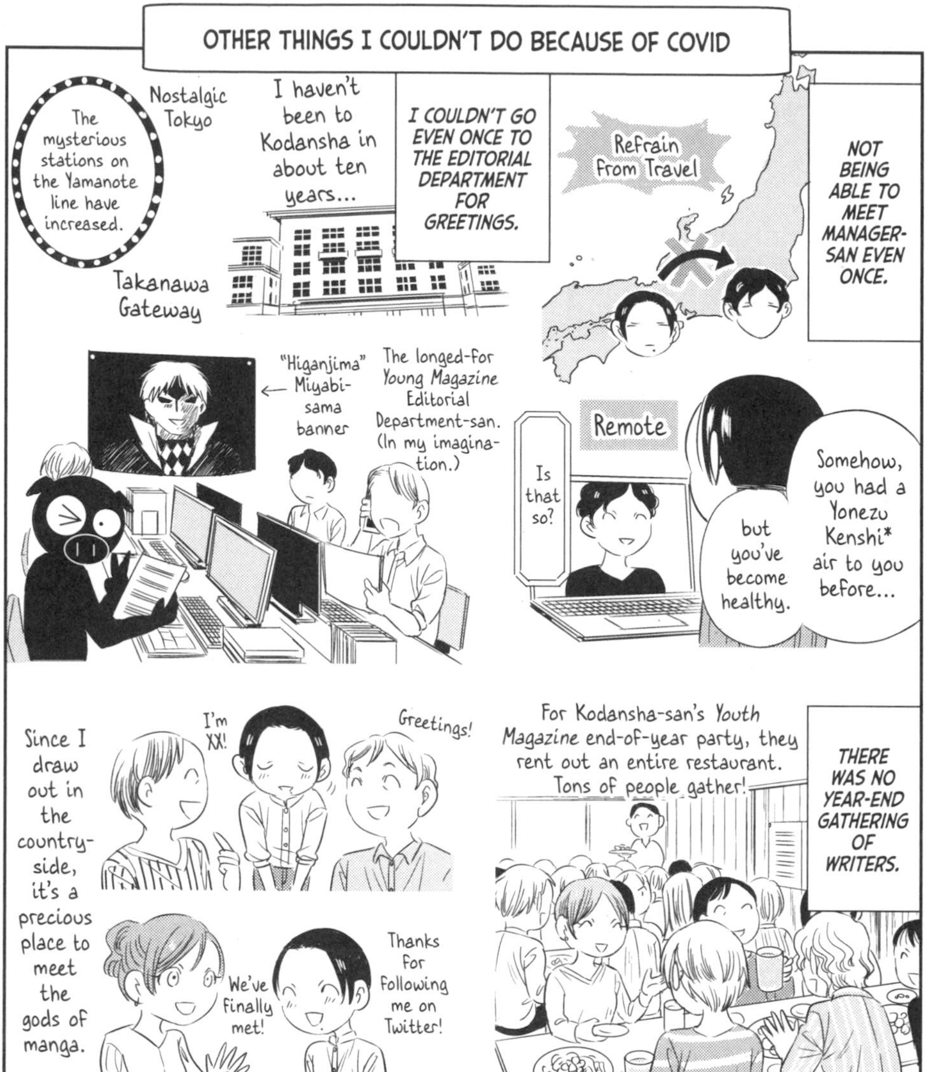
OTHER THINGS I COULDN'T DO BECAUSE OF COVID
NOT BEING ABLE TO MEET MANAGER-SAN EVEN ONCE.
Refrain From Travel
I COULDN'T GO EVEN ONCE TO THE EDITORIAL DEPARTMENT FOR GREETINGS.
I haven't been to Kodansha in about ten years...
Nostalgic Tokyo
The mysterious stations on the Yamanote line have increased.
Takanawa Gateway
Somehow, you had a Yonezu Kenshi* air to you before...
but you've become healthy.
Remote
Is that so?
The longed-for Young Magazine Editorial Department-san. (In my imagination.)
"Higanjima" Miyabi-sama banner
THERE WAS NO YEAR-END GATHERING OF WRITERS.
For Kodansha-san's Youth Magazine end-of-year party, they rent out an entire restaurant. Tons of people gather!
Greetings!
I'm XX!
Since I draw out in the country-side, it's a precious place to meet the gods of manga.
Thanks for following me on Twitter!
We've finally met!

From start to finish, Covid made me bitter. Ever since the Young Magazine the Third June 2020 Issue and the release of Episode 1 got postponed.

**Yonezu Kenshi is a Japanese musician, singer, songwriter, producer, and artist.*

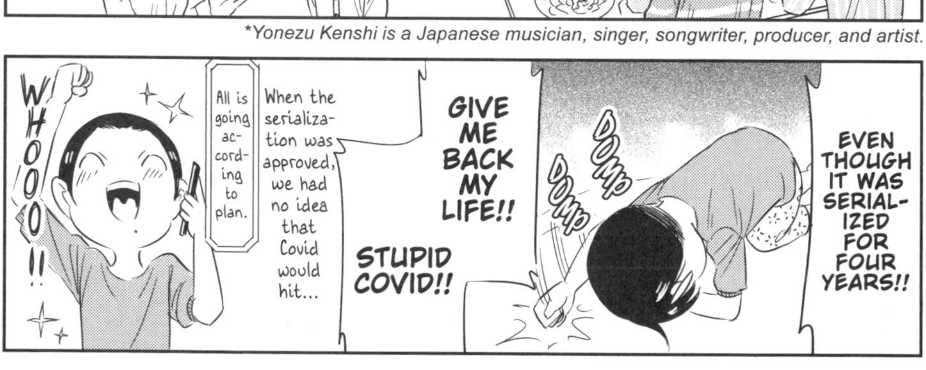
EVEN THOUGH IT WAS SERIALIZED FOR FOUR YEARS!!
DOMP
DOMP
GIVE ME BACK MY LIFE!!
STUPID COVID!!
When the serialization was approved, we had no idea that Covid would hit...
All is going according to plan.
WHOOOO!!

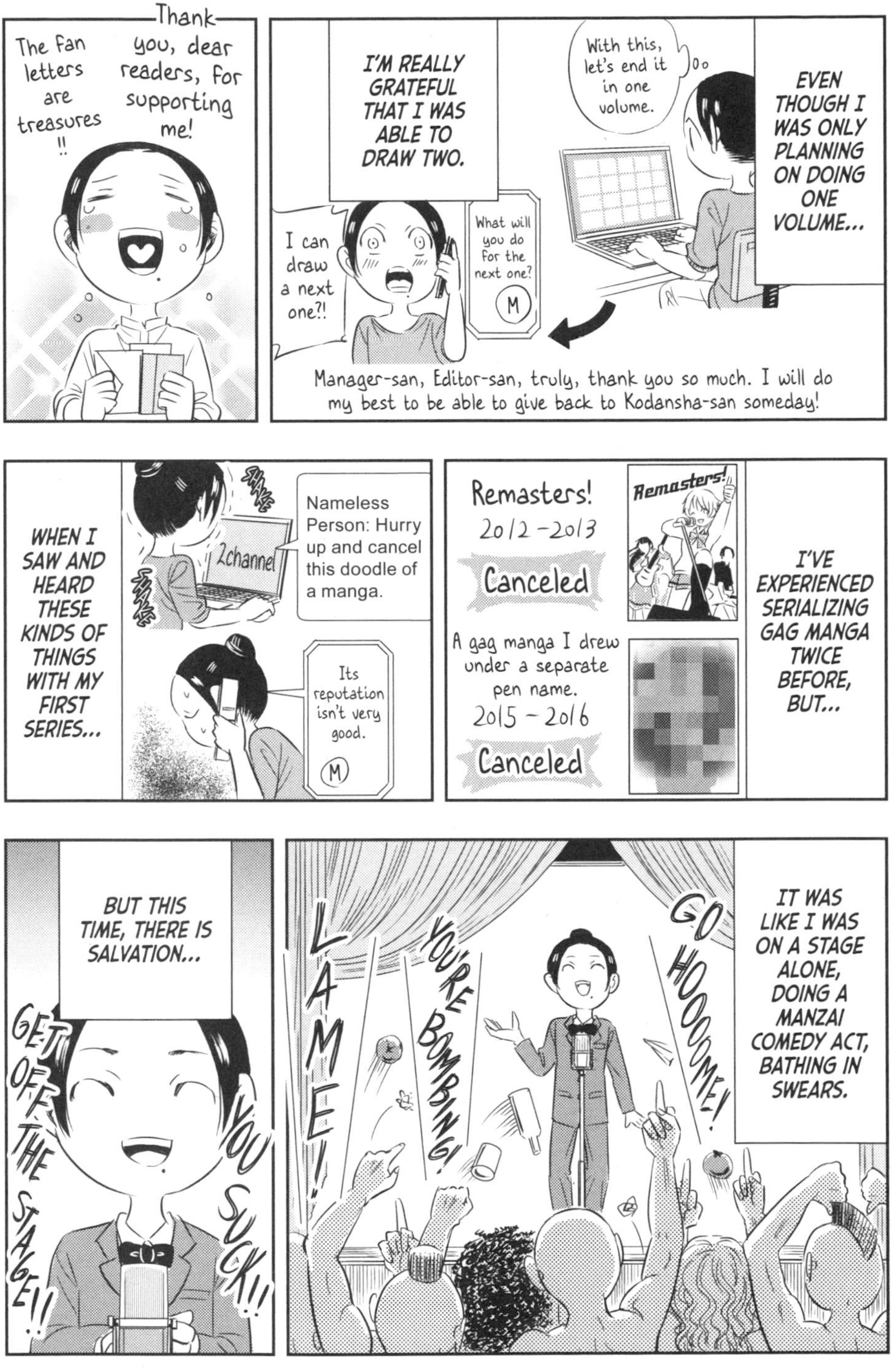
EVEN THOUGH I WAS ONLY PLANNING ON DOING ONE VOLUME...
With this, let's end it in one volume.
I'M REALLY GRATEFUL THAT I WAS ABLE TO DRAW TWO.
What will you do for the next one? M
I can draw a next one?!
Manager-san, Editor-san, truly, thank you so much. I will do my best to be able to give back to Kodansha-san someday!
Thank you, dear readers, for supporting me!
The fan letters are treasures!!
I'VE EXPERIENCED SERIALIZING GAG MANGA TWICE BEFORE, BUT...
Remasters!
Remasters! 2012 – 2013
Canceled
A gag manga I drew under a separate pen name. 2015 – 2016
Canceled
WHEN I SAW AND HEARD THESE KINDS OF THINGS WITH MY FIRST SERIES...
SHAKE
SHAKE
2channel
Nameless Person: Hurry up and cancel this doodle of a manga.
Its reputation isn't very good. M
IT WAS LIKE I WAS ON A STAGE ALONE, DOING A MANZAI COMEDY ACT, BATHING IN SWEARS.
GO HOOOOOME!
YOU'RE BOMBING!
LAME!!
BUT THIS TIME, THERE IS SALVATION...
YOU SUCK!!
GET OFF THE STAGE!!

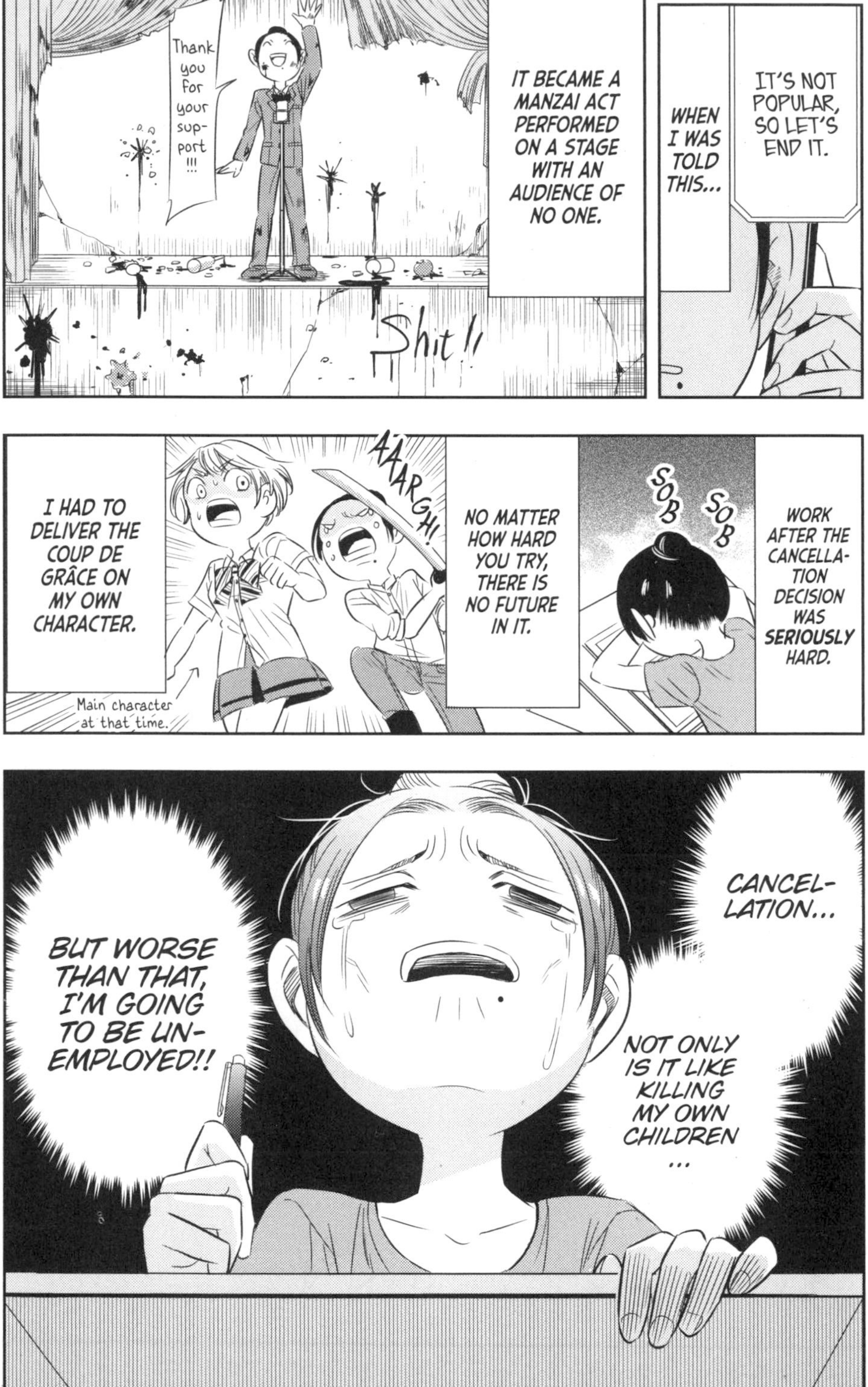
IT'S NOT POPULAR, SO LET'S END IT.
WHEN I WAS TOLD THIS...
IT BECAME A MANZAI ACT PERFORMED ON A STAGE WITH AN AUDIENCE OF NO ONE.
Thank you for your support!!!
Shit!!
WORK AFTER THE CANCELLATION DECISION WAS SERIOUSLY HARD.
SOB SOB
NO MATTER HOW HARD YOU TRY, THERE IS NO FUTURE IN IT.
AAARGH!
I HAD TO DELIVER THE COUP DE GRÂCE ON MY OWN CHARACTER.
Main character at that time.
CANCELLATION...
NOT ONLY IS IT LIKE KILLING MY OWN CHILDREN...
BUT WORSE THAN THAT, I'M GOING TO BE UNEMPLOYED!!

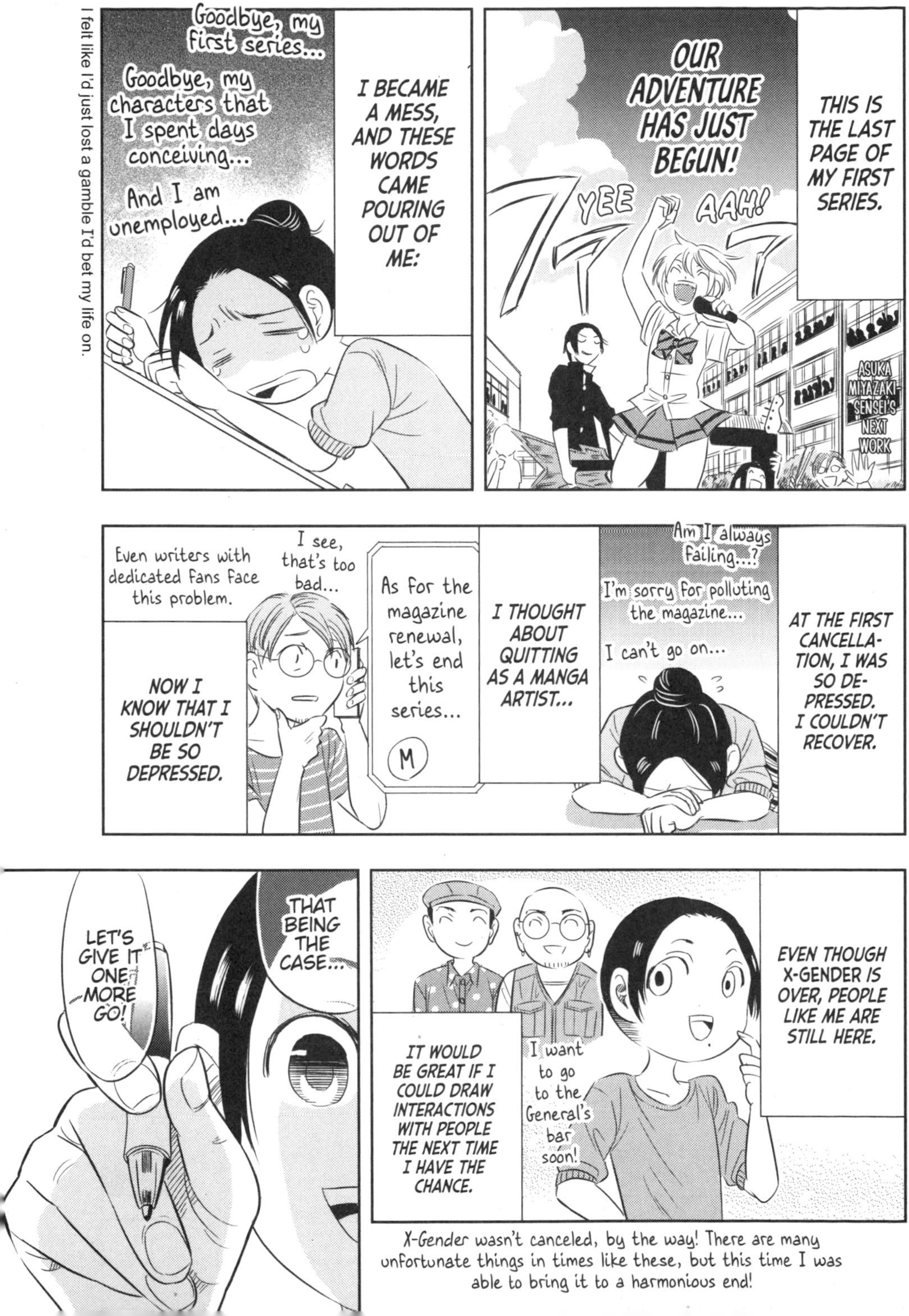
THIS IS THE LAST PAGE OF MY FIRST SERIES.
OUR ADVENTURE HAS JUST BEGUN!
YEE
AAH!
ASUKA MIYAZAKI-SENSEI'S NEXT WORK
I BECAME A MESS, AND THESE WORDS CAME POURING OUT OF ME:
Goodbye, my first series...
Goodbye, my characters that I spent days conceiving...
And I am unemployed...
I felt like I'd just lost a gamble I'd bet my life on.
AT THE FIRST CANCELLATION, I WAS SO DEPRESSED. I COULDN'T RECOVER.
Am I always failing...?
I'm sorry for polluting the magazine...
I can't go on...
I THOUGHT ABOUT QUITTING AS A MANGA ARTIST...
As for the magazine renewal, let's end this series...
M
I see, that's too bad...
Even writers with dedicated fans face this problem.
NOW I KNOW THAT I SHOULDN'T BE SO DEPRESSED.
EVEN THOUGH X-GENDER IS OVER, PEOPLE LIKE ME ARE STILL HERE.
I want to go to the General's bar soon!
IT WOULD BE GREAT IF I COULD DRAW INTERACTIONS WITH PEOPLE THE NEXT TIME I HAVE THE CHANCE.
X-Gender wasn't canceled, by the way! There are many unfortunate things in times like these, but this time I was able to bring it to a harmonious end!
THAT BEING THE CASE...
LET'S GIVE IT ONE MORE GO!

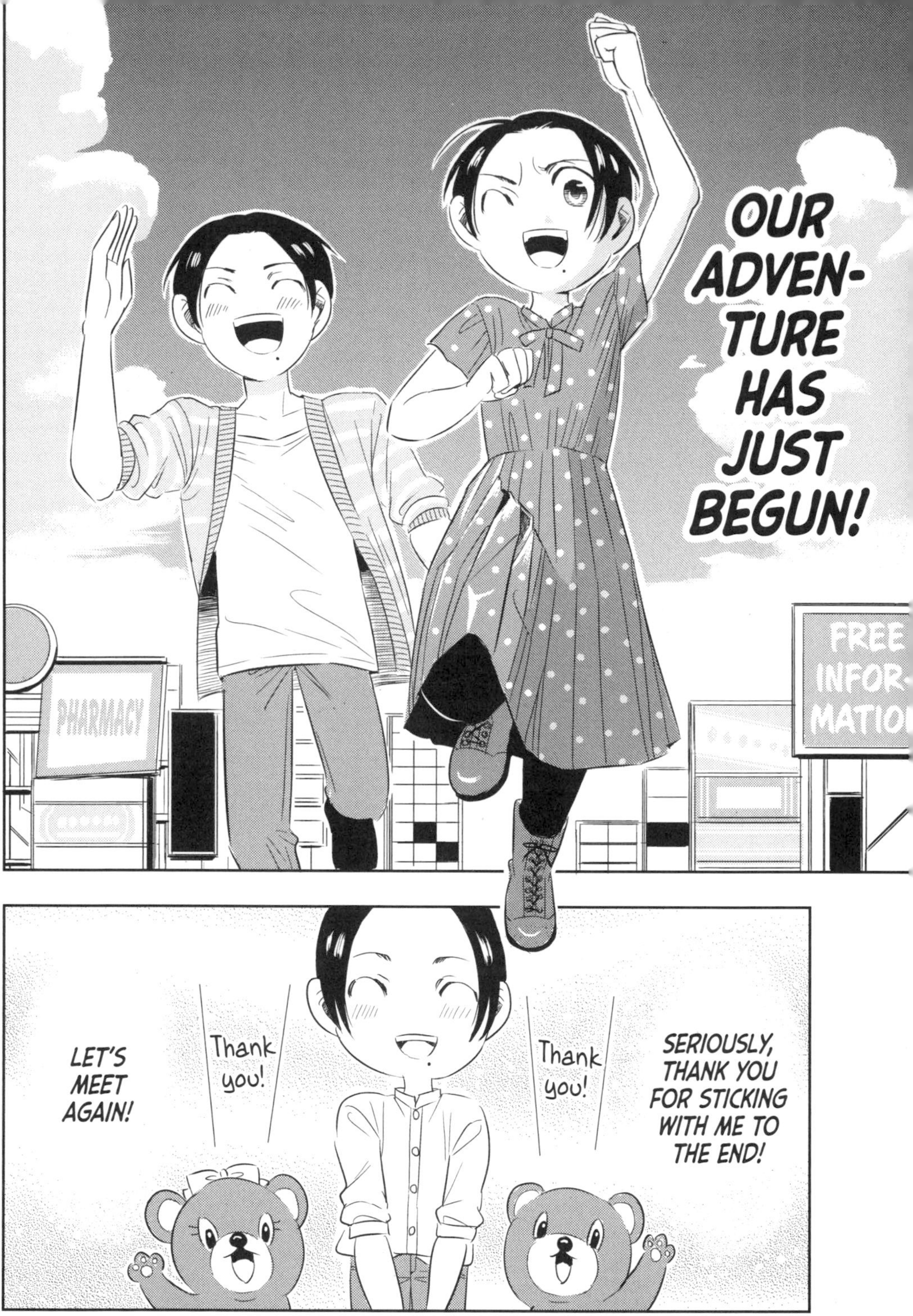
OUR ADVENTURE HAS JUST BEGUN!
PHARMACY
FREE
SERIOUSLY, THANK YOU FOR STICKING WITH ME TO THE END!
Thank you!
Thank you!
LET'S MEET AGAIN!

Afterword

Thank you so much for buying Volume 2 of *X-Gender*!

To the dear readers who cheered me on, the people who became models for characters, my managers who encouraged me when I was anxious, Kodansha, who gave me a chance to make the series, and everyone involved in the serialization, I am grateful. As of the end of this series, I'm full of appreciation.

We decided that *X-Gender* would be serialized at the end of 2019 (with publication to start about half a year later), but in Japan, the first Covid cases arose early the next year. 2020 was an unprecedented situation full of panic, limited going out, and closed bars. In 2021, right before the Olympics, Covid patient numbers increased again. In the middle of the serialization, I worried that I might catch Covid and pass it onto another person. That someone might be robbed of their life because of me! Because of that, I mostly couldn't meet with my acquaintances.

At that time, I wanted to draw interactions with people. Even though I had the chance to continue serialization past Volume 1, circumstances being what they were, I couldn't really do that. Even though it was six years of working on the series for me...

While I was desperately thinking of what I could draw, I continued with the serialization on my own. After moving publication to the web, the pace increased. Meanwhile, with the uncertainty of Covid, I felt more and more cornered, which is reflected in the work's content. That, in itself, is *X-Gender* Volume 2's notable point. I couldn't draw myself mingling with people, but I was able to draw one human being being cornered (me)! It's almost always the case that one half of my manga is made from my own suffering. I want readers to enjoy watching me struggle and having my hope crushed in the midst of working on a series during Covid!

I also want to apologize. There were many points I should reflect on about Volume 1. Consulting with my manager, there were places where I used intense words to leave a lasting effect on the readers, but my way of drawing them didn't sit well with some people, and there were parts where I conveyed the material poorly.

Likewise with this volume—I'm sure some people will find the way I draw embarrassment and ugly emotions both challenging and unpleasant.

To the people who sent me letters and tweeted at me during the series, thank you so much. You can't know how much of a comfort it has been to have people cheering on someone like me. It's surprising and joyful!

I will take advantage of the experiences I garnered during this series and do my best. My adventure has just begun! (I wrote this ten years ago at the end of my first serialization, too, though...)

Seriously, thank you so very much! I will announce any news about future work on Twitter.

If you don't mind, I would look forward to having your support from now on!

Asuka Miyazaki
February 2022

SEVEN SEAS ENTERTAINMENT

X-GENDER

story and art by **ASUKA MIYAZAKI**

VOLUME 2

TRANSLATION
Kathryn Henzler

ADAPTATION
Cae Hawksmoor

LETTERING
Vanessa Satone

COVER DESIGN
H. Qi

PROOFREADER
Leighanna DeRouen

SENIOR EDITOR
Jenn Grunigen

PRODUCTION DESIGNER
Stevie Wilson

PRODUCTION MANAGER
Lissa Pattillo

PREPRESS TECHNICIAN
Melanie Ujimori
Jules Valera

EDITOR-IN-CHIEF
Julie Davis

ASSOCIATE PUBLISHER
Adam Arnold

PUBLISHER
Jason DeAngelis

Seibetsu X
©2022 Asuka Miyazaki. All rights reserved.
First published in Japan in 2022 by Kodansha Ltd., Tokyo.
Publication rights for this English edition arranged through Kodansha Ltd., Tokyo.

Seven Seas press and purchase enquiries can be sent to Marketing Manager Lianne Sentar at press@gomanga.com. Information regarding the distribution and purchase of digital editions is available from Digital Manager CK Russell at digital@gomanga.com.

Seven Seas and the Seven Seas logo are trademarks of Seven Seas Entertainment. All rights reserved.

ISBN: 978-1-68579-461-3
Printed in Canada
First Printing: June 2023
10 9 8 7 6 5 4 3 2 1

⟨⟨⟨ READING DIRECTIONS ⟩⟩⟩

This book reads from *right to left*, Japanese style. If this is your first time reading manga, you start reading from the top right panel on each page and take it from there. If you get lost, just follow the numbered diagram here. It may seem backwards at first, but you'll get the hang of it! Have fun!!

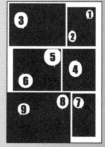

Follow us online: www.SevenSeasEntertainment.com